The Pettis Norman Story

A Journey through the Cotton Fields, to the Super Bowl, and into Servant Leadership

By

Pettis Burch Norman

Copyright © 2021 Pettis Burch Norman

All rights reserved.

No content of this book may be copied, excerpted, replicated, or shared without the permission of the author.

Published by SuburbanBuzz.com, LLC

ISBN: 978-1-7360820-4-1

ADVANCE PRAISE

★ ★ ★ ★ ★

Roger Staubach, Quarterback Dallas Cowboys

"You got the job done and had confidence in yourself that transferred to our teammates. And that's a leader."

★ ★ ★ ★ ★

The Late Charley Pride, Legendary Country Western Singer and Musician

"Pettis was a great football player and successful businessman. But did you know his athleticism extended to golf? We sponsored a lot of charitable golf tournaments, and I'm glad he captures those philanthropic memories in his book."

★ ★ ★ ★ ★

Robert Decherd, Chairman of the Board, President, and CEO of A. H. Belo Corporation, Parent Company of the *Dallas Morning News*

"Pettis is one of the true citizens of Dallas who cares, a former sportsman who devoted half his time to civic matters and never sought notoriety after his football career. He was always a person who exhibited calmness and had an innate insightfulness in his approach to very complex problems — calm and reasonable. He could lead men and women because he was just extraordinarily respected. Everyone was in the same place in their regard for Pettis. It is hard to say no to Pettis and the city is a better place because of it. I'm glad he's chronicling these moments in his book."

★ ★ ★ ★ ★

★ ★ ★ ★ ★

Ron Kirk, Former U.S. Trade Representative for the Obama Administration and Former Mayor of Dallas

"Pettis Norman was a mentor, role model and friend because he was relevant to me in all aspects of my life. If you wanted to know how to be a good father, Pettis Norman was the kind of man you looked up to. If you wanted to know how to be a good entrepreneur, Pettis Norman was one of those people you talk to. If you wanted to help bridge Dallas' racial divide and get the city to move together, Pettis Norman was one of those people you had to talk to. Any box I would want to check about the kind of man I'd like to be, Pettis checks that box for me. He just has that presence, which is apparent in his book. What a wonderful autobiography."

★ ★ ★ ★ ★

Rayfield Wright, Dallas Cowboys Hall of Fame Offensive Tackle

"A lot of my blocking skills came from the teachings of Pettis. Pettis had a great influence on players on our team because he was dedicated and committed to doing his job. And Pettis was a guy whose commitment went beyond the football field. He did a lot in his community; he helped a lot of people advance themselves. I could talk all day about what Pettis has meant to me in my life. It's a blessing for me to have this opportunity to share my feelings about this man."

★ ★ ★ ★ ★

Calvin Hill, Dallas Cowboys Running Back

"I think Pettis is the personification of a real American man, as a father, as a husband, as a teammate. If you had a daughter, he's the kind of man you would want your daughter to marry. If you're on a team, he's the kind of teammate you want to have. If you live in a neighborhood, he's the kind of neighbor you want to have. He's a wonderful man, a wonderful citizen, and a wonderful friend. In regards to opportunity, he epitomizes the best of America. He had a rough deck stacked against him, but it never stopped him from succeeding."

★ ★ ★ ★ ★

Bill Solomon, Former CEO of Austin Industries

"I came to know Pettis very well and greatly respect his character, leadership and effectiveness. Dallas was and is fortunate indeed that football brought Pettis here and that he remained to help make Dallas a better place for all. And we who have gained Pettis' friendship in the process are likewise fortunate. So many of these great friendships and collaborative accomplishments are chronicled in his book."

Erle Nye, Former CEO of TXU Electric

"I have worked with Pettis to address many civic and community challenges, some of which he includes in this book. He has achieved so much in 80 years and his service to others is notable. I have always admired how he carries himself, so thoughtful and considerate, while working for the common good. Pettis' leadership from bygone decades to this current moment has made a difference in this world, and I am proud to call him my friend."

Bob Lilly, Dallas Cowboys

"Pettis, you stood up for what you believed. Dallas was still segregated, and I don't think any of us liked it. You said, 'Let's get this changed.' And we did. That had a great deal to do with changing Dallas."

DEDICATION

★ ★ ★ ★ ★

I dedicate this book to several family members who have blessed my life and profoundly impacted my journey.

First, I thank my wonderful parents, Fessor and Elease "Eloise" Norman, for teaching me how to make life count for others.

Second, the contributions to this project by my wife, Ivette, have been endless. She led the effort through late nights and early mornings, tackled copious research for months at a stretch, and did so with utter devotion and love. She has been a true blessing to me and our family.

Third, to my beloved children, Shawn, Sedonna, Shandra and Alex, I know you must walk your own path, but the parent in me will never completely let go. Let my love be the light that guides you.

TABLE OF CONTENTS

★ ★ ★ ★ ★

FOREWORD i
INTRODUCTION iii
Chapter One: Making Life Count 1
Chapter Two: Snippy, Annie, and the Little Red Wagon 9
Chapter Three: North Carolina and a New Normal 17
Chapter Four: Golden Years of the Golden Bulls 27
Chapter Five: How 'Bout Them Cowboys! 43
Chapter Six: The Ice Bowl — Frozen in Time 59
Chapter Seven: Reflections on the Ice Bowl 73
Chapter Eight: Super Bowl V 83
Chapter Nine: San Diego Chargers 99
Chapter Ten: God and Country 111
Chapter Eleven: Civil Rights 119
Chapter Twelve: Voices of the Civil Rights Movement 131
Chapter Thirteen: Race Relations 145
Chapter Fourteen: From Texas to the White House 167
Chapter Fifteen: Eye on Education 187
Chapter Sixteen: Dallas Together Forum 197
Chapter Seventeen: Other Voices of Dallas Together Forum 207
Chapter Eighteen: One Door Closes and Another Opens 221
Chapter Nineteen: PNI Industries — We Go the Distance for You 233
Chapter Twenty: Revelations of a Serious Man 249
Chapter Twenty-One: Horse Whisperer 265
Chapter Twenty-Two: Turn of the Century 275
Chapter Twenty-Three: It's Who You Know 287
Chapter Twenty-Four: Retirement 309
Chapter Twenty-Five: Legacy 325
ACKNOWLEDGMENTS 337

FOREWORD

★ ★ ★ ★ ★

RECOGNIZING PETTIS NORMAN

United States Government
156 Congressional Record
Volume 156, Number 75, Page E861

May 2010

HONORABLE EDDIE BERNICE JOHNSON
30th Congressional District of Texas in the U.S. House of Representatives

Ms. EDDIE BERNICE JOHNSON of Texas - Madam Speaker, I rise today to recognize a truly remarkable man and exceptional citizen of Dallas, Texas, Mr. Pettis Norman. I am very privileged to consider Mr. Norman a dear friend, and it is an honor to recognize him before this Congress and the entire country.

Pettis Norman has always been a man of strong character and deep emotional conviction. He was born to Fessor and Eloise Norman in Lincolnton, Georgia and spent his formative years in North Carolina. As the youngest child in a large family, he learned early on the value of his own personal integrity, and to this day, it remains one of his most admirable qualities.

Mr. Norman received a degree from Johnson C. Smith University in Charlotte, North Carolina, and it was there that he became active in the civil rights movement. He participated in lunch counter sit-ins that ultimately spread to cities and states across the country.

These sit-ins marked a turning point for the movement and served as a spark for the African-American community to organize, be heard, and protest peacefully. Mr. Norman took part in these with a deep sense of integrity and the simple belief that all people should be judged on the depth of their character and not the color of their skin.

After Mr. Norman graduated from college, he moved to Dallas, Texas to play for the Cowboys in 1962. To this day, he is regarded as one of the greatest tight ends the team has ever had, and his resolve on the field has yet to be matched. Truly, the city fell in love with Mr. Norman just as Mr. Norman fell in love with Dallas, and I believe that the city has gained so much because of him.

As a football player, Coach Landry held him in high regard, and still says that trading Mr. Norman to the San Diego Chargers was one of the most difficult decisions he ever made.

Mr. Norman returned to Dallas after two seasons in San Diego to settle into a permanent home. He has been active in civic life ever since, and he is still highly regarded in the community. The people of Dallas consider him an all-time favorite and believe that it is his moral character and steadfast nature that so endear him to the people he meets.

Madam Speaker, Pettis Norman was an amazing football player and is an outstanding citizen today. I ask my fellow colleagues to join me in honoring this great man who has done remarkable things throughout his life and still considers his personal integrity his most variable trait.

INTRODUCTION

*Do unto others as you would have them do unto you.
Isn't that a wonderful ethic to live by?*
~ Pettis Norman

As I thought about a title for this autobiography, I knew it had to capture an incredible trajectory and the miraculous blessings in my life. *The Pettis Norman Story: A Journey through the Cotton Fields, to the Super Bowl, and into Servant Leadership* sums it up nicely.

Right from the beginning, it alludes to a journey through history and the African American experience in the Deep South while also alluding to a journey into one of America's favorite sports — football. Yet there is more to this story, much more, including the importance of an entrepreneurial spirit and the power of rolling up one's sleeves to work on behalf of just causes.

Honestly, the majority of my life has been spent outside the gridiron, yet I'm probably best known for the years I played for the Dallas Cowboys and the San Diego Chargers.

Never in my wildest dreams did I think I'd grow up to play in the NFL but was blessed to be one of the chosen few. My childhood and scholastic endeavors in Lincolnton, Georgia, and Charlotte, North Carolina, prepared me to achieve great things. Still, I assumed this would be in business roles and as the head of a family — not on television screens and championship games.

I dipped my toe into the world of commerce before my sports career ended. You see, back in the day, the NFL paid some football players very little money — a small fraction of what professional athletes earn today. You might say the limelight brought us fame, but not fortune. I signed on as a rookie for $9,000 per season, and most of us worked second or even third jobs during the off-season.

It was up to us to make names for ourselves elsewhere, either in a trade or profession, and I was no exception. However, juggling multiple jobs benefitted us since all athletes eventually face "the end" of their careers. My "end" occurred due to a knee injury. It closed one chapter but continued another, and the blessings kept coming.

I credit my parents, Fessor and Elease "Eloise" Booker Norman, for teaching me to be steadfast, self-reliant, and optimistic. My childhood as a sharecropper's son shaped the values I hold so dear. The example set by my mother, father, and nine siblings as they toiled in the dusty fields in Lincolnton, Georgia, taught me a lot about accepting, overcoming, and transcending our circumstances.

When opportunities to prosper arose outside of Georgia and North Carolina, I remained humble, as my parents would expect. In fact, their code of honor was so firmly entrenched in my soul that I followed the narrow path, the more difficult path that required me to remain a man of character no matter the temptations or obstacles. And believe me, there were many temptations and vast obstacles!

This really is the backstory — the deep roots of belief in God Almighty, planted under the sweltering sun of the Deep South and harvested in corporate America. Those sharecropping days created a work ethic and an appreciation for what we had, which was just enough to get by, and we were grateful for it.

If I have any advice to dispense after living 82 years on God's green earth, it is to be thankful for what you have and work hard for what you want. Life gains a positive perspective when gratitude is the attitude. Negativity and hate serve no purpose and only put roadblocks in front of us. We can best tackle social ills with honest dialogue, solidarity, and a focus on the humanitarian inside of us.

Being a husband and father truly changed my life. Some ask what I consider my proudest achievement. My answer is ushering three daughters and a grandson into the world — a better world, I hoped, one that would include equality, justice, and fairness. These aspirations put a whole new definition on the words "fatherhood," "grand fatherhood," and "responsibility." In hindsight, my parents undoubtedly wished the same for me, and I was so grateful that this reality was within reach for my children.

After 29 years of marriage, becoming a widower was a heartbreaking experience, especially with three daughters still in their twenties. My late wife Margaret's contribution to my life was immeasurable; we built a beautiful family together, and I praise God for placing people in my path to help me navigate the hills and valleys of grief.

Life changed again in 1995 when God restored my role as husband and gifted me with Ivette. She is a wonderful life partner and a wonderful surrogate mother for our daughters, grandson, and great-grandchildren. I cannot imagine an existence without her; we have enjoyed a loving marriage for a quarter-century and are still going strong.

The journey hasn't been easy but has brought unimaginable moments of joy and satisfaction. It has also brought deep personal loss and heartache, including my firstborn daughter, Sharneen. We called her by her nickname "Shawn." I treasure the 50 years we spent together, and there is still a hole in my heart that will never be filled. Parents who have experienced similar circumstances can attest to this sorrow. I can only say that I'm so very grateful for my Christian upbringing, which passed through me to my children. I know I'll be reunited with all my lost loved ones someday; it will be a joyous reunion.

Throughout it all, I credit my steadfast belief that doing good matters. Being of service to others, building businesses, providing jobs, and actively participating in the political spectrum matters. At my age, I have the luxury of looking back and seeing the difference my efforts have made in race relations, equality, and bridge-building. That is all the reward one can expect.

If you follow football, you'll live vicariously through my firsthand accounts of the 1967 Ice Bowl. The Dallas Cowboys, led by Coach Tom Landry, faced off against the Green Bay Packers led by Coach Vince Lombardi. This game is famous for unimaginably brutal weather — arctic temperatures — and truly demonstrates the guts and glory of the sport. I also recount the experience of playing in Super Bowl V against the Baltimore Colts in 1971 — a loss that still stings a bit, I'll admit.

It is an honor to share my volunteer work for Presidents Lyndon Johnson, Jimmy Carter, Bill Clinton, and Barack Obama. The many opportunities I've had to participate in political and social justice movements are another trip through history, although it feels like yesterday.

I also detail the wonderful charitable organizations I've been privileged to serve and the meaningful awards I've received for humanitarian and philanthropic efforts. I think it's essential for our younger generation to understand that serving others is an honor and duty in and of itself (awards or not). People must get involved through impactful, dignified, and effective means. This is how we become change agents.

This brings me to the actual hands-on creation of a manuscript. Writing is not an instantaneous craft, at least not for me. Several birthdays rolled around as the book formed, and it had me counting my blessings all over again.

Let me explain what it is like to write an 82-year story arc. First, this process began ten years ago and required going through hundreds of photo albums and reliving life's most precious and challenging moments — the births of my daughters, grandson, and great grandchildren, the loss of my first wife Margaret, my marriage to Ivette and the countless hours she has devoted to this project.

We began pulling documents from storage, and soon I was swimming in dozens of boxes, all sorted and categorized, thanks to Ivette. It was nearly mind-boggling to sift through so many varied past events, and the business notes, alone, were voluminous. After serving on many major civic boards in Dallas and forming friendships that are more than half a century old, I had a lot of history to comb through. It was an inordinate amount of reading.

One by one, we went through the folders — newspaper clippings, photos, and invitations, and relived those moments too. Reaching back in time was one thing, but recalling the finer details was another — I had nearly forgotten what I had forgotten! So much had been buried in my subconscious, and many "great awakenings" occurred as I picked my way through the data. I began to realize this would require work — work with a notepad and a computer and lots and lots of additions and rewrites. A task like this can cause temporary paralysis. I admit to some procrastination.

I now had to somehow tie my personal and professional life together in each chapter and decided a chronology was the best route. But still, I didn't have all the pieces. So, what do you do when you want to honor the nuances of the past but are still missing the finer details?

I caught up with extended relatives and close friends from the business realm in preparation for the writing. They so generously shared their insights, which became great memory joggers and pointed me in directions I had never thought to go — family lore and Army records, city archives and ancestry websites, and corporate filings that held the birth of many businesses.

It has been a joy to include this information and many voices, producing a fuller, richer book, I believe, because of the various perspectives. You will notice throughout this book, I give plenty of real estate to those who stood with me in my life's journey and others who deserved recognition for their notable accomplishments – that's who I am. My hope is that you will be educated and inspired as you read about this diverse group of individuals.

By the way, if any readers happen to be entrepreneurs-in-training, I have some behind-the-scenes thoughts on running successful businesses and managing people. There is an art and science to encouraging people to do their best. Mentoring, inspiring, and giving others a hand up rather than a handout is what defines an industry leader. If I can be a leader, you can be a leader. Educate yourself, watch closely, and go for it!

I hope you enjoy this tale that spans eight decades and that it delights and blesses you through my parent's favorite Bible verse found in Luke 6:31 — "Do unto others as you would have them do unto you." Isn't that an extraordinary ethic to live by?

Chapter One: Making Life Count

The question "How should we then live?" is best answered in Luke 12:48: "To whom much is given, much will be required."
~ Pettis Norman

For years, people from all walks of life have asked me, "Pettis, when are you going to write your autobiography?" I decided that if I ever did write a book Francis Schaeffer's *How Should We Then Live? The Rise and Decline of Western Culture* would influence it. One of my favorite quotes from Schaeffer follows, an inspirational and educational quote, but also a powerful call to action:

> *The Bible is clear here: I am to love my neighbor as myself, in the manner needed, in a practical way, in the midst of the fallen world, at my particular point of history. This is why I am not a pacifist. Pacifism in this poor world in which we live — this lost world — means that we desert the people who need our greatest help.*

I first read those words in 1976 when Schaeffer's book was published during some of the most challenging times in our nation. As you'll see, his sentiments were timely on a very personal level, but also on a professional and humanitarian level. It perfectly reflected what I aspired to do in life, which was to help "the least of these." This was something my parents taught me, but also Jesus Christ himself. Servant leadership is not a passive concept, but an active one.

No Little People

It may surprise some readers that former NFL players enjoy hobbies that have nothing to do with football. Some of us even dabble in philosophy — it's true! And although I enjoy watching games and even attending some, one of my favorite pastimes is learning more about the gifted authors who have impacted my life. That's why I decided to study Schaeffer. He did not refer to himself as a great philosopher, theologian, or scholar, although he certainly was. He simply considered himself an evangelist and pastor.

As a teen, Schaeffer sought answers to life's questions and found them in the Bible, as well as a conviction that God's Word is truth — unchanging truth. He believed in the "creation, fall, and redemption" framework of the Scriptures and welcomed people who had troubles or felt lost in despair and alienation. I admired that he didn't judge but rather helped those in need.

Photo Credit: Gittings Photograhy

I've committed his wisdom to memory. Schaeffer encouraged people by saying, "You are finite and glorious persons made in the likeness of our infinite personal Creator." I took this to mean we are all God's image-bearers whether we are young, elderly, disabled, White, Black, or Brown, or whether we have troubles, feel rudderless, or are alienated from the mainstream. I know that people of color have felt alienated from the mainstream for generations, and only through God can a healing commence.

This concept of dignity within every human person led to Schaeffer's sermon titled "No Little People." Later, his book by the same name included numerous other sermons. His book has a magnificent message — if you ever have time, I recommend that you look it up — and what did I take from it? Well, a poor janitor, a wealthy businessman, a helpless child, a drug addict, and a matron of society are equally precious and have the precise same value in God's kingdom. All are worthy of receiving time and effort, and we are worthy of giving the same.

Schaeffer is absolutely correct. There are no little people or little places. Everyone around us is important, no matter who they are or where they live, or what they look like. The fact is, there is an appearance of "the least of these" and "the greatest of these" in our communities, but socioeconomic status is irrelevant in God's eyes; for least or greatest, we are God's image-bearers just like anyone else.

It strikes me that God is the great Equalizer. He loves us all. And he tells us in Luke 12:48, "To whom much is given, much will be required." So those of us who have been blessed with opportunity are meant to help those who lack opportunity. This is an eternal truth. The fact that the powerful prey on the powerless does nothing to diminish the truth. God has wired humankind with a finer sense of right and wrong for a purpose. We are not to bow to the lowest common denominators of greed, stinginess, jealousy, and hatred; we are to rise to the highest common denominators of generosity, sacrifice, encouragement, and love. This circles back to the most compelling Scripture of all: "Do unto others as you would have them do unto you."

Taking on the System

As a Dallas Cowboy straight out of college and later a San Diego Charger, I made life count by functioning under a National Football League system. In many ways, I thrived under that system. Then I learned of another system completely removed from football and awakened to a truth: much of what happens to us is due to the larger societal system under which we live and do business.

This has everything to do with our institutions, our churches, and how we operate our cities and national government. It has to do with the way we shape our foreign policies. The "system" should be inherently based on the notion that "there are no little people," but in reality, this isn't always the case. In fact, it is rarely the case.

As a young man, I had to make life count despite the system. I ventured out on my own and raised my family while building my career and opening several businesses. I examined what society did or did not do regarding the manner in which justice was administered and how we educated our people. I considered our prisons, which reflected this reality. I considered the way we gerrymandered our districts and practiced both overt and covert discrimination in the workplace. All of the blood, sweat, and tears from the Civil Rights Movement and the legislation in place to bring balance and equality to the forefront … well, it was and continues to be diluted by the system.

These problems continue to plague us, but once again, servant leadership is never passive. We cannot sidestep, whitewash, ignore or pretend these problems don't exist today. We must make life count through persistence and by seeking solutions, no matter if we've tried and failed before. Our problems will never be reconciled until society overcomes the limitations imposed by "the system" and the nature of the system itself.

It just so happens that I cherish some deep and long-term friendships forged through social, business, and humanitarian causes, many in Dallas. The remarkable thing about my friends is that they are all so varied. Male or female, Democrat or Republican, Black, White, Hispanic, Asian, Indian or Native American, famous or not, involved in sports or not — what matters is that my friends share a social conscience. Some marched, some volunteered, some joined committees, most hired minorities, and they all attached their names to endeavors that put their reputations on the line.

Many have retired from public life but still care about the people around them. In big and small ways, they've managed to rattle the system. How fortunate for readers that they share their insights in this book, dispensing wisdom and a clear view of what they consider vital.

I want to mention my dearest friend, my pastor, the Reverend Zan Holmes Jr., who disrupted the system in his own manner and for his own reasons, heeding a finely tuned higher sense of right and wrong. He will tell you that racism, sexism, and classism remain ingrained in every system in the world and contribute to our problems today. Others may have invented it, but we buy into it, often unconsciously.

Sometimes our reactions may seem counterintuitive, perhaps even hypocritical. For instance, we all seek wealth and often resent those among us who have it. We seek excellence in education and often resent those among us who have it. We seek political power and autonomy and too often resent those who have it. We seek recognition and respect and resent those who attain it.

Perhaps successful people achieved their accomplishments through hard work and strategy, or perhaps they were simply lucky, or perhaps someone offered them a helping hand. Whatever the formula, their success puts them in a position to help others. Imagine how improved our communities would be if the successful achievers collaborated with those once in their shoes. Success should not be hoarded; it should be celebrated as an opportunity to make this world a better place. Don't you agree?

It would have been easier for the Reverend Holmes to maintain the status quo. Instead, he railed against it — sometimes diplomatically and subtly, and sometimes quite vocally — all with the goal of effecting change. That was his calling, and it brings to mind an anecdote that challenged me to find my own calling outside of the NFL.

Answering the Call

The Reverend Dr. Herman L. Counts was a civil rights leader and my mentor at Johnson C. Smith University. He taught religion and philosophy classes and pastored a series of small churches in the Charlotte, North Carolina region. I thank him for honing me into a philosophical thinker. Once, he asked, "Pettis, what do you really want to do?"

My answer was, "I want to make life count."

"Exactly how will you make life count?" he asked.

This led to a discussion about the notion of "a calling." As a youthful student, I thought I was called to teach and coach. I envisioned myself in the classroom and on the field, shaping young minds. That was the plan. I didn't know at the time that I'd spend a dozen years in the NFL or go on to be a businessman. I had no clue that humanitarian causes and economic reform initiatives were in my future.

Later as an entrepreneur, I was blessed that many business mentors stepped forward to help me succeed. I realized I could do the same — I still had the ability to teach, not in classrooms, but one-on-one in corporate America and behind podiums. And so I welcomed opportunities to speak in various platforms as a way of giving back.

It's worth mentioning that I make it a habit to tuck Scripture into some of my speeches. Why? Because I believe that is the greatest gift of all — a heart open to God and receptive to His word. I owe everything to God Almighty — every blessing, every opportunity, every friendship, and every tribulation as well. How could I, in good conscience, not spread this good news?

I once spoke in front of a young audience and based my message on the inspirational words of Michael Novak. His book *Business as a Calling* explores the characteristics and nuances of what is required to answer our various calls in life. I referenced the book as an opportunity to mentor others, especially young hopefuls who had their futures ahead of them. I have always enjoyed speaking to a room full of eager faces and had many opportunities in the past to share *Business as a Calling* that went beyond day-to-day business tips and advice.

I channeled my thoughts around three important areas: a calling with "preconditions," a "true calling," and "multiple callings." I always stressed that each inner calling is unique to individuals and is not usually easy to discover but driven by a strong impulse, a revelation unveiled in God's good timing.

So, let's begin with "preconditions." This calling is more than just a desire; it requires talent. For a calling to be right, it must fit our abilities. Not everyone can be a professional athlete or an opera singer. Take, for instance, Andrea Bocelli. Though blind, he's also the world's most beloved tenor; his calling is to sing like an angel. His God-given talent fit the precondition.

Next, a "true calling" reveals its presence by the sense of enjoyment and renewed energy. A true calling yields love and passion for what we are doing. To quote Logan Pearsall Smith, "The test of a vocation is the love of the hard, boring work which that vocation necessarily includes." This does not mean that we don't inwardly groan at the weight of the burden — long hours, frustrations, small steps forward, two steps back, and struggles. Unless these too are welcomed with a certain joy, the calling has a hollow ring.

Finally, some of us may have "multiple callings" — major callings, smaller callings, some even overlapping. It leads us to totally new careers, each in its season. I'm an example — football player to sports agent to real estate developer to restaurateur to broadcaster to fuel distributor… and you can throw a hair care product enterprise into the mix.

Conversely, we might stumble across a false path, but that is an opportunity too — a chance to reevaluate and self-correct. Experiments, painful setbacks, discernment, prayer, and much patience become our North Star, eventually guiding us to where we belong and where we are needed.

Myths and Reality

Many can attest that life for disenfranchised people has been full of challenges since the beginning of time, specifically in the United States' Deep South. Places like Dallas are no exception. You'll see throughout this book that my adopted city has been ground zero for many injustices, but also a place where people have endeavored to set things right. The volume of issues may seem overwhelming as I document these battleground moments in various chapters, but peeling back the layers is important. I think we need to expose the wrong to prevent history from repeating itself. I think we also have to document the victories. But to do so, we have to separate myths from reality.

Dallas has always been big, bold, and home to a fair share of millionaires — and billionaires — and the city's name might bring to mind more than just the Dallas Cowboys. I'm sure millions of television viewers have misperceptions thanks to the television show *Dallas* that ran from 1978 to 1991. That's a long haul of weekly fantasy. I often wondered what the people in Wisconsin, Maine, Oregon, and Kansas thought about the big hats, cowboy boots, cattle ranching, oil empires, and feuding Ewing family members.

Don't be fooled by the stereotyping. Although I, too, wore cowboy boots, it wasn't a fashion statement. I owned thoroughbreds and was out in the muck, tending to my beloved horses. And I haven't personally met anyone remotely like the mythic J. R. Ewing. I did, however, know many struggling Blacks and Hispanics, as well as some Fortune 500 CEOs who were progressive enough to care about poverty and prejudice.

Today, I call these affluent decision-makers some of my best friends, and I believe God placed me in the "Big D" at the right time to work alongside them and thousands of ordinary salt-of-the-earth citizens who made a big impact. Together, slowly but surely, we tackled the lingering and shameful problems that plagued our city, which might reflect the same "righting of wrongs" in other cities throughout the U.S.

By the way, due to the perilous South and a seemingly endless uphill climb toward racial harmony, people have asked why I chose to return to Dallas from San Diego after retiring from the NFL. My answer is always, "Why not Dallas?" After all, there is no perfect city, but I saw the potential of what "could be." I assure people that the realities of racism, workplace discrimination, school district failures, and troubling politics in no way diminished my love for this great place. I entrenched myself in the heartbeat of it all, and each victory made Dallas more inclusive for generations to follow.

The crux of my message is that we can move mountains if we use our "calling" to better others. We should be driven to pay it forward, accomplish something individually and collectively, contribute to society, add something of value, test our talent and character, problem solve, and build our communities. I see it as a way of giving back to society through goods, services, sweat equity, and servant leadership. I believe that if Dallas can heal itself, any city on earth can do the same.

Making Life Count, Anyhow

I am not sure if it's grammatically correct, but one of my favorite sayings is "Make life count, anyhow." If you are poor and disenfranchised, make life count, anyhow. After all, impoverishment of the bank account does not equate to impoverishment of the spirit. If your glass is half empty, I hope this autobiography inspires you to make life count, anyhow. Adjust your way of thinking and consider the glass not half full or half empty but refillable. This is such simple advice, but effective. You'll see traces of this mindset throughout the book, through some very tough challenges and "refillable" moments.

This has been my vision for writing an autobiography — not overly focusing on football conquests or accumulating wealth, but revealing the simplicity of complex notions and exposing the unnecessary complications in what should be straightforward progress. I hope that by this example, people will absorb history, value the efforts of their forebears, be inspired to do more, and embrace the special missions that God has tasked them with — always with God's best for us in mind.

The truth has always been right in front of our noses from ages past until now — we are one big, beautiful human race, beloved by God in all our diversity. Not the Black race or the White race or the Brown race, but the human race. Not Democrat or Republican or gay or straight, but human beings. The system seeks to categorize us, society seeks to compartmentalize us, but God seeks to bind us. We are to love each other as God loves us. Period.

But this wasn't the first time I had been taught these concepts. My parents spoke these truths in the cotton fields of Georgia. Schaeffer simply confirmed my parents' wisdom, and from these examples, I accepted the torch that was passed to me.

I wish to honor the special people who formed and shaped me into a decent human being even before I was fully "cooked." I am about to introduce you to my family.

Chapter Two: Snippy, Annie, and the Little Red Wagon

"Blessed is the child who inherits a legacy — not riches or fame, but the example of loving, upstanding Parents."
~ Pettis Norman

At the tail end of the Great Depression on January 4, 1939, I was delivered in Lincolnton, Georgia, formerly known as Goshen. I had almost forgotten my father's unusual name, "Professor," for he was always referred to as "Fessor" or "Buddy." His formal name fit him well and foreshadowed what he would become — a brilliant and gifted person born in 1890. He could read and write in a day and age when many could not. The conduct of this selfless, trustworthy person had a ripple effect in the community and greatly benefitted our family; he was the best daddy in the world.

Back in those days, many young men crossed county lines to find their brides, which was the case for my parents. My mother, Elease "Eloise" Booker, was from Danburg, Georgia, in Wilkes County. Affectionately known as "Mami," she was beautiful inside and out, always smiling and gracious and beloved by Blacks and Whites alike in our community. Our little town of Lincolnton seemed to be an anomaly in this regard — not perfect (no town in the segregated South was without its racial problems), but an unusual example of racial harmony. As you will see, my father had a lot to do with the sense of goodwill in the community.

Life in Lincolnton

I know my relatives credit my grandmother, Ma Helen, as the rock of our family in Lincolnton. The impressions she made on me personally were profound. Ma Helen loved people and was a Christian lady who was loved in return by Blacks and Whites. One of my fondest memories was the food she always had on the table, no matter how many were in her house. Her big garden overflowed with collards, sweet potatoes, and strawberries. We loved her strawberry pies and bread pudding. She had a smokehouse and prepared a lot of pork that rivaled any restaurant.

Ma Helen kept up with it all, thanks to one of her daughters who lived with her and had no children. The rest of the children pitched in as well, so she always had help. I remember her grandchildren visiting often, coming and going in waves. On Sundays, there would be 35 to 40 of us. The memories we made are priceless, and I'll never forget the sights, sounds, delicious aromas, and welcoming atmosphere that permeated her house. These experiences were a rich part of my childhood.

My father's mother, Ma Helen, sitting on the porch with her half-brother, William Murray

My father became a farmer of cotton, corn, and wheat. He sharecropped and was an excellent carpenter, building a reputation for his attention to detail and the quality of his craftsmanship. Many older residents in Lincolnton remember him building a large bridge. He trained my brother Fessor Lee (nicknamed "Bish") in the carpentry trade as well. Daddy also built rocking chairs and yard chairs that were popular with both White and Black customers. People relaxed on their porches or invited people into their yards to sit on those chairs. I can still see the sweat glistening off his shoulders as Daddy crafted these sturdy masterpieces and painted them white. I felt a swell of pride every time I spotted his handiwork dotting the landscape of our community.

I considered Lincolnton, the county seat of Lincoln County, a wonderful place to grow up. Lincoln County is known as Georgia's freshwater coast, and the City of Lincolnton is known as the heart of the Clarks Hill area. My relatives will tell you it was — and still is — the friendliest town on earth. I recall the sounds of people driving by and honking or shouting out greetings. We'd wave at the wagons pulled by mules and exchange pleasantries with whomever happened by.

We initially lived in a crowded two-bedroom home. I remember it was wood-framed with a tin roof and owned by Dr. Burch. He hired my parents as sharecroppers; they must have thought highly of him, for they chose my middle name in his honor. There was no indoor plumbing — an outhouse sat in the back — but these were small inconveniences. Our life felt rich because of the love and pride our parents instilled in our family. My parents were a hardworking pair and self-sufficient, thanks to my dad's farming and carpentry abilities and the garden my mother and siblings tended.

During those early years, my sister Sarah and I were too little to be of much use on our farm. We played around the house, made up games, did our chores and other tasks. We had a good time together, sometimes teaming up to play tricks on each other, which added so much fun to our childhood memories.

I vividly remember pulling my little red wagon around the yard and how I cherished this favorite toy. I kept it with me constantly. I also played with Snippy, my beloved terrier mix. She was soft and grey and no bigger than a rooster — what fun we had as she followed me everywhere. I taught her to sit in the little red wagon and pulled her around the yard. I taught her to twirl around and around by offering her treats. She remained underfoot when I rode Annie, my horse, which was daily.

Throughout this book, time and again, I credit my lifelong love of horses to Annie. She was mid-size, not too big or too small for a growing boy. I can still see her light beige coat and the whitish stripe down her face. What a bond we forged. It reminds me of a quote from well-known horse trainer Ray Hunt: "The horse will teach you if you'll listen." Indeed, Annie taught me so much with her uncanny ability to sense my moods and feelings. Even at that young age, she taught me to be self-aware. How I acted around this horse affected how she acted around me — a life lesson that I would later apply on the football field and in corporate America.

From Annie's back, I watched my father as he worked in the fields. I was at such a tender age, yet knew he labored to keep a roof over our heads and food on the table. I respected and loved him for all the sacrifices he made for our family. I was always respectful to my elders; that was for certain.

Dad only spanked me twice, very lightly, and what really hurt was that I had disappointed him. The first time, I leaned over the water well to draw water. The second time, I scared the mules my brother was leading. Both were dangerous situations, and I understood why I was reprimanded. Dad was a giant in my eyes, and I wanted to please him. In fact, I wanted to be just like him. Today, my sister Gladys constantly reminds me how much I favor my father, from his stature to his looks and personality; Daddy is still an omnipresent figure in my life.

I fondly recall playing with my siblings and friends outside. My first cousins Bertha Norman Hill and Jesse Norman recently reminded me that I was a competitive child and had to be the best at whatever I did. "If we were jumping across a branch, you had to jump farther," they claimed. "You always had to win, or you weren't happy." They further commented, "You were so little at the time, it was fun to watch your bravery."

Well, I guess I was a little competitive, but I strived to do my best and always have. After all, I was the youngest and tried to keep up with my siblings. We had little money for toys and created our own games — hopscotch and hide-and-seek come to mind. It wasn't all play and no work; we had our fair share of chores. I rubbed the dairy cows and milked them with Snippy by my side. The buckets of milk I brought to my mother and the fresh vegetables picked by my siblings from our garden were used to prepare delicious home-cooked meals.

My wonderful mother

Family members commented on her natural beauty, but in my eyes, Mami was a nurturer. She cooked, cleaned, did the laundry, attended to our bumps and bruises, and occasionally worked in the fields. I'm not sure how she kept up with it all, for there were many moving parts in a family our size.

I suffered from pounding headaches throughout my early childhood and recall that my mother was never too busy to massage my head and temples. Her fingers were soothing and helped dull the pain. My siblings laid wet towels across my forehead and sometimes wrapped my entire head. If ice was available, they put it in a bag and laid it where it hurt the most. Thankfully, I outgrew this condition.

Snippy the dog, Annie the horse, my parents, siblings, and beloved aunts, uncles, and cousins showed me unconditional love. Together, they laid a great cornerstone for a little boy who was quick to soak up the examples and attitudes around me. There simply aren't enough words to thank my family, especially my parents, for my character development. They were careful to instill values and emphasized strong morals, anchored in the Bible verse Luke 6:31 — "Do unto others as you would have them do unto you."

As I reflect to those early days, their words, deeds and that scripture made a lifelong impact.

Memories of School

There was just so much beauty in everyday living. I call it sustainable living, for we always had plenty of homegrown food. My favorites included pan-fried sweet potatoes, homemade biscuits prepared daily, chicken drumsticks, sausage, and eggs. I can still taste it. Those hearty meals certainly caused me to grow, and soon it was time to enroll in school.

The original school for Black children burned down, so I enrolled in the makeshift school held in a building at the New Tabernacle Baptist Church. We attended seven months a year from September through April because we were needed on the farm. My sister Ida was my favorite teacher — no one could hold a candle to her, even as I advanced through high school and college. She had all the finer qualities that made learning fun — kindness, interest in her students, manners, and the ability to connect the lessons to our everyday lives. Thanks to her, I enjoyed academics. The bonus was that I went to school with built-in playmates, including cousins, nephews, and nieces.

We walked one mile to the schoolhouse, and, weather permitting, I chose to walk in my bare feet. I liked the sensation of the warm dirt between my toes — good ol' red Georgia dirt. But my relatives are quick to remind me that I didn't always walk and I wasn't always in the classroom. Sometimes I rode Annie alongside a friend, and we whooped and hollered at full gallop past the school. Then we made a beeline into the woods and pretended to be trail-riding cowboys. Looking back, I see the irony in those childhood hijinks, for I grew up to be another type of cowboy altogether — a Dallas Cowboy.

Everyone in Lincolnton was familiar with the "big rock" — a landmark boulder that measured about 12 feet across. Once anyone reached the big rock, they knew the church and school were just a stone's throw away. It holds fond memories as a playground, and we had a lot of fun scaling its odd shape. Sometimes we even held "church" on the big rock. I remember my brother Bish preached at the top of his lungs as the rest of us clapped and sang. We made such a commotion that the White children wanted in on the action. They stopped and stared and stepped up and paused, looking hopeful. We knew they wanted to play and invited them to "the service." Every time I visit Lincolnton today, I stop by to pay homage to the "big rock;" those childhood memories are priceless.

Two of my aunts lived down past Tabernacle Baptist Church, which held a prominent place in our lives scholastically and spiritually. Many of my relatives are buried there, including my parents. My father (known as "Uncle Buddy" to our relatives) served as a deacon and taught Sunday school. His brother Isaac "Bull" Norman was named after the original Isaac on our family tree and was also a deacon. Visitors today will see a plaque at the church bearing his name. Another uncle, Clifford, nicknamed "Bo," was a photographer. So, "Buddy," "Bull" and "Bo" were the three B's in our family and ensured the Norman name was held in high esteem.

"Be men and women of prayer," they always told us. "Love God, and when you tell someone you'll do something, keep your word."

As I mentioned, Lincolnton was benign compared to other southern towns, but we did face bigotry. I remember playing with both Black and White children. In my opinion, children are taught to be prejudiced, and apparently, this was the case for a close friend whose White parents owned a grocery store. Out of the blue, one day, he insisted I call him "sir." It hurt, especially since we had grown up together and were inseparable. That friendship ended because the innocence of childhood was somehow tainted with racism.

Perhaps reaching school age in Lincolnton caused the White kids to feel superior — they rode the bus, but Black kids could not, and that was just how it was at that time. But even with this glaring chasm between the haves and have nots, we were taught never to think less of ourselves. When my parents told me I was a child of God and anyone's equal, I believed them.

Then one school year, the White kids decided to hang out the bus windows and spit on us. I remember walking along unaware and then scrambling for the drainage ditch to avoid the spit. Anger flashed through my soul. We weren't about to tolerate it and schemed up a plan to stop them.

Several boys cut thin huckleberry switches and were ready the next time the bus came around. Sure enough, the White kids hung out the bus window, but they caught a switch this time. I'm certain it left a mark. When the White parents heard about this, my dad intervened. He explained that his children were being spat upon and had justly defended themselves. And that was the end of it. You see, when my father spoke, people listened. He had a unique presence in Lincolnton and, perhaps the closest thing to a "City Father" we had in the Black community. Daddy was a noble man, and indeed, there was something powerful about him. I still remember thinking that it's a wonderful thing when your parents stand up for you.

My sister Gladys remembers Daddy as follows:

> *He was respected throughout the town because of his integrity and trustworthiness. He was well-liked and the only Black man I saw going to White churches to pray and fellowship with members. When*

people in the community recognized Fessor's children, we too were respected because of his stature. We did not have many clothes, but we were always well dressed, clean, and carried ourselves with great pride.

People of the Land

When I was old enough to help in the fields, I played in the cotton bins and helped pick cotton. Not much was expected of me, but even a small amount of physical labor brought a new appreciation for my parents. They managed to maintain a happy home under strenuous work conditions.

The Clarks Hill area includes Strom Thurmond Lake. The Corp of Engineers constructed a dam to keep the water from washing out my relatives' houses. The homes would have flooded many times without it. The water runs down through Lincolnton to McCormick and throughout Savannah, and finally to the ocean. The area is still so water-dense that some of my relatives have learned to live with weak signals on their cellphones.

If memory serves me, the bridge my dad helped build became a dead-end boat landing. My cousins backed the mules to the water's edge so they could fill the 55-gallon drums loaded onto the wagons. Then the mules pulled the wagons out and hauled the water back to my aunt. She insisted on washing clothes with fresh water because the well water was sometimes tinged red. Good well water was crucial — we needed it to drink and provide water for the animals. We used pulley ropes to haul buckets up and down and cleaned the well to keep the water drinkable.

A nearby stream provided a fishing spot. There were, and still are, a lot of fishermen in Lincolnton. We didn't have the money to buy fancy poles, but my Daddy, being the craftsman that he was, built small cages that he dropped in the morning. He returned after plowing the fields to find a cage full of freshwater fish. The youth in my family were creative, too, and went into the woods to hunt for homemade poles. They carefully selected tree branches with just enough flex to spot a fish pulling on a hook; while unconventional, it worked in the country. We attached string and worms dug up by the barn, then applied hooks and went fishing. We bent down and snatched up the fish and then put them on another string until we had collected quite a few. Then we cleaned, cooked and enjoyed them.

Those fish were a freshwater treat. I know from experience that everything tastes better when you grow it, catch it, or raise it yourself. Yet even with wildlife all around us, we never hunted for sport or wasted any of God's bounty. Everything was consumed.

Speaking of homegrown, if a farmer fell behind, we'd all pitch in to get his crops caught up before fall set in. We slaughtered hogs on the coldest days and for our Thanksgiving feasts. It was always a community event. Everybody dressed the meat, sharing equally no matter how many hogs each had. The ladies kept the stove going, and men brought in the trimmings to grind into sausage. Some of my male relatives commented on what a beautiful thing it was to see the women making sausage and liver mush. They worked elbow-to-elbow and created different batches with different seasonings, some with lots of peppers and some without.

These memories are priceless, and I frequently reflect on this fellowship with my beloved family. But what impressed me most was that we were people of self-reliance and self-sufficiency. From my father's example, I learned a lot about sharecropping and navigating the decaying economic engine of the Deep South. He worked multiple jobs six days a week — sometimes seven — and was professional and dependable. That meant people reached out to him whenever jobs became available. So, he balanced his work in the fields and his carpentry side jobs, and this became an important means of survival for my family during this segregated time in history.

I believe this is what got us into the "big house." We were the only African American family with a large, spacious home, and you might wonder how this happened.

The Big House

By then, Dr. Stevenson had hired my parents as sharecroppers. He owned the "big house," and before transferring to another town, invited my parents to live in what was, honestly, a mansion — two bedrooms downstairs and five upstairs. I recall it had a space set apart as a doctor's office but no indoor plumbing. We were used to that. What impressed us was the square footage. This space, the interior, and the large yard accommodated our large headcount and certainly made an impression on me, not to mention the neighbors. It demonstrated that people could move outside the status quo. Not only did it reflect well on my father, but it also reflected well on our whole family. I would describe us as the "salt of the earth" type of people — God-fearing, accountable, and always mindful of the mantra "Do unto others …"

We were the first Black family to have a pair of matching red mules, called "Cadillac mules." They were considered the prettiest variety. Daddy bought them for about a $100 each, which was quite expensive in that day and age. The bank loaned him the money. My sister Gladys, ten years my senior, also remembers the 1929 Whippet Daddy drove to church. Wooden spokes, gray color — it was definitely a step up from our wagon and mules. Gladys remembers my siblings filling up the car as we headed to church. My brother Tony stood on the fender, and Mami put her arm around him so he wouldn't fall. My brother Bish stood on the other side. What a sight we must have been as we rolled into the church parking lot! Dad often dropped us off and went back to pick up another group.

I remember that it gave my parents great joy to entertain family and friends. With all that room in the big house, my mother invited the townswomen who were avid quilters. Quilting was always a festive occasion, and I enjoyed the hustle and bustle of those quilting bees. I watched my mother's busy fingers and the flash of the needle as she handcrafted art forms from scraps of old clothes and leftover fabric. I overheard them talking and joking and smelled the food simmering on the stove. When the quilting bees finished, everyone enjoyed a good dinner and good company. My mother was an excellent hostess and was always generous to everyone. This was another example that stuck with me throughout my life.

Chapter Three: North Carolina and a New Normal

I lost my father when I was ten, but can still hear his soft-spoken voice telling me to be an honorable human being.
~ Pettis Norman

My father had a stomach condition, a "sick stomach," as some called it, and was diagnosed with ulcers. The only thing that soothed the pain was milk, and my brother Bish made the trek every morning to my Uncle Isaac's house to collect the special sweet milk produced by his cows. Mind you, we had our own cows, but the milk they produced was ordinary. There was something special about my uncle's herd, and therefore Bish made the trek without fail, rain or shine. He left behind an empty bottle and picked up a full bottle, and then traveled back home so Daddy could coat his stomach.

This demonstrated to us the level of devotion Bish had for our father. The love and care my uncle Isaac and cousin Jesse showed by sharing the sweet milk gave Daddy comfort. We all worked together and did everything within our power to help our parents and relatives maintain good health.

Even with ulcers, you'd never know that my father had health issues. He seemed unstoppable, an industrious man who never complained, and I thought he'd live forever. Then tragedy struck like a bolt of lightning. I will never forget the day he returned from working in the field, slumped over the plow and barely moving. We panicked, brought him into the house, and quickly took Daddy to the hospital. There was little that could be done. We're still not sure if he suffered a stroke or a heart attack. Tragically, he died the following day when I was just ten years old.

It was a tradition in the South that a loved one's body was brought home and laid in an open casket for final viewing. I quietly sat in the room, alone, peering over at my father's casket and hoping it was all a dream. With tears streaming down my face, I wanted him to get up and carry on in some miraculous way. I did not understand why he would leave me at such a young, impressionable age and remained very sad for a long, long time. I'm certain he worked himself into an early grave, but I consider this to be a noble death. He gave his all for the ones he loved and left behind a great legacy.

The community mourned with us as hundreds of people, regardless of race, lamented the loss of my father. The townsfolk brought food and shared their condolences with my mother, and the funeral was well attended. Daddy was buried in the cemetery at New Tabernacle Baptist Church, where he had devoted so much of his time. His gravestone is maintained to this day. It declares:

FATHER
Fessor M. Norman
Jan. 13, 1890
Apr. 20, 1949
**LOVE
YOUR CHILDREN**

At my father's gravesite in Lincolnton, Georgia

I'm sad about losing my father. I have no photo of him — he didn't have access to a camera back in his generation. Yet, I can still see him plowing the fields and bringing the mules to the barn in the back of my mind. I miss our special time together as we rode in the wagon. I miss his loving touch — his hand on my head as he walked with me. Every evening I'd sit on the porch and await his arrival, and he'd approach the steps and run his hand down my arm.

"How are you, son? Did you have a good day?" he'd ask. I can still hear his voice, so gentle, and feel his hand as it radiated warmth, love, and encouragement. His touch relayed approval, too — he was as proud of me as I was of him, and this thought gave me comfort after he died.

The Move to Charlotte

This great loss affected our family, and it fell to my mother to persevere. We had plenty of family support, but she decided to leave the farm and relocate to Charlotte, North Carolina. She wanted to live near her sister Sarah and took all of us with her except my sisters Winnie Pearl, Eva, and Elizabeth, who were married. This meant the years 1950 through 1956 were a time of adjustment for us all.

Charlotte, North Carolina, was a big city compared to Lincolnton, Georgia. I enrolled in Biddlesville Elementary School for two years but was overwhelmed and afraid of the size of the school, not to mention the larger city. My beloved dog Snippy had died of old age, so I didn't have the comfort of my life-long companion. My horse, Annie, was put in the care of relatives in Georgia, and I missed her too.

I must have appeared miserable, and my mother took pity on me. She allowed me to go back to Lincolnton to live with my sister Elizabeth. After I completed the 6th grade, my mother moved me back to Charlotte, this time permanently, to finish junior high and high school. I didn't want to leave Lincolnton, but she insisted. She wanted her youngest child in the nest. Years later, after becoming a parent myself, I understood this so well and would have done the same thing.

Fortunately, at this point, I was ready to acclimate. We adopted another dog, although this was a family pet and not entirely mine. Still, there's something special about dogs and their ability to boost spirits, and our new pet did just that. I made friends in school and earned good grades at Northwest Junior High. The school was segregated, and no athletic programs were available to students. Although I was familiar with baseball, I did not see a football until I was 14.

My father's passing left a void emotionally but also financially. When people ask me what I did for fun in junior high, I tell them I worked. Aside from playing occasional makeshift baseball, that's what I did after school and on weekends and holidays. I took odd jobs to help my family as best I could. Luckily for me, I had great role models in my industrious siblings, including my brother Bish. I worked at the lumber house with him, loading and unloading trucks. It was a strenuous workout for a kid, especially out in the heat and elements. But the upside was that it built my physique and endurance. Little did I know the advantage I gained early on by handling heavy lumber alongside my brother. In hindsight, I was being primed and conditioned for the gridiron without realizing it.

My favorite job was working at a bakery. I was the cleaner and took this role seriously. Those enormous oven racks got coated with baked-on oil, flour, batter — you name it — and I scraped, scrubbed, and polished them until they gleamed. One day, the owner paid me a compliment. "I wish every employee did as good a job as you," he said. These simple words meant more to me than my wages. It validated the high standards that my parents had instilled.

After all, my dad always taught us, "Whatever you do, do it well. If you're planting, plant well. If you're plowing, plow well." I felt personally responsible for applying this notion to every endeavor I undertook.

I enjoy telling this story because it is a gift that keeps on giving. Those kind words from the bakery owner spurred a life-long work ethic that followed me throughout high school, college, and the NFL, and later as a business owner. Young people tend to live up to the words they hear. When kids are told they are "less than" or failures, they often achieve that label. If they are told they are important and appreciated, then they achieve that standard as well. Even today, I look for opportunities to praise young people when I notice them doing a good job, knowing it makes a huge psychological impact.

I met my future wife, Margaret Ann Clinkscales, in seventh grade. She was a very pretty girl, but what really struck me was her smile. It was generous, contagious and matched her personality, which was friendly and polite. My heart leaped in my chest, but being an unsophisticated farm kid, I was just too shy to say much. She was one year younger and, luckily for me, we became more serious over the next six years. We walked to school hand-in-hand every day. It was no wonder that my relatives loved Margaret and treated her like she was part of the family.

My future wife, Margaret Clinkscales

High School

I graduated junior high in 1955, still playing makeshift baseball with my friends, and enrolled in West Charlotte High School. I was happy when Margaret became a freshman at West Charlotte High the following year. She put up with my very busy schedule, and in the back of my mind throughout high school and later in college I kept thinking, she's the one.

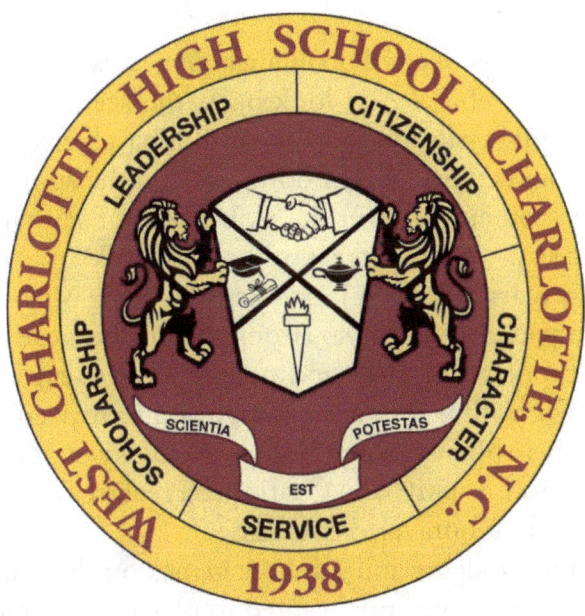

I continued to work odd jobs, and some were quite interesting. My brother Bish and I were part of the construction team that built the 1959 Motor Speedway in Concord, North Carolina, about 13 miles from Charlotte. I'll never forget hauling bags of cement to the motorsports complex and the excitement when the first World 600 NASCAR race was held there in 1960.

I accompanied both of my brothers, Tony and Bish, as they delivered building materials to various businesses in the vicinity. I learned a bit about custom cabinetry and home remodeling by tagging along and absorbing their craftsmanship, knowing they had learned the finer points from my departed father. There is something so special about a trade that is passed down through the generations. A side bonus was that once again, the manual labor kept me in shape.

Another favorite job was at a grocery store. Within a short period, I became the #1 bagger. It was a point of pride, organizing groceries for customers and ensuring their eggs and produce arrived home in good condition. Even today, I enjoy watching young baggers work their magic. Most take pride in a job well done. Admittedly, I sometimes give the weaker baggers a few pointers just in case it helps.

One of my other high school jobs was as a porter for Woolworth, earning very little money but meeting lots of interesting people. I think that's when I became a people watcher, learning to size up who would and would not leave a tip regardless of how courteous and quick I was. I'm thankful for that experience. It allowed me to study human nature and determine what kind of adult I wanted to be. The concepts of "Do unto others" and "For the least of these" were deeply ingrained, thanks to my family, and that's the path I chose.

A less than favorite job was as a janitor at various restaurants and grocery stores, not that I didn't appreciate the work. I cleaned, mopped, and tinkered with leaky faucets. It wasn't as interesting as construction jobs or even the porter job, but it was honest work. Most importantly, it brought income into the household.

Baseball

Best of all, the world of sports opened up in a whole new way for me in high school; there were real baseball bats and baseballs! As I look back, the seeds of my athletic success were sown in baseball, which might be surprising to some. But baseball legend Jackie Robinson was so popular, how could I not become a fan of both him and the sport? He was a hero to Black communities across the nation and all over the globe, and a fair share of Whites adored him too. I believe his dynamic skills changed the world of baseball.

I remember being eight years old when Jackie began playing Major League Baseball for the Brooklyn Dodgers. His impact on me was so strong, mainly because he broke baseball's color barrier. He signed with Brooklyn in 1947 and proved he was an artful Dodger — a slick-fielding infielder who hit for both power and average and terrorized opposing teams with his speed on the base paths. My nephew George Bolton was lucky enough to get a signed baseball from Jackie during his visit to the YMCA in Charlotte, a real treasure. As I recall, George kept that ball in close quarters until it unraveled over time.

Growing up, I listened to Dodgers and Yankees games on the radio. Jackie was the player who got my undivided attention. Everyone wanted to play just like him. But the Dodgers had professional equipment while we made do with socks stuffed with grass and a piece of wood. Sometimes rocks were substituted for baseballs; catching those rocks toughened our hands. It's a wonder we didn't break our fingers or lose an eye!

That may sound dangerous and even odd by today's standards, but it wasn't all that uncommon to improvise with whatever was available. We were extremely resourceful kids. In fact, around that same time, another son of the South, Hall of Fame baseball pitcher Jim "Catfish" Hunter, used corncobs as baseballs on his daddy's farm in Hertford, North Carolina.

Although we didn't have organized sports as kids do now, we did have neighborhood teams. The competition was good — lots of kids loved baseball — and we really enjoyed playing the game. It was fun to run the imaginary field and bases, pretending to play in the World Series. Those experiences would follow me onto a formal baseball team — the West Charlotte Lions.

Football

I did find time to join a few clubs — the French club, Junior Boys Honor Club, and Photography Club. I was fascinated with cameras, film, and images and wanted to learn more. My dear friend Wilson Counts, a classmate and outstanding football player, also participated in these clubs, which turned out to be fortuitous for me. He played a big role in my life in high school and later in college.

Photography club yearbook photo

At that time, I didn't know a whole lot about football. A bunch of kids played sandlot football — I watched them from a distance for a couple of weeks, trying to understand the blocking and tackling, and learned on my own. I did this because I wanted to be as good as possible before I ever stepped foot on the sandlot. I think I've always been wired that way; I study, absorb, practice, assess my own abilities, and then perform.

Wilson Counts took me under his wing as I joined him in the sandlot games. Since football was the only sport Wilson ever played, he was phenomenal and played quarterback at West Charlotte High and then at Johnson C. Smith University. It was no coincidence that his father, Herman Counts, was my favorite professor when I later attended Johnson C. Smith University.

As Wilson continued to mentor me in football, I recall observing the other players and watching their every move enabled me to do things the other kids could not. It dawned on me that I might be successful at football, although baseball was still my favorite sport. So, I attempted football in the 10th grade but quit. I honestly liked baseball better, and my penchant was pitching.

I'm so thankful that I forged a very special friendship with Wilson from the moment we met. We were close until his passing; God rest his soul. I remain close to Wilson's sister Dorothy to this day and call her my little sister; she calls me her big brother. Dorothy Counts is phenomenal and played an important part in the school desegregation battle at Harding High School in Charlotte, North Carolina. I call her a true civil rights pioneer, beginning when she was 15 years old. Her story is so significant, jaw-dropping, and important, especially now, that I expand on it in the "Civil Rights" chapter ahead.

Junior and Senior Year

As always, I made tremendous effort to earn good grades and picked up football again in the 11th grade, despite my initial failure. After learning the finer details about the game while still enjoying baseball, I began to feel good about football. I joined a summer football league, although, honestly, I was still better at baseball than football at the time.

I had a good record as a pitcher and threw a perfect game in a playoff. I had an incredible fastball and good curveball and developed a reputation as a strike-out pitcher. I was pretty good with a bat, too. Several major league teams were interested in me, and scouts came to watch me play. There was talk at the time of me signing to play for the Charlotte Hornets in the minor leagues. But God, in His wisdom, intervened. Baseball, as much as I loved it, was not in my future. Instead, I was set on a path to the NFL.

As a high school senior, I played baseball, football and ran track. I had pretty good speed for the sprints and ran the 400-meter run as well. Track interested me because it combined strategy with my God-given talents. When I ran the sprints, I relied on the speed and quickness I had been blessed with. When I ran the 400, I had to pace myself until the proper moment when it was time to sprint for the finish line.

I should mention that Margaret made the cheerleading squad and was a very good cheerleader. No matter what sport I played, I loved spotting her on the sidelines, cheering my teammates and me on. Sometimes we'd walk to Johnson C. Smith University to watch the football players in action. We'd joined my siblings, cousins, nieces, and nephews behind the wire fence, sometimes enjoying a picnic as we soaked up the adrenaline-filled practices. As high school graduation loomed, it never once occurred to me that I'd ever been on the other side of that fence. I had zero expectations of playing college football anywhere, including JCSU. I simply could not afford it.

Leroy "Pop" Miller

As I reflect on the administration at West Charlotte, one teacher made an indelible imprint on my life – Leroy "Pop" Miller. He was an industrial arts teacher who had the academic skills and leadership presence to help the school navigate the turbulent period of desegregation.

Pop Miller was like a second father and looked out for my best interest with tough love and high standards. He encouraged students to develop their talents and took note when they struggled. His legacy was simple and reflective of what my parents taught – "Be the best that you can be." He helped shape generations of Charlotteans, including myself, and I still remember a prediction he made about me one day at school when I chose a shorter route to avoid the crowds heading to the auditorium. "Norman, I see leadership skills in you —you wisely chose a shorter path to achieve the same goal. You are going places!"

A Serendipitous Scholarship

My heart led me to the Air Force after graduation. It was both a patriotic and economic choice since we needed the income. As an Airman, I would earn a much-needed salary and good benefits. There was also the Margaret factor. I was very serious about her and knew I'd propose one day. The Air Force made sense as I thought ahead to the new responsibilities that marriage would bring. I took all the required tests and was accepted. My future now had security and stability, and I was joyous.

While preparing for boot camp, I continued to work part-time at a gas station, pumping gas, washing cars, and doing engine work. I still had various other jobs as well. My mother suffered a stroke and was not well, and the $35 to $40 a week I earned helped us survive.

One day, a man pulled into the station to get some gas, none other than the new head coach at the nearby Johnson C. Smith University, the second oldest Historically Black College in the nation. I'll never forget his beautiful, brand-new Pontiac Bonneville. The car was light blue and gray, either a coincidence or a foreshadowing of the colors I would one day wear as a Dallas Cowboys player.

My coworker, Nate Edwards, assisted the customer, who introduced himself as Coach Eddie McGirt on his first scouting trip to recruit players. I was inside washing a car when Nate pointed at me. He said, "Coach, Pettis is the best player in the state." That was quite a stretch. I had played fourth string in the 11th grade and caught one pass. Of course, I improved immensely in my senior year but did not consider myself the "best player" at all! So Nate, who was older than me and a family man, very kindly went out on a limb to inflate my qualifications.

Coach McGirt walked into the garage, introduced himself, and asked about my plans. I told him I had been accepted into the Air Force and would be leaving soon. He responded by offering me a scholarship without ever seeing me play.

Well, my heart sank and rose at the same time. I didn't want to break my contract with the Air Force since I had given my word, but I had just been handed a free ride to college and a chance to play football two blocks from my mother's apartment. I decided this was an opportunity too great to pass up, especially since no one in my family had ever gone to college. I contacted my recruiting officer, explained my dilemma, and could not believe it when he listened sympathetically and then released me. He didn't have to — I belonged to the Air Force lock, stock, and barrel — so the whole situation was surely an example of God's Divine intervention.

I tried out for the team as Coach McGirt's first recruit, made the cut, and immediately signed a new set of paperwork, this time for JCSU's football scholarship program. Never in my wildest imagination could I have predicted how my future would unfold.

Eddie McGirt wasn't the only coach who was about to impact my life. The football coaching staff also included William McCollough, Byrd Crudup, and Jack Brayboy. These fine men were known as inspirational leaders who endeavored to pull the best out of their players. I knew I'd be participating in an exciting football program and could not wait to be a Golden Bull.

I remember how amazed my mother was at this turn of events. My entire extended family praised God many times for bringing this opportunity to my doorstep. As I reflect on this incredible blessing, I am so grateful that my coworker Nate Edwards lobbied for me at the start of it all. If he had not exaggerated my football credentials, Coach McGirt would not have recruited me. Before his passing, I recognized Nate as a valuable part of my life during the JCSU "Arc of Triumph" ceremony in 2010, when several alumni and I received this distinguished award.

Chapter Four: Golden Years of the Golden Bulls

What a blessing it is to be an alumnus of Johnson C. Smith University.
~ Pettis Norman

I think in this current climate of racial division and renewed strides for social justice, it's important to note the contributions of Historically Black Colleges and Universities. To offer some history, Johnson C. Smith University was established on April 7, 1867, as the Biddle Memorial Institute.

Mary D. Biddle, a devout churchwoman, donated $1,400 to the school. In appreciation of this first contribution, friends requested that Mrs. Biddle name the newly established school; she did so in the name of her late husband, Captain Henry Jonathan Biddle, who had been mortally wounded during the Battle of Glendale in 1862.

In 1923, the Board of Trustees voted to change the name of this institution to Johnson C. Smith University, in memory of Johnson C. & Jane Berry Smith, for their generous gifts to the school. The school's charter was amended on March 1, 1923, by the State of North Carolina legislature.

In 1924, the James B. Duke Endowment was established. It named Johnson C. Smith University as one of four institutions of higher education to benefit annually from the foundation's philanthropy that states: "4% of said net amount not retained as aforesaid for addition to the corpus of the trust shall be paid to the Johnson C. Smith University (by whatever name it may be known), an institution of learning for colored people, now located at Charlotte, in said State of North Carolina, so long as it shall not be operated for private gain, to be utilized by said institution for any and all of the purposes thereof." Over the past 100 years, the endowment has made gifts to JCSU of more than $85 million; what an amazing blessing.

In 1932, the university's charter was amended, providing for the admission of women. The 65-year-old institution for men then became partially coeducational. The first residence hall for women, named in memory of James B. Duke, was dedicated in 1940. In 1941, women were admitted to the freshman class. In 1942, the university was a fully coeducational institution.

In 2017, JCSU was ranked 18th among 100+ HBCU's by U.S. News & World Report. It is a private liberal arts university with proud HBCU traditions and a future aimed at diversity. The enrollment has approximately 1,500 highly talented and motivated students from various backgrounds.

Those enrolled today have a choice of 22 degree options for undergraduates and one graduate degree. Students earn their degree through one of three colleges – the College of Arts and Letters, the College of STEM (Science, Technology, Engineering, and Mathematics), and the College of Professional Studies. In addition, JCSU offers opportunities to study abroad in countries such as Egypt, Russia, Brazil, Dominican Republic, Turkey, Cape Verde, and Cuba. Equally unique, the faculty and staff members come from all over the world.

Clarence D. Armbrister, the new President, leads Johnson C. Smith University today. He is doing transformational work to reposition my alma mater for growth in today's competitive global environment. As a result of his efforts, there's renewed energy on campus. New partnerships are developing and a foundation is being laid that will provide long-term sustainability for JCSU. It's refreshing to see the city, government, and local businesses in Charlotte support and embrace JCSU, ensuring the university will continue to educate the leaders of tomorrow.

I'm honored that President Armbrister had this to say about me, an alumnus of nearly 60 years:

> *All-around excellence and the ability to continually reinvent himself – these are two characteristics to describe Pettis Norman. As a standout student-athlete and graduate of Johnson C. Smith University, he exemplifies the JCSU Golden Bulls spirit. The JCSU Loyalty Song implores us to Hold High the Gold and Blue. Throughout his life, Pettis has been proven to have the golden touch of King Midas. After playing for more than a decade in the NFL, Pettis utilized his JCSU education to start a successful career in banking and then entrepreneurship. He is a steadfast servant leader who has*

advocated for civil rights and social justice. His impact and contributions to American athletics, business, and philanthropy deserve to be recognized and celebrated. The JCSU family is forever grateful to our very own Pettis Norman.

With kind words like that, it's easy to remain an enthusiastic and loyal Smithite. I often shout out JCSU on Facebook, which allows me to connect with young students who will blaze trails for decades to come. I find it remarkable that they have the same feelings for the university that I've had all these years and will become supportive alumni after graduation and well into the future.

JCSU has graduated quite a few politicians, corporate and higher education leaders, and some renowned international track, NFL, and NBA athletes, including former Harlem Globetrotter Fred "Curly" Neal, an important part of the university's basketball program. Not everyone may know that Curly's nickname at the university was "Scrip;" he was dubbed "Curly" after joining the Globetrotters. During his time at JCSU, he averaged 23.1 points per game and was named an All-CIAA guard. He was inducted into the CIAA Hall of Fame in 1986 and the North Carolina Sports Hall of Fame in 2008.

As one of the greatest all-time dribblers and masterful shooters, he played more than 6000 games in 97 countries from 1963 to 1985. The Harlem Globetrotters presented him with the team's prestigious "Legends" ring in 1993 and retired his #22 jersey in 2008. When Curly passed away on March 26, 2020, he left behind classmates, former Golden Bull teammates, alumni, staff and faculty who remember him as a global goodwill ambassador; well done, good and faithful servant.

I appreciate our former President, Dorothy Yancy as well, another lifelong friend who became an accomplished academic and the twelfth president of the college. She led JCSU for 14 years and was widely lauded for her fundraising skills, growing the school's endowment, and wiring the campus for Internet access. In the year 2000, JCSU became the first Historically Black University to be labeled a "laptop" campus, issuing IBM ThinkPad's to all its students.

I commend Dorothy for her outstanding leadership. We stayed in touch by way of my service on Smith's Board of Trustees for two decades and "Homecoming," which continues to be a magnet for alumni. Dorothy kindly told me, "Pettis, you were able to bring the perspective of a student, student-athlete, and a businessman to the board." It is an honor to serve my alma mater; JCSU is a terrific institution of higher learning, and I remain devoted to JCSU even today.

After I graduated and signed with the Dallas Cowboys, Dorothy shared that a lot of Smith students became Cowboys fans. She recalls rarely missing the Cowboys on TV when I was playing. After I left Dallas, she says her interest and the interest of her friends in the Cowboys waned. Dorothy remembers my return trips to Smith and affectionately stated, "It was like having a rock star on campus." I appreciate those kind words from Dorothy, whom I nicknamed "little sis" during our years at JCSU.

Football

One of my fondest recollections as a young man was the start of my scholarship at JCSU. The 100-acre campus had a few buildings and a small student body of 800–900 when I arrived. The campus buildings had a classic look with large columns, a Carnegie library, and a warm, inviting atmosphere. I settled into my small but prestigious university and was proud to be a part of the most exciting team at the conference.

I became Number 82, a two-way player, offense and defense, and was nicknamed "Stone Wall." After a brief demonstration of my athletic ability, I was a starter and named team MVP at split end as a freshman. I was also appointed team captain and a two-time All Central Collegiate Athletic Association (CIAA) selection. The CIAA was known for producing great players, among them future Pro Football Hall of Famer Leroy Kelly and NFL star defenders like my great friend and Cowboys teammate Jethro Pugh; God rest his soul. Roger Brown, too, was a tremendous defensive lineman for the Detroit Lions and one of the members of the Los Angeles Rams' famous "Fearsome Foursome."

Photo credit: Johnson C. Smith University

Nate Allen was a teammate and two-way player, lining up at halfback on offense and cornerback when we were on defense. May God rest his soul. He arrived at Smith a year behind me, and we had some notable battles in a scrimmage. We laughed about these plays — a fond memory — just before his passing, but at the time, Nate said I had him spinning like a top during some of our scrimmages. He had trouble dealing with my speed and blocking abilities at times and shared a nice recollection of me blocking my opponents into the ground.

"Pettis, you clearly demonstrated how an effective leader can lead in different settings — on the playing field and on campus," he recently told me. "You were the best football player I've ever seen, catching, blocking, and running — a triple threat."

Nate, too, was an excellent player, and he had the brains. We spent a lot of time studying together on the team bus — Nate quizzed me and was quite the taskmaster. In hindsight, that's no surprise for he became Dr. Nate Allen with a Ph.D. behind his name, an accomplished leader in the field of social services, urban development, and political action. We were long-term buddies and remained great friends over the years. I'm so very proud of him, he was a loyal friend, and I miss him terribly.

Three things Nate and I will forever share is our love of football, a passion for winning, and admiration for Coach McGirt, whom we adoringly called "Cut." I wanted everyone to perform at peak level, and so did Nate. As captain of the Golden Bulls, I sought to show how we could all set our goals high by making a difference on and off the field.

My good buddies at JCSU still talk about an incident they will never let me forget. We led the nation in small college defense in our sophomore season but lost a game 54-12. Some of the guys on the team bus started joking about the loss, and I got angry. They claim my anger was over the top, and that was putting it mildly. I began to challenge every one of our players for the regrettable loss. After I chilled a little, several players said, "Wow! Pettis, I'm glad you are on my team."

Truthfully, I'm not sure whether they said so out of fear or admiration. I hope it was admiration, although, in reality, I made an impression as a tough, no-nonsense defender with a temper on the field. I always practiced as hard as I played, knocked the player opposing me into the ground, and then helped him up. Coach McGirt saw my intensity and said on several occasions, "If I had ten more Pettis Normans, I would never lose a game," a prelude to what Tom Landry would say years later when I was playing for the Cowboys.

Nate frequently teased me about one intra-squad scrimmage. He tried to block me, and things got a little heated. He had a big mustache at that time, so I nicknamed him "Stasche." During our exchange, I told him, "Don't push me, Stasche!" Our brief shoving match made news around the campus, and we laughed about it often. I honestly don't remember what the tug of war was about, but it never impacted our friendship. I just wanted to win, and losing was never an option. I guess you could call me an intense young man and these values laid the foundation for my future, much of my success at Smith, and later the NFL. Thankfully, Coach McGirt took an interest in me and worked on my rough edges.

Yes, Coach was a great man, the kind of person who had patience and taught me the best way to play ball and conduct myself as a student. He was vocal but didn't have to raise his voice to get his point across to his players. In fact, my teammates cannot recall a time when he yelled at any of us.

Coach gave another close friend of mine, James "Butch" Walker, a four-year scholarship sight unseen — scouting and film review back in the late '50s and early '60s was nothing like it is today. Butch certainly didn't disappoint, earning a coveted quarterback starting position his freshman season and remaining a starter for four years. They say dynamite comes in small packages — he stands five-foot-eight, but his small stature paid huge dividends as the starting quarterback at Smith. Butch and I still talk frequently, and I can hardly express how much I admire him.

At the beginning of our freshman year, Coach McGirt had just returned from a coaching clinic that emphasized the Shotgun offense. The Shotgun would later be brought into the NFL by San Francisco 49ers head coach Red Hickey in 1961 and then again by Tom Landry at Dallas in 1975. Today, almost every high school, college, and NFL team use the Shotgun as its base offense, an advantage that benefits quarterbacks who are mobile.

Front Row, L. to R.: Jesse Oden, Thomas Brown, James Harrison, Jimmie Lawrence, Ernest Wade, Seldon Chiles, James Willis, Thomas Wright, Herbert Singleton, James Dyson. Second Row: Thornwell Watson, Joe Adams, James Little, James Walker, Andrew Barrett, James Shamberger, John Steele, John Butler, Henry Simmons, William Joyner, Robert Moore, Pettis Norman. Third Row: Charles Butler, Walter Largent, Nathaniel Aiken, Nathan Allen, Frankie Barnes, Norman Muldrow, Herman Fisher, Robert Mallard, Howard Goode, Lewis Stephens, George Dorman. Fourth Row: John Burns, Frank Spivey, Ed Grant, Sammie Casley, Lenwood Edwards, Thomas Leach, Wilson Counts. Fifth Row: Ernest Robinson (trainer), Tracy Barrett (trainer), William Johnson, Henry Kelley, Ervin Toms, George Blalock, Ivan Sweeting (manager), Theodore Johnson (cleat cleaner).

JCSU football team. Photo credit: Johnson C. Smith University

By his own admission, Butch was No. 6 of six quarterbacks on our depth chart in his freshman season, but he was undoubtedly the most mobile — incredibly so — and a great runner. He could roll out with speed and quickness, throw on the run or keep the ball and sprint. During preseason practice, Coach McGirt became frustrated with the inability of other quarterbacks to run the Shotgun. In Butch's words, "They were as slow as molasses running uphill in the winter."

"Damn it," Coach said, "is there anybody here who thinks he can play quarterback?"

One of Butch's friends, Henry "Malzone" Morgan, spoke up, "Butch can, Coach."

Butch, Coach McGirt's first quarterback, got the starting position because he was adept at calling his own plays. For the rest of his tenure, JCSU ranked near the top of the CIAA. During that time, Butch gave me a lot of credit.

To illustrate, I recall one phenomenal game in a heavy rainstorm, when once again, Butch proved his worth. It was our freshman year; we were playing Winston, and the field became a sea of mud. We had the ball on the 25-yard line, and Butch called an "option right." I was the "left-end," and the defense gave chase. Butch fumbled the ball; it went over the defender's head and back into Butch's hands. I sprinted across the opposite side of the field and not only landed a crushing block but flipped a player in the air (not planned, just my passion), giving Butch a clear path to complete a 75-yard touchdown. That's one heck of a play, and I commend my brother for his outstanding performance. This play went down in the history books.

"You were a team player all the way," Butch still tells me, "and a tremendous competitor."

"Butch," I always reply, "you were a formidable quarterback who made me a better player on the field."

It's true. There was some sort of synergy between us, and I'm moved that teammates like Nate and Butch and many others forged such a special bond. We call each other brothers, even today. From our first meeting in 1958, we've stood in each other's corner in every one of life's battles along the way, including the recent loss of Butch's beloved wife Betty, who has gone home to heaven; may God rest her soul.

I am so proud of Butch's recent induction into the 2019 Commemorative Classic Hall of Fame. His message that evening was, "Winning is great, but I hate to lose." This award was long overdue and well deserved. Butch retired and relocated to Charlotte after a successful career with the Department of Justice and Immigration. I include him as part of my family visits when I'm in Charlotte.

Coach McGirt often told us, "The guys you're competing against today in football practice will become your friends for life." That has been very true. Recently, several of us reconnected at Butch Walker's 80th birthday party in Charlotte, six decades after we met in college. It was a blessing to fellowship with my friends and former teammates George Dorman, Frankie Barnes, Leroy "Buzzie" Scott, and good friend Nate Allen before he passed. On a personal note, I was so happy to celebrate Butch's 80th. Friends like him are hard to find.

Making the Mark

The fact that Coach McGirt gave me, and so many others, a chance is just one of many reasons we performed so well for him. The most remarkable thing was that Coach always thought of us as students first and athletes second. If we didn't keep our grades up, we didn't play. If a player wasn't a great athlete but maintained his grades, Coach kept him on scholarship. In fact, I don't recall him ever taking anyone's scholarship away, for he told us, "Most of you aren't going to become professional football players, so you're going to need your education." We loved him for that.

Coach McGirt graduated 93% of his players, a testament to his emphasis on education. He told us that when we left the campus, we represented ourselves and Johnson C. Smith University. Many of us feel that our years at Smith shaped us into successful people for reasons like these. Honestly, because of Coach, those of us on his football team weren't seen as dumb jocks. Fellow students respected us for our intelligence; when we spoke, people listened. Our conference was loaded with talented scholars who happened to be athletes. More importantly, we became the leadership group for African Americans in the arts, sciences, humanities, and business.

Under Coach's guidance, my grades were a priority. He knew that I was juggling multiple part-time jobs while balancing coursework and football. I worked at an Esso Gas Station, contracted myself out as a painter, and painted the stadium bleachers at JCSU. In addition, I contracted with several dry cleaners to deliver clothes and continued to work for my brother Bish in his remodeling and cabinetry business. Nevertheless, Coach encouraged me to focus on academics, no excuses. With a lot of determination, I found the time to keep my grades up and support my family and myself.

My teammates noticed the effort. They commented that I put the same energy into my studies as I did football, but without the temper. Thanks to the influence of my father and later my mother, I was raised to be a gentleman off the field and a voracious competitor on the field. Isn't that the way it's supposed to be?

As a senior, I played a game with five receptions for 133 yards, two touchdowns and was credited with 14 tackles. My opponents avoided my side of the field and rarely ran their plays in my direction. We went 8-1 my senior season in a conference that was loaded with talent and just missed out on playing in the Orange Blossom Classic. Following the football season, I lettered in track and field, once posting a 9.7-second 100-yard dash, and was voted one of the All-Time Great Athletes.

Here's an interesting bit of trivia — one of my competitors in the 100-yard dash was Bob Hayes, an Olympic gold medalist who would become known as the "World's Fastest Human." We later became good friends and teammates on the Dallas Cowboys team and frequently talked about the races we ran against each other in college. During our time together on the team, we lived just down the street and spent a lot of time together. I miss him.

As you can see, this treasure trove of talent wasn't limited to the football field. Winston Salem State University's men's basketball team, coached by Clarence "Big House" Gaines, boasted future NBA Hall of Famer Earl "The Pearl" Monroe and Cleo Hill, a St. Louis Hawks draft. North Carolina Central's Sam Jones would play for the Boston Celtics. Virginia Union University's Bruce Spraggins was a star in the American Basketball Association, and "Jumping" Jack Jackson played for the world-famous Harlem Globe Trotters. As shared earlier, the late famous Globe Trotter Freddie "Curly" Neal was instrumental to the basketball program.

Coach Eddie McGirt's Legacy

I must mention how much it meant that Coach McGirt set the example and cared about us like a surrogate father, as if we were his own sons. This was important to me, having lost my father at such a young age. Coach had a way of working with me that inspired my best, and I gave him credit when I was named All-Conference tight end for three years (1959-1961) in the 18-team CIAA. I credited him as well when I became First Team All-American in 1961 and received the J.M. Murphy Award — the "Most Outstanding Football Player Award."

Coach Eddie McGirt. Photo courtesy of the Inez Moore Parker Archives, Johnson C. Smith University

I cannot thank Coach McGirt enough for guiding me toward these achievements. It had a ripple effect and literally changed the direction of my life. The athletic skills I honed at Smith allowed me to be the model for future Cowboy tight ends, including Billy Joe Dupree, Doug Cosbie, Jay Novacek, and Jason Witten.

Coach remained as the university's Athletic Director and Head of the Department of Health and Physical Education until 1985. After he retired, he continued to support JCSU athletics until his passing on December 21, 1999. The JCSU football field was named The Eddie C. McGirt Field in his honor. His endowed scholarship fund continues to support student-athletes who maintain a 3.0 GPA.

When our beloved coach passed, his service was held in South Carolina. It seemed almost everyone who had played for him showed up; it was a very difficult funeral. Coach Eddie "Cut" McGirt left behind an incredible legacy at JCSU and in the hearts of his student-athletes.

In 1940, he enrolled at Johnson C. Smith University and was one of the school's greatest athletes of all time, eventually becoming an All-CIAA selection. His hard work and commitment to excellence paid off after being selected as Johnson C. Smith's eleventh modern-day head football coach in 1958.

For 20 years, Coach's teams remained in the first division of the final CIAA standings. He was considered the "Dean of Coaches" in the CIAA, winning 118 of 191 games at JCSU. Within three seasons, Coach McGirt led the "Golden Bulls" to an 8-1-0 and a second-place finish in the CIAA. I will never forget my Coach, father figure, and true friend.

Dr. Jack S. Brayboy

Dr. Jack S. Brayboy was another person who influenced my life at JCSU. He was another one of JCSU's respected and beloved administrators who became the Athletic Director during my tenure at Smith. I was blessed to have two strong mentors while in school, Coach McGirt and Dr. Brayboy, who kept a very steady hand on me both on and off the field. Dr. Brayboy spent quality time talking and guiding me; he took me under his wing and kept a watchful eye on me. I remember soaking up his wisdom on life.

Dr. Brayboy was a stellar athlete himself and earned a place on the football all-star team of the CIAA in each of his four years while attending JCSU in the 1940s. By 1960, he was Director of Athletics and later became Executive Dean at the school. He graduated from JCSU with a triple major in chemistry, mathematics, and physical education. He later achieved an M.A in physical education and a Ph.D. in teacher education at the University of Pennsylvania. In addition, Brayboy Gymnasium, JCSU'S 2500-seat basketball arena, was named in his honor.

It's not every day you come across someone with this level of intellect and overflow of positive energy. Dr. Brayboy was a respected, selfless leader who operated with his heart and cared deeply about the well-being of students. I am so pleased to have crossed paths with this noble leader, a man who inspired many others and me during his tenure at JCSU.

When I transitioned to the NFL, I was determined never to let Dr. Brayboy and Coach Eddie McGirt down; they remained omnipresent in my life as I carried the mantle forward.

The Pettis Norman Award

The Department of Athletics honors student-athletes at an annual "Smitty Golden Awards" presentation for all sports, including football, tennis, volleyball, track, and basketball. Each sport gives awards to deserving Golden Bull student-athletes, including team MVP, Most Improved, Top Newcomer, Coaches Awards, and The Pettis Norman Award, for the student-athlete judged to have had the best overall season. The Pettis Norman Student-Athlete of the Year Award is the highest athletic honor from Johnson C. Smith University, awarded to the outstanding athlete every year.

It is with great pleasure to acknowledge and commend past student-athletes who have been recipients of this award dating back to its inception in 2007:

- 2007 Desirae Riddick (volleyball) and Ed Wilson (football)
- 2008 Jennifer Lee (tennis), Shermaine Williams (track), and De'Audra Dix (football)
- 2009 Shermaine Williams (track) and Leford Green (track)
- 2010 Demetria Bell (basketball) and Leford Green (track)
- 2011 Trevin Parks (basketball), Leford Green (track) and Shermaine Williams (track)
- 2012 Trevin Parks (basketball), Leford Green (track), Shermaine Williams (track)
- 2013 Trevin Parks (basketball) and Danielle Williams (track)
- 2014 Rolando Berch (track) and Danielle Williams (track)
- 2015 Tovea Jenkins (track) and Austin Jacques (football)
- 2016 Fellan Ferguson (track) Carlo Thomas (football)
- 2017 Blaire Thomas (basketball) and Carlo Thomas (football)
- 2018 Halle Parker (tennis) and Robert Davis (basketball)
- 2019 Tavian Stewart (track) Alisha St. Louis (track)

Congratulations to these outstanding student-athletes. I am proud of their commitment to excellence at JCSU.

Alumni Leadership

It's amazing that after 58 years, I am still connected to my alma mater and many of my classmates who are living today. While there were only about 800 - 900 students when I was in school, there was a deep kindred spirit among my classmates who became lifelong friends. I am blessed to have been a part of this university and grateful that JCSU has a strong alumni association to keep Smithites connected.

I was greatly honored when Wanda Foy-Burroughs, a member of Smith's Class of 1973 and currently the Director of Alumni Relations, wrote the following about me in 2019:

> *Pettis Norman, an outstanding alumnus, has had a longstanding relationship with Johnson C. Smith University (JCSU), and has demonstrated exceptional financial commitment and dedicated service to his alma mater. A 1962 graduate, Pettis was a standout on the Golden Bulls football team and was*

a major contributor to the success of the track and field team during his undergraduate days. The Pettis Norman Award, the highest honor conferred by JCSU Athletics, is given annually to the University's male and female athletes-of-the-year.

Pettis later served on the University's Board of Trustees with distinction and excellence, earning emeritus status upon retirement from the Board. He was a key donor and architect of the Eddie C. and Minnie McGirt Endowed Scholarship, which provides financial aid to deserving JCSU student-athletes. The endowment honors the legacy of the University's most successful football coach who recruited Pettis to JCSU and helped to develop his talents as a future NFL star. In 2010, Pettis received the University's Arch of Triumph Award recognizing his distinguished service to JCSU, stellar professional football career and outstanding success as a businessman/entrepreneur.

Pettis Norman is a very powerful resource for our students at JCSU. He offers real tangible testimonies that impact them to set their goals high.

I want to thank Wanda for her kind words and share a few of my own. First, JCSU is blessed to have Wanda as our current Director of Alumni Relations. For the fiscal year ending June 30, 2020, she spearheaded JCSU alumni to raise over a million dollars during the COVID-19 pandemic, a notable accomplishment that had not been achieved in the past decade. While I commend our generous Smithites for their unfailing love for our university, I don't believe this could have been accomplished without Wanda's leadership.

Wanda is an expert in the field of education and has served as an adjunct professor at several Universities. In addition, she worked in the Newark Public Schools and New Jersey Department of Education, bringing extensive experience to JCSU. I thank Wanda for being there for me and lending her selfless support and involvement in my life.

Another important individual has been tasked with keeping Smithites loyal to our alma mater, Mr. Ron Matthews. Ron graduated in 1978 and was elected as President of the National Alumni Association. While in that role, his mission was to foster and maintain a strong spirit of loyalty to JCSU and develop a strong liaison with a spirit of cooperation between the administration and alumni. I commend Ron for the great job he did with the Alumni Association, and I especially thank him for the many things he has done to support me and my family.

From the Outside Looking In

My niece, Lynda Gresham-Moore, has an interesting take on those days. I knew my family members came to watch me practice, just as I used to watch practices as a high school student. But seeing it through her eyes as a young girl touched my heart. She weighs in below.

Uncle Pettis has always been a giant of a man to me. I remember when I was much younger and he attended Johnson C. Smith University. My younger siblings and I would pack a little picnic lunch in brown paper bags and walk through the path in our backyard on Sparrow Street that led to the outskirts of the JCSU practice field. We would sit outside the fence and watch the football players practice.

To us, he was already a star. The first in our family to not only play college football (or any college sport), but the first to even attend college. It was so exciting to sit on the grass outside the football field and watch Uncle Pettis practice. Who knew that the best was yet to come!

I love and honor him not for his status as a Dallas Cowboy, but because of the care he has for his family; because of how he stands for what he believes is right... because of how he built his personal career and established himself as a well-respected fixture in the Dallas community and beyond. For never changing who he is, but rather standing on the principles and the teachings of his upbringing.

Pettis has, is, and always will be Uncle Pettis. He will always remain the same Pettis Norman, a proud man who loves his family. I so admire how he loves on his sisters, especially my mother Gladys, who he adoringly calls 'Gippy.' Even today, he always attends to her wellbeing.

Pettis demonstrated to us all that it doesn't matter how you start, but rather how you finish.

Another Niece, Teresa Ray Hasty, also reflects on my past. She describes how my family united around football when I played for the Cowboys.

After Grandma Eloise became ill, she and Pettis moved in with his older sister Gladys, and later with my mother Sarah, his youngest sister. All of his sisters and brothers and lots of nieces and nephews came to our house every Sunday to watch the games and cheer him on. It was so much fun; we all looked forward to cheering for Uncle Pettis.

Shortly before leaving to play for the Cowboys, we all saluted him off to Dallas from my mother Sarah's house, and it was an excited yet emotional moment to watch Uncle Pettis leave. Our whole family knew in our hearts and minds that he was destined for greatness. He discovered at an early age the secrets of success by working extra hard and turning dreams into a reality.

We were all so excited and proud of him, and our family became a large group of Cowboy fans in the Charlotte, NC area.

In Retrospect

Graduating from JCSU was a huge milestone and left an indelible mark. With all humbleness, I am pleased and grateful for my achievements; they are debts payable to my mother, father, siblings, JCSU professors, Coach McGirt, teammates, and others. I look back now and say thanks with warm gratitude to all who helped me along the way.

As I look back at my formative years at Johnson C. Smith University, I recall our loyalty song that became a beacon of hope, our guiding star embedded in our minds, even today:

We love thee Smith, with all our hearts!
To thee we'll e'er be true

And in the light of truth and right
Hold high the gold and blue.

Refrain:

Proudly we hail thy name, our Alma Mater, Old S.U.
Johnson C. Smith, our own! Our Hope, our guiding
Star, our light unfailing!
Pride of our loyal hearts, we'll love and honor thee
Our whole life through
On, ever on! Dear old J.C.S.U.!

Fair Smith, where'er on earth we roam
Send forth thy constant ray,
And let it beam with steadfast gleam
To lead us o'er life's way.

The next few chapters capture the 12 years I spent playing for the Dallas Cowboys and the San Diego Chargers, applying the life skills and football finesse that I honed at Smith. Life happened on and off the field — moving parts of an adventure that I attempt to record chronologically.

Chapter Five: How 'Bout Them Cowboys!

The shelf life of an NFL player is fleeting. It's important to build a legacy outside of football that won't expire.
~ Pettis Norman

In 1961, newly elected U.S. President John F. Kennedy declared that America was seeking a "New Frontier," the exploration of space. One year later, I was seeking a new frontier of my own, having graduated from Johnson C. Smith University with a Bachelor of Science degree in physical education. My favorite courses were zoology, kinesiology, and biology.

By now, there were three pro football leagues in North America: the established National Football League, the fledgling American Football League, and, north of the border, the Canadian Football League. I had watched the NFL on television for years and was impressed by many of the great players who were already legendary, like Jim Brown of the Cleveland Browns, Johnny Unitas of the Baltimore Colts, and Sam Huff of the New York Giants. I was honored to receive a lot of interest from pro teams during my senior year — my hard work paid off.

The American Football League was less known in 1962, having been inaugurated only two years earlier. The AFL's Dallas Texans, owned by league co-founder Lamar Hunt and coached by the colorful Hank Stram, drafted me. Lamar Hunt was a Texas multi-millionaire, thanks to the dealings of his tycoon father, H. L. Hunt. It was reported that the Dallas Texans lost a million dollars in their first year of operations, pocket change for a pro sports team today but a lot of money at that time. H. L. Hunt commented that Lamar would go broke in about 100 years at the rate of losing a million dollars a year.

I admired what Lamar Hunt and other members of the "Foolish Club" were doing, opening up new jobs for pro players, coaches, and personnel, as well as expanding pro football into cities like Boston, Buffalo, Denver, Houston, Oakland, and San Diego to rival NFL teams in New York and Dallas. The AFL would eventually expand into Cincinnati and Miami.

The AFL was also expanding opportunities for athletes from traditional Black colleges like Grambling and southern schools like my own Johnson C. Smith University. The Texans drafted me and then spread the word that I had signed with them. This was during the AFL-NFL signing wars that existed from 1960–66, when the merger between the warring leagues signaled the start of the common draft. I feel confident the Texans said I signed with them to scare off potential NFL suitors who may have had interest in me.

Whatever the reason, I didn't like them spreading the word that I had signed a contract with them when I had not. Around that same time, Dallas Cowboys' Gil Brandt contacted me.

I met with Gil, and he offered me a $500 signing bonus to join the Cowboys as an undrafted free agent. To this day, Gil remembers my refusing a check and insisting on having the payment in cash. Gil had to rush to a nearby bank to secure the necessary money. I vividly recall receiving $500 in one-dollar denominations; Gil shuffled the bills like a deck of cards and then waved them at me. Today, I frequently joke about the dollar bills, but I can't thank Gil enough for finding me at little JCSU. I became one of ten Black players on the team.

Some may not know that Gil helped pioneer many of the scouting techniques used by NFL clubs today and later adopted by teams throughout the NFL. I am so proud of his induction into the Texas Hall of Fame, and in 2019, the Pro Football Hall of Fame. After six decades in the NFL, he earned it, and I consider him a good friend today.

The Dallas Cowboys, also called America's Team, is well known around the world today, with thousands of enthusiastic and faithful fans. But at that point, it was a new franchise, founded in 1960, an expansion team by oil baron Clint Murchison. The Cowboys rose to greatness under Tex Schramm, Gil Brandt, and Coach Landry, the most adored coach in football history.

Loss of My Mother

Amidst this excitement, tragedy struck once again. That dreaded bolt of lightning appeared out of nowhere when my mother died of a stroke. It's difficult to articulate the sense of being orphaned after just graduating from college... perhaps orphaned isn't the right word, for I was a young adult and independent. However, having lost both parents was significant. The support of Margaret, my siblings, and my large extended family helped me through that difficult time.

My mother's passing so deeply saddened me; she never had the chance to see me play for the Cowboys. I was crushed that I couldn't share this enormous blessing with her. Just as I shared my father's headstone inscription, I'm sharing my mother's — both emphasize the sentiment: "Love Your Children." Not surprisingly, the family spelling of her name "Elease" is used rather than the formal spelling "Eloise." Official records in that timeframe were handwritten with obvious phonetic interpretations, some more accurate than others, resulting in her name variations. Interestingly, I have always referred to her as Eloise, while other siblings referred to her as Elease. We probably didn't notice because her most endearing name was "Mami."

MOTHER
Elease Norman
Dec. 9, 1901
Feb. 11, 1962
**LOVE
YOUR CHILDREN**

My beloved mother

I credit my mother, just as I credit my father, for the love, guidance and support that helped me achieve some remarkable accomplishments and prepared me for a future that none of us could have envisioned.

Training Camp

I left my fiancée Margaret in Charlotte and flew to the Cowboys' temporary training camp at Northern Michigan College in Marquette, Michigan — it was my first plane flight, and I took my Bible with me. It was quite shocking to step off the plane into 50-degree weather when the temperature in Charlotte was quite a bit warmer.

John Henry wrote of our training camp locale in the *Fort Worth Star-Telegram* on August 01, 2015:

> *It was too cold for the liking of Tom Landry, who despaired taking his team out of the 50-degree climes of summer Michigan for the typical 100-degree Texas summer day for preseason Game 1. Tight end Pettis Norman was the darling of the rookie class, though he was hardly the only good prospect. Defensive end George Andrie, 6-7, 252, was another rookie, from Marquette, poised to set anchor at right defensive end and be a companion to Bob Lilly on the other side. 'He's big, strong, has speed and good hands. I'll stake my 10 years' experience that he'll be a good one,' quarterback Eddie LeBaron said of Norman, who played at Johnson C. Smith University in Charlotte, N.C.*

Several established players were present, notably, the veteran LeBaron and rising young stars in Bob Lilly, George Andrie, running back Don Perkins, and linebacker Chuck Howley. Lilly's impact on the organization was such that even today, he is referred to as "Mr. Cowboy," quite a tribute considering the Cowboys have fielded such stars as Roger Staubach, Tony Dorsett, Emmitt Smith, Troy Aikman, and Michael Irvin.

For football trivia buffs, Chuck Howley would make his mark during his 15-year career. He would also make NFL history in Super Bowl V by becoming the first defensive player to win the Most Valuable Player Award, the only player on a losing team to be named Super Bowl MVP.

I started camp as a split end, blocked well, and knocked people down on the run. After a scrimmage, Coach Landry called us in to debrief the team. "If you all want to know how to play football, watch Pettis Norman in this film," he said. That was quite a compliment, coming from Coach Landry.

Then Coach mentioned one day, "I really want to move you to tight end."

"Why do you want to do that?" I asked.

"Because I want to take advantage of your blocking," he answered.

I was 6'4" and 225 pounds of lean, mean muscles and never questioned his wisdom. I made the team and became a starter. I recall the media approaching Coach Landry about me, the kid from little ol' JCSU, the second oldest Black school in the union. Coach said, "Let me put it this way. I can throw a football on the field and don't have to coach him." By the way, I didn't make any extra money being on top; we were all paid the same. I was just driven — not a perfectionist, but definitely detail-oriented. I picked up this trait while sharecropping. Dad wanted us to plow the field a certain way, cut wood a certain way. "Do it like this," he said while demonstrating what he meant.

So, my siblings and I lived up to the expectations and assumed everyone else should take it upon himself or herself to do the same.

Lodging

Cornell Green and I were assigned a room together because we were both Black. In case you are not aware, he was a two-time All-American basketball player selected in the 1962 NBA draft. However, he had inborn talent as a football player. Coincidentally, our wives later became very close friends over the years, and we lived a few blocks away from each other for at least 40 years.

We experienced the racially-charged decade of the 1960s. A very real problem of segregation existed in our neighborhood, as well as on the Cowboys team. Players were segregated based on skin color, and I'm fairly certain this was the tradition on every NFL team at that time in history. Our room assignments at training camp reflected this policy, not surprisingly. I was aware of the Black-White issue from the beginning. We ate together, played together but slept segregated by race.

I was also given survival advice when I arrived at camp: (1) don't ride in cabs driven by White people; (2) don't eat myself off the team (get too heavy); and (3) don't date White women. These were just some of many hard, cold racial realities in the Deep South, not hidden at all, but out in the open. It was indicative of the civil rights struggle that permeated every facet of society, something I address ahead in the Civil Rights chapter.

Salary Per Season

Amidst the excitement of becoming a Cowboy, I was even more excited at the prospect of becoming a husband. My family was ecstatic when I married Margaret on the first available Saturday following my rookie season on December 22, 1962, in Mecklenburg, North Carolina. We had a beautiful wedding and Wilson Counts, the friend who taught me the intricacies of football, was my best man. My siblings and relatives already considered Margaret family and welcomed her as my wife. Due to football, we did not take off on our honeymoon after the wedding, but eventually travelled to Maui, our favorite Hawaiian island. I remember our drive to Hana, a 68-mile stretch of curving, scenic roads with breathtaking views of the Pacific. If you have not been to Hana, it's a real treat to see the picturesque mountains, waterfalls and nature at its best. We enjoyed this very special trip and our new beginning.

I was paid $9,000 as a rookie Cowboy (including the signing bonus) — the base pay for players in those days. People have a hard time believing we were paid such a low amount in light of current NFL salaries, but that $9,000 salary is a well-documented fact. It was certainly more than what I earned working three jobs and was a welcome raise. My salary increased to $10,000 in my post-rookie season. I gladly gave my heart to the Cowboys and played for God, country, and Dallas for that amount.

I guess you could call me one of the foundational players, along with Sonny Gibbs, Harold Hays, Sam Baker, Monte Clark, Dale Memmelaar, Jerry Norton, Dick Nolan, and Lee Folkins. The Dallas Cowboys' official fight song, "Cowboys Stampede March" by the Tom Merriman Big Band, began playing at Texas Stadium the year before I signed.

My fellow rookies included good friends like Donnie Davis, George Andrie, Guy Reese, Amos Bullocks, Lynn Hoyem, Don Talbert, Dave Edwards, Joe Isbell, Cornell Green, Mike Gaechter, John Meyers, Clyde Brock, and John Cornett. With this much talent, we were onto something big. I made the starting team as a tight end and watched through the years in amazement as the Dallas Cowboys became "America's Team," "Dallas Nation," and would inspire Coach Jimmy Johnson to fire up his players by shouting, "How 'bout them Cowboys!"

Getting to Know the Coach

Playing for Coach Landry, who served as the only head coach in Cowboys history from 1960 until 1988, was a great experience. For those who are not aware, he played in the NFL as a defensive back with the New York Giants from 1950-55 and was a player-coach under Coach Steve Owen. Coach Landry devised and implemented what became known as the modern "4-3" defense as an answer to the balanced offense run by Paul Brown's Cleveland Browns in the early 1950s.

Dallas Cowboys vs San Francisco 49ers, 1971 NFC Championship. Getty Images. Photo credit: Neil Leifer

Contrary to his public image as a stoic, unfeeling man, Coach Landry was very personable. It didn't matter if a player was a top draft choice or an undrafted free agent; Coach Landry spent time with players to help them learn their positions. Even though he was known for being a player and coach whose specialty was defense, Coach Landry was very innovative when he implemented the Cowboys' offense in our formative years.

Coach Landry instituted a man-in-motion offense, which he disguised by having our offensive linemen stand up prior to settling into their three-point stance. In later years, Coach Landry would popularize the Shotgun offense that every NFL team has used for the past several decades. He also instituted an offense that put a tight end at running back and gave us an onslaught of pass receivers to throw at a pass defense. At the time, I found it ironic that we stacked the passing deck. I was fighting hard to make it as a tight end, and my fight became more difficult as our offense eliminated the tight end position for some plays.

I was a fast study and learned Coach Landry's complex offense quickly. He recognized this and continued to tell players on the team when we were watching game films or practice films, "Watch how Pettis does it." One thing I always did was practice as hard as I played on offense and special teams. On occasion, I led our receivers in pass catches during scrimmages.

To me, practice was as thrilling and exciting as a game. During my first scrimmage at training camp, I broke my left ring finger. It required a cast that would have put me out of training for weeks. I could not allow this; I worked too hard to get to training camp and was not about to blow it. So, I told the trainer that I planned to remove the cast, tape my middle finger and ring finger together, and rejoined practice. While I had pain, I remember thinking that nothing would impact my ability to make the team. So, I demonstrated my readiness to play, and my determination paid off. I became a starter and my finger healed, though it remained crooked. To this day, it is my war wound and a topic of conversation.

Rookie Challenges

I was happy to sign with the Cowboys because I believed the NFL was superior to the AFL at that time. Stepping on the same field with the NFL's greatest players and teams of that era was exciting. I knew that if I learned my assignments, concentrated on doing them correctly, and executed the tactics properly, I could succeed regardless of whom I played against. This was something I learned and believed at Johnson C. Smith University. I felt confident it would work for me at the pro level as well.

I welcomed challenges, especially one in particular against the New York Giants, when I came across middle linebacker Sam Huff. My initial impression was that he was a "bully" who did not just tackle ball carriers but left his opponents with battle scars after the encounter. Our first on-field meeting came in the Cotton Bowl on Sunday, November 11, 1962. I was a rookie, played clean, but stepped up to any challenge on the field that involved my teammates or me.

Huff yelled, "Norman, if you come across this section on the next play, I will (expletive) you up."

My response was, "Landry calls the plays. I will be back."

Well, Landry called the play, and I took Sam Huff to the ground. Without going into detail,

I encourage you to see the film footage. There was no question of who won the fight, which was a defensive squabble and not offensive on my part.

Cornell Green and I joined the Cowboys at the same time in 1962, and he still chuckles at the memory of my meeting with Sam. I'll let Cornell tell you all about it.

> *Pettis was tough and physical. He would compete. He was a physical player, and if something needed to be done, he would do it. He could block, and he could block anyone. In the Cotton Bowl he came across the middle against Sam Huff and flattened him. It was one of the hardest hits I've ever seen. And it was clean; it wasn't dirty. It was a hard, legal hit. Sam got up mad, pointing his finger and all that, and they started pushing and shoving because Sam had never been hit like that. And I mean, Pettis creamed him.*

With Coach Landry. Photo taken by a friend

From that point forward, Huff respected me as a rookie player. Ironically, Sam and I both loved horse racing and have run into each other in Florida and New York at different racetracks. Our meetings have been cordial and reminiscent in a fun way, and he is quite a gentleman off the field.

We were in the pits record-wise, but we would improve every year as we continued to add talented players. In my first year with the Cowboys, I started three of our 14 regular season games, and we went 5-8-1. I learned that as outstanding as many of the NFL players were, I wasn't intimidated by them, even though I had been watching them on TV for years. I just kept my focus on what my assignment was on each play and executed that assignment. I didn't focus on the reputations of the defensive stars I was playing against, even though they had famous names like Deacon Jones, Merlin Olsen, Rosey Grier, Willie Davis, Ray Nitschke, Alex Karras, and Night Train Lane. I just wanted to earn their respect. It was a tremendous compliment when Chicago Bears tight end Mike Ditka, one of the all-time greats at the position, called me "an excellent tight end."

Loss of a President

In 1963 we moved our training camp to Thousand Oaks, California, which became a permanent site for us during my tenure with the team — thankfully, a much warmer locale. I started nearly half of our 14 games and upped my number of receptions during my rookie season from 2 to 18. I also scored my first official NFL touchdown and recorded three for the season. Unfortunately, we slipped to 4-10, and I believe a part of that was due to the sadness and gloom that came over the team following the tragic assassination of President Kennedy in downtown Dallas.

Our young president was beloved by so many, and it traumatized our city when he was shot and killed in Dallas. The weekend of the president's death, we played the Browns in Cleveland's cavernous Municipal Stadium. That we played at all was extremely controversial. The AFL did what most people considered to be the appropriate thing and postponed their weekend slate of games.

NFL Commissioner Pete Rozelle, however, noted that the fallen president had been a football fan and that White House Press Secretary Pierre Salinger believed JFK would have wanted the game to be played as scheduled to help soothe the nation's grief. Rozelle was roundly criticized for his decision and later called it the biggest regret he ever had as commissioner.

Many people across the nation connected the killing of the president to Dallas and blamed the city for what happened. The team was blamed by default as well. When we played the Browns in Cleveland on Sunday, November 24, 1963, just two days following JFK's death, the stadium's public address announcer referred to us only as the "Cowboys" and not the "Dallas Cowboys" as would have been the case under normal conditions. It would take a long time for the city of Dallas to shake its stigma of the Kennedy killing if it ever truly has.

Teamwork

The 1964 season was the most productive in my nine-year career with the Cowboys. I had 24 receptions and ranked third on the team. I was also becoming one of the team leaders, a mentor to younger players like Mel Renfro. Mel was a defensive back who was drafted by the

Cowboys and the Raiders and signed with us. He became an impact player his rookie season, starting every one of our 14 games, as well as one of three future Hall of Fame players we drafted in '64. The other two were Bob Hayes and Roger Staubach, who was drafted, but did not join the team until 1969 due to his Navy commitment.

Photo courtesy of the Dallas Cowboys

Mel tells the story of how he, Frank Clarke, Cornell Green and Amos Marsh lived in the

Cedar Crest Apartments in South Dallas:

> *I got to know Pettis really well. We went to work out many mornings on one of the fields near downtown Dallas. I was very unfamiliar with Dallas, and he taught me some things, told me where to go and where not to go. Pettis kept an eye on me so I wouldn't get myself into any trouble. I really appreciated that all those guys looked after me. We played a lot of golf together and got to be good friends.*

Mel is a great guy who remains a good friend today. We share a lot of history on and off the field, namely business ventures. He became a legend in football and as a fair housing advocate, described later in the book. I admire him so, and it's humbling to hear him and my teammates speak highly of me as a player and a person. He told me recently that I was a great teammate, always cheering on the players and calling for the defense to do well and make plays. I can say the same for Mel, by the way. He added another compliment by saying I was a strong, tough, tight end and excellent blocker who caught the ball well — high praise from an athlete of his caliber.

Mel's stardom rose in college football, and he spent 14 years in the NFL, tough as nails. He was selected to the Pro Bowl in each of his first ten seasons in the league. He was inducted into the Dallas Cowboys Ring of Honor in 1981 and elected to the Pro Football Hall of Fame in 1996. That's impressive.

Another teammate, halfback Dan Reeves, recently mentioned that he appreciated my work ethic and leadership abilities. "You don't have to be a talker to be a leader," Dan commented. "Pettis, you led by how hard you worked to improve yourself." Dan paid me another terrific compliment when he said that after he became a head coach in the NFL, he looked to draft a tight end like me. That was a generous comment — Dan is a great guy and quick to give credit. He was a legendary lifer in the NFL, serving 38 years as a player and coach, spanning nine Super Bowls; absolutely remarkable.

I did a lot of blocking for running back Walt Garrison, who told me, "Tight ends in Coach's offense had to block. That was a big part of our offense, and Pettis, you were a hell of a blocker. You could catch too, you could catch anything." These were kind words from a guy who was a Cowboy twice over — on the football field and as a professional rodeo competitor.

Walt grew up in Lewisville, Texas, riding steers and horses. He earned a scholarship to Oklahoma State University, fitting since their nickname is also the "Cowboys," and twice gained All-Big Eight Conference honors. He also competed for the university's rodeo team. When Walt signed with the Cowboys, he pushed for and received an unusual signing bonus — a two-horse trailer so he could go to rodeos in the off-season.

Walt is an extremely interesting guy and great friend who still calls me by my middle name "Burch." Many of my teammates did back then, and some still do. Walt was a tough, durable inside runner for us, a perfect complement to our elusive outside runners Calvin Hill and Duane Thomas. Don Meredith had an oft-repeated funny line about Walt when he said if it was third down and we needed four yards for a first down, he'd give the ball to Garrison, and Walt would get five. If it was third down and we needed 20 yards, if you gave the ball to Walt, by God, he would get you five.

Walt's celebrity extended beyond Dallas and the Cowboys. He did national television commercials for products like SKOAL smokeless tobacco, talking about the benefits of a "little pinch between cheek and gum." Over the course of 20 years, he used his celebrity as a Super Bowl champion and Pro Rodeo champion to raise more than $4 million for multiple sclerosis through his Walt Garrison All-Star Rodeos. Walt's charitable causes also included serving more than two decades on the Justin Cowboy Crisis Fund board. I was delighted to see my friend get inducted into the Pro Rodeo Hall of Fame in 2018.

Bob Lilly and I grew up together as Dallas Cowboys, and he recalls how hard we competed on special teams. Bob put his heart and soul into the game, one of the greats and an even greater friend. I was so proud of him as the first inductee into the Dallas Cowboys Ring of Honor and recall that he was a professional in front and behind the camera lens. Yes, Bob was a fantastic photographer and author of *Bob Lilly Reflections*, a book filled with black-and-white photographs of his teammates. He also wrote a memoir in 2008, *A Cowboy's Life: Bob Lilly*.

Bob generously shares the following:

> *Pettis and I were always competing on the kickoff teams to see who could make the tackle. I've always thought the world of him and remember when he first joined the Cowboys. Gil Brandt told us, 'I've got a guy coming in named Pettis Norman. He's a big guy, good hands, a hell of a blocker, and good on special teams.' Yes, he was really good on special teams, and when Coach Landry ran the films of the games, he would always praise Pettis and tell us, 'This is how you play special teams.' He was a great all-around player for a number of years.*

Middle linebacker Lee Roy Jordan and I butted helmets a lot in team practices and scrimmages, and he shares a beautiful reflection, one I will always cherish. "Pettis, you were a hard worker and showed people how to do the job and set a great example for everyone. You were a great leader and instrumental in improving relationships with the Cowboys. You stood tall."

Lee Roy was an inspiration to me as well, an astoundingly talented player and friend who played for the Cowboys from 1963 to 1976. He was inducted into the Alabama Sports Hall of Fame in 1980, the College Football Hall of Fame in 1983, and was the seventh on the Dallas Cowboys to receive the Ring of Honor. In fact, he was the first to be inducted for that honor by Jerry Jones.

Mid-Sixties

At the end of my 1964 season, I became a proud father to my first daughter Sharneen on December 3, 1964. She was beautiful! Margaret and I were so happy that she was healthy and I had plenty of time to spend with her since my off-season was approaching. She had many of Margaret's features with a blend of mine, just adorable.

The 1965 season was historic for marking the first non-losing season in Cowboys history. We drafted impact players in quarterback Craig Morton and defensive tackle Jethro Pugh. With the help of talented young players like Mel and established veterans like Bob Lilly, our defense became one of the best in pro football.

Dick Nolan, who would later rebuild the San Francisco 49ers into a Super Bowl contender, helped coach our defense into the feared "Doomsday" unit that ranked with the Packers, Colts, the Los Angeles' Rams famed "Fearsome Foursome," and Minnesota's "Purple People Eaters," as one of the great defenses of all time. And while the Fearsome Foursome, People Eaters, and a few other players would rain terror on opposing teams, I too was known as a fierce defender of my space and teammates if they came in my territory.

Don Meredith, God rest his soul, stated, "If I was going into battle and they'd only let me take one guy with me, I'd pick Pettis Norman every time." Don was a great friend and always a delight to have around. I can still hear him singing, "It Wasn't God Who Made Honky Tonk Angels," and I enjoyed watching him call games with Howard Cosell and Frank Gifford on Monday Night Football for ABC.

Former 49ers head coach Red Hickey helped coach our offense. Hayes, Meredith, Dan Reeves, Don Perkins, and I averaged better than 23 points per game. We went 7-7 to finish second in the Eastern Division behind the defending NFL champion Browns. We had climbed out of the pit of mediocrity and were turning a corner. Suddenly, we felt like we could compete with anyone in football and carried that belief into the 1966 season.

Coach Landry built us into a team that was explosive on offense and stingy on defense, and we won the Eastern Division title for the first time in team history. The drafting of guard John Niland and Walt Garrison gave us depth on offense, and rookie end Willie Townes added to our talented defense.

The Cowboys played our first postseason game against Vince Lombardi's seemingly invincible Packers. I learned an interesting thing about Lombardi in those years — he tried to trade for me. The tight end was an essential part of the Packers' power running game, basically seen as a third guard in Lombardi's game planning. Ron Kramer had been the Packers' tight end during the early part of the decade when their ground game was the best in football, one of the best ever seen. Lombardi traded Ron Kramer, a University of Michigan graduate, to his hometown Detroit Lions and needed a similar type of tight end for his offense. I was regarded as one of the better blocking tight ends in football, and Lombardi wanted to make a deal for me, but it never happened.

Off-Season

As I mentioned, many professional football players in the Sixties juggled overlapping roles as athletes, family men, volunteers, and employees in off-field jobs. In 1966, I was 27, playing in the NFL, serving on the Southern Christian Leadership board, and working off-season at South Oak Cliff State Bank, initially in public relations. This novelty does not exist today, but not working a second job was not an option back then.

I quickly rose to Assistant Vice President in Business Development and was promoted to Vice President. I believe I shattered a glass ceiling by becoming the first African American banking officer in Dallas. I learned a lot about financial markets and helped church leaders, business owners, and entrepreneurs get loans, start businesses, and build better lives. Many of these businesses are in operation some 50 years later, and I am gratified when former bank customers thank me for helping them with their start-ups.

I continued to do my best to mentor our younger players and help get them acquainted with the NFL, the Cowboys, and the City of Dallas. Cornell Green states, "Pettis took time to talk with the younger players and guide them on what to do and how to do it, show them around, get loans for homes, all those things."

Cotton Bowl Memories

We played the Packers on New Year's Day in 1966 at the Cotton Bowl; it turned out to be a classic contest. For the first time in NFL history, something more than a championship was at stake. A berth in the first Super Bowl against the AFL champion was also on the line.

Pettis Norman (84) is pushed out of bounds by Green Bay Packers defensive back Dave Hathcock (45) during the 1966 NFL Championship Game in Dallas, Texas, Jan. 1, 1967. Associated Press. Photo credit: Vernon Biever

The experienced Packers were the defending NFL champions and took a 14-0 lead before our offense even got on the field for the first time. We rallied and tied the game before the end of the first quarter. Green Bay led 34-27 late in the fourth quarter, but we drove toward the game-tying touchdown. If we could tie the game and force it into overtime, we believed we would win. I've heard that some of the Packers believed the same and thought we'd have the momentum heading into OT if we could score a touchdown on our final drive.

I had four catches in the game, none bigger than the one that put us at the Packers' 2-yard line in the waning seconds. We were poised to score and push the Packers into overtime, but linebacker Dave Robinson, who was one of a record six future Hall of Famers on defense and coached by outstanding defensive coordinator Phil Bengtson, forced Meredith into an off-balance throw that was intercepted in the end zone by safety Tom Brown.

It was a disappointing defeat since it prevented us from facing our former AFL neighbors in Dallas, the Texans who had moved to Kansas City and became the Chiefs in Super Bowl I. It would have been interesting for me personally to line up against the AFL club that had drafted me, but it wasn't to be.

Four Divisions

The 1967 pro football season would be different than any prior season. It was a year of expansion, both personally and professionally, for my second daughter, Sedonna, was born. Her eyes looked just like mine, they were the same color, and she had beautiful features like Margaret. We nicknamed her "Boobie," a name we use today. She brought lots of joy to our lives and was a welcome playmate for Sharneen.

The AFL had been expanding as well, adding the Miami Dolphins in 1966 and Cincinnati Bengals in 1968. The NFL added the Atlanta Falcons in 1966 and New Orleans Saints in 1967. The NFL now had 16 teams, and Rozelle knew it was time to change the league from its longstanding format of two conferences — Eastern and Western — into four divisions of four teams each.

We were in the Capitol Division along with the Philadelphia Eagles, the Washington Redskins, and New Orleans Saints. The Century Division included some of our biggest rivals — the New York Giants, Cleveland Browns, Pittsburgh Steelers, and St. Louis Cardinals — and some of pro football's biggest stars, future Hall of Famers like Leroy Kelly, Fran Tarkenton, and Larry Wilson.

While the Capitol and Century Divisions made up the Eastern Conference, the Western Conference included the Central Division (Chicago Bears, Detroit Lions, Green Bay Packers and Minnesota Vikings), which came to be known as the "Black and Blue Division" for the physical play of Ray Nitschke, Dick Butkus, and Minnesota's "Purple People Eaters" defense. The Coastal Division included the Atlanta Falcons, Baltimore Colts, Los Angeles Rams, and San Francisco 49ers and was known for the glamorous quarterback play of Johnny Unitas, Roman Gabriel, and John Brodie.

Since the NFL first split into Eastern and Western Conference in 1933, the NFL's postseason had consisted of a single game – the Eastern and Western Conference champions meeting in the league title game. That all changed in 1967 when the two conferences were broken down into four divisions. Expanding the league led to expanding the postseason from a single championship game to include Eastern and Western Conference playoffs.

Once again, our draft yielded a future Hall of Famer with rookie offensive tackle Rayfield Wright joining our team. We also drafted a multi-sport star named Pat Riley, who would eventually choose the NBA over the NFL and sign with the Los Angeles Lakers. This same Pat Riley would become head coach of the Lakers in the 1980s, and his "Showtime" stars — Magic Johnson, Kareem Abdul-Jabbar, and James Worthy — would dominate the decade.

Just as I had mentored Mel and other players during my years in Dallas, I worked to build a solid relationship with Rayfield as well. I take it as a great compliment when I hear him say today that I was a groundbreaker for him and many of our Cowboys teammates. I believe Rayfield was a groundbreaker, too; it was exciting to see him inducted into the Pro Football Hall of Fame in 2006. I was there in person; well deserved!

The relationship between Rayfield and me was unique because he was drafted as a tight end — the same position I played. Some players might have felt threatened, but I did all I could to help Rayfield learn the ropes in the NFL. To this day, he talks of those early years:

> *Pettis was a great example as to what you could do while playing the game as well as leaving the game. I was a backup to him, and he helped me tremendously in learning the system and advancing my play at the tight end position. He showed a path for me to follow, and I tried to do the very best I could in following his direction to help the team win.*
>
> *I was just happy that I came to a club that had someone like Pettis, who would teach those after him and not be afraid of anyone trying to take his job. He taught the younger guys certain things about the game. Back in that day, many players felt threatened by younger players, but Pettis was not that kind of a player. He was very personable. He wanted you to do your best, whether it was blocking or running your routes. I can't say enough about his influence. He was committed, dedicated, and had confidence in himself and the ability he was blessed with.*

I appreciate "Big Cat's" generous comments. He was known for his quick feet, being a dominant blocker, and was named to the NFL's "All-Decade Team of the '70s." In addition, it was exciting to see Rayfield get inducted into the Cowboys Ring of Honor and the Texas Sports Hall of Fame. That's talent, and we have been good friends since our playing days.

We won our second straight division title in '67 and first playoff game in team history when we defeated the Browns in the Eastern Conference championship game. The iconic Ice Bowl followed, a game I discuss in great detail in the next chapter. We continued to add tremendous talent to our team through excellent drafting, and we won two more division titles in 1968 and '69.

Soon we would be contenders for the Super Bowl, a game worthy of its own chapter. But first, let us recap the legendary Ice Bowl.

Chapter Six: The Ice Bowl — Frozen in Time

Even today, the Ice Bowl remains frozen in time as the NFL's most iconic and legendary game.
~ Pettis Norman

I've played in hundreds of football games, but the Ice Bowl of 1967 is one I remember over all the others, even more so than Super Bowl V at the end of the 1970 season. To me, it's the greatest game in pro football history and was a tremendous sensory experience — the sights, sounds, and sub-zero cold of that New Year's Eve afternoon in Green Bay have stayed with me to this day. It's a legendary game that remains frozen in time.

At the time, nothing could top the wonder of being a happily married family man — not even the Ice Bowl — but duty called, and I had to leave Margaret and our daughters to catch a flight to Green Bay, Wisconsin. I said my goodbyes and left to face the battle on Lambeau Field. It was the Cowboys against the Packers and Coach Tom Landry against Coach Vince Lombardi — another NFL championship game that was watched on television by breathless fans. People still talk about it as though it was yesterday.

When people find out I played with the Dallas Cowboys in the '60s, it's amazing how many times I'm asked, "Did you play in the Ice Bowl?" They see my Super Bowl ring but ask first about that day in Green Bay. Usually, they want to know how we got through it without freezing to death.

The year before, in the 1966 NFL championship game against the Green Bay Packers in the Cotton Bowl, we came within one yard of scoring the tying touchdown, forcing overtime, and earning a berth in Super Bowl I against the American Football League champion Kansas City Chiefs. We came up short, but that game proved we had advanced to the point where we could play against the best teams in pro football. Previously, we were not at that point and had never played in a championship game. But in 1967, we felt we could compete at the top level.

We advanced to that point gradually, evolving out of the almost pit-like place we had been in the beginning. We built on this process for several years, learning how to win and how to make the plays it took to win. We no longer went out thinking about losing; we went out thinking about winning. We're winning this game was the mindset, and then we would think about winning the next one.

We came so close to beating Green Bay and playing in the first Super Bowl in 1966 and used that as fuel for our fire when we opened training camp in the summer of 1967. We dedicated those draining practices to getting a rematch with the Packers.

The Houston Oilers

One of our biggest games was our first meeting with the Houston Oilers. The 1967 preseason was the first time that the NFL and AFL teams met in exhibition games. On September 2nd, we played Houston on their home field in Rice Stadium. The Oilers were still a year away from playing in the Astrodome, which at the time was called the "Eighth Wonder of the World."

The Oilers were a good team. Like us, they would go on to win their league's Eastern Division championship and play in the league title game. On New Year's Eve 1967, Houston would play for the AFL championship just as we would play for the NFL championship. If things had gone a little differently, Super Bowl II could have been a Texas-style shootout.

Looking back, our game against the Oilers served as not only an All-Texas showdown but also a potential preview of an AFL-NFL World Championship game, as the Super Bowl was still officially known at that time.

Our preseason game against Houston was for bragging rights in Texas. That added another level of intensity to it. The Oilers were our state rivals, just as the Giants and Jets were rivals in New York, and the 49ers, Raiders, Rams, and Chargers were rivals in California.

As a team, we felt like we could compete against the top teams in the NFL and the AFL. In our game against Houston, we led 27-3 and won 30-17 after Houston scored two fourth-quarter touchdowns. A crowd of 53,125 was at Rice Stadium, which shows how intense the NFL-AFL rivalry was at that time.

For our NFL teams, it was a chance to demonstrate further the Packers' dominance in Super Bowl I. AFL teams, meanwhile, were hoping to prove that they weren't inferior to the NFL. Boston fullback Jim Nance, who set an AFL rushing record in 1966, spoke for a lot of AFL players when he said, "We've heard a lot about the National League players. Well, we found out they're just men, not supermen."

Highs and Lows of the Season

We followed up our win over one of the AFL's best teams by beating our NFL opponents. We opened our regular season by beating the Browns, 21-14, in Cleveland's cavernous Municipal Stadium, a Depression-era structure whose moniker was the "Mistake by the Lake." The following week we opened our home schedule by beating another longtime rival, the Giants, 38-24.

The third week of the season brought the Los Angeles Rams to the Cotton Bowl for the kind of highly anticipated matchup that only comes along once or twice in a regular season. The pregame publicity focused on the collision between two of football's more famous defenses – the Rams' "Fearsome Foursome" and our "Doomsday" defense – and the possibility of this being a preview of the NFL title game. Our game with the Rams was featured in the NFL's weekly TV highlights show – NFL Film's "Game of the Week." Unfortunately for us, the Rams had more highlights that day and won 35-13.

Highs and lows marked our 1967 season. Don Meredith, our starting quarterback, was sidelined for all or parts of four games by injuries that included broken ribs, a broken nose, and pneumonia. Third-year quarterback Craig Morton quickly matured and took over for Meredith. Center Dave Manders was injured and replaced by Mike Connelly, and halfback Dan Reeves fought injuries as well.

Fortunately, we had depth few teams could match. We also had a defense filled with five All-Pro performers — Bob Lilly and George Andrie on the line, Chuck Howley at linebacker, and Mel Renfro and Cornell Green in the secondary. We bounced back from the loss to the Rams with a 17-14 win at Washington in our first Capitol Division game of the season. Meredith had been buried by a Redskin blitz late in the game, but he picked himself up and found Reeves all alone for a 36-yard scoring pass. We were thrilled by the win but subdued when we learned that Meredith was injured and would be sidelined for the next three games.

We improved to 2-0 in the division the following week with another close win, a 14-10 victory over the expansion Saints on a dreary Sunday in the rain-soaked Cotton Bowl. Continuing to live on the edge, we alternated Morton and Jerry Rhome at quarterback at Pitt Stadium. We survived the Steelers 24-21 when I caught a 5-yard pass from a scrambling Morton in the fourth quarter for the winning touchdown. Even in Pittsburgh's lean years, Coach Landry always said, "If the Steelers don't beat you, they beat you up."

That appeared to be the case the following week when we stayed on the road and spotted the Eagles 21 points and lost 21-14. It was our first defeat in the division, but we returned to form at home in week eight with a 37-7 win against Atlanta. It was our best offensive showing of the season, and Reeves had the best single-game performance in the NFL in 1967 when he scored four touchdowns. Meredith returned to our lineup, and we showcased our explosive, exciting offense with a number of razzle-dazzle plays, including a tight end reverse that I carried for 18 yards.

We headed to the Big Easy the following week and won a big game with ease, downing New Orleans 27-10. The next week we hosted Washington and Meredith started the game before Morton took over. Craig and I connected for a 6-yard touchdown in the fourth quarter, but Jurgensen's four scoring passes paced the Redskins, 27-20. Lance Rentzel, who was having a great season in his first year as a starter for us, had 13 catches for 223 yards that day against the Redskins, the best performance by an NFL receiver that season.

The Lead Up

A short week followed since we were once again hosting what was becoming an annual event for us, the Thanksgiving Day game. There was a lot of scoring to feast on in this night game, as we combined with the Cardinals to score 67 points. "Bullet" Bob Hayes, known for his flying feet and flashing smile, paced our blistering attack. We scored in every way imaginable – offense (5 touchdowns), defense (Lee Roy Jordan's safety), and special teams (Hayes' 69-yard punt return and Danny Villanueva's 22-yard field goal). This Thanksgiving Day game featured a buffet of big plays – Meredith threw touchdown passes of 59, 74, and 34 yards; the Cards countered with scoring plays covering 67, 38, and 36 yards.

The following week, we were back on the road, heading to Baltimore for another big game and a potential championship game preview. This game featured one of the all-time great coaching matchups – Coach Tom Landry versus Coach Don Shula. The two legends would combine to coach their teams to 578 victories, 11 Super Bowl appearances, and four world championships. Landry would get the better of Shula in Super Bowl VI when the Cowboys beat Miami 24-3, and the "Doomsday" defense became the first in Super Bowl history to not allow a touchdown.

On this day in Baltimore's Memorial Stadium, nicknamed the "world's largest outdoor insane asylum" because of its frenzied fans, we led 17-10 heading into the final quarter. But Baltimore, showing why it was unbeaten at 10-0-2, rallied to score 13 points. The Charm City held little charm for us that day as legendary Colts like Johnny Unitas, Raymond Berry, and Lenny Moore combined to give Baltimore a 23-17 victory.

We closed our campaign in an up-and-down fashion, clinching the Capitol Division crown as Reeves and Perkins each scored two touchdowns to fuel a 38-17 win over the Eagles in our final regular season game in the Cotton Bowl. Our last game of the regular season was a nonconference date in San Francisco's historic Kezar Stadium in our first and only Saturday game of the year. We lost 24-16 but little did we know that rookie running back Craig Baynham's 1-yard touchdown run in the fourth quarter would serve as a preview of what was to come in the first-ever conference playoffs the following week.

The 9-5 record we posted in 1967 wasn't quite as good as the 10-3-1 from our 1966 season. We scored 342 points, good for an average of 24 per game and 6th in the NFL. But that was more than 100 points less than the 445 we scored the previous season when we led the league and averaged 32 points per game.

Our Doomsday defense was not quite as impenetrable as the year before, allowing 268 points and an average of 16 per game. In 1966, we allowed 239, an average of 17 per game. Still, our defense was the best in the NFL against the run.

After winning our division, we were now determined to earn the first postseason victory in Cowboys' history. We hosted Cleveland in the Eastern Conference championship game in the Cotton Bowl on a sunny, Christmas Eve afternoon. We already knew going in that the winner would head to Green Bay for the NFL title game the following Sunday, New Year's Eve. The Packers had stunned the Rams 24-7 the preceding afternoon in Milwaukee County Stadium.

Like us, the Browns won their division with a 9-5 record. Leroy Kelly led the league in rushing and combined with Ernie Green to give the Browns the NFL's best rushing attack. Except for retired fullback Jim Brown, Cleveland was the same team that had won the NFL title just three years earlier and played in the championship game in 1965.

Having beaten the Browns by one touchdown to start the season, we were expecting another close game. Our chances took a hit early when Reeves was sidelined in the opening quarter with an injury. Baynham came on, and he and Perkins scored on short touchdowns to give us a 14-0 lead heading into the second quarter. Hayes' 86-yard scoring pass from Meredith made it 21-0, and we led 24-7 at halftime. Hayes also set up two scores with punt returns of 68 and 64 yards, and we outscored Cleveland 28-7 in the second half to win 52-14.

Baynham, our rookie who had scored one touchdown in the regular season, scored three

TDs this day, and Perkins added two. Hayes excelled on special teams, and Cornell Green scored for our Doomsday defense when he returned an interception of a Frank Ryan pass 60 yards to the end zone. Our scoring ended the same way it started, with a Baynham touchdown, and we had our second straight Eastern Conference crown.

Green Bay

I felt like the victory over Cleveland was a turning point for us. Beating the Browns gave us the rematch with Green Bay that we had waited for all season. This would decide the NFL championship and a berth in Super Bowl II. Getting back to the championship game and playing the Packers again was the driving goal for us that season. We wanted to go up against them and see which was going to be the best team. We had reached a level where we could play as well or better than anybody. We went to Green Bay believing we could beat the Packers. We were younger, faster, and healthier than they were.

We arrived at the airport to board the plane to Green Bay in an upbeat and confident mood; we were ready for the battle. Everyone on our team was laser-focused on the plane ride, quiet and comfortable. We were ready to count this game as another win.

When we landed, the temperature was around 30 degrees Fahrenheit. It was a little nippy, but we were pleased with the weather. It was actually a nice ride to the Holiday Inn outside of Green Bay, where we would spend the next couple of days.

The Saturday before the game was relatively warm in Green Bay and Lambeau Field was in great shape. That night, however, a Canadian cold front swept into Green Bay and caused temperatures to plummet in a matter of hours to sub-zero levels. The wake-up call the next morning informed us that it was 13 degrees below zero.

I put on my suit and tie as expected by Coach Landry, who was always professional. The journey began to the most famous game in pro football history, knowing this would be the coldest day I have ever experienced.

At Lambeau Field, we slipped and slid as we walked toward the field that was now frozen hard as a cement slab. It was an incredible experience – the extreme cold, the brightly colored clothing of the crowd, the frosty breaths of steam coming from the fans, players, and coaches, and the tremendous excitement of playing for the NFL championship with a Super Bowl berth at stake all served to heighten the experience.

At the same time, we wondered if we could play in such cold weather. We were facing not just a great team in Green Bay but the elements as well; a double battle. The field had been nice the day before, but now it was frozen. It was an incredibly quick turn of events. We went back into the locker room and put on all the pads and clothing we could find. I was trying to keep the heat in my body and keep the cold out, but the wind cut right through my clothes.

Our equipment manager went to local stores in Green Bay on the morning of the game to get Saran Wrap so we could wrap our feet to keep the heat in. We looked to Coach Landry for assurance. He was focused; the weather was not a problem for him. His priority was winning the game, not worrying about the weather.

1967 DALLAS COWBOYS

11 - Danny Villanueva, 13 - Jerry Rhome, 14 - Craig Morton, 17 - Don Meredith, 19 - Lance Rentzel, 20 - Mel Renfro, 21 - Dick Daniels, 22 - Bob Hayes.
23 - Mike Johnson, 25 - Les Shy, 27 - Mike Gaechter, 30 - Dan Reeves, 34 - Cornell Green, 35 - Pete Gent, 37 - Phil Clark, 43 - Don Perkins.
46 - Craig Baynham, 50 - Jerry Tubbs, 52 - Dave Edwards, 53 - Mike Connelly, 54 - Chuck Howley, 55 - Lee Roy Jordan, 56 - Harold Hays, 57 - Malcolm Walker.
62 - Leon Donohue, 65 - John Wilbur, 66 - George Andrie, 68 - Jim Boeke, 71 - Willie Townes, 72 - Tony Liscio, 73 - Ralph Neely, 74 - Bob Lilly.
75 - Jethro Pugh, 76 - John Niland, 77 - Ron East, 82 - Frank Clarke, 83 - Harold Deters, 84 - Pettis Norman, 85 - Rayfield Wright.

Photo Credit: Dallas Cowboys Football Club

The stands were largely empty an hour or so before the scheduled kickoff time of 1 p.m. Eastern Standard Time – noon in Green Bay time. It wasn't until the approach of the first kickoff that the stands began to gradually fill to their capacity of nearly 51,000. Packers fans are a hearty breed and they love their team. It wasn't until Green Bay became a championship team again in the mid-1990s, that Packers fans would gain national fame as "Cheeseheads" for wearing rubberized blocks of cheese on their heads.

The "Electric Blanket"

The Ice Bowl was so different from any previous game. The Packers were used to playing on frozen fields, but we weren't. It was just an incredible situation and the closest thing to hell on ice. We had played in cool weather, but nothing like this. The question in our mind was, "How in heaven are we going to get through this?"

It was a battle for survival; we couldn't focus on the game. Instead of thinking about plays, we were thinking about how cold it was. It was unbelievable, just unbelievable. We had gone from thinking, *How did we get here?* to *How do we survive?* We wondered how we'd get through the next play.

Prior to 1967, Lombardi, the Packers' general manager and head coach, had purchased an "electric blanket" and had it installed beneath the Lambeau field surface. The belief was that the electric grid would prevent the field from freezing in the Wisconsin winters and provide better traction for both the Packers and opposing players.

General Electric manufactured the underground electric blanket and promised in a press release that its installation guaranteed that "September-like" playing conditions would prevail throughout the season and postseason. The press release stated that instead of playing on a rock-hard frozen field, the Packers would be playing on a soft, frost-free turf.

GE installed the cables six inches below Lambeau's playing surface. Lombardi's electric grid actually worked, and a plastic protective tarp was placed over the field the night before the championship game. It kept the field moist and in good playing condition. The problem no one could predict was that when the tarp was removed the morning of the game, the moisture generated by the electric cables flash-froze in the sub-zero temperatures. That was the reason Lambeau Field froze as quickly as it did that day; minus-13-degree temperatures caused the moisture from the underground cables to harden and crystallize.

Lombardi learned before the game that the underground heating system wouldn't be operational because of the intense cold. He also learned that the engineer who installed the grid had decided to shut it down because it was doing more harm than good. Lombardi hated failure in any form and believed he would be blamed for the failure of the electric grid. He said it was going to be known as "Lombardi's Folly."

I didn't blame Lombardi for the failure of the heating grid beneath Lambeau Field. What I couldn't figure out was how it could get so cold so quickly. It was one of those moments when you lose any notion of where you are and why you're there.

You don't think about those things in a regular game, but we just couldn't focus under these unique circumstances. It was a matter of who stayed alive long enough to score one more point than the other team and win the game.

I have replayed the Ice Bowl numerous times in my mind. No professional football game had ever taken place in conditions like that — minus-13 degree temperatures and 25 mile-per-hour winds that dropped the temperature to minus-35. When the sun began to set late in the fourth quarter and temperatures continued to drop, it was estimated that the wind chill was minus-50. This was nothing short of Arctic conditions.

Mel Renfro stated that every player who was on the field that day was suffering. Ten minutes into the game, Mel's hands were so cold he didn't have any feeling in them. He had to use his arms and shoulders to tackle because he couldn't grab with his hands; they were frozen. Our middle linebacker, Lee Roy Jordan, saw that Coach Landry was so focused on the game that he forgot to wipe his nose and had two-inch icicles hanging from his nostrils.

To my knowledge, this was the only NFL game ever played without referee whistles. On the first play of the game, the referee blew his whistle, and when he tried to remove it from his mouth, he tore off half his lip. But due to the cold, the referee's torn lip barely bled. From that point on, the officials stopped plays by shouting, "Play's over!"

Here's a bit of trivia. It wasn't just the referee's whistle that froze — I later heard the Wisconsin State University-La Crosse band director had the same problem with his whistle. The band was the halftime entertainment, a huge opportunity for the student musicians and the pom pom squad in front of a national television audience, but they could not perform due to the extreme weather conditions.

The referees, players, and coaches had to keep jars of Vaseline close to keep moisture on their lips, nose, and mouth. That same referee had a frozen blood icicle hanging from his lips, and the players, too, started getting icicles in their noses. We were told not to pull out the icicles or wipe our noses because it would cause damage to the membranes.

It was a hard-hitting game, and the physical play was intensified by the cold. Dan Reeves was hit so hard on one play, his facemask broke, and his lip busted. Dan put his hand over his mouth, but there was no blood. Even though the hit had been hard enough to drive his tooth through his lip, Reeves didn't bleed because of the extreme cold.

The cold weather also kept us from bleeding after being cut by the shards of ice on the field. Packers fullback Chuck Mercein spoke of the ice chipped by players' cleats that became like slivers of broken glass. It cut our uniforms and our skin every time we fell to the ground. Here again, because of the freezing temperatures, a lot of players didn't start bleeding until they began thawing out in the locker room after the game.

Green Bay started fast and took a 14-0 lead on Bart Starr's two touchdown passes to Boyd Dowler. We came back and made it 14-10 at halftime on George Andrie's fumble recovery and Danny Villanueva's field goal.

Landry and Lombardi

As the game wore on, the weather got so numbingly cold that Meredith's mouth froze, and he had trouble calling plays in the huddle. Also giving us trouble that day was the Green Bay defense, one of the best I ever played against. They featured six future members of the Pro Football Hall of Fame, a higher number than Pittsburgh's "Steel Curtain" of the 1970s, the 1985 Bears or 2000 Ravens. The Packers played clean football and had the mentality that their players and their coaches could adjust to anything. That's because they had Coach Lombardi. We had the same kind of team because of Coach Landry.

Every time we played Green Bay, there was a little extra motivation because Landry and Lombardi were good friends and great competitors going back to their years of coaching on the same New York Giants staff a decade earlier. In New York, Lombardi was the offensive coordinator and Landry, the defensive coordinator for head coach Jim Lee Howell. They combined to coach the Giants to a victory over the Bears in the 1956 NFL championship and a title game appearance in 1958 when they lost to the Baltimore Colts in the famous "Sudden Death" overtime classic in Yankee Stadium. To this day, it's still one of the greatest games ever played.

Lombardi was hired as Packers head coach in 1959, and Coach Landry became head coach of the expansion Cowboys in 1960. Lombardi quickly built Green Bay into what became known as "Title Town, USA." While the Packers were winning NFL championships, we were steadily building a contending team that would challenge the Packers in the 1966 and '67 championship games.

Fourth Quarter

In the fourth quarter of the Ice Bowl, Reeves, a triple threat running back who could run, catch and throw, rolled to his left and threw a 50-yard pass to Rentzel on a halfback option play. It gave us our first lead at 17-14 and was the same play we had used three weeks earlier to score against the Eagles in the Cotton Bowl. Meredith said in the huddle, "We're going to throw the halfback pass." We had been running a sweep in that game, but the Packers kept blocking the plays. So when Meredith told us we were going to run the option pass during a timeout at the end of the third quarter, Reeves put his hands as far down his pants as he could to try and keep them warm.

We believed we could come back against the Packers. We knew that we had to go out during the next few minutes and play harder than we had ever played before. I had the feeling we could win, but my teammates were so cold and were suffering. Though they were giving 100%, it was only 75% of what they were able to do. We were in a mindset that we were playing against three opponents: the Packers, cold weather, and the frozen field.

The Packers got the ball at their 32-yard line with just under five minutes to play. The weather was even colder. One gentleman died in the stands from the extreme conditions. Walt Garrison was sitting on our bench with linebacker Dave Edwards and said we had to be crazy to be out there when it's 13 below zero.

Starr mixed running and passing plays to march his team downfield. Everyone talks about what an incredible championship drive that was, and we agreed. Even today, Reeves is still amazed by it. He says Starr did an unbelievable job taking his team 68 yards in those sub-zero conditions and against our Doomsday defense with the NFL championship on the line.

We thought we would be on the winning side in Green Bay even as Starr was driving the Packers into our territory. Our great defense was having trouble getting traction on the icy field, but they were confident they would stop the Packers. The problem is that Green Bay's offense knew the running and passing plays, but our Dallas defense had to guess and then try to recover on an icy field.

When the Packers got down to our 1-yard line with 16 seconds left, I think Lombardi and Starr were thinking about the negative impact from the conditions affecting both teams. They believed a quarterback sneak was the right play to call. Because everyone was slipping and sliding, the Packers would rely on their center Ken Bowman and guards Jerry Kramer and Gale Gillingham to move our line. It was the best play they could call to win the game. If I had been their coach, I would have called the same play.

Starr called the quarterback sneak and wedged into the end zone behind Kramer and Bowman, who combined to deliver a great double-team block on Jethro Pugh. After the game, Lombardi acknowledged that Starr's quarterback sneak was a gamble. He said the Packers had their field goal team ready to go if Starr didn't score, but Lombardi also knew it was questionable whether they would have sufficient time to get the field goal unit on the field.

In our locker room, Coach Landry, a defensive mastermind, was stunned that his old friend Lombardi risked everything on such a dangerous call. Coach Landry had expected Starr to call a rollout play and, if his receivers were covered, throw the ball away to stop the clock and save time for the Packers' field goal unit to take the field.

"I can't believe that call, the sneak," Coach Landry told reporters in our locker room after the game. "It wasn't a good call, but now it's a great call."

"Amazing," he said more than once. "An amazing gamble."

Ice Bowl finish line. Photo courtesy of Dallas Cowboys Football Club

Jethro Pugh

Every time I see that Ice Bowl picture of Starr sneaking at the goal line, it reminds me of Jethro Pugh. Jethro and I were close friends. We played against each other in North Carolina, and later, he was the best man at my wedding. Jethro passed away in 2015, and I still miss him.

Today when I think of Jethro and the Ice Bowl, I wonder if he has been fairly judged on that play. Lombardi's Packers were known for their meticulous film study; it was one of the things that set them apart from other teams in football. Kramer stated that the Packer offense noticed while studying films of our defense the week before the game that Jethro, our left defensive tackle, tended to come off the ball a little higher than Bob Lilly, who played right defensive tackle. The Packers determined that if they were to run a "wedge" play in a short yardage or goal line situation against us, it should be run at Jethro rather than Bob.

Lombardi and Starr stored this information away and used it at exactly the right moment in the game. It's a credit to Starr and the Packers. For years, Jethro felt bad that the Packers had scored by running in his area. But Lilly, a Pro Football Hall of Famer says, Kramer and Bowman executed a great double-team block on Jethro, and because the field was frozen, there was no way to get traction on the ice. He also says that if the Packers had double-teamed him instead of Jethro, he would have been the one going backward because it was such a perfect block and the field was in such poor condition.

Another thing that bothered Jethro about that play is that he was convinced Kramer was offside. Jethro said he saw Kramer's right hand lift up and off the ground a split-second before the ball was snapped. Jethro looked around at the end of the play for a penalty flag on Kramer, which would have negated the touchdown and likely forced Lombardi to try for a field goal to force overtime. Jethro always said he was stunned there was no penalty called, but he took solace several years later when Kramer admitted he might have jumped offside on the quarterback sneak.

The film of the play has been slowed down to fractions of a second and seems to show Kramer's right hand moving a millisecond prior to the ball being snapped. Since Kramer was an interior lineman, it would have been impossible for any official to see such minuscule movement with the naked eye.

The fact is that Kramer and Bowman delivered a great double-team block, and they won the game. We can't take anything away from the Packers. They had a great team and great players.

Battered and Bloody

A photo was taken of me standing at my locker after the game. That one photo speaks a thousand words — my head down, hand on the top of the locker, replaying an unbelievable game that took the life out of my teammates and me. We left the icy field feeling like we had just exited the football equivalent of a war zone. We were battered, bloodied, and exhausted, as were the Packers.

Meredith had a black eye; Reeves' facemask was busted and a tooth driven through his lip from the force of a shattering blow. Several of my teammates had frostbite and damaged lungs. On the Packers' side, Starr and many of their players had frostbite and lung damage as well. Bart's fellow Pro Football Hall of Famer, middle linebacker Ray Nitschke, nearly lost three toes to frostbite.

In the locker room after the 1967 Ice Bowl game, dejected at the loss to Green Bay on the icy Lambeau Field.
Photo credit: Bettmann / Contributor – Getty Images.

I was fortunate not to have suffered any frostbite from the Ice Bowl. But I'll never forget the intensity of the hard hits and sub-zero cold, a field frozen as hard as concrete, the effects of the extreme conditions, and the emotions of the game. This game took a toll on me physically and mentally, and I had to regroup and get myself together.

The plane ride home was quiet. It was my final vision of the battle we just endured. I reflected on the unbelievable quarterback sneak, several players with frostbite, other players with injuries to their mouths and noses, and others with damaged lungs from the bitter cold.

All in all, the Ice Bowl is the most incredible game I ever played, an unbelievable experience that I've never forgotten. I look back and wonder how I got through it. I tell players now, "Be thankful you don't have to play in those conditions."

Chapter Seven: Reflections on the Ice Bowl

The impact of the Ice bowl left scars, but also a sense of wonder that we survived at all.
~ Pettis Norman

Looking back, it was a blessing to play in the greatest game of all time. My memories of the iconic event are just that — one player's anecdotes. But when I run into players who also played in the Ice Bowl, either with or against, other details emerge. I'm so happy that some of my fellow players have weighed in with their bird's-eye views, adding detail and clarity to football's most famed moments. Some of these stories are priceless and never before told.

Dallas Cowboy legends and Ice Bowl Players reunite in 2009 for Pettis' birthday party. Back Row: Rayfield Wright, Walt Garrison, Mel Renfro, Tom Landry, Jr., Jethro Pugh, LeeRoy Jordan and Dale Hansen. Front Row: Bill Mercer, Gil Brandt, Pettis Norman, Willie Townes, Jim Ray Smith, Dave Manders, Mike Connelly, Cornell Green. Photo credit: Jesse Nogales Photography

Contributed by Gil Brandt

There have been some famous games in the NFL over the years, but no one contest has drawn more continued interest than the Ice Bowl. Unlike the one million-plus people who have claimed they were there over the years, I was actually on the sideline at Lambeau Field on Dec. 31, 1967, when the Cowboys (for whom I was working at the time) lost to the Packers in the NFL Championship Game. It was a high-profile showdown with a trip to the second Super Bowl at stake. And, yes: It was cold.

How cold, exactly? Consider that everyone always wants to be on the sideline of an NFL game -- except for that game, where the temperature dropped to minus 15 degrees Fahrenheit. I heard that they had to use an ice scraper in the press box to keep the windows clear of ice. If you got a cup of coffee or hot chocolate, it was frozen by the time you got back to your seat. We had multiple players suffer frostbite.

Half a century after it happened, people are still talking about this one, and I think they'll keep on talking about it for another 100. In honor of the 50th anniversary of the Ice Bowl, I've compiled some of my more vivid memories from that game:

We arrived in Green Bay on the Saturday before the game, and when we went and worked out at Lambeau Field, it was very clear and sunny. It was cold -- it felt like it was about 35 degrees -- but really, it was a nice day for the region at that time of the year. Also, on Saturday, there was an NFL Championship party, held at the Oneida Country Club, which members of both the Packers and Cowboys could attend. Green Bay coach Vince Lombardi and Dallas coach Tom Landry were both there. One topic of conversation that night was the field, and Vince talked about how he had this heating system installed under the field, and the field would be soft and in very good condition the next day. It did not work out that way.

The geniuses who built the Holiday Inn in Appleton, where we were staying, designed the building so that the doors to each room opened to the outside. Thus, when you stepped out of your room, you were hit immediately by the elements. At 8 a.m. on game day, I woke up, stepped into the cold, and came across starting offensive tackle Ralph Neely, who was going on about the temperature being 15 below zero with a wind-chill factor of 40 below. I didn't believe him at first, but then I walked down the steps to the lobby and asked the woman behind the desk, and she confirmed it: 15 below with a wind-chill factor of 40 below.

So I looked over to the left of the desk, and there was a big fireplace. Around the fireplace sat five bus drivers. I walked over to the bus drivers and asked them where they got their boots. One of them said, 'These aren't boots; they're galoshes.' I said, 'Where did you get your galoshes?' He said, 'Prange's,' which was a department store of note at the time — one that also happened to be closed on Sundays. I asked how much the galoshes cost. He said $9. I said if anyone had a size 12, I'd rent them for $25. One of the drivers said, 'I have a size 12! I'll rent 'em to you!'

There's a picture of me from that day all wrapped up in a scarf and gloves.

The funny thing is, because of the heat of the battle, I didn't truly realize how cold it was until I took those galoshes off and gave them back to the driver.

Our equipment man had made arrangements and gone to all the stores in town to get Saran wrap, and everybody wrapped their feet, which was great, except it made your feet sweat like heck. I walked out onto the field about an hour before the game, and there was not a fan in the stands -- but about five minutes before kickoff, I noticed that the entire place (listed attendance was 50,861) was full.

A fairly competitive game unfolded despite the weather. We were leading, 17-14, with a few minutes left to play when the Packers mounted a drive that would go down in history. Everyone remembers the Bart Starr touchdown to give Green Bay the game, but one of the biggest plays that people don't talk about as much was the swing pass that Packers receiver Chuck Mercein — whom I tried to recruit before he signed in Green Bay — caught right in front of our bench and turned into a 19-yard gain, taking Green Bay to our 11-yard line. Mercein then took a handoff of 8 yards to put the Packers on the doorstep. And, of course, after we stopped Packers running back Donny Anderson three times, Starr sneaked into the end zone to win the game in the closing seconds. To this day, when I look at footage of that last play, it makes me sick -- it looks like guard Jerry Kramer left a tick early, and they scored.

I think everybody was too cold to realize what had happened immediately after Starr scored, and I don't think anybody had any idea whatsoever that this game would become as famous as it is. But the experience definitely stuck with me. In fact, I still remember it like it was yesterday. Whenever I see anyone who was also there — whether at a party a few years ago for Cowboys tight end Pettis Norman, which was loaded with alumni from the game or when I'm just running into guys like Kramer, Anderson or Forrest Gregg — there's a tendency to reminisce about the Ice Bowl, and for good reason.

Contributed by Mel Renfro

Every player who was on the field that day was in misery. It was a horrible experience. We went out to practice the day before the game, and it was 25-to-35 degrees, and it was great. We were chomping at the bit and looking forward to the next day because there was no way Green Bay could beat us because we were a better team, a faster team.

And we woke up the next morning and heard that it was like 13 degrees below zero. And everybody kind of just said, 'What the heck is this?' It was just unbelievable, but we didn't really realize how bad it was until we got to the stadium and went on the field for the pregame warm-up. There was some ice as we went down the ramp to the field, and we slid a bit. When we got on the field, it was frozen, it was just like concrete, hard as a rock, and the wind was blowing. So, needless to say, when we went back into the locker room, we put on every layer of clothing we could find. I put on a sweatshirt under my jersey, every possible thing I could to try to keep warm, but to no avail, because it was so cold. And the wind cut right through us.

Ten minutes into the game, my hands were so cold I couldn't feel them. I played the game, not feeling my hands, not being able to grab; I just tackled with my arms and shoulders. Everyone was suffering; many of the guys got frostbite. I felt sorry for our receivers trying to catch the ball and for poor Don Meredith trying to throw the ball under those conditions. What was so remarkable was that the Packers came out on the field for pregame warm-ups wearing tee shirts. I guess they were used to that type of thing. It didn't seem to bother them at all. I don't know if it was a mental thing or a psych thing for us, but it took effect.

The type of coach that Landry was, the cold didn't matter to him. It was a mind thing, and you had to get it out of your mind and move forward. Landry was the type of guy who felt you could overcome anything, but you couldn't. But that was his mindset. Just forget about the cold and play football.

We played a gallant game; we probably should have won the game. We were excited after taking a 17-14 lead on halfback Dan Reeves' touchdown pass to wide receiver Lance Rentzel at the start of the fourth quarter. We never, ever thought we would lose until the quarterback sneak went in. We thought we were going to stop them there.

The elements really played a big part against us because we couldn't get any traction on defense during the Packers' final drive. Our linemen couldn't get any traction to come off when the ball was hiked. It was a no-win situation, but I was confident until the last play of the drive that we were going to stop them on that 1-yard line, and we were going to win the game. But it wasn't to be, and I attribute that mainly to the conditions and the cold weather. It was late in the game, and the cold had really gotten to us. I couldn't feel my hands, and I'm sure it was that way with a lot of the guys. But we gave it everything we had. And like I said, if it had been 20 degrees and sunny, Green Bay would not have had a chance. We had the speed, the power, the talent to run all over them, but it was not meant to be. They were blessed, and we were not.

The Packers were a dominant team. They weren't always the best team, but they always won. They knew how to win under any circumstances. They would lose a couple of games during the regular season, but they would always win when it came to the playoffs and the big games. There was just something about that Packers head coach Vince Lombardi thing.

We couldn't battle the Packers and the elements and the weather at the same time. They couldn't get the heating function beneath Lambeau Field to work. It mysteriously malfunctioned. In my opinion, it was no mystery. Lombardi pulled the plug on that electric grid, no doubt in my mind. He knew he had to have leverage because he knew how talented we were. There was no way they could win unless something like that happened. We lived in Dallas, Texas, where it's 90 degrees, 100 degrees. We're used to warm weather. The cold was not our friend. Lombardi knew that and took advantage of it. I'll believe that to the day I die.

But you can't do anything about it. The game shouldn't have been played, but it was played, and we all suffered for a long time. It was three weeks before my fingers thawed out.

A lot of stories have been written about it, and it will go down in history as one of the most iconic games that has ever been played.

Contributed by Dan Reeves

It was a little bit of extra motivation every time we played Green Bay because Lombardi was there, and he and Coach Landry had coached together with the New York Giants in the 1950s and were good friends and great competitors.

Green Bay had beaten us the year before 34-27 in the 1966 NFL championship game in the Cotton Bowl. They were a better team that year, but we felt we were better the next year in 1967. I don't think Lombardi would do anything illegal with the underground heating grid beneath Lambeau Field to help his team gain an unfair advantage.

The day before the Ice Bowl, it was 20 degrees and the sun was shining, and that was the forecast for the next day. We went out and worked on Lambeau Field, the field was in great shape, and you could actually work up a little bit of a sweat. I remember waking up the next morning. Walt Garrison and I were roommates, and we got dressed for our pregame meal and put on our coat and tie — Coach Landry made you wear a coat and tie — and we opened the door and took about two steps and were like, 'Dang, it's cold out here!'

We turned around and said, 'We better put our overcoats on!' So we put our overcoats on and walked back outside, then we started jogging, and then we sprinted to the restaurant. When we got inside, we said, 'Damn, it's cold out there.' And a guy said, 'Well, it ought to be, it's 17 below zero!'

It had dropped like 32 degrees overnight. I grew up where you'd get some cold weather, and it would be below freezing. I thought we could handle it, but I didn't realize that when it keeps getting colder, you keep feeling it. I got hit in that game and busted my facemask, busted my lip. I'm putting my hands over my lips, and it's not bleeding, and I try to put my tongue between my upper lip and my teeth. I couldn't get my tongue in between there because the hit knocked my lip through my tooth. It wasn't bleeding, and I had never been in a place where you get your lip busted, and it doesn't bleed. I found out real quick, it's cold.

The field the day before the Ice Bowl was just perfect, and we weren't prepared for an icy field. We didn't know what kind of shoes we were supposed to wear. It was hard to get our footing. I remember throwing the halfback pass to wide receiver Lance Rentzel for a touchdown on the first play of the fourth quarter. Don Meredith told me, 'We're going to throw the halfback pass.' We had been running a pitch-sweep a great deal in that game, and the Packers were coming up and doing a great job of stopping that. So Meredith told me we were going to run the option pass, so during a timeout at the end of the third quarter, I put my hands as far down my pants as I could put them, trying to keep them warm because you couldn't feel the doggone football.

So I came out of the huddle with my hands down my pants, trying to keep them warm. It was unbearably cold. It's hard to explain. I still don't have any feeling where that tooth went through my lip. When I shave, I don't have any feeling in my upper lip; it's a dead area.

It was a great game because it was a close game. I think because of the conditions, they show that game on TV every year. The Ice Bowl lives on. I've had more people come up to me and say, 'I saw you in the Ice Bowl!'

Green Bay quarterback Bart Starr did an unbelievable job taking them down the field on the game-winning drive. I mean, there's no way you're going to drive 68 yards in those conditions. I don't care if you're on your home field or not. That was just amazing what he did. Amazing.

During the Packers' final drive, I was thinking that our defense had been playing so well that we would make a play. When you look at it, the last thing in the world you think they're going to do is run the quarterback sneak. You're figuring they're going to run some kind of play-action pass, and if it's open, they'll hit it. If not, they'll throw it away, kick the field goal and go into overtime.

They had no timeouts, so they can't stop the clock, and then they run a quarterback sneak. You talk about a gutsy call. If it hadn't worked, what do you think the Ice Bowl would be like now? They'd be talking about how dumb Lombardi was and what a dumb call! And that was the gutsiness of Bart because he was supposed to give the ball to the fullback Chuck Mercein. It was a bold call by Lombardi and Bart.

Contributed by Lee Roy Jordan

I think the Ice Bowl would never have been played today. They would have called it off and rescheduled it. The NFL commissioner Pete Rozelle was out on the West Coast in Oakland for the AFL championship game between the Raiders and Houston Oilers. And he wasn't cold out there.

It was an unbelievable experience. We don't know how many frostbite cases we had, how many had lung damage. We got the wake-up call on the morning of the Ice Bowl, and it's, 'Hello, it's 7:30 and 17 below zero.' I had never heard of below zero.

We'll never know what happened to the electric grid installed beneath Lambeau Field to prevent the field from freezing. I wouldn't be surprised if Lombardi did something to give his team an advantage, playing on a skating rink rather than a football field.

Coach Landry was so busy trying to call plays and operate the team that he forgot to wipe his nose. Two-inch icicles were hanging out of his nose, two white streams of solid ice.

Tom would say things like, 'They've got to play in the same weather.' But they may be a little more used to it than we were. I was proud of our team. We came back and made a great game out of it. We never gave up. We kept working the entire game and gave ourselves a chance to win.

We were very optimistic. It just didn't work out for us. That last drive, we were on too much ice and couldn't keep guys standing up. The Packer offense knew absolutely where they were going on running and passing plays, and we had to guess and try to recover.

We had most of our defenses set up formation-wise; we let Green Bay's offensive formations dictate what we were going to do on defense. It was tough defending the Packers on the final drive. We were having trouble with our footing on a frozen field. They didn't run the quarterback sneak a lot, but we were always expecting that. I was too far away from Starr to get a shot at him. They double-teamed defensive tackle Jethro Pugh, and he kind of had to rise up when they double-teamed him, and it made it hard for us to see Bart and what he was doing.

Contributed by Bob Lilly

The Ice Bowl is something I'll never forget. It's almost like President Kennedy's assassination; everybody remembers what they were doing. And that Ice Bowl, I'll never forget it.

We stayed at a Holiday Inn. It wasn't in Green Bay; it was outside of Green Bay. My roommate was defensive end George Andrie; we roomed together for 11 years. George was Catholic, and he always got up at 6:30 a.m. and went to Mass. When he came back, I was all dressed and we were ready to eat pregame breakfast at ten o'clock. George came in and didn't say anything, didn't say it was cold or anything. He just got a glass of water and said, 'Watch this.' He threw the water at the window, and most of it froze before it hit the windowsill.

George said, 'It's already nine below zero, and the wind is blowing at about 35 miles per hour. It's supposed to get down to 20 or more below zero.' George was from Michigan, and he said, 'Bob, we've got to go out there and show these guys it's not really that cold. A lot of these guys have never played in weather like this.'

And I'm thinking, I've never played in weather like this. We go out there on the field for pregame warm-ups, and immediately everybody started getting icicles in their noses. The trainer from Green Bay came over and told Coach Landry, 'Take your team in (the locker room) and let them thaw out their noses naturally. If you try to pull the icicles, you'll pull a membrane out of your nose.' He gave us jars of Vaseline to put on our noses and our mouths.

We went in and put everything we could find under our uniforms; we did have some long-handle underwear, and we put on an extra tee shirt. Some wrap that you might put on your knee — I put that on my ears. It was cold for Green Bay too, but they were a little better prepared.

The referee blew his whistle first play of the game, and that was before they put the plastic on the metal whistle. It stuck to his lip and tore part of his lip off. He had an eight-inch blood icicle hanging down his face. They called timeout, stopped the game, gave all the referees some Vaseline, and told them to keep their lips, mouths, and noses full of Vaseline. That's what they told us, too.

We had two really nice hot air blowers on the sideline. But the NFL Films people who were taking

35 mm pictures blocked the hot air from us. It was colder at the end, and we had that last goal-line stand, and we didn't stand very well. My impression of that game is that it should not have been played. It was too cold and hurt everybody's lungs; some of our guys smoked, and they gave up smoking after that game due to damaged lungs from the intense cold. We had five guys on defense that I know had frostbite. They had to have skin trimmed off.

I can give you the final picture. We were on the airplane, we were taking off, the sun had gone down, there was a beautiful glow, a pinkish-red glow, and we were thanking God that we had gotten out of Green Bay alive.

That one hurt us. We really felt like we could beat them. On Saturday, the day before the game, we worked out, and the grass was green, the field was soft, and it was wonderful. And the weather was supposed to hold until late afternoon the next day, and it didn't. The cold front came in early the next morning. It was just one of those things.

I've heard a lot of stories as to why Lambeau Field iced up even though it was equipped with an underground heating grid. We just thought it froze. I don't think Lombardi would tinker with the underground heating unit. I think the weather did it. Green Bay's favorite play was the outside running play, the Power Sweep, and they tried some outside running plays; they slipped down too.

We were on a roll, having beaten Cleveland 52-14 in the Cotton Bowl in the Eastern Conference championship game the week before on Christmas Eve. And that's where you want to be at that time of the year. I don't know what would have happened if we had played the Packers on a good field. They might have beaten us anyway.

We were down 14 points and overcame that. We had a feeling of determination in Dallas' defensive huddle during Green Bay's last-ditch drive. I told middle linebacker Lee Roy Jordan, 'We've got to call timeout, get us a screwdriver and dig some holes in the ice because they're going to run up the middle from the 1-yard line.'

And Lee Roy said, 'We don't have time, Bob.' I was kicking the dirt, trying to kick it, and hell, it wouldn't move. If fellow defensive tackle Jethro Pugh and I just had one little hole to put our cleats in, the Packers' offensive line would not have moved us. They couldn't. They would've been just spinning their wheels.

The feeling was, we didn't know if they could push us or we could push them. It was just like standing on glass, very slick. We knew they didn't have far to go, just one yard. They double-teamed Jethro; they could have double-teamed me and done the same thing. It was just one of those deals. You look back on it and say, 'We wish we'd won it, but we didn't.'

Bart did the quarterback sneak, and they won the game. I'm not going to take that away from them. They had a great team and great players.

Contributed by Walt Garrison

The Ice Bowl was cold. I was returning punts and kickoffs and covering punts and kickoffs in that game because Don Perkins was the starting fullback. I didn't get to start until he retired because he was a hell of a guy and a hell of a fullback.

I remember freezing my ass off, sitting on the bench in between punts and kickoffs. I'll never forget that Dave Edwards, a linebacker, and I were sitting side-by-side on the bench. I said, 'Fuzzy'—that was his nickname — 'we've got to be crazy to be out here when it's 13 below zero.'

He said, 'Look behind you.' I said, 'What, at the stands?'

He said, 'Yeah. They paid to get in. We're going to make money whether we win or lose. They're going to lose money whether they win or lose. They're going to freeze their asses off.'

That Ice Bowl game was something else. They sold out Lambeau Field. It wasn't a big field in 1967 and looked like a high school stadium. But they've got a lot of great fans up there if you're a Green Bay Packer. They hate everybody else.

I remember playing against Green Bay Packers Hall of Fame middle linebacker Ray Nitschke. I'd talk to him and some of the other guys after the game and get to know them. I'd talk to them while walking to the dressing room, and they were good guys.

Contributed by John Niland

There was some sort of problem with the hotel accommodations when we arrived in Green Bay. They couldn't get us in a certain area and moved us around. Finally, the team settled in. The weather was mild, probably in the 30s or 40s, but the temperature dropped overnight. The humidity from our breathing must have caused icicles to form in the door seals. The doors froze shut, and on game day morning, they had to kick them open from the outside.

We had no clue it would get that cold. I grew up in New York and was very comfortable in cold weather, but this was shockingly cold. The players talked about layering with flannel clothing or long pajamas underneath their uniforms, and some overdid it. My uniform was too tight to layer — all I wore on Lambeau Field was my jersey over shoulder pads. It turned out to be a good thing, at least for me. I warmed up rapidly due to all of the running being done by the offensive line. Every time the ball snapped, Pettis ran all his patterns, and he seemed to warm up quickly as well.

We had a better game and were confident we would win. Green Bay was known for their running game, and we did shut that down. Still, on that ice, we couldn't play to our performance level. We didn't have the passing game we needed. The slipperiness of the ground itself and a couple of fluke plays and interceptions meant that Dallas fans got robbed. The game should never have been played in those conditions. I don't remember playing in weather that cold since.

Chapter Eight: Super Bowl V

They may have called it the 'Blunder Bowl,' but only a small percentage of players were blessed to play in Super Bowl V.
~ Pettis Norman

I'll share a quick backstory before I delve into Super Bowl V. During my career with the Cowboys, Black football players were relegated to living in South Dallas, a far commute from the practice field in North Dallas. We would have preferred to live in North Dallas but were not welcome. This issue bubbled to the surface throughout the 1960s. Those of us who were raised in the Deep South understood that this was how it had always been, but some of the players from northern states were shocked.

My teammate and wide receiver, Peter Gent, was from Michigan. May Peter rest in peace. He played for the Dallas Cowboys from 1964 through 1968 and was appalled at the racism in Dallas. If you've ever watched the movie *North Dallas 40*, you might be aware that the film was based on a book written by Pete. However, you may not know that the book's title, *North Dallas 40*, alludes to the fact that Blacks could not live in North Dallas. We raised our families far away from the neighborhoods and schools that were exclusively filled with Whites, quite a commute from South Dallas.

While Pete's book and the movie were filled with controversial and questionable topics such as drug use and partying, the picture he painted of the NFL was completely foreign to me.

I believe it was the fair housing issue that inspired him to write his novel. In 1968 the Fair Housing Act became law and banned discrimination in the sale, rental, and financing of property, the same year that Martin Luther King Jr. was assassinated.

Suffice it to say, racial tensions were high over Dr. King's death, and even more so when Blacks in Dallas attempted to lease or purchase homes outside South Dallas without much luck, despite the new legislation.

I began thinking about the rent I paid while leasing apartments. I looked at the quality of housing available. Then it dawned on me that I should build an apartment complex and become a landlord of affordable, quality apartments.

With what became approximately a half-million-dollar loan (an extraordinary amount of money back then), I worked with architects, engineers, and construction companies to build 74 units in South Dallas.

With Mel Renfro at the Golden Helmet Apartments grand opening

I still keep some of the plat maps as a memento of those exciting days, as well as a few news clippings that covered the fanfare. I named the apartment complex The Golden Helmet and opened it with pride. It felt terrific to pay off that loan years later. All the while, I constantly worried about the state of race relations in Dallas. Housing was part of a bigger problem, and that bigger problem was racism.

Don't get me wrong — some White people lived outside of North Dallas, and their presence in South Dallas made it a diverse part of the city. The Golden Helmet apartments were open to all regardless of skin color. I tried to make our advertising inclusive and kept the units filled because the complex had great upkeep and management.

Speaking of housing, I should mention that Mel Renfro's name became synonymous with fair housing. He certainly battled for it. In 1968 after the Fair Housing Act passed, he tried to rent a duplex in North Dallas near the Cowboys' training facility. The owner withdrew the offer, and Mel accused him of violating the Fair Housing Act. Mel sued in federal court and won — a true hero on and off the field. Peter Gent later noted that the housing situation didn't change until Mel Renfro won his lawsuit.

The Late Sixties

I believe the loss in the Ice Bowl left a lingering effect on the Cowboys for the following two years. We continued to add tremendous talent to our team through excellent drafting, and we won two more division titles in 1968 and '69. Despite our regular season success, we continued to struggle in the postseason. In 1968 we drafted future starters Blaine Nye, D.D. Lewis and Larry Cole and won what was then a franchise-record 12 games. The 1968 season was one of my best seasons but also one of my most painful. I jammed my left shoulder against Washington and pulled a hamstring muscle against New Orleans. But any inclination to sit out a game or two was resisted because I had just regained my starting tight end position from Frank Clarke.

When Dallas reporters asked about playing with pain, I told them, "Pain is relative. Some people can take it, others can't." I wasn't saying I was a strong man, but I was able to play with pain. One Dallas writer described me as being "usually the toughest guy on the field." I had plenty of war wounds to prove it too.

We faced the Browns in Cleveland for the second straight year in the Eastern Conference championship game. Unlike our lopsided win in 1967, we were upset 31-20 in 1968.

Here I share a page from my 12/21/68 playbook that illustrates the complexity and variety of Coach Tom Landry's offense and the numerous pass routes I was involved in as a key member of the Cowboys' offense. I believe the Cowboys were one of the more innovative teams in pro football.

It turned out to be the last game in Meredith's career, with Dandy Don retiring after the game. He went on to greater fame than he had enjoyed as an All-American at Southern Methodist University or as a Cowboy when he became an original member of the Monday Night Football announcing crew in 1970. I never forgot another song Don made famous after a key play ended the possibility of the other team to win the game: "Turn Out the Lights, the

Party's Over." Those days bring a smile to my face.

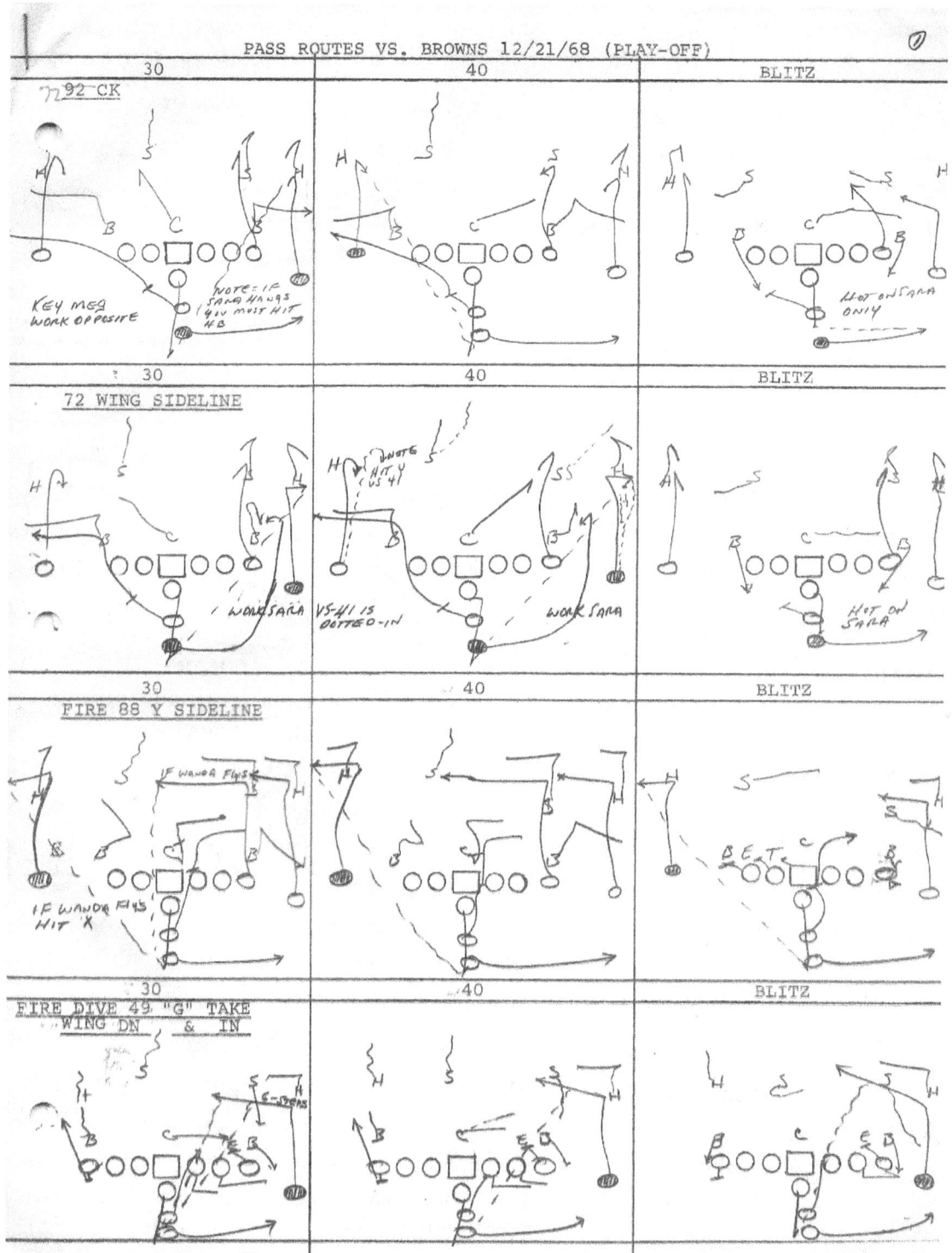

A page from my 12/21/68 playbook that illustrates the complexity of Coach Tom Landry's offense and the numerous pass routes I was involved in as a key member of the Cowboys' offense

The following year was more of the same. Craig Morton was our quarterback, and we added high-quality rookies in Roger Staubach and Calvin Hill, both close friends today. Roger and Calvin have kind words to say about our years together as teammates on the Cowboys.

"Everyone respected you, Pettis," Roger told me. "You were a real strong blocker, a very good blocker, and a solid receiver. You got the job done and had confidence in yourself that transferred to our teammates. And that's a leader. You were at the heart of an expansion team becoming a winning team."

This from the man nicknamed "Captain America" — a 1963 Heisman Trophy winner, U.S. Naval Academy graduate, and Supply Corps officer who volunteered for a tour in Vietnam. Roger was hero material on and off the field. I'm proud to call him my good friend.

The Cowboys drafted Calvin Hill in 1969, straight from Yale University. While NFL teams did not believe they could find excellent talent at elite universities, Calvin was the exception. During his tenure with the Cowboys, he received NFL Offensive Rookie of the Year, All-Pro, and Pro Bowl honors. By the way, his son is Grant Hill, former pro basketball player and co-owner of the Atlanta Hawks. I know Calvin is so proud, and I am too. Calvin is still today a very good friend and credits me as a mentor. That means a lot to me as well.

> *Pettis was a role model, especially for the Black players, in the way he conducted himself, in the way he valued education, and in his involvement in the Civil Rights movement and in local government. I admired the way he carried himself on the field and off the field as one of the best blocking tight ends I've ever seen. He was a great competitor. I remember a game against Houston. Pettis got into a fight with one of their players and said, 'I'm just protecting my daughter's father.' As great a competitor as he was on the field, he was mild-mannered off the field. Pettis was very civic-oriented very prominent in the Black community.*

In 1969 we earned our fourth straight division title. We won 11 games and met the Cleveland Browns in the Eastern Conference title game for the third consecutive year. Once again, we were favored. Playing in front of our partisan fans in the Cotton Bowl had us feeling confident. Yet we were upset by the Browns for the second straight year, this time by 38-14 on a rainy, muddy afternoon. It was a frustrating feeling for all of us, especially since we were now being referred to as "Next Year's Champion," the team that "couldn't win the big one."

Many of us believed the close losses to the Packers in the 1966 and 1967 NFL championship games affected us so much, they negatively impacted our playoff games with Cleveland in 1968 and '69. At the same time, it's important to remember that those Cleveland teams were very talented. Coach Blanton Collier had won an NFL championship in 1964 and would take the Browns to league title games four times in six years from 1964-69. The Browns had future Hall of Fame players in halfback Leroy Kelly, wide receiver Paul Warfield, and guard Gene Hickerson. Their defense, led by linebacker Jim Houston, was strong and tough. They were experienced pros just as we were, and they wanted to win as much as we did. And as the saying goes, on any given day, any team can beat another.

The 1969 season was also the season Roger Staubach formally joined the Cowboys. I feel privileged to have been on the receiving end of Roger's earliest completions in the NFL. With

Don Meredith having retired, Staubach and Morton, the latter Meredith's former backup, dueled for the starting quarterback position. Roger was given the opening game start against the St. Louis Cardinals on September 21 in the Cotton Bowl. It was a picturesque day in Dallas; sunny, 77 degrees and with a slight breeze blowing. Staubach gave us an early lead with a 75-yard scoring strike to Lance Rentzel in the first quarter. In the second quarter, I hauled in an 8-yard square out pass from Roger, getting both feet down just before stepping out of bounds.

Roger completed 7 of 15 passes by the game's end for 220 yards with one touchdown and zero interceptions. He also ran four times for 22 yards and a TD. The result was a 24-3 victory as Roger rose to the occasion and made his lone start of his rookie season a memorable one.

Roger and I still communicate and meet on occasion for lunch. During our visits, whether at lunch or in my office or his, we have supported each other in real estate sales and development and fundraising for just causes. In 1993, he committed to one very memorable trip to Charlotte to be the keynote speaker at a fundraiser in support of my former alma mater JCSU head coach scholarship fund: "A Tribute to Eddie C McGirt."

To me, Roger is not just a big name; he is truly a good friend.

With my good friend Roger Staubach

New Decade

The new decade marked a new chapter for the Cowboys and the NFL. Once again, our scouts improved our team greatly through the draft, bringing future stars and starters in running back Duane Thomas, defensive backs Charlie Waters and Mark Washington, center Pat Fitzgerald and defensive end Pat Toomay.

I recently caught up with Duane, who was an exceptional talent, a six-foot-one, 200-pound blend of size and quickness that the NFL hadn't seen since the great Jim Brown. Duane was a native son of Texas, having been born in Lincoln and playing college ball for West Texas A&M. The Cowboys drafted him in the first round, the 23rd pick overall, and he proved his versatility by playing multiple positions — fullback, halfback, and kick returner.

Interestingly, Duane didn't want to play for the Cowboys. He didn't like what he had heard about the team and its cold, corporate image and low salaries relative to other NFL teams. Duane heard at that time that our great defensive tackle Bob Lilly was making far less money than the Rams' star Merlin Olsen. Duane also didn't want to play in Texas because of the civil rights issues in the state at that time. Duane said he didn't know how people in Dallas could say they loved God and still have so much hate in their hearts.

Duane grew up in California and loved the weather and the laid-back atmosphere. He hoped to be drafted by the San Francisco 49ers. Ironically, his rookie season would see the Cowboys play the 49ers in San Francisco for the NFC championship and a berth in Super Bowl V. Upon joining the Cowboys, he gravitated toward me as being part of what he called the "heart" of the Cowboys along with Lilly, Cornell Green and other team veterans.

I certainly admired Duane's style on the field, and he felt the same about me. Duane said I'd knock an opponent on his butt, but off the field saw me as the nicest guy one could meet, and I appreciate that. He also likes that I was the kind of guy who, when I believed in an issue, I went all out. "That's the kind of heart you have, Pettis," he told me recently and noted that he appreciates this quality as a friend, player, and teammate. Duane certainly went all out when it came to issues close to the heart. He has always marched to the beat of his own drum, a person with his own principles, perspective, and unique way of looking at the world.

Duane's running style blended beautifully with our offensive line's blocking abilities. Our line isn't as well-remembered as "The Hogs" in Washington, but center Dave Manders, guards John Niland and Blaine Nye, and tackles Rayfield Wright and Tony Liscio comprised one of the great offensive lines. They were agile, mobile, and excelled at precision blocking. Duane, Walt Garrison, and Calvin Hill made for a deep and versatile backfield, and they were adept at reading the blocks and running to daylight.

Duane's rookie season saw him rush for a team-best 803 yards, 5.3 average, and 5 TDs, and he was named NFL Rookie of the Year. Interestingly, he and I would later play together as San Diego Chargers, and then work together in the World Football League (WFL), him as a player and me as a broadcaster.

The 1970 season also saw us bring in another outstanding player as tight end and future Hall of Famer Mike Ditka, who would become the first man to win a Super Bowl both as a player and head coach. We also made another big deal in getting Packers' All-Pro cornerback

Herb Adderley in a trade. Adderley was a winner and an all-time great. He was also the vocal leader we needed and brought that "Lombardi attitude" with him.

Cornell Green, who moved from cornerback to safety to accommodate Adderley states, "Adderley made plays for us and gave us confidence because he knew how to win big games." In 1970, our secondary was one of the best ever. Adderley, Renfro, Green, and Waters were perennial NFL All-Pros, and Herb and Mel would be enshrined in the Pro Football Hall of Fame.

The Merger

The 1970 season was the first of the merger era, and saw the NFL and AFL divided into two conferences, the NFC and AFC, under the NFL umbrella. The NFL adopted the AFL's custom of putting players' names on the backs of their jerseys, and the AFC adopted the NFC's use of the Wilson football, which was fatter than the AFL's slimmer Spalding ball. We saw two of our former rivals, the Browns and Steelers, join the AFC, along with the Colts. With the merger, NFC and AFC teams now played each other in regular season play.

Coach Landry took a different approach for the 1970 season. He told us before the season started that he wanted more dedication, seriousness, and hard work. There was to be no kidding around during practices, which were going to be strictly business. Coach Landry also decided there would be less emphasis on big plays, such as the long bomb to Bob Hayes, our speedy wide receiver. A greater reliance on the running game suited me fine; blocking was a strong suit of mine.

We got off to an uneven start, going 3-2 against NFC teams before playing our first game against an AFC team in Week Six. Our first inter-conference game just happened to be against the defending Super Bowl champion Chiefs in Kansas City. We won 27-16. For those of us who had been there in 1966, it was a reminder of what might have been if we had played them in the first Super Bowl.

Still, we struggled for much of the regular season and were almost knocked out of contention a couple of times. The low point came in a 38-0 loss to the St. Louis Cardinals before a national television audience on Monday Night Football. The loss dropped our record to 5-4, and the next day Coach Landry was near tears when he told us, "Y'all can just play flag football if you want," and tossed his clipboard before walking out of the room.

Lilly and linebacker Lee Roy Jordan called a team meeting on the spot. They reminded us that everyone had given up on us, and that if anything was going to happen, it would happen in this room or not at all. After that, we had a sense of unity. Coach Landry helped by relaxing practices a little bit and told us to "Have fun the rest of the year."

We started playing touch football or volleyball on Mondays, and the team began to gel. The final two games of the regular season included a victory over Cleveland 6-2 in a mud bowl at Municipal Stadium. It was an important win for us because it was the first time we had beaten the Browns in two years.

Blunder Bowl?

We gained added confidence the following week when we handled Houston in the regular season finale, 52-14. The Oilers had been an AFL playoff team the season before and had played for the AFL championship three years earlier. They had great talent, including linebacker George Webster and safety Ken Houston. Defeating our Texas rivals gave us great momentum heading into the playoffs.

Next up were the Lions, seeking their franchise's first postseason victory since 1957. It was a tremendous relief to claim our first postseason win in three years when we defeated Detroit by the baseball-like score of 5-2. It was a historic occasion, marking the final NFL postseason game ever played in the Cotton Bowl.

We were back in the championship game for the first time in three years, once again just a step away from playing in the ultimate game — the Super Bowl. This time, we took that big step and beat the 49ers and our former assistant coach, Dick Nolan, 17-10, in the final NFL game played in San Francisco's Kezar Stadium.

Finally, we were in the Big Game, but the experience was a bit of a letdown for me. The two weeks between the NFC championship game and Super Bowl V were filled with a lot of interviews that became repetitious and a bit boring after a while. I expressed my feelings to the media in Miami, especially the two-week layoff between the NFC Championship Game and the Super Bowl as a factor in how Dallas played.

The NFC Championship game was better from an emotional standpoint than the Super Bowl. First of all, there was a two-week lag time. To me, you lose some edge when you wait like that, and then you try to get it back. Honestly, some of my teammates and I got tired of going through numerous interviews and posing for pictures.

Still, we were confident going into our Super Bowl showdown with Baltimore. Coach Landry had given every offensive player a 45-page playbook, dissecting the numerous defenses the Colts liked to use. But there was more to our confidence than strategy. We had a more relaxed, upbeat attitude than in past years. As I told the media at the time, I had never enjoyed an NFL season like the 1970 season.

"It used to be if you dropped a pass, you'd come back to the bench, and 30 heads would turn away from you," I told reporters. "Now, you get everybody rushing up to tell you, "It's okay, forget it, don't worry about it. Catch the next one." We were also buoyed by the confidence that came with beating some of our old playoff nemeses – Cleveland and Green Bay – during the 1970 season.

Super Bowl V occurred on January 17, 1971. We were going up against the Baltimore Colts in the most important game of my NFL career. We were very familiar with the Colts from having played them for years in the old NFL, but the atmosphere at the Orange Bowl in Miami was not quite real. Not having a former AFL team in the Super Bowl took a little bit out of the game. The rivalry between the leagues had added something extra to the Super Bowl for the players, coaches, and the fans, much as the World Series did prior to interleague play.

I think NFL commissioner Pete Rozelle realized that not having a team from the old AFL was taking away from Super Bowl V because he ordered the Cowboys to wear our blue jerseys for the game, even though we were the designated home team. Like the Browns, the Cowboys always wore white for our games at home, but Rozelle believed that allowing us to wear our white jerseys and the Colts their blue jerseys would make the Super Bowl look too much like an NFL regular season game between Baltimore and us in the 1960s. So, we had to wear our blue jerseys, even though we considered them somewhat unlucky.

Super Bowl V would undoubtedly have generated greater interest among fans and even my Cowboy teammates if we had played an AFL representative, like the defending champion Kansas City Chiefs or the AFC runner-up Oakland Raiders. A Super Bowl between the Cowboys and Chiefs would have matched two teams that had previously battled for the heart of Texas during the fledgling years of both franchises in the early 1960s. The Chiefs had originally been the Dallas Texans, and from 1960-62 the Cowboys and Texans sought to win over the fans of the City of Dallas and the state of Texas.

The Texans were more successful early on. They won the 1962 AFL championship in a classic double-overtime victory over the two-time defending champion Houston Oilers. The Texans' win was the longest game in pro football history, eclipsing the Baltimore Colts' famous overtime victory against the Giants in Yankee Stadium in 1958. The success of the Texans prompted the Cowboys' public relations department to lure fans to our games by promoting the fact that our opponents were great players like John Unitas, Jim Brown, Jim Taylor, Bart Starr and Y.A. Tittle. The AFL just couldn't match that star power, and Texans owner Lamar Hunt knew it. Even though his team was winning more on the field, the Cowboys were winning at the box office. That prompted Mr. Hunt to move his team to Kansas City.

Had we played Kansas City in Super Bowl V, this history between the two franchises would have added extra spice to the game. Even more spice might have been added had we played other great AFL teams like the Super Bowl III champion New York Jets and their flamboyant quarterback "Broadway" Joe Namath or the Oakland Raiders and their maverick owner Al Davis. Unfortunately for the Jets and for football fans everywhere, Broadway Joe broke his passing hand in a Week Four loss to the Colts early in the season, and the Jets missed the playoffs. The Raiders, on the other hand, were just one win away from returning to the Super Bowl for the first time since January 1968, when they lost to Green Bay.

A Super Bowl between the Cowboys and Raiders would have represented the polar opposites of pro football. Tom Landry was seen as the squeaky-clean coach, Al Davis, the rebellious owner. The Raiders were a colorful crew coached by a young John Madden, who would gain even greater fame in later years as an NFL color commentator. Quarterback Daryle Lamonica was a classic pocket passer whose rocket-launching right arm earned him the moniker "the Mad Bomber." Defensively, the Raiders featured "Big" Ben Davidson, a mustachioed giant, and Willie Brown, arguably the greatest cover corner in AFL history.

A Cowboys-Raiders showdown would have matched "America's Team" against "America's Most Wanted" and would have kept alive the NFL-AFL blood feud. Unfortunately, it didn't happen, and that affected the hype and emotion going into the game.

Pettis Norman (84) takes the field during Super Bowl V against the Baltimore Colts in Miami.
Photo credit: AP Images / NFL Photos

My approach to the Super Bowl was the same as every game; I played hard. I had played against these people before, and I knew that Johnny Unitas, John Mackey, Earl Morrall, Bubba Smith, Mike Curtis, Billy Ray Smith, Rick Volk, and company were savvy veterans and outstanding players. Like us, they had been in big games and lost and were trying to shed the label of "Next Year's Champions." It was the Colts who had suffered the humiliation of being the first NFL team to lose to the AFL in the Super Bowl — they dropped a 16-7 decision to Namath and the New York Jets just two years earlier in Super Bowl III.

The Orange Bowl

Yet, this was not exactly the same Baltimore team that had been embarrassed by the Jets. They had a new coach, former offensive coordinator Don McCafferty nicknamed "Easy Rider" by his players for his low-key style. He replaced hard-driving Don Shula, who had moved on to Miami. Don Klosterman also took over as general manager, allowing Baltimore to boast if it wanted, that it had more Dons than the Mafia.

The Colts had also gotten younger, bringing in talented players like receivers Eddie Hinton and Roy Jefferson, running backs Norm Bulaich and Tom Nowatzke, linebackers Ted Hendricks and Ray May, defensive end Roy Hilton, and place kicker Jim O'Brien. Now the Colts were returning to the scene of their greatest defeat, Miami's fabled Orange Bowl.

Our experience in the Orange Bowl was limited; we played there in postseason games called the "Playoff Bowl." Held in early January, the Playoff Bowl matched the Eastern and Western Conference runners-up and was a game few really wanted to play. The perks were a paid vacation on famous Miami Beach and the opportunity to close the season with a win. We went 1-2 in the Orange Bowl, bowing to Baltimore in 1966, beating Minnesota in 1969, and losing to Los Angeles in 1970.

The difference this time was that the Orange Bowl's spongy grass field had been replaced by artificial turf, which was still relatively new to the NFL at that time. This would be the first Super Bowl game played on an artificial surface. The historic stadium also had some quirks, notably swirling, gusty winds that would blow unpredictably down on the field. These winds were known to wreak havoc at times with punts and field goals.

Unpredictability turned out to be a big factor in our Super Bowl with Baltimore. It was an extremely hard-hitting and physical game, not surprising since we were two teams desperate to win and playing for a prize only one team could claim. The result was a combined 11 turnovers, which led some critics to call Super Bowl V the "Blooper Bowl" and the "Blunder Bowl."

That was an unfair label since several of those turnovers had been caused by bone-jarring hits. It was a bright, beautiful day, and the sold-out stadium was filled with vibrant colors and fired-up fans. We took the opening kickoff, and on the first play from scrimmage, I was lined up on the left side of the line and helmet-to-helmet with outside linebacker Ted Hendricks. He was nicknamed the "Mad Stork" early in his Hall of Fame career because of his tall, gangly frame. At the first snap, I fired out and hit Hendricks squarely, driving him back a couple of yards.

Hall of Fame sportscaster Curt Gowdy, at that time the voice of NBC-TV Sports, told viewers early in the first quarter, "You'll be seeing the tight ends alternate for Dallas, Pettis Norman Number 84 and Mike Ditka Number 89." That's exactly what happened as Mike and I both saw action. It was all part of Coach Landry's system of using his tight ends to bring the plays in. It was similar to what Paul Brown had done a couple of decades earlier when he was coaching the Cleveland Browns, except Paul employed what was known as "Messenger Guards." One of those messengers was Chuck Noll, who would go on to a Hall of Fame coaching career as the builder of Pittsburgh's "Steel Curtain" Super Bowl champions of the 1970s.

On our second series on offense, I wrangled with middle linebacker Mike Curtis, nicknamed "The Animal." Curtis was a quick, intelligent, and fiery player. He was probably Baltimore's best player that day and a candidate for the game's Most Valuable Player. Curtis once clubbed a Baltimore fan who had run onto the field at Memorial Stadium and tried to take off with the football. Some of Mike's teammates criticized him for belting the fan, but Mike's response was, "That guy broke a city ordinance, and I enforced it."

To show the intricacies of our offense, our third series saw me lining up on the left side of the line again but this time blocking down on Colts' right defensive end Roy Hilton to clear a path for Duane Thomas. On our next series, set up inside the Baltimore Red Zone following a fumble recovery on a punt. I flexed out from right tackle Rayfield Wright and then cut across the middle and cut down Curtis. A couple of series later, I blocked down on big Bubba Smith, the massive Colts left defensive end.

Mike Clark's 14-yard field goal gave us the first points of the game, and we led 6-0 in the second quarter when Clark connected on a 30-yard kick.

The Colts tied it on a controversial play that saw tight end John Mackey haul in a 75-yard touchdown reception from Unitas on a tipped ball. The ball had bounced off the hands of wide receiver Eddie Hinton and right into the hands of the alert Mackey, who then raced untouched to the end zone. The rules at the time stated that a pass was not complete if the ball deflects from one offensive player to another. A defensive player would have to touch it in between the two offensive players. Officials claimed that right cornerback Mel Renfro nicked the ball as it sped from Hinton to Mackey.

We got that score back when our great Doomsday defense pressured Unitas out of his protective pocket on a pass play and forced him to scramble. Lee Roy Jordan jarred the ball free from Johnny Unitas, and Jethro Pugh recovered the fumble at the Baltimore 28. It was the third of four turnovers in the first half for the Colts, who hadn't turned the ball over once in their AFC title game victory over Oakland. It seemed that the Colts were suffering the same fate in Super Bowl V that they had in Super Bowl III.

On the play immediately following Jethro's fumble recovery, I blocked big Bubba and was shaken up a bit. NBC-TV cameras showed me limping on the sideline, but two plays later, I knocked down linebacker Ray May and cleared a path for Duane Thomas to score on a screen pass from Craig Morton. On the NBC-TV telecast, Curt Gowdy paid tribute to my contribution on the scoring play that gave us a 13-6 lead, saying, "Duane Thomas got a great block by the tight end, Pettis Norman."

Unitas was hurt and left the game for good later in the second quarter, following a hard hit to the ribs by George Andrie. Unitas was later diagnosed with torn rib cartilage and was replaced by Earl Morrall, the NFL's MVP, two years earlier when he led the Colts to a 15-1 record and a berth in Super Bowl III. Earl had a nightmarish afternoon against the Jets and was replaced by Unitas. Now, the situation was reversed, with Morrall replacing Unitas.

Second Half

As you can imagine, the Super Bowl halftime shows of the '70s were light years different than what we see today. Super Bowl V featured the star power of Anita Bryant, a Top 40 hits singer who toured with Bob Hope and was the Citrus Growers Association ambassador and Florida orange juice spokeswoman. Anita was no stranger to Super Bowl performances, having sung the "National Anthem" at Super Bowl III. She was introduced as "the voice of America" at Super Bowl V and sang a stirring rendition of "The Battle Hymn of the Republic." The Southeast Missouri State Marching Band also performed.

We were close to scoring what could have been the clinching touchdown in the third quarter when we recovered another Colt fumble, this on the opening kickoff of the second half. Duane Thomas was hit hard by Mike Curtis and Jim Duncan at the goal line and fumbled. But although our center Dave Manders emerged from the pileup with the ball, the officials awarded the ball to Baltimore. It was the second controversial call of the game, and both had gone against us.

Still, our lead remained 13-6 in the fourth quarter before Baltimore tied it. Safety Rick Volk intercepted a tipped pass – the second crucial tipped pass of the game – and returned it to our 3-yard line. Tom Nowatzke bulled in from the 1, and with 7:35 remaining, the Super Bowl was suddenly tied. A late interception by the ubiquitous Curtis, who played an outstanding game, set up Baltimore for the win with just seconds remaining in regulation. Rookie Jim O'Brien, whose long, shaggy hair prompted the nickname "Lassie" after the famous TV dog, kicked the winning field goal from 32 yards out, and the Colts won 16-13.

We had played the closest and most competitive Super Bowl to that point, but it did little to ease our disappointment or soothe our frustration. Once again, we were the team that "couldn't win the big one" even though we had won plenty of big games to get to the Super Bowl. Lilly was so anguished at game's end, he took his helmet off and flung it high and far into the air. It landed an estimated 30 yards downfield, prompting an observer to call it the best Cowboy throw all day.

Duane Thomas had a penchant for putting things in proper perspective and did so with Super Bowl V. He said it was a learning experience for us and taught us to be ready for unexpected situations and how to deal with them.

It was a lesson I would soon take to heart personally. I didn't know it at the time, but the Super Bowl, the "Ultimate Game," turned out to be the last game I ever played in a Dallas Cowboys uniform. Recalling what Duane said, it was an unexpected situation, and I would have to deal with it. I did receive a Super Bowl ring and cherish it to this day.

I was about to heed Horace Greeley's famous advice: "Go West, young man." My "West" happened to be San Diego.

Revisiting the Cotton Bowl. Photo Credit: Lawrence Jenkins Photography

Chapter Nine: San Diego Chargers

I guess I've just tried to live up to the expectations of the people who had faith in me.
~ Pettis Norman

I played a total of nine magical years in Dallas and left for San Diego with fond memories of my time spent on an outstanding team, including the seasons I played with four starting quarterbacks: Eddie LeBaron (1960–1963), Don Meredith (1960–1968), Craig Morton (1967–1971), and Roger Staubach (1969–1971).

Suddenly, I found myself on a new path in a trade to the San Diego Chargers. As I've mentioned previously, some attributed this trade to my participation in a political march. However, I've never believed that. A lot was going on with the Cowboys at that time, and not all may be aware of the backstory; it was a perfect storm.

We had traded troubled receiver Lance Rentzel for another all-star receiver named Lance, this being Alworth of the San Diego Chargers. Recognized by everyone as one of the all-time great wideouts and along with Don Maynard, the best receiver in the pass-happy American Football League, Lance Alworth was nicknamed "Bambi" for his unparalleled grace and fluidity in the open field.

Alworth being as great as he was, I felt honored that the Chargers insisted I be included in the trade in return. Coach Landry paid me great respect when he went out of his way to come across town to the bank where I worked in the offseason and told me about the trade in person before it went public. He informed me what the Cowboys were going to do and why. Coach Landry told me, "I came to you because I need to explain something to you. It doesn't have anything to do with the march you led in downtown Dallas. I had to involve you in a trade, and my wife (Alicia) is going to kill me."

I greatly admired Alicia Landry (God rest her soul). What a special wife, mother, and dear friend. She and Coach Landry lost a daughter, Lisa, in 1995 and established the Lisa Landry Childress Foundation in her memory to raise awareness for organ donation. Alicia once shared, "Pettis Norman was a good football player and an even better person — he was always one of my favorite Cowboy players." I'll cherish those words forever.

I was also a favorite of Tom Landry Jr., who came to practice and helped the players carry our helmets down a dirt road and back to the locker room. Tom Jr. was 12 at the time and recently told me that he remembers the 1960s as being tough years, especially for Black players. He saw me as a "special guy" because I made it on my own. I was undrafted by the Cowboys, yet I made the team and became a fixture in the starting lineup for years. Tom Jr. says he admired the way I came up because it wasn't an easy thing to do.

"Pettis, you are a really good guy," he told me, "a solid guy, no bravado, very respectful, and you worked hard at your career. You were a team player and a great man."

With my good friend, Tom Landry Jr.

Tom Jr. also recalled how difficult the trade was on his father. He remembered how his father insisted on telling me about the trade in person as a gesture of the respect his father had for me as a person and a player. Tom Jr. says he carries that same respect, and of course, I feel the same way about him and his iconic dad. What a wonderful family.

I wasn't alone in the trade between the Cowboys and Chargers. The deal also involved our offensive lineman Tony Liscio and defensive lineman Ron East. Both were versatile pros who could play more than one position. Tony played guard and tackle for us, and Ron was a defensive end and defensive tackle. Their versatility added to their value and made them attractive to a Chargers' team that was actively seeking veteran experience.

Just as Redskins Coach George Allen was stockpiling veteran players for his "Over the Hill Gang" in Washington, Chargers head coach Sid Gillman and his eventual successor Harland Svare were doing the same in San Diego. In short order, the Chargers would add David "Deacon" Jones and Coy Bacon from the Los Angeles' Rams celebrated "Fearsome Foursome"; Lionel Aldridge, a former starter on the great Green Bay championship teams of 1965-67; and Dave Costa, an AFL stalwart who had previously played for Oakland, Buffalo, and Denver. East would become a three-year starter and play alongside Deacon, Aldridge, and Costa in his move west.

Off to California

Margaret and I had a lot of packing to do as we prepared to move to California's second-largest city. We found a new home in San Diego, situated our daughters in school, and settled into our lives as southern Californians. We discovered that the cooler oceanfront weather warmed up the further inland we went. The summers were warm and dry and the winters mild. Our girls soon learned to appreciate the white sand beaches in our new locale on the Pacific coast. Before long, we felt like natives instead of tourists.

Our three daughters

With Margaret

Being a baseball fan, I had heard a few years back that the San Diego Padres moved from the minor league into the major league and debuted their first game in the new San Diego Stadium. I looked forward to visiting the stadium and attending some of those games.

I had met some of the San Diego Chargers as opponents during games when they faced the Cowboys, making the transition easier. I fit in with my new teammates and was immediately chosen as co-captain and later named San Diego Charger's Man of The Year.

A word here about California — it did not have the racial issues that I experienced in Texas because, in my opinion, it wasn't a southern state. I had no problems when I played in San Diego and believe that's why I became team captain and was voted by fans as their favorite player, even though I was a Black man in a predominantly White city.

My main thought on my trade to the Chargers was, I'm going to go out to San Diego and be the best player I can be for this team. I knew the Chargers played a much different brand of ball than what we did in Dallas. Sid Gillman had coached the Rams in the NFL in the 1950s and was one of pro football's leading innovators when he took over the Los Angeles Chargers in 1960 in the AFL's first year of existence.

Gillman developed an offensive attack based on speed and quick-striking ability. The jagged lightning bolt that adorned the Chargers' helmets and uniforms perfectly symbolized the electric attack Gillman had created. His Chargers could strike instantly from anywhere, just like a bolt of lightning.

The Chargers' uniforms reflected not only our strategy but our surroundings as well. The bright blue jerseys and yellow-gold pants resembled the brilliant blue skies and golden sunshine that San Diego is known for. Because of their wide-open offense, the team became the standard-bearer of AFL football. When they relocated to San Diego and won the 1963 league championship with a record-shattering 51-10 victory over the defense-minded Boston patriots, Sid's squad became the first AFL team to invite serious comparisons to the NFL's best.

In fact, Otto Graham, the quarterback of the Cleveland Browns' title teams in the 1940s and '50s, broke with his NFL brethren and openly predicted that if Gillman's Chargers could play George Halas' NFL champion Chicago Bears, the Chargers would win.

It was exciting for me to join the Chargers and learn Sid Gillman's system as an offensive player. It was intricate and advanced, so much so that it influenced future San Francisco 49ers coach Bill Walsh to build on it and develop the great Joe Montana-Jerry Rice offenses that dominated the 1980s. Fans credit Walsh with creating the famed "West Coast Offense," but it was really Gillman's offense.

In time, I would play alongside the legendary John Unitas, the aging quarterback who joined the Chargers in 1973. His star teammate with the Colts, all-time great tight end John Mackey, and halfback Mike Garrett, the 1965 Heisman Trophy winner from USC and former Kansas City star, helped lead the Chiefs to Super Bowls 1 and IV.

Tony Liscio, drafted by the Packers in 1963, was part of the College All-Star squad that handed Vince Lombardi and his two-time defending NFL champions a humiliating defeat in the annual summer game held in Chicago's storied Soldier Field. Tony was released by the Packers and signed by Dallas. Knee injuries sidelined him, but Tony battled through a long recovery and became an all-pro and a starter in our two classic title games with Green Bay.

Tony played for us in Super Bowl V, and although he was traded to the Chargers, he never played a game for San Diego due to recurring back injuries. But, it was not over, injuries to starting offensive tackle Ralph Neely prompted Coach Landry to reach out to Tony in November 1971. Despite numerous injuries to his legs and shoulder, Tony moved into the starting lineup and did an exemplary job.

Ironically, Tony was a teammate to the man he was traded for — Alworth – in Super Bowl VI, and both contributed mightily. Alworth hauled in a touchdown pass from Roger Staubach, and Tony's blocking on Bill Stanfill, the Dolphins' outstanding defensive end, helped Duane Thomas head a ground game that gashed Miami's famous "No-Name" defense for 252 yards rushing.

Tight end Pettis Norman #88 of the San Diego Chargers is contained by the Denver Broncos after a reception at San Diego Stadium on September 24, 1972 in San Diego, California. Getty Images. Photo credit: James Flores

Fans and Acclaim

My hard work and steady play won over the fans in San Diego as it had won over the fans in Dallas. In the stands at Chargers home games, fans gave me standing ovations, and I soon built the same kind of bond with the San Diego community as I had in Dallas. San Diego is a beautiful city, and everyone, especially the fans, were so nice to me. They voted me their Number One player, and it was a great honor. So was being named the Chargers' "Man of the Year" and co-captain. I liked the community, and the community liked me.

Just like in Dallas, I tried to do things to bring the community together. I spent hours after games signing autographs for fans, and word quickly spread that I did these kinds of things. I saw myself as more than just a football player; I was an ambassador as well. My thoughts on football and the community were to try and do everything better.

I had not seen a lot of AFL games in the 1960s or many AFC teams since the merger of the two leagues in 1970, but I adjusted to their playing styles. It helped that we had great chemistry on the Chargers. It also helped that I was a good blocker and was recognized as such by my new teammates and our fans.

I saw this fresh start as a great opportunity, and things were quickly falling into place for me. The guys on the team were nice, the coaching staff was good, and I felt we could build something similar to what we had built with the Cowboys.

We had guys on the Chargers who were great football players. When he got to San Diego in 1972, Deacon Jones told me, "I'm so glad to have you on my side." I felt the same way about Deacon and Unitas. Johnny was one heck of a football player, one of the greatest of all time. If you played against him, most of the time, you were going to lose.

Mike Garrett was a great running back who had come to San Diego from the Super Bowl champion Chiefs. If I had signed with the Texans out of college, Mike and I would have been teammates much earlier. He starred at USC and won the Heisman Trophy in 1965 as the best college football player in the country.

Mike was a two-time All-AFL choice and was so talented athletically he was also drafted by the Los Angeles Dodgers and Pittsburgh Pirates. We arrived in San Diego at a very interesting time. The Chargers were bringing in a lot of "name" players, including Mike, myself, Deacon, Johnny Unitas, Jerry LeVias, Coy Bacon, Dave Costa, et al. It was a menagerie of football people and talent, but we all got beyond our egos, and even got beyond our old AFL-NFL rivalry. Our whole deal was to get together and help the San Diego Chargers win. It was a lot of fun playing with those guys.

Even though we played in different leagues, Mike says he knew I was a good tight end and couldn't wait to play alongside me. He knew of my blocking abilities, and as a running back, he knew that when he ran to my side of the scrimmage line, I would be at the point of attack, helping to clear an avenue of daylight for him.

"Pettis, you were a great addition to the team," Mike says now. "And you're as nice a person as you were a good football player."

As much as Mike admired my exploits on the field, he says he came to admire me off the field as well. "You were always doing good things for people," he mentioned. "You're just a good human being."

Another teammate, Jerry LeVias, echoed Mike's comments. Jerry was a true son of Texas, born in Beaumont and starring at Southern Methodist University and then the AFL's Houston Oilers. At 5-8 and 177 pounds, Jerry was considered too small to play major college football but proved otherwise and helped the Mustangs to their first Cotton Bowl appearance in nearly two decades. Jerry's speed afoot helped him make up for his lack of size on the football field, and he impressed opposing players and coaches, including the great University of Texas coach Darrell Royal.

Deeply religious, Jerry wore No. 23, for Psalm 23, at SMU and in the pros. One of the few Black students at SMU in the mid-1960s, Jerry experienced racially motivated abuse from contemporaries and opponents. Still, Jerry excelled on the field and was named All-America his senior season. Along with Baylor's John Westbrook, Jerry was instrumental in helping integrate the Southwest Conference.

Jerry joined the Oilers and was named to the All-AFL team his rookie season as he helped Houston reach the AFL playoffs. The following season, Jerry was responsible for nearly half of Houston's total yardage. Jerry's athletic abilities have earned him induction in the College Football Hall of Fame and Texas Sports Hall of Fame. He prepared for life after pro football and became a successful businessman. Today, he works as an ambassador with the Houston Texans.

Jerry and I touched base recently. As he looked back at our time together in San Diego, I'm gratified that he remembers me not only as a football player but as a great guy who played football. Here's an interesting anecdote — Jerry and my San Diego teammates called me the "Rev," short for "Reverend." Jerry says it was because I was revered by other members of the Chargers. Whenever I spoke to the team in a meeting, Jerry and some others would wait until I finished speaking and then say, "Let's get an Amen!" It was a sign of respect and very moving to me.

Highlights

In my first year in San Diego, I started 12 of our 14 games and caught a career-high 27 passes for 358 yards and one TD. We opened at home with a 21-14 win over Kansas City and then lost four straight, including games against the Raiders and the "Steel Curtain" Steelers. My most productive game of the season came against "Mean" Joe Greene and Co. when I had seven catches for 48 yards.

One of our 1971 season highlights came in early December when we defeated the vaunted Vikings and their "Purple People Eaters" 30-14. John Hadl, along with Joe Namath and Daryle Lamonica, was one of the renowned deep passers of that era and threw for over 330 yards and four TDs against Minnesota's great defense.

Coach Gillman went 4-6 before resigning for health reasons, leaving Svare to take over as head coach. I renewed acquaintances with Phil Bengtson, our defensive coordinator, who had held the same post for the Packers during their glory years. We finished 6-8 and in third place in the AFC Western Division but struggled even more the following season when we went 4-

9-1.

I started 11 of our 13 games and had 19 catches for 262 yards. My best game came in Week 13 when I hauled in 5 catches for 69 yards. We played one of the great teams in NFL history in 1972 when we faced the Miami Dolphins in the Orange Bowl in Week Five. We lost 24-10 but were one of 17 teams to lose to the Dolphins in their historic undefeated and untied season.

We closed our campaign at home with a loss to Pittsburgh. It was a historic game for the Steelers, who clinched their first division title in franchise history and punched their first ticket to the playoffs. One week later those same Steelers had a date with destiny. Franco Harris made his famous "Immaculate Reception" in the final seconds to stun the Raiders in a playoff game in Pittsburgh.

Here's a piece of trivia. In 1972, San Diego was chosen as the site of the Republican National Convention, which was exciting for many people both politically and economically. However, plans changed, and the convention was moved to Miami Beach. Mayor Pete Wilson handled the loss of the convention in a unique way. Rather than get upset, he declared San Diego "America's Finest City." Suddenly, at least according to the mayor, I was playing football in the finest city in our nation, and the moniker has stuck ever since.

Final Season

The 1973 season, my final in pro football, saw the Chargers finish a disappointing 2-11-1. We underwent a coaching change when Svare was replaced after a 1-6-1 start by our offensive coordinator Ron Waller. We had another change in leadership as rookie Dan Fouts took over at quarterback for the 40-year-old Unitas. Fouts has since joined Johnny U. in Canton, Ohio, in the Pro Football Hall of Fame. I started 11 of the 13 games I played in 1973 and caught 13 passes for 200 yards.

After 12 years in the NFL, I was ready to move on. The Sunday wars on NFL gridirons had left me with a degenerative knee condition. Still, I was able to retire with 182 receptions in 162 games and had totaled 15 TD receptions and 2,492 receiving yards. I was also named NFL Man of The Year first runner-up, which was gratifying.

I was prepared for life and had acquired businesses outside of football and wasn't sad when I left the NFL; instead, I focused on growing my businesses and being the "change agent" in my community. It was another dynamic that helped me to move on from football.

Today, my post-retirement relationship with pro football revolves around being a fan of the sport — and the Cowboys in particular. I purchased season tickets at Texas Stadium and went to as many games as I could, cheering on former teammates Roger Staubach, Bob Lilly, and Lee Roy Jordan. In time I welcomed new generations of great players like Tony Dorsett, Drew Pearson, and Randy White in the 1980s; the celebrated "Triplets" of Troy Aikman, Emmitt Smith, and Michael Irvin in the 1990s; and Dak Prescott, Ezekiel Elliott, and Jason Witten in the 2000s. These are players who not only wear stars on their helmets; they're stars on the field as well.

A Shout Out to the Players' Wives

There were "other" stars in football, namely, the wives who held down the home front. They functioned as the glue that kept our families together and on track. These players' wives deserve special recognition as a vital part of the success of the NFL. Their famous football-playing husbands often overshadowed their roles, and I want to shine a spotlight on their importance as spouses, mothers, and support systems.

Back row: Mary Breunig, Biddie Jordan, Diana Gaechter
Middle Row: Margaret Norman, Jan McIlhenny, Annette Liscio, Marianne Staubach
Front row: [guest], Nancy Howley, Betty Green, Betty Manders

My late wife Margaret sat on the sidelines in the '60s and '70s with her fellow wives, cheering us on. She had plenty of practice from her high school days as a cheerleader at West Charlotte and used these skills in the stadium stands. She'd shout, "Go, Pettis! All right, Pettis! Get 'em, Pettis!"

Her friendships with her fellow Dallas Cowboys wives were important, for the wives developed a special bond in a storm of uncertainty. They never really knew if their husbands would make it from one season to the next. There was always a chance that they'd have to pack up children, pets, and furniture and move to a new city. Thus, the wives stayed emotionally connected and supported each other — those who were new to Dallas and others like Margaret, who had been there for years.

The early Cowboys wives did not have flashy cars, big homes, and loads of money like the significant others today. They were ordinary people, working extra jobs and raising families while in an industry with flashy lights and cameras. They united over many special causes that included fundraisers, fashion shows, cookbooks, and charities. Margaret was very active in these causes and enjoyed the special camaraderie she had with player wives.

One very special friend was Cornell Green's wife, Betty. We were neighbors, and they leaned on each other in many ways, not just as football wives but as best friends. They shopped, cooked, and celebrated special occasions together and were inseparable friends. Even our children grew up together, became friends, and are still connected today. We lost Betty in 2019, a huge loss to me and my family, and all Dallas Cowboys wives.

Most wives could not travel with us, and some joined together to watch the televised out-of-town games. If our wives decided to travel to a game, the airline tickets and hotel were at our own expense, not easy considering our salaries in the '60s. Back then, the players flew on a private plane via American Airlines, used only by the Cowboys at Dallas Love Field. Another bit of interesting trivia — the wives could not visit their husbands at our hotels during home or away games; we had to stay focused. So, it was easier for Margaret to stay home when I traveled out of town, especially because we had young daughters.

While Margaret considered many of the "players' wives" good friends, she was also very close to Beverly Pugh McKiver, Jethro's wife. Jethro and I were great friends too; we both came from North Carolina and quickly bonded when he joined the Cowboys. Our wives were members of the Dallas Cowboys Wives Club who met monthly at different homes.

Beverly recalls, "Several wives, including Margaret, carpooled to these meetings. It was a wonderful way to network and bond with players' wives. Before heading home, Altamese Hayes (Bob), Pat Renfro (Mel), Betty Green (Cornell), and Andria Wright (Rayfield) stopped at a restaurant or the Hilton Hotel and extended our fellowship – we had a great time."

Beverly remembers Margaret as a "Proverbs 31 woman," saying, "She was a Christian who was a loyal wife, excellent mother, and great cook with a very sweet spirit, but also a loyal fan who would get hyped up when cheering for Pettis and the Cowboys."

It just so happened that Annette's husband, Tony Liscio, and I were traded to the San Diego Chargers at the same time. Margaret and Annette, along with our children, flew to San Diego together. Margaret adored Annette and thought it was nice traveling to a new city with familiar friends. Annette states, "Margaret became a good friend and was a fine individual."

I was happy that we could "start over" in California with the Liscios, but fate intervened. Just before the new season started, Tony was traded to Miami. Now Annette faced yet another move, this time to Florida! Tony decided to retire instead of uprooting his family once again.

Calvin Hill and I became great friends both on and off the field. He has always been there for me, and his wife Janet established a nice friendship with Margaret too. Interestingly, Janet's college roommate from Wellesley College was Hillary Clinton, with whom she remained friends over the years. In 1969, Janet and Calvin became engaged. They would become the proud parents of Grant Hill, former NBA player, sports broadcaster, and co-owner of the Atlanta Hawks. Janet has enjoyed an illustrious career and remembers Margaret as being such a nice person. "Margaret attended every home game and always had her very young girls with her. She was a great cook, and I remember the parties we enjoyed, especially after the players returned from an away game. We will always remember Margaret."

In 1970, Marianne Staubach became the president of the Dallas Cowboys Wives Club. All the members, including Margaret, continued to be involved with various charities. The club once hosted a famous casino party for a good cause; it was a very successful event. When I was traded in 1971, I remember the player's wives wished Margaret the best in San Diego. But it wasn't goodbye — the players and their wives tended to keep in touch.

Chronic Traumatic Encephalopathy (CTE)

I endearingly called Tony Liscio "Ton-I," and he called me "Pet-I." He remained a very, very good friend after football. Ivette and I connected on many occasions with the Liscio's, and always enjoyed their company.

Tony began to have unusual symptoms and was eventually diagnosed with amyotrophic lateral sclerosis (ALS), also known as Lou Gehrig's disease. It was heartbreaking when he succumbed to the disease just 14 days shy of his 77th birthday in 2017. With Annette's permission, I can share that the medical professionals attributed Tony's deteriorating condition to his football career. After he died, she donated his brain for testing both in Dallas and Boston. Results were concerning and showed that Tony had chronic traumatic encephalopathy, CTE, and it started in his forties. He was diagnosed with the onset of Alzheimer's 20 years later. This was a very difficult loss for Annette and her family and a significant loss to me too.

It gives me pause as I reflect on CTE and other illnesses that have taken many close friends and teammates over the years — Jethro Pugh, Dave Edwards, Bob Hayes, Mike Gaechter, Mike Clark, Frank Clark, and Willie Townes, just to name a few. While not all of my teammates died of brain concussion challenges or CTE, this condition is a real concern in the world of football today. It's a dangerous and debilitating disease brought on by damaging blows to the brain, resulting in dementia, mood disorder, memory loss, and other brain-related problems.

It was common to use smelling salts and finger counting to determine a player's neurological stamina during my era. If we bounced back with these tests, we were put back in the game. Concussions were not taken seriously back during the '60s, and as a result, many

NFL players today have personal neurological challenges in addition to the physical impact of football.

A 2017 study published in the Journal of American Medical Association found that 99% of deceased NFL players whose brains were examined (110 of 111) had CTE. While the NFL has struggled to deal with the tragic deaths and diminished lives of hundreds of its former players, the fact remains that no one really knows how many NFL players past or present have CTE because these conditions can only be confirmed through postmortem brain autopsies. The players or their families have to donate those brains. If we want to know the extent of CTE in the NFL, we'd have to test current players as well, but that's beyond our medical capabilities at this point.

Current NFL athletes are stronger, faster, and bigger than their counterparts of my era, and there are more regular-season games and playoff games than ever before. Therefore, some observers, like longtime NFL agent Leigh Steinberg, believe injuries to NFL athletes are more severe than ever before. In 2007, Steinberg called the NFL's injury situation a "ticking time bomb." If it's not adequately addressed, Steinberg said, the NFL might be relegating this generation of athletes to cognitive problems in their retirement years.

In 2013, the NFL reached a financial settlement with 4,500 of its former players or their estates if they were already deceased. These players were plaintiffs against the league for concussion-related injuries suffered during their professional careers. The lengthy list included Hall of Famers and All-Pro players.

A newer study published October 2019 in the Annals of Neurology takes a closer look at the relationship between duration of football played, CTE risk, and severity. The NFL decided in March 2020 to explore several options, such as increasing its regular-season schedule from 16 games to 17 in 2021 and further expanding the postseason by adding more teams. This means that players will continue to expose their brains and bodies to the risks of long-term damage.

Still, the rules have changed for the better. Players are protected and sidelined more quickly in the event of concussions. I hope the league can and will continue to improve the health of our NFL players today by implementing additional rules to minimize the impact of concussions.

So, the question you are probably asking is, "Would you play the game again?" My answer is, "Absolutely!" While it truly saddens me to have lost many teammates, I still love the game of football. While I have some aches and pain today, I thank God for blessing me with the opportunity to play 12 years of pro football.

Chapter Ten: God and Country

I served proudly while absorbing important lessons about discipline, duty, and the price of freedom.
~ Pettis Norman

I'll pause here and reflect on my family members who served in the military and my own military service as well — no, not the Air Force as originally planned, but in the Texas Army National Guard. People have asked why I signed up for the National Guard while playing professional football. The answer is simple — the Declaration of Independence inspired me:

We hold these truths to be self-evident, that all men are created equal, that they are endowed by their Creator with certain unalienable Rights, that among these are Life, Liberty and the pursuit of Happiness.

~ The Declaration of Independence, July 4, 1776

The concept is noble, but the equality of "all men" wasn't applied justly in 1776 or in 1865 at the end of the Civil War, or later in the Deep South. Equality became something we strove for in the 1960s — not just minorities, but women as well. Some people reached for this goal through protest and some through military service, and some (like me) through both.

I loved my country fiercely and still do, as a land of opportunity. The potential was there for free people to reap the blessings of free trade and free markets without the stain of discrimination. I enrolled as a private in the 49th Armored Division in November of 1962 and advanced to Sergeant First Class in short order. Once again, my father's lessons about "doing things the right way" helped me succeed in the Army just as I succeeded in the NFL.

I held that rank until May of 1968, when I was honorably discharged after earning the qualification of marksman and the Texas Faithful Service Medal for honorable service in the Texas Military Forces. If you are able to serve full-time or in the National Guard, I encourage you to do so. It was a great experience that further molded and shaped me into a disciplined, highly responsive person and an even better team player. The experience paid dividends in the corporate world, as well.

There was an interesting backdrop to that time in history. The year before I enlisted, the 49th Armored Division, part of the United States Army National Guard, was activated to federal service due to the 1961 Berlin Crisis. It reverted to state control in August 1962 as the Texas Army National Guard. In the year I was honorably discharged in 1968, the 49th Armored Division deactivated and became three separate brigades and was then reactivated

Getting vaccinated in the Texas Army National Guard. Photo courtesy of the U.S. Army

Talking about football with fellow National Guardsmen. Photo courtesy of the U.S. Army

My big brother, Bish

and headquartered at Camp Mabry in Austin, Texas, in 1973 where it remains today. I contacted Camp Mabry to gain permission to use the Army-issued photo in this book.

Military buffs might also be interested to know that *Stars and Stripes*, an American military newspaper, featured several Dallas Cowboys games and followed the exploits of other athletes enlisted in the Armed Forces as well. Some of the stories appeared in overseas editions so that military members in Europe, the Pacific, the Mediterranean, and North Africa could enjoy the sports coverage.

A Brother Who Served

My brother Fessor Lee, or "Bish," registered for the draft at the age of 18. I feel compelled to honor his service, for he certainly exemplified the "Greatest Generation" by living through the Great Depression and fighting in World War II. Bish enlisted in the Army at Fort Benning, Georgia as a single man with no dependents at the tail end of the war, serving as a truck driver and technical sergeant from April 11, 1944, to April 16, 1946. I recently noticed a coincidence — he enlisted on April 11 and died exactly 68 years later on April 11, 2012.

His service meant the world to him, and his tombstone commemorates the following:

FESSOR L. NORMAN
TEC 5
US ARMY
WORLD WAR II
AUG 9 1925
APRIL 11 2012
LOVING FATHER AND FRIEND

Many WWII veterans didn't speak much about their war involvement, and this was true of Bish. Young farm boys left their mules behind and thought they'd see the world but experienced trauma and bloodshed that weighed heavily on their hearts and minds. Bish was stoic about these experiences and only once mentioned a near miss when he had to jump behind a tank. We will never know the full details of that story, for he didn't expand on the harrowing nature of the battlefield.

These veterans went through a lot and were fortunate to arrive home safely. Thankfully, Bish did return and started a family of his own, as well as a business. Norman Woodworking continues today through his sons Chauncey, Kent, and Eugene. Notably, Bish was the first African American to finance a business through Mechanics and Farmers Bank in Charlotte. He became a sought-after master craftsman in the cabinetry-making industry, worked on high-end projects, and helped design the "disappearing stairs" that led to the attics in many homes.

Bish credited his woodworking skills to our grandfather Jesse and father Fessor. Many of the Norman males, including my brother Tony, worked as carpenters and woodworkers all the way back to our forefather Isaac. Another thing I admire about Bish was his role as a father and grandfather. His door was always open, and his home overflowed with loved ones. He didn't just tolerate the comings and goings of his children and grandchildren; he welcomed it. There was always room under his roof, not to mention his hugs and encouragement as a father figure to me after we lost Dad. I believe these were Bish's greatest legacies — a patriarch and renowned craftsman who served his country well.

By the way, Bish received a letter from President Harry S. Truman thanking him for his service to his country. Perhaps it's a coincidence, or maybe it's fate, but President Truman is tied to my family in more ways than one. Below is an interesting story about the President and my late father-in-law.

The USS Missouri Buttermilk Pie

Many stories have circulated about my father-in-law Harry Hightower and President Harry Truman. The lore centers on the "USS Missouri Buttermilk Pie" recipe, also known as the "USS Missouri Pecan Buttermilk Pie."

President Truman once sailed aboard the USS Missouri from September 7-20, 1947, known as the Rio-Washington cruise. This occurred as the President was returning from the Rio Conference — the Inter-American Conference for the Maintenance of Continental Peace and Security — held near Rio de Janeiro.

My father-in-law, Harry Hightower, happened to be Chief Steward at the time and had the honor of creating and baking an original pie according to President Truman's preferences. He had a beloved family recipe memorized but had to alter the ingredients somewhat due to the resources available on the ship. This made-from-scratch buttermilk pie delighted the President so much that he asked for the recipe. My father-in-law politely declined (it was a guarded and treasured family recipe), which I believe took some nerve. After all, who says "no" to a sitting president?

Obviously, my father-in-law enjoyed telling this story very much. The "two Harrys" had a stalemate; my father-in-law held onto his recipe, and Harry Truman settled for a second slice of pie. It wasn't until my father-in-law transferred to civil service that he gifted the recipe to the Navy. At that time, it received its official name — the "USS Missouri Buttermilk Pie."

Just browse the Internet for stories about the famous pie recipe, and you'll find Harry's role in this "slice" of naval history. In fact, check out the Harry S. Truman National History Facebook page for posts of the story and a photo of the President with the crew. The Missouri State Museum's Facebook page also posted the story with a different image of the President and crew enjoying the pie!

In preparation for writing this section of the book, my wife Ivette reached out to the Harry S. Truman Library in Independence, Missouri. Randy Sowell, Archivist, was a helpful resource as we sought to fact-check my father-in-law's "confectionary" role in U.S. Naval history. He offered to put a copy of my autobiography on the library shelf and remembered some of the games I played with the Dallas Cowboys. It was a great walk down memory lane.

Ivette also reached out to the Truman Library Institute in Kansas City, Missouri, for details about the buttermilk pie backstory and shared the great honor her father felt while serving President Truman. Alex Burden, Executive Director, and Lisa A. Sullivan, CFO/CAO, of the

Truman Library Institute, graciously invited us to the reopening of the Harry S. Truman Library and Museum in the fall of 2020 after undergoing a $30 million massive renovation project in preparation for the 75th anniversary of Truman's presidency. Unfortunately, Covid 19 delayed the opening of the museum.

On display are the many conflicts President Truman faced and the decisions he made — ending the war in Japan, the Marshall Plan, United Nations, NATO, the recognition of Israel, desegregating the military, and the Korean War. I am certain the reopening of this fantastic museum will increase visitation and tourism. The new exhibitions of our 33rd President of the United States present an opportunity for younger generations to walk in the footsteps of a great leader.

Throughout this wonderful chain of events, Lisa A. Sullivan of the Truman Library Institute put us in touch with Clifton Truman Daniel, grandson of President Harry S. Truman. Clifton is a wonderful person — former Director of Public Relations for Truman College in Chicago, former feature writer and editor for the Morning Star and Sunday Star-News, honorary chairman of the board of trustees of the Harry S. Truman Library Institute, and a sought-after lecturer on various aspects of the Truman presidency, as well as U.S. and White House history. We were thrilled when he called us, for up to that point, he had been unaware of the USS Missouri Buttermilk Pie story and enjoyed hearing about it.

During our phone conversation, we learned a lot about Clifton's background. As an actor, he portrays his famous grandfather on stage around the country and has appeared in more than a dozen theatre productions and television roles. Also, he was cast to play the role of President Harry S. Truman in the independent film *Second Samuel*.

Ivette and I were honored to receive the lovely note below from Clifton:

> *On the surface, what you have here is a nice story about a president who loved a pie and wanted the recipe, and the chief master steward who wasn't quite ready to give it up, even to his commander-in-chief. But if you look a little deeper, what you see is two men, both named Harry, who served their country ably and honorably and, when they met, treated each other with respect and good humor. If that isn't an example for the rest of us, I don't know what would be.*

A Personal Salute to Harry

Who would have ever thought that by marrying Ivette, I would gain such a great father-in-law? I'm very proud of Master Chief Harry Hightower (God rest his soul). He was a proud naval officer, and what an incredible military career he had. His combined active duty and civil service period total more than 50 years, and his name is legendary in the Bachelor Officer's Quarters of the Navy.

Hightower Hall at the Naval Station Norfolk is named in Harry's honor. A bronze sign at Hightower Hall vividly describes why he earned this honor.

Mr. Harry T. Hightower
U.S. Navy Retired

My distinguished father-in-law, Harry T. Hightower. Photo credit: Sears Photography Studio

Throughout the period July 1941 to August 1992, Harry T. Hightower served the U.S. Navy faithfully and with distinction. During his 30-year active-duty career he achieved every pay grade in the steward rating including Master Chief Petty Officer and earned nine continuous good conduct medals following his transfer to the fleet reserve in 1971. He assumed the duties of Bachelor Officer Quarters Manager at Naval Station Norfolk and served in that role superbly. For more than 20 years his superlative achievements and far-reaching impact to all who resided in Navy Bachelor Housing set a benchmark of excellence for all who succeeded him.

On December 18, 2011, we visited Hightower Hall, named in my father-in-law's honor, on what would be his final visit. He had cancer and would die the following month. It's a poignant memory that we'll cherish forever. Command Master Chief David Carter, 3rd in command at the naval station, personally met the family and arranged for a naval photographer to be on hand and capture this special family gathering. We still smile at the images of Harry standing upright and proud beneath the Hightower Hall placard and the bronze sign — he was such a dedicated Navy man.

Command Master Chief David Carter has become a family friend. We are indebted to his kindness, from the tour of Hightower Hall to the 21-gun salute he arranged at my father-in-law's funeral. We recently caught up with him and asked him to weigh in on his military service and his memories of Harry Hightower. He shares his insights below:

It was an extreme honor to get to know Harry Hightower, who also experienced many promotions and monumental responsibilities in the Navy. He was a humble servant-leader and lived his life with a high level of character and ethical values that people of all stripes should strive for. For Harry to earn the prestigious Zumwalt Award as many times as he did says something about the man and his abilities.

I am so glad I could spend time with Harry before his passing and talk about his achievements. As the Command Master Chief for Naval Station Norfolk, I met his family when they flew to Norfolk, Virginia, for a tour of Hightower Hall, and I was immediately impressed with their graciousness and pride in their father's legacy. I immensely enjoyed meeting and getting to know Harry and his family. Harry even brought me two of his famous buttermilk pies, a special treat which I shared with the staff at my office. It is truly my honor and pleasure to help celebrate Harry Hightower's life and legacy.

Chapter Eleven: Civil Rights

Has racism been eradicated? If the answer isn't an immediate yes, then the struggle continues.
~ Pettis Norman

The theme song "We Shall Overcome" quickly became a trademark song for the Civil Rights Movement in the '60s. From the pulpit of the Washington National Cathedral in Washington, D.C. on March 31, 1968, Dr. Martin Luther King Jr. delivered the following words:

We're going to win our freedom because both the sacred heritage of our nation and the eternal will of the almighty God are embodied in our echoing demands. And so, however dark it is, however deep the angry feelings are, and however violent explosions are, I can still sing 'We Shall Overcome.'

The cause was so crucial, the situation so dire, that I thank God for Dr. Martin Luther King Jr. He became an emblem for millions of Blacks and many young people, including Whites who felt strongly about the Civil Rights Movement. You will soon read firsthand accounts from those who lived through the Civil Rights Movement. Below is a portal into the dark days of oppression and our response, which lit up the world.

I think it's appropriate to begin with the school desegregation struggle of the 1950s and 1960s. One of the most important issues to me is education, which has been intertwined with civil rights, race relations, and politics for more than half a century in Dallas and the nation as well.

In those days, discrimination was entrenched in society; White children knew nothing else. They were innocent sponges who absorbed a strong societal message: White people thought they were superior and believed the races must be kept separated in schools, restaurants, churches, buses — you name it. Even separate drinking fountains were set up for "Colored" and "White."

This racist indoctrination was nothing more than spoon-fed poison inflicted on one generation after another. It affected the educational opportunities of Black children who were taught with second-hand textbooks in dilapidated buildings by underpaid teachers. The lack of integrated schooling and other obstacles did not prevent Black children from learning, however. They learned because this was all they had ever known and they adapted to the surroundings given them.

The ability of Black children to learn in an inferior environment had parents wondering what they would do in a better environment. Shouldn't Black children be entitled to equal education and equal learning conditions?

The Start of It All

Perhaps some readers are only vaguely familiar with the desegregation battle in America, while others remember it like yesterday. I believe history and context are important, so I reflect on the early attempts at integration. We can never forget the price paid by the children who changed the course of our educational institutions.

In 1951, nine-year-old Linda Brown of Topeka, Kansas, was refused admittance to Sumner School on racial grounds. It sparked the *Brown v. Board of Education of Topeka* case and resulted in the U.S. Supreme Court's ultimate overruling of the "separate but equal" doctrine. It should be noted that Supreme Court Justice Thurgood Marshall was the NAACP lawyer at the time who argued the case before the Supreme Court, resulting in the landmark decision.

The Supreme Court required that schools throughout the United States desegregate in two decisions in 1954 and 1955. Members of the Black community in Dallas sued to be able to enroll their children in White schools in 1955; United States District Court Judge William H. Atwell ruled against one of these plaintiffs, holding that the United States Supreme Court had overstepped its authority in *Brown v. Board of Education*. He ruled the same in 1957 against a case brought by the NAACP on behalf of two Black children who wanted to attend a White school closer to their home.

Judge Atwell was overruled by the Fifth Circuit Court of Appeals both times and was ordered to integrate Dallas public schools immediately. Two months later, DISD was in front of the Court of Appeals once again, claiming it would lose accreditation and State Education Foundation funding if it integrated.

On September 17, 1960, Superintendent W.T. White announced that he anticipated some form of school integration in 1961 — a "salt and pepper'" plan also described as a "stair-step" plan in which a slow integration would occur, testing the waters, so to speak. Dallas attorneys W.J. Durham, C.B. Bunkley, and Thurgood Marshall challenged the "salt and pepper" plan in court, claiming it was unfair to Black children. In 1961, Judge Atwell passed away; the Federal court ordered DISD to desegregate fully.

A photo of little Willie Pratt and his mother still tugs at my heart, taken at Roger Q. Mills Elementary after the first day of Dallas school integration on December 6, 1961. He was the only Black student. The year before, Ruby Bridges attended her first day of first grade, also as the only Black student at William Frantz Elementary School in New Orleans. These little ones were the first pioneers of integration.

The Little Rock Nine

I recall nine teenagers — six females and three males — who enrolled at Central High School in Little Rock, Arkansas, in 1957. I was a junior in high school, and my eyes were glued to the television screen as the "Little Rock Nine" stepped toward their high school entrance.

I remember reflecting on my school in Charlotte, North Carolina — all African American — and the level of comfort and protection I was blessed with during that same period. I also had a flashback to Lincolnton, Georgia, when White students hung out the windows of a bus and spit upon my schoolmates and me as we walked to school. My heart pounded as I watched the Little Rock Nine scenario unfold, and I empathized with the emotions those students must have felt as they embarked on this treacherous journey.

I was disheartened when I heard that Governor Orval Faubus called in the Arkansas National Guard to block the Black students' entry into the high school. These Black students were exposed to hostility, screams, and frightening intimidation. While the police and military presence prevented bodily harm, they incited the crowd of White students when they were denied entry to the school. This empowered the White students to hurl hate and disrespect at the Little Rock Nine.

I continued to stay connected to this story and watched President Dwight D. Eisenhower weeks later send in federal troops to escort the Little Rock Nine into the school amidst an angry White mob. They were protected as they walked up the school steps and were escorted to class by U.S. Army troops — nine in a sea of 1,900 White students.

Later that morning, the nine Black students were removed from the school because their safety was at risk, and none too soon — a riot had erupted outside. The students went to the basement and were driven away by the police. Later, television coverage showed the mob going inside the school; newspapers reported it around the world.

This shameful display prompted President Eisenhower to send in 1,200 paratroopers from the 101st airborne division. The students were brave enough to go back again and were escorted in single file up the steps and through the doors. The soldiers dispersed the protesters, and the nine survived a full day on campus.

As you can imagine, their high school years were tremendously difficult. They continued to endure ridicule and bullying, which profoundly affected me as a junior in high school across the country in North Carolina. While my activism did not begin until I reached college, this incident unearthed deep anger within me and planted the seed for my future exploits in activism and support of just causes in sports, business, and life.

We owe these students tremendous thanks for enduring this abuse and achieving a breakthrough that became a turning point in public education. They and other brave students made a huge difference in people's lives, especially children who would continue the integration effort. In some cases, it required lawsuits and court battles that lasted for decades — Dallas is an example.

Bill Clinton later awarded these students the Congressional Gold Medal in 1999, well deserved.

Walter Cronkite's Video

Desegregation was a powder keg throughout the nation. The news media covered the outraged White citizens who stood outside schools in Louisiana, Arkansas, and elsewhere. White parents screamed loudly and vehemently against integration, some holding babies in their arms. It was appalling — we watched as hate was planted in the hearts of innocent children who were at the mercy of their crazed mothers and fathers.

The Dallas White Citizens Council, to their credit, produced a film in 1961 narrated by Walter Cronkite titled "Dallas at the Crossroads" that included interviews with prominent

Dallas citizens. It emphasized the rule of law and the importance of White adults setting examples for their children — an attempt to desegregate peacefully by exposing the terrible behavior of parents in other states and the impact their violence and hatred had on their kids. The film was aimed at the better judgment of Dallas citizens, specifically, parents who would set the tone for their offspring.

One segment featured Dr. P. E. Luecke of the Dallas County Medical Society, who stated, "We wouldn't knowingly hurt or frighten a child. And yet, as we have seen, violence does frighten children. They become uncertain and insecure. When children are frightened and insecure, they look to their parents or those they respect for reassurance and guidance."

The legal validity of the Supreme Court Decision was emphasized by J. W. Ream of the Southern Methodist University Law School: "The law is a system where the unfortunate stand as peer and equal with the most privileged."

Judge Julian Hyre stated: "Once a decision has been made, it is the law. On April 6 of this year [1961], the federal court decision became final that some degree of desegregation must, by law, begin in Dallas, in the schools, this fall. In spite of arguments, in spite of criticisms, in spite of personalities, the law is the law. Disagreement or dissatisfaction with the law should not, and must not be expressed by citizens with violence. In a democracy, there are always legal channels open to those who would be preferred to change the law. These are the methods that a good citizen uses, not with bats, and stones."

That year, eight Dallas public schools integrated peacefully with 18 Black children enrolled in all-White schools. The City of Dallas remained under court orders to continue desegregation.

Judge William Wayne Justice

I recently came across a cherished autographed copy of the January 20, 1978 issue of the Texas Observer, sent to me by a wonderful judge. He signed it: "To my friend Pettis Norman, with kindest regards. — Wm. Wayne Justice."

This involves quite a backstory. Judge William Wayne Justice sat on the U.S. Court for the Eastern District of Texas. In 1970, he ordered the Texas Education Agency (TEA) to desegregate its schools in United States v. Texas. This extraordinary case covered more than a thousand school districts, and the quality of education for two million students was at stake. Judge Justice and I became acquainted due to my interest in the Dallas Independent School District (DISD) and struck up a friendship.

Perhaps the most notorious landmark case in Dallas' desegregation was Tasby v. Estes, filed in 1970 in federal court 15 years after the Supreme Court ruling. It involved a complex series of injunctions, court orders, and appeals and was finally assigned to United States District Court Judge Barefoot Sanders in the Northern District of Texas in 1981. He oversaw the Tasby litigation for the next 22 years until he declared that DISD was a unitary district.

You read that right — 22 years.

This meant that it took nearly half a century after *Brown v. Board of Education* for my beloved City of Dallas to fully commit to desegregation. The long road was frustrating, but I must say that many of us were activists and railed against this ridiculous and unnecessary turmoil. We pushed for minority representation on the school board and in the classrooms. We worked on behalf of the kids, the teachers, the bus drivers, and the administration, often arm-in-arm with parents.

Students of Change

Historically Black Colleges and Universities (HBCUs) played a pivotal role socially, academically, and athletically. Many of our country's most gifted young men and women chose to attend HBCUs, largely because these colleges were sensitive to the plight of African Americans and mandated a standard of excellence.

The professors had degrees from many of the nation's most prestigious northern schools — Harvard, Yale, Columbia University, New York University, Boston University, and the University of Chicago. Their job was to polish students into astute and capable citizens who could compete in a world of White privilege.

The topic of civil rights circles back to Johnson C. Smith University for this very reason. The professors taught us that everyone, regardless of ethnicity, was due equal privilege. When I reflect on my time as a student and athlete at JCSU, they truly were golden years. I took important steps to become who I am and change our world for the better, where and when I had the opportunity.

Just a stone's throw from my beloved mother's apartment, the university enabled me to grow academically, athletically, and in activism. The Civil Rights Movement touched me deeply and personally. I was raised to be nice to people, work hard and give more than expected to people regardless of skin color. I did the same in my new college environment. Unfortunately, Charlotte and the nation as a whole didn't always reflect these values.

I happened to be in the right place at the right time to do something about it. I was fortunate to be influenced by Smith's exemplary leaders, Coach McGirt, Dr. Jack Brayboy, and civil rights icon Dr. Reginald Hawkins. Almost from the time I first registered in Biddle Hall (named for the original name of the school – Biddle College), they saw in me a sense of promise; my goal was to live up to it.

Thousands of brave students tackled racism and discrimination in their communities. My earliest hands-on involvement in civil rights occurred on February 1, 1960, with my fellow Johnson C. Smith University students. We followed the news out of Greensboro that four Black male students at North Carolina A&T State University were conducting the state's first sit-in. They sat in at a Woolworth's lunch counter, defying the "Whites only" food service policy. Ezell Blair Jr., David Richmond, Franklin McCain, and Joseph McNeil were denied service but refused to move from their seats.

The police arrived but did not take action. The media was called and televised the event. The four young men stayed seated until the store closed, and then came back the next day with more students. Their audacity and bravery caused quite an uproar and inspired me to travel to Greensboro and join the cause.

Dr. Dorothy Yancy was a dear classmate and friend who would become the President of

Johnson C. Smith University from 1994–2008 and was among many who participated in the protests. As she notes today, there was a protocol to protesting that included not physically fighting back against those who opposed us. We acted as a team, all non-violent foot soldiers at the crossroads in history, and certainly stuck together.

My commitment to social justice deepened at Smith and later led me to help change the Cowboys' policy of assigning roommates according to race. This is why the Johnson C. Smith University's motto — "Become yourself. Change our world" — has always been more than mere words to me. It has been my way of life.

Change, Indeed

It just so happened that young Jesse Jackson, a freshman at North Carolina A&T at Greensboro, had also joined the demonstrations. Over the course of our lives, we developed a solid friendship, continued the fight for equality, and noted that the foundation of it all was built on student activism. He became an integral part of my life story, which I detail throughout this book.

Our cause was just. Throughout the month of February, we were joined by hundreds of Black students across North Carolina who sat-in at lunch counters. By March, the protests expanded into Nashville, Baltimore, Houston, and New Orleans.

Today, people ask if I was worried about losing my football scholarship or ruining my chances to play in a professional league based on my participation in student protests. I tell them I didn't let those thoughts bother me (not then or later in the NFL), even with a football scholarship riding in the balance. We were encouraged, not discouraged, to protest by our university administrators.

I had spent my life doing the right thing. Standing up for civil rights — or in this case, sitting down for civil rights — definitely was the right thing to do. Why shouldn't my mother, sisters, brothers, or future wife Margaret be able to sit at a counter and enjoy lunch? Our money was the same green as anyone else's. Our hearts pumped the same red blood. It was time our country embraced the notion that people are people, no matter their skin tone.

As thousands of students rallied against prejudice and bigotry, some paid a high price. We heard that arrests were made for whatever offenses the authorities could lodge, such as disorderly conduct, disturbing the peace, trespassing, and even vagrancy. The students' sacrifices weren't wasted, not by any means. By the end of the summer, Woolworth changed its policies and served four Black employees — Geneva Tisdale, Susie Morrison, Anetha Jones, and Charles Best — at the lunch counter. This was more than symbolic; it was a victory and ushered in, slowly but surely, equal treatment at restaurants nationwide.

Discrimination in the NFL

For me, football was never an end in itself. It was an opportunity to provide an example to others that we can all make a difference, regardless of the unrelenting problems in our path. Civil rights demonstrations, specifically the lunch counter sit-ins, taught me the impact of peaceful but powerful action.

I think it's important to stop here and memorialize the efforts made to eradicate discrimination in the NFL. In the '60s it was a common practice to separate players by race, and I addressed the issue of segregation, which percolated beneath the surface of the Dallas Cowboys franchise with both Coach Landry and Tex Schramm. First, I went to Tex to discuss it.

"It's really time we change it," I told him. "We are a team. We cannot separate by color. It sends the wrong message to us and the community."

"Thanks, that's a good idea," he said. "We'll address it."

Sure enough, a month or so later, just before the next training camp, Tex Schramm called me in and said, "I want to follow through on your idea. You and Dave Manders will room together, set the tempo, and we'll pair everybody up alphabetically at the end of training camp."

Fortunately, Dave Manders' name and mine fell in alphabetical order on the roster, so it was an easy transition when the players were informed of our new arrangements. I later talked with Coach Landry, and to his credit, he addressed the segregation as well. We were once in a southern city for an exhibition game. There was a policy that Blacks and Whites could not eat together, and Coach Landry simply said, "Well, we don't play where we can't eat and sleep together as a team." Suddenly, the arrangements were made, and we did play the game.

Bob Lilly remembers me as being pretty vocal when I needed to be. "You would say what was on your mind," he recalled during a recent conversation. "Pettis, you stood up for what you believed. Dallas was still segregated, and I don't think any of us liked it. You said, 'Let's get this changed.' And we did. That had a great deal to do with changing Dallas."

Legislation

I rejoiced in 1963 when Martin Luther King Jr. gave his "I Have a Dream" speech at the March on Washington. It primed me for a future as a minority business owner, humanitarian, and bridge-builder in race relations. The Civil Rights Act became law in 1964, two years after I signed with the Cowboys, and coincided with the birth of my first daughter, Sharneen. It ended segregation in public places and banned employment discrimination based on race, color, religion, sex or national origin. Martin Luther King Jr. said it was nothing less than a "second emancipation." As African Americans, we were joyous that this legislation was finally a reality. As a father, however, my underlying emotion was relief.

It was a comfort to know that Sharneen, and later my younger daughters Sedonna and Shandra, would grow up in a country where racial discrimination was no longer legal. The fact that it was illegal did not mean that racism would magically disappear, but at least the Black community had legal protection.

I focused on the concept of equal rights and inclusion in my community through open dialogue and joined causes off the field that I believed could address the anger and outrage that still simmered, sometimes boiling over. In the midst of this turmoil, Dick Nolan named me the "Fastest Tight End" in the league in 1964, but this did not affect my salary. I continued to work multiple off-season jobs, and in my case, the cause of civil rights became a "job" of its own.

The next year on August 6, 1965, President Lyndon B. Johnson signed the Voting Rights Act into law at a ceremony in the Capitol Rotunda. Live footage was captured of this event, which gave us hope. We watched the entirety of the President's speech, the signing of the act, and the President shaking hands and distributing pens to Reverend Martin Luther King, Jr. and Senator Robert F. Kennedy.

The 1965 legislation was a follow-up to the initial legislation that prohibited literacy tests and other discriminatory voting practices. It was painfully obvious that the new Civil Rights Law would take time to "sink in" to the nation's consciousness. Some segregationists vowed to oppose any positive advances in civil rights and continued to ignore the new laws.

NAACP Picket

There may be a general tendency to believe that only African Americans experienced discrimination and have ownership in the struggle. Still, the fact is that many Whites, Hispanics, Asians, and Native Americans linked arms with us. They put themselves in harm's way to fight prejudice. The Jesuits of Dallas were no exception.

During these difficult times, Dr. Martin Luther King Jr. called for clergy and religious leaders to join civil rights marches. Members of the Society of Jesus (the Jesuits) marched in their own towns, most notably in downtown Dallas in 1965, with about 100 Jesuit high school students. Marching in peaceful protest was a hallmark of those times. I participated in an NAACP picket that coincided with the Jesuit march and invited some Dallas Cowboys players — Jim Stiger, Tony Davis, Amos Marsh, Cornell Green, and Frank Clark. We followed behind the students, and Councilman George Allen marched with us as well.

I'll never forget Amos Marsh's speech at the plaza: "They tell us to wait a little longer. Can we wait another 300 years for our rights?"

The crowd shouted in response, "No! No!"

I remember a photo taken by famed African American photographer Marion Butts, who captured the event. Thankfully, I was able to trace it to the History & Archives Division of the Dallas Public Library. With the library's permission, I am sharing the historical image and remember it like it was yesterday.

A Promise Broken

I cannot tell you how many times I was urged to run for public office, but unlike Black leaders who stepped up to serve as elected officials, I led behind the scenes and supported candidates who cared about "the least of these." George Allen, a former member of the City Planning Commission and local Black businessman, was one such leader. In 1968, he exemplified the political progress made by Blacks when a citywide election ushered him onto the Dallas City Council.

I might add that White community support made this possible; George was well-liked by many. I was proud to call him a friend and lent him my full support, especially when he was later denied the position of Mayor Pro Tem. This pulled me from behind the scenes into an extremely public protest over a promise broken by the Citizens Charter Association in 1971, comprised of town leaders who controlled appointments to offices, particularly City Council.

Marching in the NAACP Picket, Dallas, Texas, 1965. Front row: (left to right) C. Jack Clark, Travis Clark, Roosevelt Johnson; Second row: C. B. Bunkley, unknown, George Allen; Third row: Tony Davis; Fourth row: (right) Pettis Norman; Fifth row: Frank Clark. Courtesy of the Dallas Library. Photo credit: Marion Butts

As background, the Citizens Charter Association had assured us that they would appoint George Allen as Mayor Pro Tem. I remember standing up and seconding his nomination. George was eminently qualified, and we were excited that an African American would serve in this prestigious position. But a White council member was chosen instead, to the dismay of many.

I knew this was racially motivated and stood up again, this time in outrage. I demanded that each councilman justify his vote. It was something we could not allow, not without making our voices heard. I called on the church community and the NAACP. We held a news conference to announce that we were going to organize a march.

On Mother's Day in 1971 — and in the middle of a tornado alert — the community supported George by marching through downtown Dallas, exercising our constitutional right and shining a big media spotlight on this betrayal. When I was asked what we hoped to accomplish by demonstrating, I said it was to dramatize the displeasure of Black people in Dallas. I stated that we were there because we had witnessed the previous Monday's arrest, death, and burial of justice and fair play.

I led more than 250 fellow citizens and civic leaders in this demonstration, holding an American flag. I think I was tapped to display the flag because I was an Army veteran and a passionate, vocal leader of the civil rights movement.

Marching with the flag, May 1971. Photo Courtesy of the G. William Jones Film and Video Co.

The controversial news coverage continued after the march. A reporter asked, "What do you think about being traded to Kansas City?" I knew he was implying that my social activism might have consequences.

"If that's what it takes to be a man, then Kansas City, here I come," was my answer.

I do not believe there has ever been a march like it in Dallas, before or since. As a footnote,

George did eventually serve as Mayor Pro Tem. It turned out that I was traded to the San Diego Chargers almost immediately. Some believe my activism prompted this decision, but I do not believe that is the case at all. I still believe in Coach Tom Landry, who assured me that he traded me reluctantly from a business perspective — a decision that included player dynamics within the NFL rather than politics.

The Dallas County Court building at 600 Commerce Street was posthumously renamed the George L. Allen Sr. Courts Building in his honor — 21 years after our historic march. This is just one of many anecdotes in the saga of Dallas politics.

Chapter Twelve: Voices of the Civil Rights Movement

We won the war for civil rights but are still negotiating a fair settlement half a century later.
~ Pettis Norman

We have been blessed in Dallas and throughout the nation because courageous men and women battled injustice. I am proud to call many of these civil rights icons my friends, and some are my best friends who have kindly weighed in on this sensitive and very necessary section of my book. I am delighted also to share my views on their importance in our struggle against bigotry and prejudice and their views on the Civil Rights Movement.

These servant leaders celebrate the accomplishments of others, give credit where credit is due, and applaud those who go out of their way to better humankind. Their insights are noted below.

Dorothy Counts-Scoggins

I would venture to say that all Black students in the 1950s faced racism and discrimination in the public school system. That did not stop Dorothy Counts, a lifelong friend. She is now known as Dorothy "Dot" Counts-Scoggins after becoming the face of civil rights in Charlotte, North Carolina, the nation, and the world. It was a very courageous path for a 15-year-old girl who stepped into an all-White high school and paid a price for us all.

Dorothy became the first African American student to enter Harry Harding High in the Mecklenburg County public school system. She was like a little sister to me and still is. I mentioned her and her brother, my good friend Wilson Counts, previously. Wilson was my football buddy and mentor and became a football star in high school and college; their father, Herman Counts, was my professor of religion at JCSU. Basically, the family took me under their wing when I was new to the area. This was my first exposure to a family of academics; I will never forget their kindness and the example they set.

Dorothy became known in her own right as a teenage civil rights pioneer for helping to integrate Harding High. She broke the color barrier at great personal cost and suffering. As context, the court order to integrate had been in place since 1954; the school district dragged its heels. In 1957, Dorothy's father applied for transfers for all three of his children, Dorothy, Wilson, and Howard, into White schools.

But only four students were allowed to transfer, Dorothy among them. Hers was the only application granted for Harding High. Thus, 1957 would become an unforgettable year — a year that set the world on a different course.

Kids are natural optimists, and Dorothy was no different. Sure, she anticipated a bumpy start but assumed everything would be fine once she settled into Harding. What hurts me, even to this day, are the many photos of her on her first day of school. They are difficult to behold. Charlotte Observer photographer Don Sturkey captured the shocking moments, and another image by photographer Douglas Martin won the 1957 World Press Photo of the Year. These photos documented the vast crowds mocking and abusing Dorothy as she walked toward the school with spit on her dress. Dorothy fell ill with a sore throat and fever the second day of school and could not attend — I personally believe it was due to the flying germs.

The images quickly made their way around the world. Dorothy's ordeal was documented with brutal honesty and showed everyone what the integration battle was like in the Deep South. It did not speak well of Charlotte's school system or the parents who egged the students on, or the students themselves.

Worse, no teacher, administrator, or police officer attempted to keep Dorothy safe as she walked toward the school entrance. She was pelted with trash, sticks, and rocks. If you browse images of Dorothy Counts online, you will see a tall, slender, lovely, demure, and harmless-looking teenager followed by a hoard of maniacal students and adults. Considering the look on their faces, I'm still struck by Dorothy's composure and dignity. She held her head high.

In 2010, Harding High School renamed its library in honor of Dorothy, an honor rarely bestowed upon living persons. In addition, May 31, 2019, was proclaimed as Dorothy Counts-Scoggins Day, so very well deserved. Below she shares the experience of being the first Black female student at Harding High. What a story of bravery. I feel privileged to be able to share it and am so very proud of Dorothy.

Contributed by Dorothy Counts-Scoggins

The night before I went to Harding High School, my father, Herman Counts, told me, 'Remember who you are. Remember that you're inferior to no one. Remember that you can be anything you want to be, and don't hold your head low for anybody.'

Before I left for school that morning, I prayed. Then I put on a dress my Grandmother Emily had made for my first day at Harding High, within walking distance of our home. My father wanted to drive me to school that first day and our family friend, Dr. Edwin Thompkins, rode with us. They had to drop me off two blocks from the school because the entrance was blocked. There was a large crowd in front of the school. I wanted to walk to the entrance alone, but Edwin escorted me. Dad said, "Hold your head high," as I left the car, and I did.

The crowd was huge and full of students, but there were adults too — the police, parents, teachers, and administrators. I followed the sidewalk as the crowd moved in closer. The jeering started, and they began spitting on me from behind. Spit dripped from my special dress.

Most of the abuse occurred behind my back, not to my face, and I think that spoke volumes. They threw sticks and small rocks and trash. I anticipated some protesters because we lived in a traditional neighborhood; White people were taught that they were superior. But I was shocked at the level of vitriol and hatred.

I was raised in a family of educators and had a high regard for teachers. I was taught to be kind and respectful. While walking to the school entrance, I was never afraid a serious injury would happen to me, even with the pushing, shoving, and name-calling. What really hurt wasn't the physical abuse, but that no adults helped me. It bothered me that no teachers stepped in on my behalf.

I came down with a sore throat and fever the next morning and missed one day of classes. My father picked up my homework; apparently, people believed I was not coming back, so there were no crowds when I returned. I received even worse treatment in the hallways, the lunchroom, and my locker — slurs and pushing and things thrown at me. A sharp object pelted me in the back of my head, and an eraser hit me in my back. The teachers ignored me when I raised my hand to answer questions.

I had asked my parents to pick me up for lunch after having students spit in my food the day before. Back then, we could go home for lunch and return to the campus. "Someone will pick you up," they said. That someone was my brother Howard — a surprise because he was working in New York. He picked up the newspaper and saw his sister on the front page of the New York Times and took the train home. He was worried about me.

As I left the school, I noticed that the window of my father's car was smashed into a million pieces; this was the first time I was afraid. Now, they were targeting my family. My father spoke with the police chief and superintendent of Charlotte-Mecklenburg Schools, and they shared that they could not guarantee my safety.

Grownups allowed this to happen to me, a young girl, and that's when my father decided to withdraw me from school. He first met with several friends, our pastor, and Black civic leaders, before making the decision. He then made a statement to the media:

> It is with compassion for our native land and love for our daughter Dorothy that we withdraw her as a student at Harding High School. As long as we felt she could be protected from bodily injury and insults within the school's walls and upon the school premises, we were willing to grant her desire to study at Harding… Contrary to this optimistic view, her experiences at school on Wednesday disillusioned our faith and left us no alternative.
>
> In enrolling Dorothy in Harding High School, we sought for her the highest in educational experience that this tax supported school had to offer a young American. Yet, when a continuous stream of abuses undermines this objective our purposes are nullified and the effects are damaging to ethical and religious training.

Needless to say we regret the necessity which makes the withdrawal expedient. This step, taken for security and happiness, records in our history a page, which no true American, can read with pride.

Dorothy has received communications from hundreds of Americans and from at least a dozen foreign countries since her first day at Harding High School. This indicates that this historic event will be read simultaneously in England, Holland, Korea, and Charlotte — reflecting credit or discredit according to the individual's understanding of and attitude toward American democracy.

In view of this fact, we wish to express our most sincere gratitude to the many friends of democracy and Christianity in America and abroad, for their understanding and appreciation of our daughter's modest efforts to enjoy full citizenship in the country which we all love.

The true part of America and the faith in human rights expressed by telegrams, telephone calls, local police power, and letters from friends in American and foreign countries comfort us and strengthen our belief that our cause is just and ultimately must win.

I wanted to stick it out; leaving Harding High after just four days felt like a failure. However, my parents were not getting support from the school administration or the police and were concerned about safety — my family's and my own. Considering the danger, I reluctantly agreed with my father that enough was enough. My parents sent me to Pennsylvania to live with relatives for the remainder of that school year and then to a private boarding school in Asheville, North Carolina to finish high school. Then I returned to Charlotte to enroll at Johnson C. Smith University.

A former Harding High student contacted me after the 50-year celebration of the integration by the name of Woody Cooper. His father was on the police force that first morning and told him, 'Don't you get involved,' and he didn't. But Woody felt guilty for being in the crowd of students. 'I didn't cause you harm,' he said, 'but I should have stepped forward.'

I didn't respond to his email right away; I had to process his apology. It was heartfelt, and Woody and I became friends. Our families became friends. Once in his Sunday school class, Woody's teacher asked, 'Is there anyone you would like to ask forgiveness from?' and he thought of me. We talked about the importance of forgiveness and that we'd grown up in a different day and time. I mentioned that we had different childhoods and upbringings; I had been taught forgiveness and love while he had been taught hatred. He agreed.

In 2010, a Garden of Forgiveness dedication was held at Freedom Park in Charlotte. A forgiving bench was dedicated; Woody could not attend due to illness, but his family was there to represent him. Woody and I for years spoke of that day, and we traveled throughout the CMS System speaking to students about the importance of forgiveness. We gathered on many occasions to share meals together.

Woody had been diagnosed with cancer and was not well. He went into hospice. I visited with him; the nurse said he could hear me but would probably not respond. I spent two hours with him, and he died two hours after I left. The next day his wife called and said, 'He was waiting for you.' Our friendship was so very special.

I live within walking distance of the school today. I hold onto the memories of Harding High and the racial divide of the Southeast, but not the bitterness. I have a forgiving spirit and hope my journey has improved the lives of others.

Pettis was a friend throughout it all. When he first moved to Charlotte with his mother, my brother Wilson befriended him and helped him fit in. Pettis was in and out of our house, and we all became very close. He was such a protector at JCSU and kept an eye out for me. I still call him "big brother."

Reverend Zan Holmes

My close friend, Reverend Zan Holmes, is a walking example of the civil rights struggle. More properly known as The Reverend Dr. Zan Wesley Holmes, Jr., he is a great leader and is famous for building bridges instead of walls. I mentioned him in Chapter One — he is at the top of the list as someone who marched, preached, served in the Texas House of Representatives, and became a brilliant author as well.

In my opinion, that old saying, "Never discuss politics or religion in polite company," just doesn't apply when it comes to his approach to service. He doesn't separate religion and politics — he merges them under an umbrella of servant leadership.

Together, we have tackled some of the toughest issues in our society: discrimination, education reform, diversity initiatives, workplace fairness, and better government. We are still actively thinking, working, and rallying to forge a better system — an inclusionary system — despite the lingering obstacles. Even in our twilight years, we haven't given up. Only collective action will cure our social ills and create a colorblind society. I continue to believe we can shape the system under which we operate into something that better reflects God's loving will for His beloved children.

Reverend Holmes' selfless pursuit of "what is right" has helped solidify our community, harkening back to his service in the Texas House of Representatives from 1968–1972. I remember when he won reelection as a state legislator — Hubert Humphrey shook his hand. I was so proud of Reverend Holmes' political victories and still cherish a letter he sent me (with the State of Texas Seal) on August 6, 1968, after his reelection:

State of Texas
House of Representatives
Austin 78711

August 6, 1968

Mr. Pettis Norman

1415 E. Illinois
Dallas, Texas

Dear Pettis:

When one feels as close to someone as I feel toward you, it seems trite to say "thank you" for kindnesses shown. However, I am sincerely grateful to you for all the ways you aided my campaign. Victory would not have been possible without you.

Sincerely,

Zan W. Holmes, Jr.

In 1971, Judge William Taylor of the United States Court for the Northern District of Texas appointed Reverend Holmes to serve as chairperson of the Tri-Ethnic Committee, which oversaw the implementation of public school desegregation in the Dallas Independent School District. In 1991, Governor Ann Richards appointed him to be the first African American to serve on the Board of Regents of the University of Texas System, a position he held from 1991 to 1997.

In 1990, I nominated Zan for the Linz Award, one of the oldest and most prestigious civic honors presented to individuals whose community and humanitarian efforts have greatly benefited Dallas during the last decade. He earned the award that year as the second African American to win such an honor, and I was very proud of my good friend.

In 2001, the National Voting Rights Museum and Institute in Selma, Alabama, recognized him as one of the Civil Rights Movement's "Invisible Giants." In 2012, the Dallas Independent School District honored him at the dedication ceremonies for the new Zan Wesley Holmes, Jr. Middle School. The school's mission statement ensures student success by creating a well-structured, student-centered environment where effective, high-quality instruction is in every classroom, and rigorous student learning is the norm.

At the same time he served in the House of Representatives, Zan served as the United Methodist District Superintendent, and later as Senior Pastor of St. Luke's from 1979 to 2002. He is now pastor emeritus of St. Luke "Community" United Methodist Church in Dallas. I consider him my personal pastor.

Contributed by Reverend Zan Holmes

I'm proud to say that Pettis is one of my best friends. The City of Dallas owes a lot to him. He's the center of attraction at a party — people see that Super Bowl ring and want to hear about his NFL career. But the real story is his involvement in civil rights.

I came to Dallas in the '60s to study at the seminary at SMU and rented a room in South Dallas. I heard a commotion and noticed a lot of people rushing to the Central Expressway — an automobile had hit a Black man. Two White ambulance drivers and two White policemen did nothing to minister to that man. I learned they were waiting for ambulance services from Black & Clark funeral home, which had the contract for that part of the city.

While waiting, the man died. It's important to note that the White ambulance drivers and police officers were troubled by these circumstances. The ugly disease called racism bound them. I made a vow that if my ministry didn't deal with this ugly disease, I didn't need to be in seminary. On that day, I made the decision to show up and break down barriers.

Pettis feels the same way. I first met him when he and I helped Joseph Lockridge get elected, one of the first African Americans to serve in the Texas House of Representatives since Reconstruction. That was momentous. Lockridge was tragically killed in a plane crash, and we met to see who would fill his unexpired term. "You run!" I told Pettis, knowing he has never been interested in public office although so many have urged him to run. He looked at me and said, "You run!" Reluctantly I agreed, and Pettis put his reputation on the line as my campaign manager. There he was, this big, strong, physically imposing Dallas Cowboy, pulling my political signs out of the trunk of his car on the streets in the Bishop College area, an under-represented community. He worked tirelessly in that campaign, and I won.

The church has been the center of the movement. I served as pastor of St. Luke United Methodist Church when we had just 50 members. We added the word "Community" to the church name and watched it grow to a congregation of more than 12,000. We minister to people and support the path toward justice and liberation, as all churches should.

Interestingly, Pettis is one of few laypeople I know who can bring numerous pastors together for powerful initiatives to mobilize many people. I remember the downtown march in 1971 when he carried the American flag, demonstrating on behalf of political fairness and human rights issues in the City of Dallas despite the risk to his football career.

One of his crowning achievements was his work in banking that emphasized funding for programs in the Black community. He never got so caught up in his own business career and self-achievements that it interfered with his community involvement. He remained consistent in the struggle, being outspoken when necessary. He did it out of a love of bringing people together.

We've worked on several social justice issues from the Civil Rights Movement onward. Later, our work in the Dallas Alliance and the Dallas Together Forum was instrumental in bringing business leaders together to commit to do their part in hiring people of all races and reporting their progress. Pettis was so important to that aspect of accountability. People trust and appreciate him.

Dallas' highest civic award, the Linz Award, was presented to Juanita Craft in 1969, a beloved civil rights activist and the first African American person given that honor. I know both Pettis and I hold her in high esteem. The only other African American recipient was me — and I thank Pettis for his part in it. It just so happens he was serving on the committee and supported my nomination.

We have seen progress. Thank God I have lived long enough to be invited to speak at a graduation ceremony at the Police Academy when the mayor of the city, an African American, was a member of my church. It was the most inclusive graduation session to date, with recruits from the Philippines, Black men and women, Whites, and Hispanics. In fact, this has been Pettis' vision all along — unity in the community and jobs, opportunity, and fairness for all, including minorities. The struggle is still ongoing, however. Both Pettis and I hope and pray the day arrives that racial issues are finally resolved.

Pettis and his wife, Ivette, make a great team and are role models for new generations and those in the trenches today. I'm so pleased he's written an autobiography that includes such great perspectives and life lessons. I'm partial, but he deserves this praise.

Reverend Peter Johnson

Reverend Peter Johnson was — and is — deeply involved in the Civil Rights Movement and the Congress of Racial Equality at Southern University, a historically Black university in Baton Rouge. He worked for the Southern Christian Leadership Conference and came to Dallas on a filmmaking project in the '60s and planted deep roots.

I remember him being extremely concerned with structural inequality, urban hunger, and the socio-economic issues that plagued minorities in Dallas. But he was also focused on human dignity and was a part of the Anti-Apartheid Movement in North Texas, a global effort supported on the campus of Southern Methodist University,

Peter is now an adjunct instructor at the University of North Texas and teaches a course titled "The African American Civil Rights Movement 1954-1970." His students are fortunate to receive his view on those historical days, for Reverend Johnson can speak on behalf of "the least of these." He witnessed monumental events that impacted our nation, and his concern for human dignity worldwide has never diminished.

Peter has been a friend for more than 50 years. I admire him as a civil rights leader, including his devotion to just causes. His work in the movement is commendable in the City of Dallas and other cities across this nation, and I am blessed to have crossed paths with this great man. He is a wonderful family man, husband, father, grandfather, and loyal friend; well done, good and faithful servant.

Contributed by Rev. Peter Johnson

It's important to describe the history Pettis and I share in relation to the African American experience and civil rights. In 1969, I was working full-time in the Civil Rights Movement and was sent to Dallas by the Southern Christian Leadership Conference in an effort to support Dr. Martin Luther King Jr.'s widow. He died without insurance, and through a film project, we aimed to raise funds so that Coretta Scott King could raise Martin's children.

Samuel Livingston, Sidney Poitier, and others were behind the project, and the movie was slated to premiere in 800 cities around the world. Only one city on earth resisted, and that was Dallas. The movie was to show citywide, but the White benevolent power elites were unsupportive, and very little could be done without their approval. It just so happened that Andrew Young (later well-known as a politician and diplomat) was also involved in the project. His uncle, George Allen, sat on the Dallas City Council, and still, we had to fight tooth and nail to make a success of the film.

Three days before the movie was to premiere, Sam Livingston told the City of Dallas that there would be no more dealings with Hollywood if the film was not shown. The city gave us only three days to put tickets on sale. I knew two football players, Frank Clark and Pettis Norman, who could help mobilize the effort. Frank called me and said, "Peter, I have someone who wants to help you — philanthropist Peter McGuire. How much will it cost if he made the movie admission free?" Indeed, Peter McGuire wrote a check to cover the admission price in three movie theaters, and it was a success.

I'll never forget one Sunday in 1971. Pettis was on the Southern Christian Leadership board and worked as a vice-president at a local bank in addition to playing for the Dallas Cowboys. Despite the potential risk to his multiple careers, he helped rally the Black community to city hall in a street protest to support Dallas City Council member George Allen, who had been passed over as mayor pro tem despite assurances to the contrary. The whole state saw a pro football player carry the American flag and lead the protest through downtown Dallas.

Pettis was traded almost immediately to the San Diego Chargers. It seemed to many of us that this was a high price to pay for his contributions to the civil rights cause, but he put everything on the line to do the right thing. I and many others appreciate and admire Pettis for the sacrifices he made.

Many people are not aware of how generous and selfless Pettis has been in my life and the lives of many others. As most people know, Civil Rights leaders do not have regular income and are dependent upon organizations and people to fight for justice.

Pettis fed me when I was hungry; he gave me a van when I needed transportation and a key to a home for my family and me so I could remain in the fight for Civil Rights. He helped me stay steadfast as an agitator in the movement during a very difficult time in our history and risked his career to fight for justice for all people.

Rene Martinez

Rene is a wonderful humanitarian with a perspective that encompasses all races, particularly the Hispanic and Latino communities. He is mentioned throughout this book as someone I admire for involvement in educational leadership, mentorship of young adults in both high school and higher education, political activism, and past chairman of the Dallas chapter of the League of United Latin American Citizens (LULAC).

So much of his selfless sacrifice has everything to do with the larger issues in this book, from school desegregation to his service on the Tri-Ethnic Commission, and especially his continued focus on minority inclusion during the Civil Rights Movement. As a co-chair on the Dallas Together Forum, he forged alliances between small businesses, particularly Hispanic businesses, and the larger corporations. He later served as vice president of the Park Board and was recently appointed to the Dallas Mayor's Task Force on Safe Communities.

Rene has been a very good friend to me personally. We also shared many mutual friendships — Reverend Zan Holmes comes to mind — and worked for common causes. He has never forgotten his roots and stands up for what he believes is right. I appreciate his reflections below.

Contributed by Rene Martinez

I'm a few years younger than Pettis and entered North Dallas High School in 1962, old enough to be aware of the civil rights struggle from the lens of a Hispanic youth who lived in a less than accepting society. When my brother and I were young, my father told us a story about a lynching in Waco. He had grown up in Waco and witnessed the horrific event that included not just the lynching itself but the torture, burning, and dismemberment involved. He did not know the victim's name and only vaguely remembered that it occurred around the 1920s. It had a tremendous impact on him as a young immigrant from Mexico.

Years later, I shared this story with Zan Holmes, who has been a very good friend and mentor. After I described it, we realized my dad had very likely witnessed the infamous murder of Jesse Washington, a teenager in 1916, one of the last lynchings in Waco. It was such a vile and barbaric act, yet it was celebrated and photographed. Those images were published in the media and turned the stomachs of people throughout the United States.

I believed this lynching changed the country. It influenced the way my parents raised us. They believed in civil rights and that people should be treated equally, no matter who they were, no matter their skin color, no matter their language or culture. That's the way we were raised.

One incident in 1973 spurred the Mexican American community in Dallas to organize a protest for the first time. Thousands marched in response to the police shooting of Santos Rodriguez, a 12 year old Mexican American boy. Prior to his murder, he had been handcuffed and detained in a police car with his 13-year-old brother. The police suspected the boys had robbed eight dollars from a vending machine at a gas station. A police officer tried to coerce a confession through Russian roulette. He held a gun to Santos' head. At the second trigger pull, the boy was fatally shot in the head. He and his brother, by the way, were innocent of the robbery. The officer was convicted of murder and sentenced to five years but was released after serving half of his sentence. It was an atrocity.

I have known Pettis for nearly 40 years, and my biggest impression of his footprint is that he is an outstanding athlete who pushed for civil rights in mainstream Dallas. When I think about Pettis marching through the streets, I'm thankful. Few Cowboys immersed themselves in politics in a consistent, ongoing manner as Pettis did. It distinguished him. Keep in mind; he did so as a world-class athlete playing for 'America's Team,' yet boldly spoke out on cutting-edge issues. In the '60s and '70s, many athletes just didn't have the fortitude to take such a public stand, unlike Pettis. He truly led.

Pettis and I co-chaired Jesse Jackson's presidential campaign. We were able to pull together a coalition of Blacks and Browns and generate more votes for Jesse Jackson than Walter Mondale in Dallas County. I got to know Pettis in the political arena and on a personal level. I also know his family very, very well. It was an honor to be a groomsman at his wedding to Ivette. The Mexican custom is to call a groomsman a compadre, and I am Pettis' compadre — his brother and friend.

★ ★ ★ ★ ★

It is vital to expand on the roles of three notable people whose names are synonymous with civil rights — Congresswomen Eddie Bernice Johnson, Barbara Jordan and the Reverend Jesse Jackson. May Congresswoman Jordan rest in peace. As public officials, their importance in the long, painful and necessary journey is undeniable and has forever impacted where we are today. I weigh in with personal glimpses into their remarkable service, grateful for what they have accomplished on behalf of the poor, the downtrodden, and the marginalized.

Congresswoman Eddie Bernice Johnson

I admire Congresswoman Eddie Bernice Johnson. She has faithfully represented me and the people of the 30th Congressional District of Texas in the U.S. House of Representatives for 15 terms as I write this book.

In 1993 when the district was first created, she was elected and has served ever since — and with the distinction of being the first registered nurse elected to Congress (the chief psychiatric nurse at the Dallas Veterans Administration Hospital). I believe her staying power derives from constituents who appreciate her decorum and wisdom. They prove it by consistently casting their ballots and re-electing her. It's remarkable.

Prior to the U.S. House of Representatives, Eddie Bernice Johnson served in the Texas State House of Representatives, scoring a landslide victory in 1972 as the first Black woman to win electoral office from Dallas. Again, remarkable, and I was proud to be her treasurer.

I was impressed at her appearance on C-SPAN in 2015, speaking about U.S. civil rights and referencing Selma as the "crowning walk," something to which we can all relate. As a Texan, she personally knew President Lyndon Johnson, Ladybird Johnson, and their daughters, Lynda and Luci. I believe she has quite a unique perspective regarding LBJ's difficult presidency, as well as his relationship with Martin Luther King Jr. They worked together, a president and a civil rights leader, to generate progress, all the while enduring pressure from both sides.

My congresswoman mentioned that she agreed with LBJ's tactic of separating the Voting Rights Act and the Civil Rights Act to prevent the possibility of them both being voted down. She also credits both acts for opening the door to her political career; it enabled African Americans in the South to vote and ultimately run for office. And although President Johnson had detractors, the congresswoman is quick to say he was an outstanding president for minorities — housing, education, food for children in schools, and Medicare and Medicaid were initiatives that occurred on his watch.

The congresswoman has honored me with several moving tributes (one in the Foreword of this book and one in 2019) and I thank her from the bottom of my heart. What a gifted communicator; I can only hope to reciprocate as elegantly. Within the last 20 years alone, she has supported funding for women-owned businesses and disadvantaged businesses. She has also supported legislation on violence against women, re-introduced the Equal Rights Amendment, recognized the 1961 Freedom Riders against segregated buses, co-sponsored the Paycheck Fairness Act to protect against wage discrimination based on gender, and co-sponsored the Student Non-Discrimination Act to stop anti-gay discrimination in public schools. She is endorsed by the Feminist Majority on women's rights and scores 100% by the NAACP on affirmative action.

Congresswoman Johnson has and continues to host informative roundtable discussions to bring together local business owners and key federal and state officials to help facilitate economic growth in the Dallas area. I have been closely involved with these meetings and have encouraged others to do the same. I greatly appreciate her devotion to our community and the fact that she is always there for me and her constituents.

As I reflect on her role in the Civil Rights Movement, I distinctly remember her saying during Black History Month: "From slavery to suffrage, from the Jim Crow era to the Civil Rights Movement, the struggle for progress has marked the story of African Americans in this nation."

The Reverend Jesse Jackson

I have mentioned Jesse Jackson several times within these pages — his student activism, relentless energy on behalf of the Rainbow PUSH Coalition, and selfless service to our country. But here in this chapter, he deserves a special mention.

Jesse's drive for justice has always been about knocking down barriers. He has since dedicated his life's work to providing equal opportunity to Blacks in the form of employment, housing, education, and social services. He's done this with the Rainbow PUSH Coalition, a social justice movement that began in 1971 when he created Operation PUSH (People United to Serve Humanity). PUSH's mission was to protect Black homeowners, workers, and businesses.

Jesse rightly stated, "Now the next phase of our struggle, beyond freedom, is equality. You can be free, but without equality, you can't expand, you can't grow."

It's gratifying that the successful initiatives of the Dallas Together Forum that I co-chaired played a role in inspiring a nationwide movement — Jesse took what the Dallas Together Forum achieved in Texas and created similar initiatives nationwide. Back in 1996, the Wall Street Project "challenged Corporate America to end the multi-billion-dollar trade deficit with minority vendors and consumers, while working to ensure equal opportunities for culturally diverse employees, entrepreneurs, and consumers." American business could not maximize its growth potential until all businesses had an equal opportunity to compete on an even playing field, where the rules are public and the goals are clear.

Jesse is a notable humanitarian who has always put the country first and has done good things for today's Civil Rights Movement. I was so moved when he made a gracious statement about me and my book; it is another wonderful gesture of his support and friendship. I'm proud to share it below.

> *Pettis Norman has been a man of action throughout his 82 years. From his days in the NFL, he marched for civil rights. He later volunteered his time and talent in my presidential campaigns that defied all expectations and radically expanded the role of Black voters in national Democratic politics.*
>
> *He has ardently supported Rainbow Push Coalition initiatives and involved himself in the betterment of humanity. At this moment, after a life spent in service, it is Pettis who deserves due credit and our gratitude. How wonderful that he has written an autobiography. I'm proud to call him a national treasure and my friend.*

How remarkable that Jesse continues to advocate for minorities, the poor, the disenfranchised, and the downtrodden even today. His name recognition is the byproduct of a relentless drive on behalf of the "least of these," but it is his unwavering friendship that has touched my life.

Barbara Jordan

I'm honored to pay tribute to the one and only Barbara Jordan. I remember her as a highly effective attorney, educator, politician and daughter of a Baptist minister who has gone down in history as a bonafide Texas treasure. I appreciated her so, never dreaming that I would work with her one day to help usher presidential hopeful Jimmy Carter into office. What an experience that was!

Barbara was no novice when it came to campaigning, for she had volunteered for John F. Kennedy's presidential bid in 1960 and later for Lyndon B. Johnson. Back in 1966 as I played for the Dallas Cowboys, worked at South Oak Cliff State Bank, and served on the board of the Southern Christian Leadership Conference, she became a senator and the first African American woman to win a seat in the Texas legislature. I recall that President Lyndon Johnson invited her to the White House the following year to discuss an impending civil rights speech. Her oration and reasoning skills were second to none. The way she articulated a message reminded me of my father's persuasiveness — fair, rational, and dignified.

"What the people want is simple," she said. "They want an America as good as its promise."

Hearing her speak was a transcendent experience. Some will remember her heartfelt and unforgettable eulogy of Dr. Martin Luther King Jr. This established her as a household name. Whether people lived in Texas or elsewhere, they recognized Barbara Jordan.

I have always thought of her as a pioneer in the field of politics, for her charisma drew people across the aisle to support the issues she cared about. It mattered less that she was Black and female and mattered more that she possessed bridge-building skills, time and again. She served as a congresswoman from 1972 to 1978 and sponsored dozens of bills that supported minorities, the disabled, and the underserved. It made her a hero to many, me included.

In 1976 during her very first year as a congresswoman, Barbara became the first African American woman to deliver the keynote address to the Democratic National Convention. There was talk by convention delegates that she should be Jimmy Carter's vice-presidential running mate — I'm not sure if she was shortlisted, but I wouldn't doubt it. However, she wasn't focused on herself but rather on getting Jimmy Carter elected.

She was a strong voice on his behalf, and I and many others worked in tandem with her in Texas. She was a national figure; I was a local figure. Yet there was a synergy and adrenaline in our "get out the vote" efforts, fundraising, and appearances. We attended several campaign strategy meetings with Jimmy Carter himself, and it was a true victory when our candidate was sworn into the highest office in the land.

Barbara was voted president pro tem of the state senate — another first. It was all over the news, and I remember discussing this with my daughters. Thanks to Barbara's trailblazing legacy, their futures seemed limitless. We all followed Barbara's career and admired her very much, especially her work on minimum wage laws, anti-discrimination, and fair employment practices.

Her comments during President Nixon's impeachment hearings made national news. I recall her saying that her faith in the Constitution was "whole, complete and total" and that she would not be an idle spectator in the "diminution, subversion and destruction" of the Constitution.

What a proud list of achievements she left behind. She became the Lyndon B. Johnson Centennial Chair of Public Policy in 1982, served as special counsel on ethics for Texas Governor Ann Richards in 1991, was appointed by President Bill Clinton to head the Commission on Immigration Reform in 1994, and was presented the Presidential Medal of Freedom by President Bill Clinton just two years before she passed away in 1996.

She did much more than I can possibly list, and it was an honor to know her and work with her in pursuit of equality.

Chapter Thirteen: Race Relations

For the sake of our children, I look forward to the day when the term 'race relations' becomes antiquated due to the extinction of prejudice.
~ Pettis Norman

My final involvement in presidential politics was with President Barack Obama's 2008 campaign. I mention President Obama several times throughout this book, more so in this chapter, because his nomination, election, and reelection were amazing milestones in American history.

This was an occurrence that would have seemed almost impossible back in the '60s when we struggled for basic rights. Now, we as a people sat in front of our televisions and witnessed the nation's first Black president and saw our first Black First Lady smile and wave confidently. It was incredible — a strong validation for all people in America and worldwide that African Americans are equal and quite capable of holding the highest office in the land.

I recall being very excited when President Obama ran against Republican John McCain and won. The word "excited," however, does not begin to cover the swell of feelings we had as African Americans when Chief Justice John Roberts swore our first Black president into office.

When he won his second term after defeating Mitt Romney, it confirmed that President Obama's policies were effective. He was beloved, as was First Lady Michelle Obama. It was a joy to watch them parent their two daughters. Understandably, they went to great lengths to shield Malia and Sasha from the limelight. What great role models they became for millions across the country.

I think most will agree that race relations under Obama had a profound, positive effect on people of color by dispelling stereotypes and creating fairer opportunities for Blacks and other traditionally disadvantaged groups of people. While it had a profound impact, the issues of racism continued to surface in a way that had long been thought dead. The open disrespect was shown in cartoons. Congressman Joe Wilson called out "You lie!" during President Obama's health care speech to Congress and later issued an apology. The "birther" movement, too, revealed that while the election of the first Black president showed much promise, old racist feelings were still prevalent.

Despite this, Obama's presidency proved that young Black and Brown children and women could (and will) be future Presidents of the United States of America.

Still Room for Improvement

It would be both wrong and naïve to assert that race relations have not changed; they have. However, we have a moral and ethical obligation to address the subtle yet lethal byproduct of racism and discrimination against African Americans that continues to bubble beneath cities across this nation today.

I called the '70s one of the "most dangerous times in our nation," prompting an uneasy examination of race relationships and the governance of cities throughout our country. Yes, we had (and still have) problems with racial profiling, persistent racial inequality in employment, unfair housing practices, and other social domains that were overt decades ago but are now covert and clever.

Dallas was "run" by a group of establishment Whites — the power elite, you might say — who formed the Dallas White Citizens Council (White was later dropped from the name) and its political arm, the Citizens Charter Association. I am not denigrating these servant leaders for being powerful or White. I became close friends with many members of these organizations, all the while being very aware that they held sway over a city manager, a part-time mayor, the city council, the delegation to the State Legislature, and the Dallas Independent School District.

The fact that many of these friendships exist today, spanning decades, attests to the fact that many of the powerful elite "listened." They, too, were uncomfortable with the status quo and had a social conscience. They saw an opportunity to act, and we united to right the wrongs in our city.

I felt my role was to open their eyes to the suffering of underserved communities, perhaps in a manner that had not been presented before. I was passionate about the depth of untapped minority talent and the importance of doing business with minority and women-run enterprises. In the past, I believe minority viewpoints had been marginalized, and the City of Dallas would benefit if leaders sought out perspectives from a diverse citizenry.

In stark contrast to the wealth, affluence, and centralized authority of these prestigious citizens who lived in North Dallas, a population of racial minorities in South Dallas still lived in poverty-level housing, subsisted on welfare, and attended failing schools. During this time, the White population had grown by 14%. The Black population had grown by 63%, and minorities suffered from the economic disparity and social inequality that continued to plague our communities and school system. This had to be addressed. I was determined to change the status quo.

A New Mayor

It seemed to me that establishment leaders defined race relations by the absence of tension — the less tension, the better the race relations. This was simply not true. Race relations require an inclusive approach with the opportunity to fully participate in society, be embraced as a part of the community, and be treated equally regardless of race. We certainly had a long way to go to become a more inclusive and perfect union, not only in Dallas but also across our nation.

In 1971, change was on the horizon. Dallas experienced what many called a "big event" that showed promise for minorities. Democrat Wes Wise was elected mayor by 85% of the vote. He was considered a dark horse candidate — a television personality who covered sports for CBS and reported personally from Dealey Plaza when President Kennedy was assassinated. Most importantly, he was progressive. His winning slogan was: "I'm an average man."

My friend Bill Solomon, CEO of Austin Industries, stated that Wes Wise's election was a "watershed moment." I agreed. This shift away from an entrenched "old guard" way of governing and "right-wing hysteria," as Wes stated in his memoir, bode well for those of us who sought reform. As Dallas' first independent mayor, he led the city toward racial equality, guided it through desegregation, and fought to memorialize JFK's life and death.

Wes served until 1976 as a three-term mayor. While he experienced both personal and professional challenges in office, my hope was that a new era had dawned. I believed it had people talking about the concept of power and who held that power and signaled that more inclusionary change would take place in the city. I was beginning to feel a sense of belonging, with a more just future ahead. I was cautiously happy during this period.

My Good Friend Charley Pride

I had high expectations for change in our city and the nation and began to see a glimmer of awakening within all communities, White, Black, and Hispanic. However, it was evident that more challenges faced us. This reality was brought home when one of my good friends dating back to the '70s, Charley Pride, was affected by discrimination.

Charley was a country music sensation who began his career during the Civil Rights Movement and performed until his passing on December 12, 2020. It just so happened that his country music attracted fans of all ethnicities. He rose to greatness, this son of the South, in an industry that had never seen anything like him. But everyone could relate to Charley. He bridged a chasm, was beloved by all and was a friend to all.

We were both born to sharecropping parents in the south, Charley from Mississippi and me from Georgia. We learned a thing or two about business since our humble beginnings and happened to end up in Dallas. Charley had the talent to sing, perform, and be successful in the country music industry. He also had the intellect and wisdom to make sound investments and own a recording studio.

Talk about staying power! I was so proud when he sang at an invitation-only event at the White House for First Lady Michelle Obama and President Barack Obama in 2009. It was later broadcast on television — what an exciting occasion for Charley! In 2019, his life story was featured in a PBS American Masters documentary, an impressive story with humble beginnings.

My favorite songs, "Why Baby Why" and "Kiss an Angel Good Mornin'," still play in my mind like a tape recorder, but there are many more favorites. I should also add that Charley served in the Army and was quite an athlete — a professional baseball player, in fact.

He maintained his residence and established strong ties in Dallas. My late wife Margaret and I traveled on the road with Charley and his wife Rozene and became close companions around his music, community issues, and visited each other's homes during our free time.

He and I shared a mutual love of golf. I remember how we loved soaking up the scenery on the beautiful greens and enjoying the companionship of good golf buddies during many excursions. Golfing was also an excellent way to support charitable causes. For years, the Charley Pride Golf Fiesta was instrumental in raising funds for St. Joseph Hospital's cancer therapy program, and I proudly participated in some of those tournaments. On the flip side, for years, the Pettis Norman Golf Tournament supported El Centro College, and we had a tremendous turnout for these worthy causes. About six months prior to his passing, I caught up with Charley to reminisce about old times and talk about my autobiography. He generously shared a statement of advance praise for this autobiography.

> *Pettis was a great football player and successful businessman. But did you know his athleticism extended to golf? We sponsored a lot of charitable golf tournaments, and I'm glad he captures those philanthropic memories in his book.*

Black golfers were somewhat of a novelty in those days (Tiger Woods would not come on the scene until 1996), and Black golf memberships at country clubs were almost nonexistent. By 1978, Texas lawmakers had many opportunities to enact legislation against discrimination in country clubs, but had they acted? No. True, not many Blacks applied. But those who did apply and met the application criteria should have been welcomed with open arms.

I applied for membership in the Oak Cliff Country Club (now, Golf Club of Dallas), not at all sure my application would be accepted. This was ironic since my backyard overlooks the 3rd Tee Off. I could look but not play until a decision was made to admit me as the one and only Black member. The vote was 51 to 49, indicating that a large percentage of the membership was not ready to invite me to the table. Perhaps the slight majority of voters were influenced by my willingness to speak out for the "least of these." Maybe it was my association with the Cowboys or a tug on the hearts of those who chose not to judge me by the color of my skin.

I recall saying, "Any time barriers are broken down, barriers that deny other groups for any reason — for religion, for race, or anything else — I think that's a major step for the community." Upon approval of my application, I was welcomed by most members and felt proud that I was the "first" and able to pave the path for other people of color to join.

I thought it would open doors at other country clubs and applauded Charley Pride when he applied for membership at the Royal Oaks Country Club in Dallas. We assumed Charley's application would be a slam dunk (or better yet, a hole in one). After all, he was a renowned person involved in charity golf, successful in his music career and several businesses, and could certainly afford the dues. He was also a war veteran and former professional athlete — who would not want him on a country club membership roster?

Yet, Charley was rejected without explanation. What reason could there be other than discrimination? I would not have blamed Charley if he had pursued this matter in court, but we both realized there was still more work to do. I took it personally, but he shook it off, knowing he could buy his own country club if he were so inclined.

The Pettis Norman Annual Golf Tournament sponsored by El Centro College

To his credit, Charley remained active in the Golf Fiesta for several more years, but his rejection at Royal Oaks made me more determined to help change the tone of race relations locally and nationally; Charley deserved better. I vowed to back presidential candidates who addressed "civil wrongs" and pushed for civil rights. It was (and still is) vital to support leaders in the highest offices who fight for us, not against us. I was pleased that the media gave wide coverage to this debacle, for it further illustrated how far we had to go to break down the barriers of second-class citizenship.

Today, the Golf Club of Dallas has come full circle. In May 2020, an African American visionary leader, Dr. Tony Evans, and his church, Oak Cliff Bible Fellowship in Dallas, purchased it. I applaud Dr. Evan's purchase of this iconic landmark; his church ministry has improved the quality of life for citizens in our community. I trust his visionary leadership to preserve the historical significance of the golf course and use the beautiful landscape, pool, dining, and ballroom to enrich families in the surrounding areas.

Let me close this section with a few facts about Charley Pride's amazing accomplishments. First, he was a friend to several Dallas Cowboys and enjoyed watching our games. Second, did you know that Charley, a three-time Grammy winner, was topped only by Elvis Presley in RCA records sales? Further, he racked up 52 Top 10 country hits and became a Grand Ole Opry member in 1993. He was inducted into the Country Music Hall of Fame in 2000, and the acclaim he has achieved says more about him than I ever could. I am proud to share that in November 2019, Charley was the inaugural recipient of Mississippi's Crossroads of American Music Award — well done, good and faithful servant. Charley passed away on December 12, 2020. He left an incredible legacy. May God rest his soul.

Fair Park

You would think something as positive and uplifting as a park would bring people together. Fair Park — once an 80-acre fairground on the outskirts of East Dallas — is home to the Dallas State Fair established in 1886. The City of Dallas saved the State Fair from near bankruptcy in 1904 when it purchased Fair Park.

The Cotton Bowl Stadium was built in 1930 during the Great Depression. I always loved playing in the Cotton Bowl, and it is a point of pride that our city hosts the State Fair. During those early years, the real beauty of Fair Park was that it was more than a seasonal fairground. It was a locale that could be used by the entire city year-round and eventually attracted the Dallas Museum of Art, The Dallas Opera, Hall of State, The Science Museum, The Women's Museum, The African American Museum, and other iconic cultural destinations.

Under the surface, however, Fair Park presented a challenge on the race relations forefront. I discovered this reality after accepting a position on the Fair Park Board in 1969, a position I maintained even after moving to San Diego to play for the Chargers. Serving on the board was something I could do in the off-season. Our mission was to expand Fair Park into South Dallas, populated by minority families, and stimulate the economy.

This expansion was important to me — my hope was that it would benefit everyone in the community, especially disenfranchised Blacks who desperately needed a boost. Being an entrepreneur myself, I wanted these families to have opportunities to establish small businesses, draw Fair Park customers, and lift themselves out of poverty.

The potential for good was huge, but it became obvious that the expansion did little to help minority families who lived in southern Dallas. The State Fair itself monopolized Fair Park for several months out of the year, meaning that other organizations and small businesses could not operate year-round. Most did not survive.

Worse, rather than revitalize the area, the poor were considered a threat to tourism. The low-income housing and living conditions were considered an eyesore. How did the City of Dallas address this issue? It wasn't by investing in the lives of those who resided near the fairgrounds or bridging capital into distressed communities. The "least of these" were targeted rather than uplifted. Massive parking lots were installed to separate the surrounding community from Fair Park — a concrete barrier to keep out the residents.

Enter my good friend Don Williams, former Chairman and Chief Executive of Trammell Crow. In my opinion, Don is driven by his willingness to stand up for "the least of these." For decades, he has made it his personal mission to create initiatives and implement them with heartfelt passion. He, more than anyone, exposed the disenfranchisement at Fair Park stemming from the late '60s onward, and did so in a scathing report described below.

The road toward equity has been long and frustrating, culminating in a 2017 report issued by Don's nonprofit, the Foundation for Community Empowerment (FCE). Yes, Don published some distasteful yet truthful facts. As background, well before my participation on the Fair Park board, a shameful report was issued in 1966 by the city and cited the "intense emotional discomfort with middle-class white residents of Dallas" during their visits to Fair Park:

> *The solution for all these conflicts, at least in terms of Fair Park's location, is simple. All that is required is to eliminate the problem from sight. If the poor Negroes in their shacks cannot be seen, all the guilt feelings revealed above will disappear, or at least be removed from primary consideration...*
>
> *... If all the land around Fair Park were bought up and turned into paved, lighted, fenced parking lot, would that solve the problem?*

That is precisely what happened. The city displaced poor citizens and solved "the problem" by razing homes and building parking lots. I knew Dallas' track record with minorities was woefully lacking, but to see the report written in black and white was beyond disappointing.

South Dallas was viewed as a blight and while housing in the Fair Park area decreased by more than 50%, housing in the entire city rose by 72%. It was also noted that for 15 years leading up to 2014, the property values in the entire city increased four times faster than property values in and around Fair Park. Something had to change, and Don was a significant change agent.

Don battled tirelessly as a vocal diplomat who insisted that underperformance was unacceptable and that Fair Park could and should be part of the economic engine of Dallas to revitalize low-income neighborhoods. His article published in the *Dallas Morning News*,

"Putting Fair Park in Private Hands Means City Hall can Focus on Government, not Event Planning," sums it up nicely. As Don pointed out, we can look to the Dallas Arboretum and the Dallas Zoo, both run by nonprofits, as examples of successful year-round city attractions.

Today, thankfully, we see a marked improvement. Dallas City Council listened and was in consensus regarding Fair Park management. Don notes that we now have a "fairer Fair Park" and that the Texas State Fair is a better neighbor. I can't thank Don enough for his selfless support of this very important landmark in our city. It appears we are coming full circle, back to the days when Fair Park served all citizens.

Grow South Initiative

With all the challenges we have had in our city and across our nation, allow me to shine a big spotlight on a positive initiative that infused much-needed investment into the southern sector of Dallas.

In 2011, Mike Rawlings was elected the 61st Mayor of Dallas. Under Mayor Rawlings' leadership, the economy flourished. The housing market remained hot, and new residents flocked to the city thanks to a robust job market. Many neighborhoods attracted significant business, and the city's tax base continued to grow.

I was so pleased with Mayor Rawlings' commitment to grow southern Dallas (southern Dallas is distinct from South Dallas where Fair Park is located). This part of our city has always had growth and infrastructure challenges, but it grew faster under Mayor Rawlings' leadership than North Dallas during his tenure. Land values increased by 50%, crime fell overall, schools received more attention, and there were more neighborhood associations to help build better communities.

Today, 55% of our citizens live North of the Trinity River, yet that part of our City provides 85% of our tax base or, conversely, southern Dallas is home to 45% of our population yet provides only 15% of our tax base. It comprises roughly half of Dallas' landmass with beautiful trees, lakes, and hills and is one of the most beautiful parts of the city. I have proudly lived in southern Dallas for decades and can see tremendous potential. Sadly, there has always been a psychological stain on this sector of our city because of the lack of investment, infrastructure, housing, retail, and other conveniences until Mayor Rawlings was elected.

Mayor Rawlings saw the growth potential and launched an incredible initiative called "GrowSouth," supported in part by a private equity fund that began to change the landscape of the southern sector. The results of this initiative were huge — new activity, new investment opportunities, improved infrastructure, new developments, new jobs, and energy you can sense around this exciting growth.

Today, while more work is needed to equalize the tale of two cities, I credit Mayor Rawlings with attempting to end the disparity between the North and South. Exciting plans are now in place for retail, office space, restaurants, entertainment, and high-speed rail.

There is no doubt that business people are looking harder at opportunities in the city's southern sector because of his leadership. It is imperative that our city continues to offer incentives to investors and redirect their dollars to southern Dallas.

Before Mayor Rawlings left office, I had the opportunity to personally thank him for his vision and leadership, especially the GrowSouth initiative — well done, my good and faithful Mayor. I am delighted to share his kind, parting words before he left the Mayor's office:

> *Pettis is a truly unique individual who has made a difference in our city on many levels. Not only was he an athletic star that hundreds of thousands looked up to, but he also transformed himself into a successful businessman, breaking color barriers in several professional endeavors.*
>
> *But he didn't stop there. He became a civic leader by partnering with other leaders across the city in Dallas' to grow minority contracting and minority inclusion through the Dallas Together Forum effort. And he kept working. I called upon him as we assessed our schools' performance to ensure that the African American community was heard and heard clearly. He did that job with the same sense of excellence he has carried throughout his whole life.*

The Redistricting Landscape

In 1988, I began working on a committee headed by Mayor Annette Strauss to address the redistricting dilemma that plagued the city. This hyper-local issue culminated in an initiative referred to as "Dallas Together" (not to be confused with a future initiative, the Dallas Together Forum). I imagine the backstory will be interesting to political buffs regardless of locale, for it touches voting rights, politics, and community debate.

At issue was the 10-4-1 redistricting initiative, vilified by some and supported by the mayor and others. The goal was to establish, once and for all, a system at City Hall that achieved the largest representation for all ethnicities so that their voices counted at the polls. I liken it to a Shakespearean drama, so passionate were the players involved.

Because our right to vote is so vital and our votes should mean something, redistricting has always been a hot-button topic. Dallas is not the only city that has faced redistricting issues, but perhaps ours was at the top of the list as the most highly contentious. While I draw much of this information from memory, it's complicated. I will attempt to reiterate this contentious issue in our city to the best of my recollection and a little research.

Even now, after all these years, I'm still finding small, fresh snippets of information that might be interesting to others. For instance, Dallas has always had populations of Blacks, Whites, and Hispanics. Yet, despite this diversity (or because of the diversity), intentional racism had been built into the city's first charter in 1907. "Segregation of the Races" was not repealed until 1968; it authorized City Council to pass ordinances regarding housing, amusement, churches, and schools by members of the "White" and "Colored" races. This did not bode well for minorities. Old habits lingered; institutional racism was entrenched in our society.

The Citizen's Charter Association was developed in the 1930s after Dallas adopted the Council-Manager form of government to improve citizen participation in city affairs. By citizen participation, they meant participation by Whites. Blacks and Hispanics were not endorsed, and therefore the Citizen's Charter Association gained the reputation of enforcing a "Whites-only" City Hall. That is the kindest way I can describe it.

In 1961, the City Council contracted ambulances to aid citizens according to their race and bury "Negro paupers" — something the Reverend Peter Johnson mentioned in the Civil Rights Chapter of this book. By then, especially in an era of activism, minorities began to find their voices. The key to change was in how the districts in Dallas were represented at City Hall.

This, too, was an evolution. From 1931 to 1968, nine at-large members sat on the City Council. From 1969 to 1975, the Citizens Charter Association increased the size of the Council from nine to eleven to include two minority seats — George Allen who was Black and Anita Martinez, Hispanic. This was due to Black and Hispanic growth, now about half the population, and the fact that minorities had begun to demand fair representation.

From 1975 to 1991, there were eight single-member districts plus three at-large members and subsequent lawsuits. Mayor Strauss appointed the Dallas Citizens Charter Review Committee to find a way to restructure the City Council fairly. Many pushed for a 14-1 plan with 14 council members from single-member districts and an elected mayor. Some pushed for a 10-4-1 plan in which ten council members represented local districts, four represented regional districts, and the mayor was elected. Others preferred the 8-3 system, a 12-1 system, and even a 16-1 system.

As I watched the unveiling of this redistricting debacle, I jumped into the brewing controversy to meet with various factions and help broker a compromise. With tensions escalating, I approached Mayor Strauss and suggested that we identify 75 representatives from various districts in our city to find an amicable truce. While the mayor initially had concerns with the number of people I suggested, she agreed to give it a try with hopes of finding a resolution. Well, let us just say the arguments waged behind closed doors were daunting. The acrimony was nearly overwhelming. There was zero consensus. Zero unanimity.

In a close popular vote, the 14-1 adherents lost, and the 10-4-1 adherents won. My understanding was that nearly all African American precincts rejected 10-4-1. Most Mexican American precincts felt the same way. I, however, ultimately backed the 10-4-1 plan as a compromise, putting me at odds with thousands of dissenting views.

Of course, I faced backlash. When you are out front, you have many friends and often a few critics. However, in a *Dallas Weekly* article, J. Alfred Washington wrote a piece referring to me as a maverick on the 10-4-1 plan, "unbossed and unbought." I stated that I had no political ambitions and that my obligation was to raise the consciousness level of my community.

Even during the raging redistricting debate, many knew me as a man with a great degree of integrity, honesty, and anchored with my Lord and Savior. While it is easy to embrace friends, I also embraced my critics — here's why. My goal has been to bring my detractors along with me and absorb and appreciate their constructive feedback. Their opinions are as valid and important as my own.

Thus, most White voters and a few mavericks like me brought the 10-4-1 plan to fruition. But then came a plot twist — I was not kidding when I called this matter Shakespearean. From the federal bench, Judge Jerry Buchmeyer ruled that the 10-4-1 plan did not meet a legal threshold. He implemented the 14-1 plan based on the Voting Rights Act of 1965. This caused a furious backlash, but the Justice Department approved the ruling… and that was the end of this story.

Perhaps another good adjective to describe these redistricting efforts is "passionate." Certainly, it is a case study in race relations, perhaps one for the records. As in most political situations, there was no way to please everyone. The bottom line is that Dallas functions under the 14-1 plan (at the time I wrote this section), and while there are pros and cons, it changed the future of Dallas governance.

So why should you care? I share this redistricting and gerrymandering debacle in Dallas because you, too, need to understand what is happening in your own districts and states. For those unaware, redistricting takes place in each state about every ten years, and the resulting map affects the elections of the U.S. House of Representatives and state legislative bodies.

According to a recent report by Michael C. Li, one of the nation's leading experts on redistricting and gerrymandering, "The risk for abuse in map drawing will be especially high in 2020 and 2021 in the South, where fast population growth and demographic change in Texas, Florida, Georgia, and North Carolina, will combine with single-party control of the process and weaker legal protections for communities of color."

No matter your political preference, Democrats and Republicans use redistricting alone to flip seats needed to gain party control. While redistricting and gerrymandering may be an obscure issue to most, today, more voters understand what is at stake and the importance of electing representatives who reflect their views and the population in their districts. I urge you to get fired up, demand less partisanship, less manipulation, and encourage more fairness in our redistricting process.

Police Relations

In my view, Dallas was wrestling with a lot of issues — identity politics, a school system in distress, federal courts, a growing population of ethnicities, racial tension, and a love-hate relationship with the police for many decades. Each topic could be a chapter. Suffice it to say, I have always supported the police force as a whole and credit them for working in dangerous, sometimes life-threatening, scenarios.

Support, however, involves more than blindly cheering on law enforcement. As a member of the Mayor's Taskforce on Crime, I believed that addressing egregious wrongs and demanding improvement was vital. Fixing problems rather than covering them up is always best for the community.

There was not just economic polarization in Dallas — there was a dark cloud of disparity in the treatment of minorities by the police. Excessive force was one problem; another was the lack of safety within minority neighborhoods. Often crime in Black and Hispanic neighborhoods was not addressed with the same zeal as in White neighborhoods. The truth is many African Americans did not feel safe in their own homes. Worse, the African American and Mexican American populations deeply feared the police. Whites felt just the opposite.

Rather than delve into a litany of headline stories, I will mention one (of many) that pushed me to action — one that should never be forgotten. Santos Rodriguez was murdered in 1973, the 12-year-old Hispanic boy referenced by Rene Martinez in the Civil Rights chapter. I remember feeling utterly appalled at Santos' murder; this child was yanked into a patrol car and endured Russian roulette as the officers tried to force a confession for a crime he did not commit. I remember being 12 years old and would have been either frozen in fear or shaking in terror at the first click of the gun.

Then in a tragedy that will forever haunt Dallas, the gun went off, and Santos died. It was so senseless and preventable. Even if Santos had stolen from a vending machine, which he did not, the perceived crime in no way justified an execution of a 12-year-old. This murder was a catalyst. Santos' funeral spurred a protest, and I joined in, grieving and outraged that this happened on the city's watch.

Minority leaders became vocal, especially two council members, Al Lipscomb and Diane Ragsdale, along with County Commissioner John Wiley Price. To this day, I appreciate my friendship with the commissioner and admire the good he does on behalf of the voiceless. He and others demanded accountability and answers for Santos Rodriguez's death. In response, the city council gave authority to a standing committee to investigate complaints about "police bias" — a police civilian review board — which the Dallas Police Association and hundreds of law enforcement officers opposed.

Mayor Annette Strauss, elected in 1987, walked into a firestorm of police controversy. She held eight months of continuous meetings with me, Tom Dunning, Rene Martinez, and others in what became known as "Dallas Together," a think tank for solutions to these daunting problems. Tom, Rene, and I became very close friends during the process.

It would take an entire book to capture all the good things Tom Dunning has contributed to the city. He built a small business into one of the largest privately-owned health and welfare benefit firms in the United States, the Lockton Dunning Benefit Company. City leaders have turned to Tom for help in race relations, education reform, and homelessness, to name a few.

When President George W. Bush asked mayors across the nation to help with a ten-year plan to end chronic homelessness, Mayor Laura Miller asked Tom Dunning to be Dallas' first "Homeless Czar." Mayor Ron Kirk asked him to chair the DFW International Airport Board. Tom has also served as chairman of the Dallas Citizens Council, comprised of the leading CEOs in Dallas, and so much more.

As I prepared this section of the book, Tom recalled an incident when an African American took a police officer's gun and shot him, to the cheers of some. "It caused a huge pushback," Tom noted. "Many citizens and the wives of Dallas police officers made this a police-race issue, which it wasn't because African Americans were just as concerned about what happened." I agreed.

For and against, police relations and public perception were fast becoming an overriding issue that could not be ignored. The delicate balance of law enforcement, citizen perception, and officers' lives impacted all communities in Dallas.

Tom and Rene were vocal, and so was I. "Pettis, you were never afraid to stand up and speak strongly whether you were challenged by the minority or majority community," Tom told me. I can say the same about him and am glad we were on the same team and fighting the same issues in those challenging days.

Tom was always prepared and spoke eloquently from the heart; he was ready to do the hard work on many fronts — the police, education, minority hiring, and homelessness. Rene Martinez, too, was on the front lines; his voice made a difference.

I must mention that my good friend Pete Schenkel, CEO of Schepps Dairy, was also concerned about the state of police relations in Dallas. He noted, "We had some issues with police units and White officers shooting Black citizens. It was Pettis who really stood up and said all the right things. He was involved and stayed aggressively on top of the issues, speaking up and demanding change, and I think it made our Dallas police department better." I appreciate his words, for it was difficult walking the fine line between officer's lives and citizen's lives, all the while seeking to identify the root cause of why this was happening in the first place.

In 1988, the Chicago Tribune declared the City of Dallas "a racial time bomb" — and it was due to police shootings, the media coverage, and a deep rage felt by minorities. Charles Terrell, Chair of the Dallas Crime Commission, hired consultants to make recommendations that would improve police relations and give more power to the police civilian review board. Reforms were adopted, including subpoena power (with Council oversight) and the use of investigators. Of course, the Dallas Police Association protested these measures — one valid complaint was that accused officers were being denied their right to not self-incriminate.

Many officers did not feel Billy Prince, the Police Chief, fought strongly enough against the reforms. City Manager Richard Knight and Mayor Annette Strauss supported him, while Council members felt he criticized them too much. The Chief was between a rock and a hard place. In the meantime, three White police officers were killed in the line of duty, spurring enormous White support and sympathy for the police force. It led to further polarization.

I vividly recall when Police Chief Billy Prince resigned after six years at the helm. His resignation came at a time of heightened tension between the police and the minority community.

Commissioner John Wiley Price

It was also well known that the Dallas City Council and Mayor Annette Strauss wanted more police accountability versus the police union, which opposed greater control. City Manager Richard Knight began an aggressive nationwide search for a replacement. Commissioner John Wiley Price threatened a "call to arms" if the city manager did not pick a new police chief who was up to speed on minority issues and understood the backstory of race relations in Dallas.

I did not agree with the Commissioner's choice of words; my approach to conflict was consistent with MLK's teachings — "Returning violence for violence multiplies violence." John's comments were clearly wrong. Later, to the Commissioner's credit, he backed off that comment and explained it reflected the frustration and anger simmering in the Black community over the previous Police Chief's firing. He went on to say that he used the wrong choice of words.

Fast forward to today. Perhaps Commissioner Price was ahead of his time. Was his outspokenness with this incident a foreshadowing of police brutality against African Americans in Dallas and our nation? I say yes! While we may not have been ready for an outspoken Commissioner, his agitation in our community was a prelude to the tragic death of George Floyd and many other African American men who have died in police custody. Again, while I never condone violence, I do encourage freedom of speech, and Commissioner Price has never been afraid to fight for just causes.

I met John Wiley Price in the 1980s and supported him in his bid for Dallas County Commissioner in 1985. He was elected to this influential position and has served the people of District 3, who affectionately refer to him as "Our Man Downtown" ever since.

Some may not realize that John Wiley Price was the first African American elected to the "County Commissioner's Court" and has served more than 30 years; that is impressive. While I have not always agreed with his approach to solving political controversies in our city, he has always been a vocal, unapologetic official who stood up for what he believes in. He is known as a voice for the voiceless, and his heart is in the right place. We both "pulled on the same rope" to achieve results for the "least of these."

I appreciate his service to our community, our friendship, and the respect he has always shown me. John recently shared the following and has always been a supportive friend:

> *Just about everyone in Dallas knows that a conversation with Pettis benefits everyone. He's a "solutions" type of person, calm and levelheaded. He looks beyond what separates people and focuses on what brings us together. I've always admired him as a businessman and as a person who cares deeply about the community. Dallas is a better city because of a servant leader named Pettis Norman.*

By this time, Ross Perot had stepped in on behalf of the Dallas Police, acting independently in negotiations with the mayor, city manager, and Black leadership. I, too, stepped up alongside Craig Holcombe, Chair of the Council Committee on Public Safety, and Charlie Terrell. Ultimately, a compromise was reached, and Officer Lou Caudell became acting Dallas Police Chief.

On his last day in that position, Chief Caudell announced the deadly force policy to the citizens of Dallas in cooperation with incoming Police Chief Mack Vines. It alleviated the dark cloud of suspicion hanging over questionable shooting incidents, re-crafted in simpler and more easily understood terms.

The Ticker Tape Parade

I will interject another anecdote. On February 9, 1993, around 350 officers were on hand for a ticker-tape parade downtown. Spirits were high, for the Dallas Cowboys had won Super Bowl XXVII. I remember thinking, they sure have added a whole lot of Roman numerals since we squared off against the Colts in '71!

DART, the public transit system, provided free rides. A total of about 400,000 people showed up, roughly twice the anticipated amount, and some schools reported that half the students had skipped classes. It was not unusual for people to celebrate a big home win, but for whatever reason, this time was different.

In the midst of a vast crowd, pockets of violence erupted. Perhaps 100 youths, primarily Black, attacked innocent bystanders, most White or Hispanic. Here and there, shots were fired. A few liquor stores were looted, and bottles were thrown. People climbed on top of city buses resulting in thousands of dollars in damage. Two-dozen people ended up in the hospital. An additional 100 officers were called to the scene.

I mention this incident because it caused us to wonder why the riot started in the first place. I joined a task force that investigated that very question. Our findings were that "the post-parade disturbance, assaults, and 'wilding' activities were generated by the combination of a sports-excitement atmosphere, lack of sufficient police presence, and mob psychology by groups—and also by race."

I recall saying, "The Dallas Cowboys will soon win again, and next time the city will spend three million dollars to have ten times the police force out. We should be spending three million dollars trying to solve the problems that created the climate for such violence in the first place." No, I was not giving the offenders a pass — I am all for accountability and personal standards of conduct. It is wrong to destroy property; it is astronomically wrong to assault innocent bystanders. There must be consequences in place to deal with this behavior. But we should bear in mind the backdrop of race relations in that era and the undertone of anger, which I believe manifested during the celebration. We still had a long way to go, and it was not easy.

Very few officials have served without intense public scrutiny and the spotlight that shines on perceived problems, failures, or unresolved issues. I will never discourage public service, but I do tell people that they can serve effectively as servant leaders outside of public office.

This is the path I chose — a calling to lead from behind the scenes and use my platform as an athlete, businessman, and leader in our community on behalf of the "least of these."

Bill Clinton's Forum on Sports and Race

President Clinton held a forum on sports and race at the Wortham Theater Center in Houston, Texas in 1998. There were two town hall meetings on race and sports broadcast live on ESPN. It was viewed by an audience in Dallas that were predominately African American and Hispanic residents who listened and watched Clinton's discussion live from Townview Center, an Oak Cliff magnet high school. I led and facilitated the Dallas discussion along with my good friend Rene Martinez. The Houston panel discussed several topics but often returned to the relative shortage of minorities in top sports-management jobs.

The Race and Sports Forum panel had several high-profile athletes, including retired Cleveland Browns running back Jim Brown, Dallas Cowboys wide receiver Keyshawn Johnson, track and field star Jackie Joyner-Kersee, and San Antonio Spurs player Felipe Lopez, to name a few. These panelists were subject-matter experts on the topics of sports and racial issues. They had a robust conversation with President Clinton about closing the opportunity gaps between races in our country and identifying what should be done to continue to meet the challenges that exist today.

President Clinton with his panel at the Wortham Center, Houston, Texas.
Photo courtesy of the Clinton Presidential Library. Photo by Barbara Kinney

Our President, an avid fan of college basketball and major professional sports, said that "If professional sports wanted more minority coaches but cannot find them, then there's something wrong with recruitment." President Clinton went on to say that he was optimistic that talking about race in the context of sports could help the nation deal with broader racial issues. "America, rightly or wrongly, is a sports-crazy country," he said, "and we often see games as a metaphor or symbol of what we are as a people."

This topic has been advocated by many, most notably Johnnie L. Cochran, Jr., a.k.a. O.J. Simpson's lawyer, and my good friend and NFL player John Wooten, who helped convince the NFL it needed to change by embracing the "Rooney Rule." In a nutshell, the "Rooney Rule" was named in honor of former Pittsburg Steelers owner Dan Rooney, who championed the concept among owners, mandating that NFL management must agree to interview at least one minority candidate before selecting a head coach.

In recent times, while approximately 70% of NFL players are African American, head coaching jobs are hard to come by. At the start of the 2006 season, the overall percentage of

African American coaches jumped to 22%, up from 6%, a great improvement due to the Rooney Rule. In 2018, of 32 teams, the NFL season included eight minority head coaches, seven that were African American — a record in league history.

At the time, the NFL had four minority head coaches, Rivera with the Redskins, Lynn with the Chargers, Tomlin with the Steelers, and Flores with the Miami Dolphins. The Dolphins' Chris Grier and the Cleveland Browns' Andrew Berry are the league's only African American general managers. Is this an abysmal trend due to lack of talent…or lack of opportunity? Is it an anomaly, or are we slipping back into "the way things were" despite the advancements we fought so hard to gain?

In May 2020, I became cautiously optimistic about change when the NFL owners met and agreed to expand and improve the Rooney Rule. During the meeting, NFL owners voted to enact new measures aimed at improving diversity in coaching and front office hiring. The change includes a requirement to interview two candidates from outside the organization for any vacant head-coach job, including offensive, defensive, or special team coordinator positions. In addition, teams are now required to interview "minorities and/or female applicants" for upper-level positions such as team president and senior executive-level positions.

Another significant inclusion requires that coaching fellowships be established for minority and female participants to receive hands-on training and coaching – thus creating a pool of qualified candidates for future head-coaching opportunities. While the NFL owners tabled the resolution that would "incentivize" the hiring of minority coaches and general managers, the new accepted guidelines demonstrate a level of commitment on the part of NFL owners to improve diversity, equity, and inclusion within the NFL. This is impressive!

I give heartfelt thanks to Dan Rooney, former owner of the Pittsburgh Steelers, for championing this idea among NFL owners. Additionally, I salute my good friend John Wooten for his vision and trailblazing the Fritz Pollard Alliance to push collectively for equal employment opportunities throughout the NFL.

Safer Dallas Better Dallas

In 2014, I served on the steering committee for Safer Dallas, Better Dallas. This group was headed by group Chairman Charlie Terrell (may God rest his soul) and supported by more than 100 business leaders, politicians, and public servants committed to reducing violence in our city.

The mission was to (1) Protect the citizens of Dallas from becoming victims of crime; (2) Engage citizens in a partnership with the police; (3) Support the Dallas Police Chief and officers; and (4) Make Dallas America's safest city. This group was concerned about police relations and an increase in targeted killings of police officers by civilians.

The organization raised money from Dallas foundations, businesses, and citizens to purchase equipment and security cameras, train Dallas police officers, facilitate grants, and so much more. In addition, we teamed with the Rotary Club of Dallas to present Public Safety Awards to citizens and Distinguished Service Awards to police officers, who exemplified the leadership and service necessary to reduce crime in Dallas.

Our city had an opportunity to utilize the investment of this initiative during an unprecedented event in downtown Dallas on July 7, 2016. During a peaceful "Black Lives Matter" demonstration protesting the wrongful slaying of two African American men in Louisiana and Minnesota days before, the evening turned violent. A sniper in downtown Dallas ambushed a group of police officers, specifically targeting White officers. The sniper, an African American man who began his attack on street level, took shelter on the third level of an El Centro College building while he continued shooting at police officers.

Dallas Police Chief David Brown accomplished an amazing feat after a long standoff with the sniper. In what appeared to be a scene from a thriller movie, Chief Brown directed his police to deploy a bomb disposal remote control vehicle armed with explosives, killing Johnson in the parking lot. Unfortunately, when it was all over, five officers had been shot and killed, and seven officers were wounded, along with two civilians.

Brown stated that his lieutenants were "convinced the suspect had other plans and thought that what he was doing was righteous" and was "determined to make us pay for what he sees as law enforcement's efforts to punish people of color." The incident made headlines around the nation, and I commended Police Chief David Brown, an African American, for his courageous efforts to minimize the number of deaths.

President Obama attended the funeral service in Dallas and his message was one of unity. He stated, "Scripture tells us that in our sufferings, there is glory. Because we know that suffering produces perseverance; perseverance, character; and character, hope. But sometimes, the truths of these words are hard to see. Right now, those words test us because the people of Dallas, people across the country, are suffering. We're here to honor the memory and mourn the loss of the five fellow Americans, to grieve with their loved ones, to support this community, to pray for the wounded and try to find some meaning amidst our sorrow." President Obama concluded his speech with the most profound words – "I believe our sorrow can make us a better country. I believe our righteous anger can be transformed into more justice, more peace."

I continue this thought of peace and unity in the following section. After sharing a litany of issues in this chapter, it is important to hone in on solutions. Honestly, the answer to local, national, and international race-related problems lies within us all. If our hearts are pure and we do as God instructs, we will love our neighbors as ourselves – neighboring households, neighboring states, and neighboring nations on this planet we share.

Dr. Tony Evans and the Theme of Oneness

I recently reached out to Dr. Tony Evans, Christian Pastor, speaker, author, widely syndicated radio and television broadcaster, and former Chaplain of the Dallas Cowboys.

What a wise man he is — Senior Pastor of Oak Cliff Bible Fellowship in Dallas, founder of The Urban Alternative, and one of the most influential evangelical church leaders of our time.

I believe Dr. Evans personifies the theme of unity. On Good Friday, April 10, 2020, he live-streamed Kingdom Men Calling: A Global Gathering in partnership with Lifeway, and a million viewers soaked up his message. That same month, he was invited to Liberty University, which streamed his words of wisdom and encouragement regarding how to cast worry on the Lord during the COVID-19 pandemic.

Dr. Evans has been studying and preaching the Gospel for more than 50 years. I enjoy his bestselling books and his radio program, "The Alternative with Dr. Tony Evans," broadcast every day on 1,400 stations throughout the US and in 130 countries across — Europe, India, the Middle East, South America, and the Caribbean. Ivette and I have been listening to The Alternative for a long time and continue to enjoy his lessons today.

If you ever speak with Dr. Evans, you will be moved. He recently shared his perspective on the role of the church in our communities, our nation, and around the world — not the Black church or White church, but "The Church" comprised of precious souls who worship together regardless of race, background, or geographic locale. I am honored he took the time to share the message below:

Pettis has been a treasure to our community and a great unifier. He's worked hard to bridge the anemic divide of a Black church and a White church, which reaches back to slavery. We recently spoke about the theme of unity. Indeed, the church plays a huge role in bringing people together. Jesus spoke of unity in John 17: 20-23, 'My prayer is not for them alone. I also pray for those who will believe in me through their message, that all of them may be one, Father, just as you are in me and I am in you. May they also be in us so that the world may believe that you have sent me. I have given them the glory that you gave me, that they may be one as we are one — I in them and you in me— so that they may be brought to complete unity. Then the world will know that you sent me and have loved them even as you have loved me.'

Our mission is to be visible and unite all Christians. Only that will heal our communities and nation. Dr. Martin Luther King Jr. said it best: 'The early Christians rejoiced when they were deemed worthy to suffer for what they believed. In those days, the church was not merely a thermometer that recorded the ideas and principles or popular opinion; it was a thermostat that transformed the mores of society.'

These words have influenced Pettis profoundly. He desires to see the church's influence in society, improving the lives of people through good works. Dr. King's words have inspired me, as well. My late wife, Lois, and I started our church with ten people in our living room and now have 10,000 members locally at Oak Cliff Bible Fellowship — a 'church for all.'

Throughout the years, I've written 115 books, many having to do with 'oneness,' most notably, Oneness Embraced: Reconciliation, the Kingdom, and How We are Stronger Together. Pettis and I both agree that we can open the Bible, even after doing so our whole lives, and be surprised at the loving words that God pours out on His people. God loves us in all our variations, ethnicities, and walks of life. We can find "oneness" through Him — a 'Kingdom Agenda' that I consistently share with audiences worldwide.

When we work in concert, side by side, we achieve the societal impact Dr. King spoke of. I highly admire Pettis and his devotion to the great Commandments to love God and his neighbors.

A Pivotal Moment

Back in the '60s, Sam Cook famously sang, "It's been a long time, a long time coming, but I know a change gonna come." Despite progress, I am disheartened 50 years later to say that many African Americans are still burdened by the legacy of slavery, segregation, and discrimination.

While I have tried passionately to encourage unity, diversity, and equality in my lifetime, today, our country is still at a crossroads despite significant gains. Big events occur with greater frequency, like the White supremacist march in Charlottesville, Virginia; the tragedy at the Emanuel African Methodist Episcopal Church in Charleston, South Carolina; and African American men being disproportionately incarcerated and murdered by police. It also seems that opinions and views are no longer subtle; they are loud and overt, and weapons of mass destruction are now used to silence our differences. What is going on?

If we reflect and are honest, we will admit that the hallmarks of American democracy were largely reserved for White people by the intentional exclusion and oppression of people of color, and more specifically, African Americans. We are not hardwired to hate. Racism is a grown-up disease and while children are born blameless, they learn how to process the world through the examples around them. However, we do have a lingering history of racial discrimination, and that must be eradicated.

So, how will change come? Well, it took a tragic crime committed by a cop, Derrick Chauvin, with the Minneapolis police department for our country to wake up and demand justice for African Americans. I am talking about the death of George Floyd, who experienced a slow 8 ½ minute asphyxiation by Derrick Chauvin's knee, who murdered George Floyd for no apparent reason other than being Black.

I was so emotionally moved by the outrage shown by all my brothers and sisters, White, Black, Hispanic, Asian, Native American, and other ethnicities in our country and abroad. Never have we seen this powerful sign of unity through peaceful protest for an egregious act of violence against a human being. The murder, so horrifying and denounced by most Americans, was the catalyst for sweeping change that is now in the works.

These changes include addressing systemic racism and inequality, disbanding corrupt police departments and law-enforcement policies, exposing disciplinary records of cops who use excessive force, banning police chokeholds, oversight on all police shootings, and mandatory body cameras to capture police incidents.

Changes are not only occurring in law enforcement. The NFL is increasing social justice reforms through a ten-year, $250 million commitment to combat systemic racism and support the battle against the ongoing and historical injustices against African Americans. Further, how refreshing that the Redskins have finally agreed to change their name after many years of denial, and the Cleveland Indians seem to be taking steps towards changing their name.

Finally, 11 professional sports organizations in the greater Los Angeles area have united in pursuing change in communities of color. They launched "The ALLIANCE" — a comprehensive five-year commitment to drive investment and impact social justice through sports in Los Angeles.

Corporate America has also been nudged into action by eyeing brands that perpetuate stereotypes. In addition, a joint committee was established among the nation's largest businesses to fight for racial equality, education, healthcare, and equitable justice. This voluntary group of CEOs created a "Business Roundtable" that includes Walmart, General Motors, AT&T, and JPMorgan Chase, to name a few. This group is well positioned to address these issues, and its chief executive members lead companies with more than 15 million employees and $7.5 trillion in revenue.

Tens of millions of people protested in the summer of 2020 to pronounce that Black Lives Matter and made George Floyd the new face for racial tolerance and unity. This movement is different from the '60s; today, we are bridging the racial divide and unearthing common ground no matter the color of our skin. While George Floyd died a tragic death, his legacy will remain entrenched in our hearts and minds forever as a symbol of change that we desperately need in our country.

As I close this section, allow me to share my passion for unity and equal rights; it took a varied approach. First, I enjoy many very close friendships with people of all races. When it comes to my friendships and associates, people know me as a person who judges others by the content of their character rather than the color of their skin. Many have worked by my side on plenty of just causes. Together, we diligently endeavored to stop citizens from being judged by the color of their skin, and if qualified, earned them a seat at the table.

Second, I joined forces with leaders of all races to ensure that our educational institutions for Black and Brown children are equipped with the same benefits and opportunities as other schools.

Third, it became my personal quest in the '70s, '80s, and '90s to partner with Fortune 500 CEOs who represented all races, Black, Brown, White, Asian and Native American. We implemented initiatives to address inequalities in the workplace and created more opportunities for minority and women-owned businesses.

Finally, I supported politicians who represented "the least of these" and had plans for just causes and a belief system that we are better together. Many of the challenges I embraced and championed over the past 60 years have resulted in significant improvement in our workplaces, our schools, and in our voting booths — but problems persist.

I always felt a top-down approach combined with a grassroots movement for fairness and equality would yield the best results. So I targeted corporate America, the criminal justice system, the housing authority, educational institutions, and our politicians.

I subheaded my closing remarks in this chapter as being "pivotal," meaning "vitally important" or "critical," and there is no better word to describe the precipice from which our future hangs. This leads me full circle to the Dallas Citizens Council. This White organization originally controlled Dallas in the early '70s with a closed-door policy regarding minority inclusion. It has evolved over the years to include minorities. Today, this powerful organization with chief executives from the largest companies across the DFW area has metamorphosed into something I could not have envisioned decades ago. The first Black CEO, Kelvin Walker, took the title in 2019. This is monumental, and I believe we are witnessing more pivotal progress in Dallas with him at the helm.

Let us celebrate the gains by understanding that while we do not have a perfect union, we are making great progress and learning to respect ethnic, political, and religious differences. I hope that when my work on earth is done, I will leave behind a better world and a population of more connected souls. Ultimately, I believe humanity can and will evolve to fulfill the constitutional promise of equality and justice for all.

Isn't that how our time on earth is meant to be spent — bringing people together in peace and harmony?

Chapter Fourteen: From Texas to the White House

Whether you run for office or volunteer in your community, you are demonstrating servant leadership.
~ Pettis Norman

I still think of myself as a kid from a small town in Georgia, so as you can imagine, it was wonderful to become a full-fledged entrepreneur while working elbow-to-elbow in the national realm of politics. I supported the people I admired and believed God put several presidents, presidential candidates, and other public servants in my path to support them.

As I mentioned, I refused to hold office myself; instead, I offered to use whatever influence I had for the common good. I believe God had been equipping me to serve in more prominent roles as I forged personal, professional, and political alliances. I didn't hesitate to answer several calls to duty, some of which led to the nation's capital. These efforts resonated deeply. The notion that "we have a duty" is precious to me. We have a duty to break down barriers and fight for our rights. We have a duty to serve our communities.

In my case, I had a duty to use my God-given talents, support minority-owned businesses, encourage inclusion in my community, and answer the call when presidents and presidential candidates counted on me. These "calls to duty" surfaced, one after the other, and a few certainly stood out. Below are some intertwining stories that unfolded over the decades, involving my own adventures and the insights of some notable public servants.

A Call to Politics

In 1968, the Washington D. C. Riots erupted in response to the assassination of Dr. Martin Luther King Jr. It became a national crisis, and it was quite an honor to have been called upon by U.S. President Lyndon B. Johnson to speak to the rioters and students involved. African American men were already upset about the lack of jobs and opportunity. You could cut the tension with a knife, and it pushed the Black community over the edge.

In light of the unrest associated with Dr. King's death on April 4, 1968, I along with other professional athletes joined forces on May 8, 1968, to work in teams visiting schools in the lower income areas of D.C. Our mission was to use informal talks to stress individual civic and moral responsibility to help ease the tension that existed in some areas of Washington. This initiative was called "Project AthCom," (Athletes Communicating) and brought together top professional from different sports to address junior high and high school students in the city. Athcom was the brainchild of three members of Congress, one of whom was Congressman Graham Purcell of Texas.

On the White House lawn putting green with President Lyndon B. Johnson. Photo courtesy of the LBJ Library. Photo credit: Mike Geissinger

I spoke about my sharecropping upbringing with the rioters and the sting of discrimination I felt while growing up. I shared that I understood their pain, their frustration, and their anger. After telling my story and capturing their hearts and minds, I stated:

You don't punish one because of another. The way to combat unjust racism and prejudice is to follow the message Dr. Martin Luther King gave us. Unite as an army and have peaceful demonstrations as he showed us. Follow Dr. King's example, galvanize in your churches and neighborhoods, and take the fight for social injustice outward, peacefully, and without violence and bloodshed. We will make more progress with an organized approach.

I call this trip to Washington D.C. my entrance into politics. After our strategic planning session at the White House, I joined President LBJ on the south grounds putting green, along with Congressman Graham Purcell and other athletes. While continuing our informal discussion, we took time to hit a few putts. The President also showed off his putting talent and autographed the football I was holding.

After this exhilarating meeting, I was in a hurry to get back home to my family in Dallas and, of course, to my teammates. I remember how heartwarming it was to return to Dallas and be voted one of the most popular Dallas Cowboys by fans; I endeavored to live up to the honor.

The Honorable Graham Purcell was a United States Representative from the Texas 13th congressional district. May he rest in peace. He teased me about dodging the cameras in a thank you note he sent on behalf of President Johnson, shared below:

HOUSE OF REPRESENTATIVES
WASHINGTON, D. C.

GRAHAM PURCELL
13TH DISTRICT, TEXAS

August 1, 1968

Dear Pettis:

The President has asked me to send you the attached souvenir of your visit with him, along with his best personal regards.

Pettis, you are just too bashful! Follow the lead of we politicians and don't hide your light under a bushel when there's a photographer around.

Once again, thanks for your fine effort in communicating with the school children in the District of Columbia. If I can ever be of any personal assistance to you, just let me know.

Warmest regards,

GRAHAM PURCELL

Mr. Pettis Norman
Dallas Cowboys
6116 North Central Expressway
Dallas, Texas 76206

Prayer Breakfasts in Washington D.C.

It was even more gratifying when President LBJ later invited me to the National Prayer Breakfast. During the '70s and '80s, I considered it a high honor to be invited by President Nixon to his inauguration and a National Prayer Breakfast as well. Presidents Ford, Carter, and later President Clinton also invited me to National Prayer Breakfasts, all held on Thursday mornings.

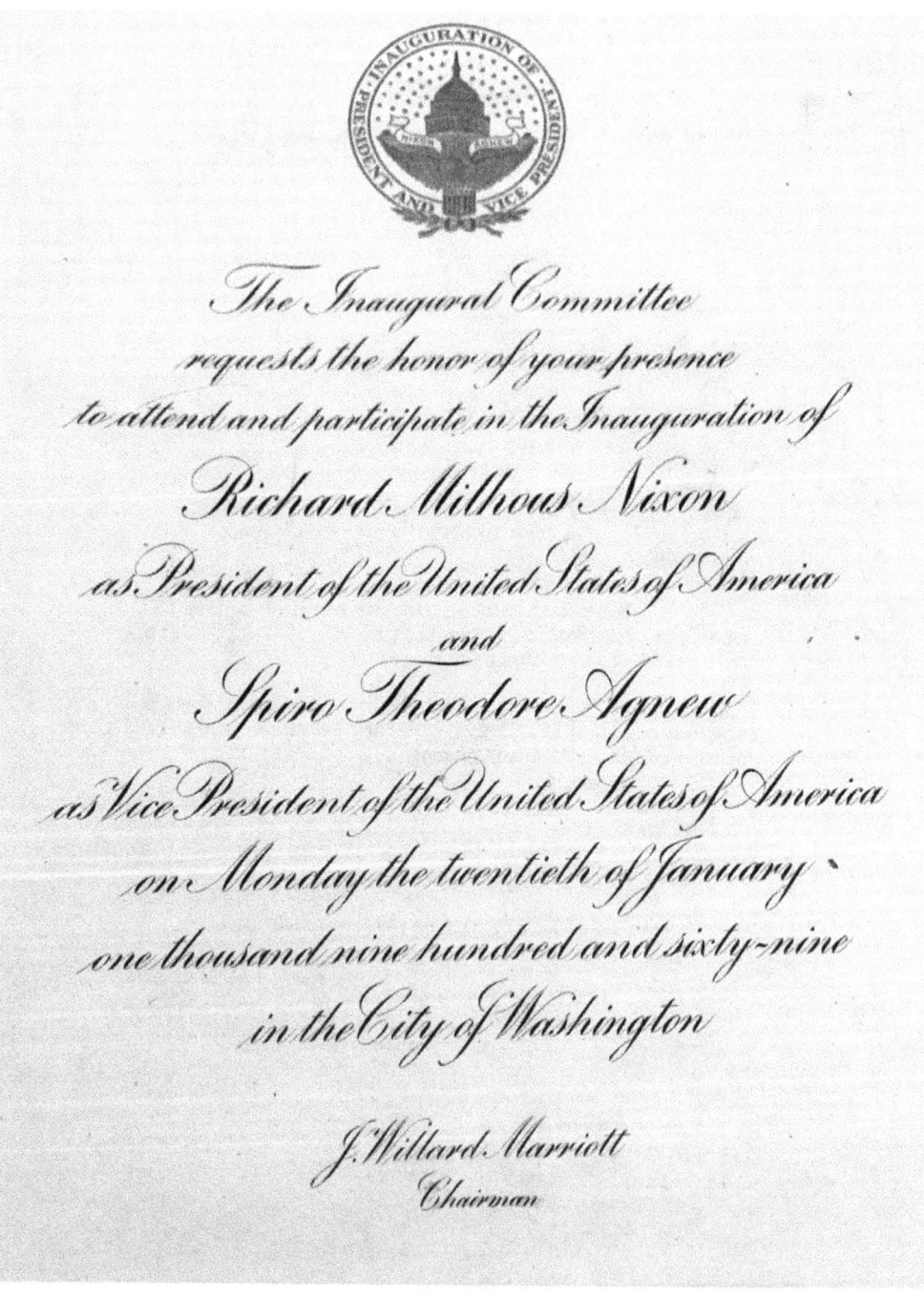

Pettis Shaking hands with President Lyndon B. Johnson
Photo courtesy of the LBJ Library. Photo credit: Frank Wolfe

In 1953, President Dwight D. Eisenhower and Billy Graham were among the first attendees. Today, these Congress-hosted events are more than "breakfast" and include luncheons and dinners. But the breakfasts are what impacted me, led by the President of the United States and a special guest each year whose name is unannounced until the morning of the event. Over the years, these keynote speakers have included Elizabeth Dole, Mother Theresa, Max Lucado, Bono, Tony Blair, and more.

I cannot rightly express how much it meant to witness our most powerful national leaders bow their heads in reverence. Attendees prayed for every influential man and woman in the room and our country and allies. An otherwise politically divided country became united at these breakfasts. It gave me hope that our elected officials would consider the common good for all in every piece of legislation. My personal prayer was that they would help bind our wounds, correct our wrongs, and fill me with the passion to address the simmering challenges awaiting me back in Texas.

Air Force One

Monetary support of candidates is crucial, but campaigns are also people-oriented. Human beings who volunteer their time, energy, and sweat equity fuel grassroots movements. I worked on behalf of Jimmy Carter during his presidential campaign in 1976; this put me in close proximity with other volunteers who supported his successful candidacy, including the remarkable Congresswoman Barbara Jordan.

I stepped up as Jimmy Carter's Co-Chairman of "Blacks for Victory," as well as Chairman of the Pro Athletes for Dallas and Texas. I did so with a deep belief that Jimmy Carter could further pave the road to equality. He had always opposed racial segregation and supported the civil rights movement. I was also very impressed with his qualifications as the governor of my home state of Georgia. After the national nightmares of Vietnam and Watergate, it was time to elect a leader who was refreshingly honest and untouched by scandal.

What pride I felt when Jimmy Carter made a two-day trip to Dallas on June 23, 1978, as the 39th president of the United States. He attended a luncheon with Senator Lloyd Bentsen, Representative Jim Wright, and Fort Worth Mayor Hugh Parmer, among many others, and observed Army tanks in training exercises at Fort Hood the following day. I recently revisited these images in the archives of the *Dallas Morning News*. It was another walk down memory lane, knowing President Jimmy Carter turned 97 years old during the writing of this book.

In 1979, I was honored with a Certificate of Merit from the Texas Legislative Black Caucus. It encouraged me to continue my support of President Carter, and I served in the same campaign roles again in 1980. I never, ever expected anything but a quiet "thank you" for these volunteer efforts, but sometimes with service comes a few special and surprising intangible rewards.

One such reward literally lifted me off the ground! I was invited to fly aboard Air Force One during the final push of President Carter's 1980 campaign. The below pictures show us strategizing on November 1, 1980, three days before the election. I, along with my good friend and teammate Jethro Pugh, was eager to help Jimmy Carter during his campaign visits to several cities throughout Texas. Between football and business ventures, I was no stranger to air travel, but there is something quite extraordinary about being a passenger in the "flying Oval Office."

I felt immersed in pride and history, for this particular plane had flown renowned leaders, foreign dignitaries, and previously transported Presidents Richard Nixon and Gerald Ford. During President Ford's term, it had been fitted with defense systems due to the early threats of terrorism, so I was aboard an extremely secure Boeing 707. It was a comfortable and memorable flight.

I was happy to receive a beautifully framed flight certificate issued by the Carter administration that proudly hangs in my office today as a memento of those long-ago adventures. This particular Air Force One would later serve Ronald Reagan, George H. W. Bush, Bill Clinton, and George W. Bush before it was retired and displayed at the Reagan Library in California. Few civilians have had the experience flying aboard this iconic plane, and I treasure the memory.

FLIGHT CERTIFICATE

This is to certify that

Pettis Norman

has flown in Air Force One as a guest of Jimmy Carter, President of the United States of America.

November 1, 1980

Presidential Pilot

With President Carter and Jethro Pugh. Photo courtesy of the Jimmy Carter Presidential Library

Aboard Air Force One. Photo courtesy of the Jimmy Carter Presidential Library

Ron Kirk

I've mentioned Ron Kirk several times in this book. He's the former U.S. Trade Representative for the Obama Administration and a former Mayor of Dallas. To me, however, he is a good friend and the embodiment of his parents' dreams. His mother and father navigated the battle for civil rights and taught him that his life was not defined by someone else's perception of what a Black man could achieve. Ron also understood the importance of civic engagement and was determined not to sit on the sidelines after watching his parents fight against the Poll Tax and Literary Tax to get the right to vote.

Ron has been a good steward of these lessons — he became a successful lawyer and partner, held multiple political and legislative positions in Texas, worked for our 44th President, and is a wonderful husband, father, and champion of many causes.

When Ron put his name in the ring for Mayor, I knew he was our guy. He was the anointed candidate of the Dallas establishment, could bridge the racial divide and change the culture at City Hall. He did not just make history as the first Black Mayor; he made a massive difference in our city. It was a pleasure supporting his bid for Mayor, and I was so proud when he was tapped for the U.S. Trade position in the Obama Administration. Below he shares his remarkable journey through life and politics.

Contributed by Ron Kirk

Pettis Norman was a mentor, role model and friend because he was relevant to me in all aspects of my life. One of the things I most admire about Pettis is that he is a father who raised three girls. I loved the way they loved him and the support he gave to his daughters. If you wanted to know how to be a good father, Pettis Norman was the kind of man you looked up to. If you wanted to know how to be a good entrepreneur, Pettis Norman was one of those people you talk to. If you wanted to help bridge Dallas' racial divide and get the city to move together, Pettis Norman was one of those people you had to talk to. If you were a Dallas Cowboy fan, Pettis was our guy. Yes, Bob Hayes was great and some of the others were great too, but Pettis was one of the Black Cowboys who stayed here, stayed involved in the community, was visible, approachable, and you could touch him. I love the fact that he never failed to remind people he came from a small HBCU, which was refreshing. Any box I would want to check about the kind of man I'd like to be, Pettis checks that box for me. He just has that presence, which is apparent in his book. What a wonderful autobiography.

For the benefit of educating other aspiring Black politicians, youths, and dreamers, I refer to myself as the 'Fifth First Black Mayor of Dallas.' This is because I'm one of five Black Mayors who are Texans. Maynard Jackson, former Mayor of Atlanta, was born in Dallas; Emanuel Cleaver, former Mayor of Kansas City, was born in Waxahachie; Willie Brown, former Mayor of San Francisco, was born in Mineola; and Tom Bradley, former Mayor of Los Angeles, was born in Calvert. So, I'm not the first, and it could have been any individual, including Pettis, who was one of the first people I talked to before running for office.

Being Mayor was not in my plan but in my heart. When Steve Bartlett stepped down, Ann Richards encouraged me to run. Pettis called a meeting to lay out the blueprint for our next Mayor — first, he asked Zan Holmes, and then all eyes turned to Pettis and then to me. I had so much respect for Pettis that I would not have run if I did not have his support. I was also encouraged by Ann Richards, who challenged me not to sit on the sidelines, but fulfill my duty to service, including the promise I made to my parents.

Pettis didn't let anyone define his dreams either. He wasn't content to wear the crown of the Dallas Cowboys and be silent on community and civic issues. It was Pettis Norman and Zan Holmes who said, 'That ain't enough.' They would not allow themselves to be put in the box as athletes, businessmen, or African Americans.

We always went to Pettis with the city's challenges, and he always answered the call, even as he was launching his own businesses. I am honored to be included in this book because it discusses in detail how Pettis Norman and others worked closely with Mayor Annette Strauss in the late '80s. She wanted to ensure that our city fully represented opportunities for minorities. Pettis Norman and Tom Dunning shined a light on prominent law firms that did not have Black partners or an appropriate number of Black associates. While it was not the singular reason I became a partner, I would be foolish not to realize that their advocacy and honesty cracked that door open for me.

I know Pettis was involved in every one of the initiatives that brought people together and leveled the playing field for women and minorities, with an initiative he founded and Co-Chaired, The Dallas Together Forum. I was drawn to Pettis, the 'go-to guy,' because there was such a huge chasm between those who lived in South Dallas and the more affluent areas in North Dallas. Pettis had credibility and could bridge the gap with activists in the African American community and speak honestly and non-threateningly to White business leaders. He always said we must do more than complain; he was a godsend to our community and me.

Gubernatorial Advisor

I received another honor from the State of Texas, this time from Rodney Ellis, a proud native Houstonian with a remarkable resume of service in the Houston City Council, Texas Senate, and now as a Harris County Commissioner, Precinct 1. There's an interesting backstory attached.

In 1999, Senator Ellis was named President Pro Tempore of the Texas Senate while George W. Bush was Governor and Rick Perry was Lieutenant Governor. It turned out that this was more than a ceremonial position, largely because George Bush was campaigning for the presidency and Rick Perry was traveling. Senator Ellis' duty as President Pro Tem was to preside in their absence.

During his time spent as acting Governor, Rodney tapped me as a Special Gubernatorial Advisor. What exactly do gubernatorial advisors do? I asked Rodney to weigh in below regarding his notable background and this special appointment.

THE STATE OF TEXAS

to all to whom these presents shall come, Greetings: Know ye, that

Pettis Norman

is hereby commissioned

Special Gubernatorial Advisor

under the laws of the State of Texas with all rights, privileges, and emoluments appertaining to said office. In testimony whereof, I have signed my name and caused the Seal of the State of Texas to be affixed at the City of Austin, this, the 8th day of April A.D., 2000.

Rodney Ellis
GOVERNOR OF TEXAS
APRIL 8, 2000

Contributed by Commissioner Rodney Ellis

When Pettis commends me for all I've done for our state and country, I tell him, 'Well, I had good teachers, including you, Pettis.'

During my time in the Texas Legislature, I was able to serve as acting Governor in 2000. Although the position was 'ceremonial,' I did not take it lightly, and I made sure to gather the best and brightest in Texas to serve as my advisors. Naturally, this included Pettis.

I tapped Pettis because of his unique experience, successfully transitioning from professional sports to the corporate world, as well as our shared commitment to fighting for equality. Through his leadership with the Dallas Together Forum, he brought powerful CEOs and business people together to open opportunities for communities of color. His record of leadership in the African American community in Dallas was unparalleled.

Throughout his life, Pettis demonstrated servant-leadership and was able to bring people together to work on pressing challenges. While serving on Jesse Jackson's board together, Pettis and I built our relationship working in trenches in the fight for civil rights. Pettis has a natural ability to build coalitions. Not many people in Dallas could pull a diverse group of people together to create a more inclusive city.

Our community needs more examples of people like Pettis, not just experiencing success as he did in the NFL and the business world, but living lives with purpose and a strong commitment to using their success to create change. Pettis' story is an important example about how civic engagement and responsibility can transcend the public sector and how important it is to be able to bring different people together to solve complex problems.

We've worked together on a number of political goals and just causes over the years, and I'm glad that he's sharing his experiences through this book. Back in the day, Pettis was 'Mr. Dallas,' and even today, he remains an important bridge builder. Pettis has had a hell of a ride.

I want to thank Commissioner Ellis for his vote of confidence in me. As I reflect on his career, Commissioner Ellis has used his power to make a difference and earned widespread praise as a leader on economic development, education, civil rights, and criminal justice reform. He was (and is) passionate about leveling the playing field for women and minorities. Amazingly, he also passed more than 700 pieces of legislation during his 26-year tenure in Congress. Well done, my friend; I am proud of your accomplishments.

As a sharecropper's son from a small town in Georgia, I would never have believed that I would interact with four presidents in my lifetime, as well as many elected officials who became my friends. It's a testimony of how God can take anyone and use them for a higher purpose.

Back Home in the Big "D"

By the time I retired from the NFL, I had already made plans to move home to Dallas. The city has so many special qualities — the skyline, the sprawling miles of infrastructure, and the people. In my mind, it was a city of promise, filled with a great cross-section of races, religions, and viewpoints. This is where I wanted to re-plant my family.

Margaret was happy to be home. Our three girls, Sharneen, then nine, Sedonna, age six, and Shandra, age three, were happy to reunite with their friends. We enrolled them in school and picked up where we left off, settling into the southern sector of "Big D."

Upon my arrival in Dallas, I became a sports agent — a good fit due to my long exposure to the NFL and multiple negotiations with teams. Eventually, I built and managed 200 apartment units and kept my finger in real estate as well, especially single-family housing. As a minority entrepreneur, I had a lot to prove. I wanted every endeavor to be a personal and professional example of excellence in Dallas. These enterprises added to the job market and helped stimulate the economy. The experience helped hone me into a tried-and-tested businessman. The possibilities were endless.

After some research, I decided to become a Burger King franchisee and bought my first franchise from Burger King Corporate in 1975 — a failing restaurant in a low-income neighborhood. It was about to shut down and had to be completely renovated. The extensive remodel lasted three months. We put up mirrors and themed it in Dallas Cowboys décor, including a big star with a helmet in it. It seemed like a brand new building once we completed the project, and my employees loved it.

These were the same employees who worked in the restaurant before I bought it. The majority were part-time youths from the community who attended high school in addition to seven or eight full-time employees. I decided to keep these employees and introduce them to a new way of doing business, which meant I was thoroughly "hands-on" and truly mastered the fine art of managing people. I oversaw their retraining — not training, but retraining.

This location was obviously failing for many reasons, including poor customer service and poor food quality. When you take on a store that is underperforming, you have to change the culture of the store itself. Therefore, I emphasized a "customer first" philosophy and led by example. My advertising motto was, "To win a customer, you have to move smart and fast," but internally, we focused on the "three H's" — (1) "Hello!" (2) "How are you?" and (3) "How may I help you?"

Along with greeting customers with a smile, these three simple little phrases made all the difference and helped us deliver a great experience each time someone set foot in our establishment. In other words: be nice and serve good food.

Previous Burger King customers were not used to this level of courtesy. I remember saying, "Hello! How are you? How may I help you?" and the customer looked behind him as if I was speaking to someone else. But soon, the community discovered that this Burger King restaurant was the place to go. Customers could count on a quick, accurate order and a pleasant staff. Of course, good food too.

Burger King Corporate hosted competitions for the fastest counter and cashier service and also drive-through service. We won three years in a row and turned that restaurant around from $300,000 in revenue to an enterprise that eventually generated $1.2 million annually within a short timeframe. The investment paid for itself, and I knew I was onto something quite lucrative.

I purchased other Burger King restaurants and bought the land as well. I recall one location was built from the ground up and themed in traditional Burger King branding. It looked like most of the franchises across the nation.

I personally trained my staff with the three "H's" there and at another restaurant, which required refurbishing and was decorated in the Dallas Cowboy's theme, much like the first restaurant. Overall, we employed 24 to 32 part-time and full-time workers per location, including day and night shifts and management personnel.

Soon each restaurant ran like a well-oiled machine. Overall, it cost me around $650,000 and was a risky venture by any standard. But I had faith that the investment would pay off and wasn't disappointed. Dollar for dollar, my franchise investments did just as well as or better than my other investments and yielded a nice return.

I think the key was well-trained supervisors who watched closely and really focused on motivating our employees to do their best. It was all about one-on-one connections. We had training manuals as well, for we employed a lot of students who came and went, and the training materials provided consistency as we hired new staff. My goal was to equip our employees with the skills to do well in my business, take those same skills, and apply them to their lives and future employment. I did not want just employees; I invested in people.

Many still remember the Christmas parties we had every year at a hotel. Even today, I have former employees tell me it felt like they were part of a family — the Burger King family. It truly was a family affair, for occasionally Margaret worked at the restaurants, as did all three of my daughters.

You might wonder why I include my Burger King franchises in a chapter on politics. Well, Jesse Jackson, too, helped with Burger King Corporate initiatives while becoming a presidential contender. Jesse is such an iconic activist for civil rights and political inclusion. He worked closely with Dr. Martin Luther King Jr., held a prominent role with the Southern Christian Leadership Conference, and did excellent work with Operation Breadbasket, Operation PUSH, the Rainbow PUSH Coalition, and the Wall Street Project. Our paths merged again when an opportunity opened with Burger King Corporate.

I was elected president of the Burger King Minority Franchisee Association at a time when only 60 Blacks and Hispanics were operators, representing 140 of the 3,500 restaurants in the chain. Herman Cain had signed on as the Philadelphia Regional Manager in 1983, just as Burger King was ramping up its Affirmative Action program. May Herman rest in peace. At the corporate headquarters in Miami, I was particularly proud when Burger King University announced it was signing a joint trade covenant with Operation PUSH, focused on creating 20,000 new jobs for Blacks, resulting in $140 million in salaries.

With my dear friend, Jesse Jackson

Jesse Jackson was instrumental in making that happen. The goal was to make 15% of its franchises available to Blacks since Blacks represented 15% of the company's business. The day after the announcement, I stood with Jesse Jackson and Herman Cain at the PUSH Headquarters in Chicago as Burger King President J. Jeffrey Campbell signed this "win-win" deal.

Jeff kindly weighs in below about our work through PUSH and some behind-the-scenes recollection of one very famous Burger King campaign.

Contributed by Jeff Campbell

My memories of Pettis extend around Jesse Jackson and Operation PUSH, starting in the early 1980s. I was the brand new President of Burger King, and our minority franchisees had requested that Reverend Jackson and Operation PUSH represent them to address some frustrations.

I was summoned to Burger King's parent company, Pillsbury, at the headquarters in Minneapolis. The senior executive room was on the 40th floor and had a circle of grammar school desks. We sat at those desks in our suits! It was comical, and I'm not really sure to this day why Pillsbury chose this seating method. Maybe it was meant to keep everyone humble and focused on the task at hand. The task at that moment was to address the concerns of the minority franchisees.

I was sitting next to Bill Spoor, Chairman and CEO of Pillsbury. 'Now, about this Jesse Jackson situation,' he said. 'You are going to give this Operation PUSH collaboration your best college try, and the board will support you.' In other words, they were leaving it up to me, the new guy, to find a resolution.

Pettis Norman was one of a handful of minority franchisee representatives who worked for six months to identify and enable a good outcome. Pettis was the person I remember most for helping keep things on track and always being the guy who minimized tension, a class act. He was great friends with Jesse Jackson and devoted himself to Burger King as well. I'm very grateful for that in retrospect.

The premise was that the Reverend Jackson was seeking procurement dollars to invest in minority franchise ownership. He asked, 'How much of your business do you think African American consumers bring in? You tell me. And then tell me what procurements dollars derive from that.' I went in expecting combat and what I got was a reasonable proposition. We worked out a deal throughout the six months, and Pettis was an honest broker for both sides.

There were some funny moments during our negotiations. The first meeting took place at the University of Chicago Hyde Park. Pettis and the other minority franchisees weren't present. Reverend Jackson came in with two or three guys, and I had my guys. 'Mr. Campbell, would you object if I open the meeting with a prayer?' said the Reverend Jackson. The prayer felt somewhat like, 'Dear God, please open the eyes of these men.' That set the tone for the second meeting in the basement of PUSH headquarters.

The regional manager of the D.C. Burger King market, Herman Cain, suggested prior to the meeting, 'What if I open this meeting with a prayer?' I thought that was a great idea.

Pettis was there when I announced, "Reverend Jackson, you did us the honor in the first meeting by opening with a prayer. To return the honor, Herman would like to open this meeting with a prayer." Everyone accepted, we prayed, and then we got down to business.

When I think back to that meeting, I never would have believed I'd be in a room with two future presidential contenders — Jesse Jackson and Herman Cain, both on the opposite ends of the political spectrum. That's what I like most about Pettis. He gets along with everyone regardless of politics. He was a great mediator, especially when things got contentious, and I appreciated that, especially because I was up to my neck in a very famous Burger King marketing campaign.

You might remember the 'Battle of the Burgers.' Burger King took on Wendys and McDonalds, claiming our burgers were bigger and better, and broiling beats frying. The media just loved it. Many did their own independent taste tests, and Burger King's flame-broiled burger won the lion's share of acclaim. Even the chef from the Waldorf Astoria in New York tested our burgers and claimed that ours tasted better. Of course, I thought we'd be sued, and we were. We won, and it generated great publicity — what a boost for Burger King franchisees, including Pettis!

Guess who came up with the 'Battle of the Burgers' campaign? The creative director for our ad agency was none other than James Patterson, today an extremely famous author. In those days, he got up at five in the morning and wrote, then went to work. He's the same guy today as he was back then. I later invited him to speak with a class at San Diego State University, where I taught. It was such a treat for the students.

I invited Herman Cain to speak at San Diego State as well. He wasn't able to, and then we lost him to COVID during the summer of 2020. The night before he passed, I emailed him well wishes. The next morning, he was gone. The memories, however, remain. My wife and I once held a holiday party in Miami that included pranks and wrapped gifts. Herman opened a tape recording of a lip-synching song and performed with choreography. His team won. Guests still talk about that fun evening.

I have great memories of Jesse Jackson too. Our brief episodes of locking horns probably forged our relationship as well. He never lied, he never took advantage, and the guy I spent six months with became a friend.

I was in Chicago on business when Jesse invited me to the PUSH Ball. Since I was in town by myself, I walked to the hotel ballroom. As I stood at the entrance, left of the stage, Jesse came out of the crowd. 'Jeff, Jeff!' he exclaimed and dragged me up on stage to meet the piano player, who happened to be the great jazz composer and radio personality, Ramsey Lewis. 'Ramsey, Ramsey!' he said, 'Meet Jeff Campbell!'

Then Jesse escorted me into the crowd. 'Bill, Bill!' he said and introduced me to Bill Cosby. I grabbed *myself a bottle of beer, and the only other white guy in the room walked my way. It was Phil Donahue. What a great night. The whole experience was positive.*

I want to stress that going on 40 years, Pettis has always remained the level-headed friend to all, the one guy in the room who can calm a storm. He's an example of 'cooler heads prevail' and is such a special person. I'm honored that he contacted me to give insights into our Burger King days. In my opinion, the reason his restaurants performed so well was because was of Pettis' devotion, business sense, and people skills. What a wonderful man, and I'm so glad we share so many memories in common.

I was happy to support the development arm of Operation PUSH through the National PUSH Chapter and was honored to receive the Par Excellence Award from Operation PUSH in 1983. By then, Jesse had announced his candidacy for President of the United States. I recall Jesse's many trips to Dallas, including our strategic "think tank" sessions. When he wasn't in town, I mailed him various Dallas newspaper articles covering his and Tony Bonilla's efforts to organize Black and Hispanic voters through PUSH and LULAC (the League of United Latin American Citizens) leading up to the 1984 elections.

Jesse recognized the Black church as a voting block. The goal was to raise a strong call to action and usher minorities into the voting booth. Those who represented us needed to walk in our shoes. Just as Dr. King merged theology and social justice, so did Jesse to impact our nation's economic, educational, and social policies.

I am most proud of being by Jesse's side during his 1984 and 1988 presidential campaigns. He made history by winning 16 state contests and millions of votes, making him the first viable African-American candidate for president. When the opportunity came to serve as Chairman of the Texas Delegation for Jesse Jackson during his campaign for president in 1984, I quickly stepped up. I fully believed that Jesse, rather than Geraldine Ferraro, would have been tapped as Walter Mondale's running mate on the ticket if Jesse hadn't already announced. I still feel that would have been a winning ticket.

In 1988, I worked with Representative Mickey Leland, chair of the Texas Jackson campaign. Jesse ran against Massachusetts Governor Michael Dukakis, who chose Texas Senator Lloyd Bentsen as his running mate. I vividly recall standing with John Wiley Price and State Representative Al Edwards of Houston at the Democratic National Convention. The Texas delegation gave Jesse 71 Texas ballots; Governor Dukakis received 135. We vowed that the Democratic leadership would not automatically get the traditional support from Black voters unless minorities were represented fairly in a Dukakis administration.

I remember that Mickey Leland indicated that Dukakis was better for minorities than anything the Republicans could offer. Representative Leland was a native Texan and true soldier in the war against poverty and homelessness — an advocate for healthcare rights as a U.S. Congressman from the 18th District of Texas. He was someone I admired, and when he spoke, I listened.

We lost him a year after the convention in a devastating 1989 plane crash during a mission trip to Ethiopia, yet his name and legacy live on. A federal building in Downtown Houston is named after him, as well as the Mickey Leland International Terminal at George Bush

Intercontinental Airport in Houston and the Barbara Jordan-Mickey Leland School of Public Affairs at Texas Southern University. His legislative work is archived at the TSU Institute of Museum and Library Services. I am proud that I knew this iconic leader and that we worked together on behalf of Jesse Jackson.

Serving alongside Jesse changed my life and the direction of our country. He lent his support to local political issues in Dallas, which was a blessing to the city and the State of Texas. His name recognition is the byproduct of a relentless drive on behalf of the "least of these," but his unwavering friendship is what touched my heart. We had another wonderful visit with Jesse when he flew to Dallas and officiated for Ivette and me at our wedding in 1995 and attended our reception as well.

What a tremendous impact he had on the diversification of corporate America while gaining the respect of both Republican and Democratic lawmakers. Recalling these milestone moments makes me realize how much of a presence he has been in my life and the life of others. Jesse is a notable humanitarian who has always put the country first.

A Cheerful Giver

My involvement with Burger King brought many opportunities to give back to the community. I believe that philanthropy, both personal and corporate, should be based on 2 Corinthians 9:6-8, which says, "Remember this: Whoever sows sparingly will also reap sparingly, and whoever sows generously will also reap generously. Each of you should give what you have decided in your heart to give, not reluctantly or under compulsion, for God loves a cheerful giver."

Burger King was, indeed, a cheerful giver and donated $10,000 to the Lou Rawls Parade of Stars Telethon to benefit the United Negro College Fund (UNCF), which I co-hosted for many years. I really admired Lou Rawls. "This is something I can embrace wholeheartedly," he explained. "It's a way of using — instead of losing — the potential of bright young minds. Through UNCF, we're helping to educate the future doctors and scientists who may someday cure the major diseases. And that means we're getting closer to the root solutions of these problems."

This worthy event was held from noon until midnight and was a blessing to Burger King. Our logo was displayed, our sponsorship was announced hourly, and our brand was covered in the newspapers, on television, and on radio. But more importantly, 42 private Historically Black Colleges and Universities and some 50 thousand students were supported by the telethon.

My wife, Ivette, will tell you that I find it difficult to take a compliment, let alone mention honors bestowed upon me by others. My parents' motto of "Do unto others as you would have them do unto you" is just hardwired into my personal consciousness. We should do our utmost for our family, friends, neighbors, community, nation, and world, not for personal acclaim but because God gave us the ability to "do good." So when Ivette mentioned that I should include my various honors, I hesitated. In fact, throughout this book, I hesitated many times before adding a compliment or various recognitions. After all, servant leadership is about giving back and shining a light on others.

Ivette, however, reminded me that every volunteer position exposed me to many viewpoints, put me in touch with extraordinary thought leaders, and provided innumerable opportunities to make a difference. Plus, the names of these organizations should be acknowledged. I had to agree, and so what follows is a list of worthy organizations I was affiliated with at that time.

I served on the board of directors of the City of Dallas Parks and Recreation Department, the Oak Cliff Chamber of Commerce Dallas, the Black Chamber of Commerce, Park South YMCA, Dallas County Democratic Forum, Dallas Commission on Children and Youth, Dallas Urban League, Martin Luther King Center, and was president of the Concerned Voters Council. I was also chairman of the African American Advisory Committee and president of the Minority Franchise Association. I served on the board of directors for Johnson C. Smith University, Operation PUSH, and the PUSH International Trade Bureau. Last but not least, I was a recipient of the Dallas Bar Association's Liberty Bell Award and the Dallas Jaycees Distinguished Service Award as Dallas' Outstanding Young Man.

Chapter Fifteen: Eye on Education

It does take a village. Not just the Black or the White or Hispanic villagers, but the entire village, every one of us.
~ Pettis Norman

In 2020, the school districts of New York City, Los Angeles, Chicago, Clark County in Nevada, and Miami-Dade and Broward in Florida were the top six in the United States. In comparison, Dallas Independent School District ranked sixteenth in the nation and is often under the microscope along with other "mega" districts in Texas. It was the second largest in the Lone Star state, with nearly 158,000 students, while Houston ISD topped the list at over 216,000.

It just so happened that I wrote this chapter during the devastating coronavirus outbreak in 2020, and marveled at the adaptability of DISD during "stay at home" orders from the government. Schools all over the United States have implemented distance-learning innovations while still providing "drive by" breakfasts and lunches for students who would not otherwise have these vital meals. I would never have imagined that we'd face such a crisis, and it's still not clear how it will transform us as a nation.

The enforced downtime has given me spare moments to reflect on the history of DISD — where we were and how far we've come. It takes me back to the 1970s when White parents began dis-enrolling their children from Dallas Independent School District and moving elsewhere, better known as "White flight." White flight wasn't unique to Dallas — cities all across the nation navigated this phenomenon as desegregation became a reality. I recall that the schools of my youth in the Mecklenburg County School District grappled for years with mandated court orders. Many other school districts, including those in Boston, experienced chaos, marches, and discontent.

As for Dallas, a 1977 article in *D Magazine* titled, "Is White Flight Ruining the Dallas Schools" cited a public opinion poll

Photo Credit: Jesse Nogales Photography

by Louis, Bowles, and Grove, Inc. It reported a 44% favorable rating of DISD overall, with a matching 44% unfavorable. Busing, desegregation, and racial conflicts were cited as major problems, and desegregation certainly led to increased private school enrollment. My hope was that this trend would reverse once the school desegregation battle was settled in 1984. But what actually happened? Well, from 1968-1978, DISD's performance with Superintendent Nolan Estes at the helm saw some of the greatest innovations emulated by districts across the country. This included world-class magnet school programs, the Skyline High School Career Center, and the DISD learning centers mandated by court order (as were the magnet schools). Many Whites returned to the district because of these innovations. Superintendent Linus Wright took the reins from 1978 to 1987 to the dismay of some and cheers from others; it was a decade of transition.

In 1988 when Marvin Edwards became Superintendent (Dallas ISD's first Black Superintendent), Rene Martinez, Tom Dunning, and I formed the Committee for Racial Healing and Understanding, similar to Mayor Annette Strauss' Dallas Together initiative but not a replica. The Committee for Racial Healing and Understanding sought to find ways to resolve the political and racial problems within the school district that Superintendent Edwards faced until 1993 when Chad Woolery stepped into the superintendent role through 1996.

Honestly, tensions weren't solely due to desegregation. Lackluster performance in DISD affected everyone, and Black parents joined White parents in pulling their children out of public schools. I was incensed that I had to send my daughters to private schools to ensure they received a decent education. Other Black parents who could afford private education often did the same. I recall the statistics were a roller coaster with the Arts Magnet receiving a Blue Ribbon designation, North Dallas schools doing well, and other schools (mainly in the southern sector of the district) at the bottom of the state achievement ladder.

This leads to a second point, specifically, that desegregated but underperforming schools had a negative trickle-down effect on employability. If memory serves me correctly, the unemployment rate for Black teens in Dallas was around 50%. Our youth were simply not equipped to hold jobs. I wanted more for my children and agonized over the students who were stuck in the system. So many were doomed to failure unless DISD could turn it around.

This became my focus, although some felt I had no right to be involved in public education decisions because my children were in private schools. Some questioned my qualifications to weigh in at all, but that did not dissuade me.

My good friend Tom Dunning was (and is) very involved in public education and well aware of the issues that continued to plague DISD during this period. His comments put it into context:

> *Pettis is a very effective leader because he is a good listener and an excellent communicator. When he speaks, people listen. Why? Because he speaks slowly, sincerely, and clearly explains his point of view, which encourages those in the room to agree with him. He's one of a kind and has never hesitated to state who he is and what he believes. While playing for the Dallas Cowboys, he started speaking out*

on public education. The press often referred to him as an activist rather than a civic leader, but this never stopped him. He has continued to address issues that are important to African Americans and all Dallas residents.

I consider Tom a subject-matter expert on the topic and appreciate his insights. He is absolutely correct to note that economic opportunities are affected by educational opportunities. Now that minority students could attend desegregated schools, shouldn't those schools offer the best possible education? I certainly thought so.

I met my good friend Pete Schenkel when he was President of Schepps Dairy. He recently reflected on those days of upheaval and uncertainty in DISD and I value his insights.

I think we have a much better school district because people like Pettis got involved and made tough decisions. He attended meetings and spoke up at times when I'd say 90% of people kept their mouths shut. He spoke up for the right causes and opened many doors, not by rebelling, but with a demeanor accepted by the White, Black, and Brown communities. The way he went about it was well-received, right on target, and done for the betterment of education. He carried that same passion into city politics here in Dallas.

Pete, too, was a proponent of change and an advocate for better education. His leadership in education and in our community was always well respected.

I also developed great friendships with two renowned Black educators, Dr. Yvonne Ewell and Shirley Ison-Newsome, who ultimately changed the Dallas Independent School District for the better. Thanks to them and other passionate public servants and volunteers, DISD found its bearings over time amidst a revolving door of Superintendents.

The constant shifts in leadership weighed heavily on the district. Yvonne Gonzalez served from January to September 1997; James H. Hughey served from 1997 to 1999; Superintendent Waldemar "Bill" Rojas served from 1999 to 2000; Interim Robert Payton served from July to December 2000; Superintendent Mike Moses served from 2001 to 2004; Interim Larry Groppel served from 2004 to 2005; Superintendent Michael Hinojosa served from 2005 to 2011; Alan King served from 2011 to 2012; Superintendent Mike Miles served from 2012 to 2015; and finally, Dr. Hinojosa came back on board in 2015.

I have my own thoughts as to why we had this revolving door of superintendents. At the top of my mind, the question is, while these past superintendents were educators, were they leaders? Did they have the political finesse to engage the board, rally the community, build consensus, and form partnerships to succeed in the position?

Now in fairness, Dallas is not the only big city with superintendent challenges. It's obviously a very difficult job with typically a short life cycle. Most successful superintendents are those who have a strong educational background, gain the respect of the board and the community early on, and mandate "student-first" innovative solutions to prepare our youth for success.

I must say that I am pleased with our current superintendent, Michael Hinojosa, who has brought stability and leadership to our school district and community.

Allow me to shine a spotlight on two outstanding educators who have fought passionately for our children.

Dr. Yvonne Ewell

We lost my good friend, Dr. Ewell, in 1998 (may God rest her soul). I would have loved to include her voice in this book, for she was a guiding light on the school board after serving as teacher, principal and associate superintendent in DISD. She had a stellar record with the schools she taught in, served as principal (Arlington Park Elementary), and was supervisor of principals (East Oak Cliff Sub-District.) This articulate, thoughtful academic forged relationships in the African American, Anglo, and Hispanic communities, and in 1978 was named an associate superintendent of the Dallas Independent School District.

In 1981, when the East Oak Cliff section of DISD dissolved, she became the court-appointed school desegregation monitor for DISD. Her oversight lasted until 1984, and it is gratifying that I was able to work alongside her.

Yvonne did a lot of good for our community and was outspoken when it came to the welfare of students. There is a backstory — U.S. District Judge Barefoot Sanders approved a 35% cutback in DISD's busing program at a time when 100 out of 178 schools were predominantly filled with minority students. This was more than troubling; Judge Sanders had developed a desegregation plan that was implemented in response to Judge Justice's ruling about a year before the bus cutback.

I can attest that Yvonne was incensed at the plight of the children who now faced a busing hardship. Out of many, many memories of Yvonne, I suppose this one stood out because she spoke so vehemently regarding the plight of students, parents, teachers, and bus drivers.

I admired Judge Sanders and did not envy his role at this time in history. I, too, criticized the busing decision but credited him highly for desegregating DISD. In 1977, he established a programmatic desegregation plan rather than simply a busing plan that included establishing four magnet schools, called "The Law Magnet" (later named in his honor). He ordered the opening of Townview Magnet Center where six of the district's magnet programs were located (later named in honor of Yvonne Ewell); the Sub-District organizational structure to focus on specific community educational needs; the East Oak Cliff Sub-District which Yvonne Ewell served as the associate superintendent for administrative and instructional oversight; and the Dallas Learning Centers in South and West Dallas.

In 1984 after desegregation was reality, Yvonne urged me to serve on the Community Advisory Committee. She felt that my continued involvement was necessary; in her honor, I have remained active in DISD issues ever since.

She retired in 1985 — what a retirement party she had, and well deserved! The Honorable Congresswoman Eddie Bernice Johnson and Dr. Dorothy Height, Former National President of the National Council of Negro Women, were present to honor Yvonne. So were State Senator Royce West, State Representatives Yvonne Davis, Helen Giddings, and County Commissioner John Wiley Price.

I am pleased to say that the Yvonne A. Ewell Townview Magnet Center is very much like a college or university setting for ethnically diverse high school students. It boasts a high-achieving student body and is among the very few with advanced curriculums in the United States that have been recognized at state and national levels. U.S. News & World Report ranked the school 16th in the nation and 2nd in Texas. Both the Science and Engineering, and Talented & Gifted schools, are part of DISD's Yvonne A. Ewell Townview Magnet Center. This complex hosts six independent high schools that offer advanced academic curricula across specific interest areas. All six schools have been designated as National Blue Ribbon Schools, one of the highest designations for schools by the U.S. Department of Education. I am truly excited about the Magnet Center's consistent recognition and the fact that other school districts seek to replicate it nationwide.

I will never forget Yvonne and credit her for introducing me to another dear friend, Shirley Ison-Newsome.

Shirley Ison-Newsome

Shirley Ison-Newsome is such a remarkable educator — tough, disciplined, and results-oriented. We share a kindred spirit when advocating for our students, our city, our district and on behalf of those watching from afar in other states. Rather than wondering what DISD would do to solve its multiple crises, Shirley did something about it.

I mentioned serving on the Community Advisory Committee at the behest of Dr. Ewell — this was when Shirley Ison-Newsome was the principal at Harry Stone Middle School. Her school had the largest poverty index in the Dallas Independent School District. She turned it around and is credited with creating DISD's model and initiative for middle schools.

Shirley recently told me, "Your involvement highlighted the importance of education for the community at large. Your contribution to folks like me inside the system was knowing that someone was advocating outside the system. We didn't feel alone. At Harry Stone Middle School, you weren't just a business leader and former Cowboy, but a role-model who cared for the kids."

As Area 2 Superintendent in the late 1990s, test scores rose under her watch. These were test scores of students who lived in extremely challenging circumstances — poor, transient, and from communities challenged by many issues such as poverty, unemployment, violence — all the "isms" designed to keep kids from learning and having a future of hope. These children were highly disadvantaged but achieved academic success, and I credit Shirley for pulling the best out of teachers and administrators to make this happen.

Shirley also reminded me of the value of community leaders coming together to talk about the needs of schools and then presenting the information to the superintendent. She mentioned Don Williams' interest in south Dallas schools, Arcilia Acosta's hard work, and my involvement with them both during our brainstorming sessions.

On a very personal note, Shirley added:

Pettis, you've done a lot in our community, a lot of giving of yourself, not only to the Black community but to the community at large. You speak your mind, and everyone knows where you stand, and you do not go along to get along. But you genuinely care. When my grandson was born prematurely at 23 weeks and was in the NICU, you came by frequently to visit, and this is the core of who you are. There was no press around, and no one knew of your kindness. I appreciate your decency and compassion — it shows in all you do.

Don Williams, Reverend Zan Holmes, and I co-wrote an article heralding Shirley's many successes after her retirement in 2012, not just because she's one of our closest friends but also because she was an effective administrator. I excerpt part of it below:

Ison-Newsome's career with DISD began with the desegregation efforts in the 1970s, a turbulent time in Dallas history. Recruited to help examine the efficacy of instruction, she authored a chapter of the 1974 report to the board titled "A Study of Instruction." Superintendent Nolan Estes then appointed her as the first dean of instruction.

Subsequent milestones include her appointment as senior planner for the nationally recognized East Oak Cliff Sub-District, under the leadership of Dr. Yvonne Ewell. In this role, she designed the nation's first programmatic desegregation efforts. She later planned, alongside Ewell, DISD's magnet programs (counted among the best in the nation) and program components for the court-ordered Learning Centers.

Ison-Newsome was then appointed principal of Harry Stone Middle School, creating the model for DISD's middle school initiative. Later, as Area 2 superintendent, she led academic gains that were so significant that her model was used throughout DISD. Moreover, the elementary schools Ison-Newsome oversaw consistently ranked high in the district, with over half designated as recognized or exemplary each year.

I believe Shirley's legacy is defined by academic excellence in traditionally underachieving schools, principal and teacher development, community partnerships, and advocacy for children. In her stellar 37-year career with DISD, Ison-Newsome set the standard of leadership that our public schools need and deserve. She did not "leave quietly" — as a lightning rod for good, she left with thunderous applause in the form of thousands of better-equipped young people. Her legacy benefits our city and society at large — a benefit we need to thrive as a democratic society. She has been weighed in the balance and been found exemplary!

Most importantly, Shirley is a wonderful friend. She has been there for me during great times and difficult times, especially when I lost my beloved daughter Shawn. She just shows up in time of need and gets busy with the task at hand. She has been a blessing to my family and the City of Dallas, and will always remain in my inner circle of very close friends.

Dallas Achieves Commission

The precursor to Dallas Achieves was the South Dallas Achieves initiative funded by Don Williams and his Foundation for Community Empowerment. Working with the principals and Area Superintendent over south Dallas schools (Shirley Ison-Newsome), the model was in place for expanding the program per Superintendent Hinojosa's request to all Dallas schools.

Hence the birth of the Dallas Achieves Commission.

There is more to my involvement in the education arena, and I credit my great Co-Chairs Don Williams and Arcilia Acosta's ongoing effort to address and solve the lingering issues. Arcilia, by the way, was CARCON Industries & Construction President and CEO, and I had come to admire her tenacity during our days with the Dallas Together Forum. Don was such an inspiring leader himself, putting in the sweat equity necessary to address a problematic school district.

Don recently commented:

> *Pettis was smart and fearless throughout the struggle with the public education system. We wanted to see if we could overhaul the entire DISD organization, especially the curriculum. Pettis, Arcilia, and I co-chaired the Dallas Achieves coalition and talked with Michael Hinojosa about assisting with putting together a transformational model. Everyone jumped on board, so we chaired a 50-five-person task force that included wealthy philanthropists to LULAC, to teacher unions — a representative slice of the community. We spent three years raising $25 million of private money to support this effort and engaged the consulting firm Boston Consulting. They created a separate arm strictly for public education for cities around America, including the Delaware school system.*
>
> *Everyone has an opinion on public education, and getting everyone on the same page is another story, but our monthly meetings were very well attended. Pettis was crucial due to his standing in the community, his presence in public and private groups, and within separate communities. We'd identify best practices around the country and bring those ideas back to our meetings. Of course, there were differences of opinions and sometimes some very serious conflict. Pettis had a separate meeting with African American commission members to navigate a compromise that made everyone happy. He's the only guy who was respected enough to pull off such big-time negotiations, and we could not have gotten unanimously through the finish line without his leadership. He brought order and peace, and his word is his bond.*

Don's Foundation for Community Empowerment took a hard look at the data and collaborated with DISD Superintendent Mike Moses to form the concept for the Dallas Achieves Commission. This would become a think tank group comprised of more than 60 community leaders. Mike Moses' reign was short, stretching from January 2001 to August 2004. Mike Hinojosa took over as Superintendent, and in 2006 the commission was co-chaired by Don Williams, Arcilia Acosta, and me — another trio of ethnicities.

Once again, the diversity in race, gender, and culture yielded results as we worked with the community. The Dallas Achieves Commission recommended reforms to the DISD school board as well as a three-step agenda: (1) the district should adopt performance targets as measured by the National Assessment of Educational Progress and the National Center for Educational Accountability; (2) the district should graduate students who are college or workforce ready; and (3) the district should reduce the dropout rate by identifying and counseling students deemed at risk.

I recall that Superintendent Hinojosa wanted very much to win the "Broad Prize for Urban

Education," a 1-million-dollar annual award to honor urban school districts making the greatest overall improvement in student achievement and reducing achievement gaps across income and ethnic groups. Awards had been granted annually between 2002 and 2014 to graduating high school students in the finalist and winning districts. Our role was to seek ways to help qualify. This became DISD's "The Road to Broad," a formal plan throughout the district.

We reported to the board of trustees and Superintendent Hinojosa and were tasked with ensuring that a transformation occurred within DISD. That was quite a tall order. It required fundraising, collaboration, and cool heads. We had to find ways that enabled the district to perform so that minority and disadvantaged students were college ready when they graduated from high school and that TAKS scores improved — reflected in the numbers so the prize could be won.

Hadn't that been the goal for decades? Looking back, it seemed that DISD had always cycled through periods of improvement and disappointments, but we kept trying. We wanted the district to win the Broad Prize and worked diligently with the community, business leaders, and district decision-makers. It was laborious, sometimes challenging, and always a study in patience and collaboration.

The DISD board of trustees adopted one 100 of our recommendations and began implementing them, which became the goal beyond the prize. Although we lost to Brownsville Independent School District, I am proud to say the number of "exemplary" and "recognized" schools rose even while the state issued more challenging TAKS tests (Texas Assessment of Knowledge and Skills).

Dallas Education Foundation

This brings to mind a recent conversation with Erle Nye, a close friend and former CEO of TXU Electric. He recalled our involvement in the Dallas Education Foundation, created to ensure donors that the school district's funding would be used appropriately. I became more involved around the same time I was active with the Dallas Achieves Commission and felt both initiatives had tremendous merit. Erle commented:

> *The Dallas Education Foundation worked with the school district on grants. It ensured oversight on large donations. Erle reminded me, 'and you, Pettis, had the context of growing up Black and experiencing challenges that the foundation hopes to address.'*

Indeed, Erle was spot on. We sought to supplement educational opportunities and meet the needs of students and staff in ways that had not been done before in DISD. The foundation has been more active at certain times than others, and I hope to see it grow in usefulness to the school district in the years ahead.

Home Rule

Back in 2014, there was an "awakening" within our community in Dallas because of a term called "Home Rule." It generally signifies a shift of governing power from the state to local counties and was the cause of tremendous upheaval and unrest in Dallas.

Texas has a charter school law provision permitting an entire school district to convert to charter school status and create a Home Rule school district charter. That is, as long as a majority vote to convert and at least 25% of voters weigh in. No one in Texas has ever actually opted to "remake" a school district in this manner. However, an organization called "Support our Public Schools" backed Home Rule and collected more than twice the signatures needed to force a referendum — 48,000. Considering that in 2014 there were 43 "Improvement Required" (IR) schools in DISD, the initiative gained traction.

Mayor Mike Rawlings supported the initiative and called it "a line in the sand moment" because thousands of upper- to middle-class parents were fleeing the district. I became concerned with his public stance on this very contentious initiative and his attempts to promote the concept to Dallas voters.

Some proponents felt it was a step in the right direction that "bad" teachers would no longer be protected, and the sense of less government seemed liberating. But others felt teachers would be vulnerable to wrongful termination, minimum salaries, and professional development could be exempted. In addition, some of the due process enjoyed by students in disciplinary proceedings would no longer apply. Parents would no longer have to be granted access to teaching materials, a charter school could request to take over a failing school, and principals and teachers could start charter schools as an alternative.

In short, if something was not specifically stipulated in the law, it could be done. A large district could be divided into smaller districts. A voucher system could be set up, and for-profit corporations could take over. John Arnold, a billionaire Houstonian and former Enron executive, was a major funder of the Home Rule push, which had many Dallas residents scratching their heads.

By law, the school district had to appoint a Home Rule Commission composed of representatives appointed by each board member (9), representatives from the school district staff, and appointees from specific organizations (the teachers' representative organizations, the PTA) and others.

The Commission was chaired by Bob Weiss, a longtime public school advocate, and Shirley Ison-Newsome, Secretary, and held public hearings throughout the community. They met for a year to research the issue and to gather public comment. The Commission eventually voted not to approve Home Rule for the Dallas Independent School District.

Mayor Rawlings made an excellent decision to step out of the limelight on this issue and appoint civic leaders to research and address this contentious issue. Hence, the Dallas Forum for Public Education was established.

Dallas Forum for Public Education

I was tapped by Mayor Rawlings, along with Rene Martinez and Tom Dunning, to lead a new initiative as co-chairs of Dallas Forum for Public Education, an outgrowth of the failed Home Rule effort. Our forum included a diverse committee of 45 parents, civic leaders, and educators who became stakeholders in our newly founded group.

In 2014, the co-chairs and stakeholders met monthly for almost one year on the best direction for operating and managing Dallas ISD. We had lively roundtable discussions and made presentations and recommendations on how to engage the public.

"I decided it was time to make a suggestion that we have a broader conversation," I told the media. "We want a balanced discussion for this city, and we want to include as many people as we can."

We recommended developing and expanding quality pre-kindergarten for all four-year-olds, improving parental involvement, implementing individual learning plans, and examining how to change the culture of struggling middle and high schools.

My thought was to consider the benefits of faith-based organizations "adopting" elementary schools. Sure, some might argue the need for separation of church and state. Some might argue that certain churches exclude other faiths. However, this misses the point. My goal was to have a faith-based initiative that wouldn't proselytize but simply bring in the strongest coalition of people — people who happened to exercise their freedom of religion to advocate for public education. Together, we could effect change.

At the conclusion of this initiative, some of the Dallas Forum for Public Education suggestions were put in place, but the faith-based initiatives were not. Since the failure of the Home Rule debacle seven years ago, we see evidence that Dallas ISD has moved in the right direction.

Today, new schools are being built, we have quality pre-k programs, investment in teacher preparation (with development as a budget priority), important dual literacy priorities, tech innovations, and other aggressive enhancements for our teachers and students. DISD made the right decision – Home Rule was not the blueprint for our schools.

Finally, the Dallas ISD Board of Trustees unanimously adopted a resolution – "A Commitment to Black Students for Educational Excellence and to Black Lives."

This signaled that the district was focused on putting students with the greatest needs on the front burner. Such a move gives hope for the district's future and how well it will serve all of its students.

Chapter Sixteen: Dallas Together Forum

To change the corporate horizon on behalf of minorities and women, we had to change hearts and minds.
~ Pettis Norman

The root of the concept and need for the Dallas Together Forum goes back in time. There was so much going on in Dallas that I can only offer a "Cliff's Notes" version of the chronology.

As background, Mayor J. Erik Jonsson took office just after President John F. Kennedy's assassination and all the turmoil surrounding it. He rolled out "Goals for Dallas" in 1965 with some world-class "public works" initiatives. I recall these initiatives specifically because I had decided to call Dallas home and felt these goals would benefit my growing family. They included:

- Public kindergarten with mandatory attendance at age five
- Quality museums for art, natural history, science, and industry
- Designated pedestrian walkways throughout the city, especially in congested areas and school zones
- Central Business District as a commercial, governmental, educational, cultural, recreational, and residential area, with multi-purpose uses linked to Fair Park with through parks, boulevards, and connections to major expressways

These may seem like basic concepts now, but at the time, they were cutting edge. It was obvious that Dallas leaders cared about our future — these cosmopolitan ideas won Dallas the "All American City" designation in 1971 by *Look* magazine, covered by WFAA-TV and other media.

In 1973, Dallas County judge W.L. "Lew" Sterrett released a report that 11% of county employees were racial minorities. This was a preliminary reporting of facts and figures — an attempt at transparency that I applauded. In fact, I took note of it as I settled back into Dallas and assessed the nuances of the city.

In 1975, the International Year of the Woman, the Dallas Commission on the Status of Women was created to advance opportunities and eliminate discrimination based on gender. Dallas City Council members each chose and appointed two people from their districts for a total of 22 members on the commission. A Spanish professor at the University of Texas at Dallas, Dr. Carolyn Galerstein, was the first chairwoman.

The commission addressed issues in task forces, held public hearings, hosted workshops, addressed the local problems facing women, provided information and resources, and made recommendations to the Dallas City Council. I thought this was a much-needed initiative and applauded the commission and council members for their efforts.

In 1979, however, the council disbanded the commission after determining the mission was complete. I will never forget the outcry from the commission's supporters who knew the mission was far from complete. As a father of three daughters who were in junior high and high school at this time, I was determined that my girls would have opportunities that prior generations of women did not.

This matter stayed with me and became a focus 20 years later. I knew, without a doubt, that the Dallas Together Forum should pick up the banner and advocate for career advancement and women-owned businesses. Women's rights were an ever-trending issue, and we were set on impacting the economic status of women in Dallas, in Texas, and throughout America.

Business leaders implemented other initiatives. As I recall, the Dallas Citizen's Council formed a strategic planning committee in 1989, but rather than public works, it focused on education, jobs, and governmental affairs. Goals for Dallas were eventually phased out and reimagined as a part of the Greater Dallas Chamber of Commerce and its economic development division.

The Dallas Plan followed in 1991 — a comprehensive nonprofit plan for the physical evolution, urban planning, and design of the city, taking into account the disparity within the geography of Dallas and how society worked.

My friend Robert Decherd, Chairman of the Board, President and CEO of the Belo Corporation, parent company of the *Dallas Morning News*, was instrumental in envisioning the Dallas Plan and getting it funded by businesses and philanthropies. It gained community-wide support, and I thought it was brilliant as a long-range strategic plan.

Other planning groups included the North Texas Commission and the City of Dallas Economic Development Council. I believed all who sacrificed their time on these boards and committees genuinely loved our city. However, each had a different focus and agenda, but no group had a specific focus on minority inclusion in the business sector.

At times it seemed we had a kitchen full of cooks who prepared ingredients for what should have been a melting pot but wasn't. A recipe of various factions, corporate power brokers, and political leadership did not always produce a dish that served all.

Could we conjure up something palatable that all would want to taste? That question became the driving force behind the Dallas Together Forum.

An Ethnic Trio

As the 1990s approached, minorities and women were still not full partners in our city's social, economic, and political bounties. This exclusion was something I decried along with my good friend Bill Solomon, President, CEO, and Chairman of Austin Industries, one of the nation's largest, most diversified U.S.-based construction companies and Joe Alcantar, co-owner and President of Alman Electric Company, one of the top 500 Hispanic-owned businesses in the U.S.

With Bill Solomon and Joe Alcantar. Photo credit: *Dallas Morning News*

There we were — a Black, White, and Hispanic trio who cared deeply about this issue. Bill, Joe, and I believed it was time that minority-owned and women-owned businesses had seats at the table. We wanted to increase their presence on boards, increase the hiring of minorities as executives, and increase minority business promotions and contracts. We envisioned a rating system that tracked and measured the progress of corporate inclusion.

As I reflect on this important time in history, it recalls the underlying theme of it all:

For where two or three are gathered together in my name,
I am there among them.
~ Matthew 18:20

Indeed, the Dallas Together Forum started with three — Bill, Joe, and me — and God was with us as it blossomed into a collaborative undertaking by Dallas business leaders. We began reexamining race relations through an economic lens, in a way the City of Dallas had never considered. It meant taking a hard, truthful look at the underclass, the underserved, and the underrepresented. I believe this was the most important cause in my entire career.

A handful of Black-owned enterprises thrived, and I'm sure they felt as much an anomaly as I did. We were challenged to work harder, perform better, and deliver more than our competitors. As minorities, we had more to prove and held ourselves to a higher standard because we were now entering territories formerly serviced by non-minorities. We were the "fledgling" competition.

In short, minority enterprises were willing and capable. If offered the opportunity, we desperately wanted to blaze trails for those who would come after us. I took these blessings very seriously and promised my Creator that I'd move heaven and earth to serve my customers, going above and beyond in thought, word, and deed. It was the only way to succeed.

Finding the Win/Win

The laser focus by Dallas leaders on various agendas simply reflected the complexity of issues facing the city. The Dallas Together Forum grew out of one specific complexity — hiring minorities and women in the business sector.

The question remained: How would minority hiring benefit all business sectors? What would it take to make a win/win for all? Well, in 1990, we looked at what the City of Atlanta, Georgia, was doing (bringing top business owners together with the city's Blacks) and adapted their model to Dallas.

Bill, Joe, and I canvassed the Dallas business sector and personally visited the CEOs of large corporations, pitching the notion that minority hiring would bring diverse talent to their enterprises and promote market growth. We didn't speak with vice-presidents; we wanted to get in front of the CEOs, presidents, and top decision-makers and talk about race relations, diversity training, and the need for inclusion.

I also appealed to the overall vision of "one Dallas undivided" — not a wealthy northern Dallas and a struggling southern Dallas, but one large thriving city. In short, minority hiring would elevate the reputation of Dallas and make it a model that could inspire other cities.

The biggest problem for minorities has always been a lack of access. The Dallas Together Forum focused on solving this problem through economics. We set goals for minority purchasing and contracts and began addressing the pressing issues of participation by minorities and women.

These efforts really paid off in more ways than one, for there were tax advantages in hiring and contracting minorities. President Richard Nixon's administration had already rolled out the first federal laws offering legislative provisions to encourage the hiring of minority-owned businesses. The federal government provided (and still provides) tax breaks for companies that procure materials and supplies from minority companies. A second tax incentive reduced tax liabilities for companies using minorities that supplied labor or services to a project funded with federal or state grants or loans.

It made good business sense, and Dallas' Fortune 500 companies agreed. We pulled them into the fold. Thus, the Dallas Together Forum became one of many entities that profoundly changed the landscape throughout Dallas, leveling the playing field regarding the way business was done. Bill, Joe, and I envisioned it as a powerful peace council of like-minded Dallas CEOs. We were ethnically diverse, inclusive, and achieved "the impossible dream."

The Covenant

The Dallas Together Forum was dedicated to promoting minority economic opportunities in the private sector and could not have done so without willing cooperation. The CEOs of major corporations literally went out on a limb by signing our "Private Sector Covenant for Workplace Diversity and Minority Economic Opportunity." It was ultimately embraced by over 200 CEOs who agreed to increase minority purchasing and hiring.

This was new and, for lack of a better word, breathtaking. The CEOs agreed to uphold the Covenant and made public statements about how and who they hired and for what purposes, year after year.

They agreed to disclose and set objectives for purchases of goods and services from minority firms. The hiring of minorities and the inclusion of workplace diversity appeared in their regular performance reviews. They published their firms' accomplishments annually, and I remember congratulating them for being amazingly progressive. I believe their corporate reputations benefitted because they became known as fair and transparent agents of change.

These companies ultimately reported $565 million in purchases from minority-owned businesses (a 68% increase in minority contracting) and more than 39% of minority new hires, including African Americans, Hispanics, Asian Americans, and Native Americans. Adopt-a-School programs, mentoring programs for college-bound minority youth, community investment, and financial lending saw increases as well.

Bill Solomon

Bill has been a phenomenal ally in the fight for minority inclusion. From 1970 through 2001, he served as President and CEO of Austin Industries. Later from 1987 to 2008, he served as chairman of the board. On his watch, Austin Industries became one of the nation's leading commercial, industrial, and infrastructure construction companies in the United States. The Dallas Together Forum wouldn't have been the same without him.

Bill began as a young businessman back in the day when even the thought of a blended forum seemed impossible. Corporations were focused on the bottom line and had not yet realized they could maintain or even increase their bottom line through alliances with minority businesses.

But Bill was always a forward thinker, a man of integrity. The chasm between the "social classes" troubled him; he saw potential in the city, a way forward that would help bridge the economic and racial gap. He weighs in on those early years with a short description of our initial efforts.

I appreciate his views very much and admire him as one of the most important business leaders in Dallas and one of my dearest friends to this very day.

Contributed by Bill Solomon

Like most people, my earliest memories of Pettis are of a tall, elegant athlete who stood out as a star player for the Dallas Cowboys. Not too long after that, as a young businessman fresh out of school, I began to notice the next iteration of Pettis. By then, he was a budding entrepreneur who was increasingly becoming engaged in community leadership in Dallas.

This was in the 1970s and 1980s, and Dallas was especially stressed with racial tension grounded in serious unresolved issues rooted deeply in current and past inequities.

The whole community suffered from the increasing divide between Blacks and Whites. Into this, Pettis inserted himself and quickly rose to a leadership role. I noticed this and was impressed by his constructive impact. I, too, was deeply concerned by these issues.

In 1990, largely at Pettis' initiative, he and I asked businessman Joe Alcantar to co-chair the Dallas Together Forum, which initially included about 30 other Black/Brown/White CEO's who were committed to work together to address the root causes of racial tensions in Dallas.

Though many of these problems remain with us today, and countless other people besides the Dallas Together Forum worked hard then to address these issues, I am convinced that much progress was made during that era. The Dallas Together Forum played a key role in that progress. Pettis' leadership was indispensable to the forum's effectiveness.

In 1993, the Dallas Together Forum asked companies in Dallas to help bolster minority hiring in a five-year effort we called the 'Private Sector Covenant.' In 1994, 168 companies voluntarily disclosed their track records of hiring, advancing and contracting with minorities; more signed on in the process that ultimately included more than 200 dedicated companies.

The Dallas Together Forum was made up of a coalition of like-minded entities — large companies, the Dallas Area Rapid Transit (DART), the City of Dallas, nonprofits, and smaller businesses with both minority and non-minority ownership.

It became a successful role model replicated across our nation and communities abroad. I felt that our city had 'grown up.' We were working together, sharing goals, and achieving something quite remarkable.

Joe Alcantar

I appreciate that Joe has weighed in below with insights on our friendship and his role in the Dallas Together Forum. He is a servant leader in every sense of the word — a person who generously gives his time and talent. Joe was instrumental in drawing people to the table and championing the cause of inclusion for Hispanics, Blacks, Whites, Asians, Native Americans — everyone.

Joe later served as Chairman of the City Plan Commission on behalf of the City of Dallas. Today he sits on the Board of Advisors for the Texas State Fair. He could have retired and enjoyed a well-deserved break from city issues, but he is still the same servant leader I know and admire, ready to step up when and where he is needed.

I am fortunate to call Joe my friend, another long-term relationship that has blessed many, me included.

Contributed by Joe Alcantar

Pettis spearheaded the Dallas Together Forum and was the catalyst for making it work. He exemplified leadership and had the ability to cross lines into the Anglo, Hispanic, and African American communities. Bill Solomon and I were co-chairs and worked with Pettis to draw upon the city's makeup, quality, and diversity. We embraced it rather than pulling against it. That's what made the Dallas Together Forum successful.

The decade of the '90s was a remarkable period, a window for Pettis to bring his leadership skills to the table. It's why the city is so great today. We started the Dallas Together Forum and brought the major CEOs of the city together — special people like Bob Crandall, Erle Nye, the major banks, and women entrepreneurs. We brought in people from all walks of life, and Pettis was the glue that held it together.

I met Pettis in the '80s. We were both serving on different boards and commissions. We became great friends, played golf, and were very family-oriented. He has such a lovely family. It was tragic when he lost his wife in 1991. I was one of his groomsmen when he married Ivette in 1995, a lovely woman. The whole community mourned with him when he lost his daughter in 2014. Throughout it all, he has remained a big-hearted, loving person.

I can't thank him enough for all the years of friendship, and I am glad to be part of his life and journey.

All Hands on Deck

When I formed PNI Industries and five additional companies in the 1990s, you can bet we took responsibility for our role in the community. I personally signed the Dallas Together Forum Private Sector Covenant for Workplace Diversity and Minority Economic Opportunity to ensure my businesses supported the initiative.

However, PNI's involvement went beyond minority and women's inclusion in the workplace and extended into the communities in which we lived, worked, and played. PNI went a step further through the efforts of my employees, who were able to devote their generous and unwavering support to the community's civic and educational endeavors — not because they had to, but because they wanted to.

Several were involved in local volunteer organizations such as Bryan's House Pediatric AIDS Foundation, Wednesday's Child, Right Alternatives for People, and Alpha Kappa Alpha Sorority. I encouraged this voluntary involvement and ambassadorship and was proud of our corporate culture.

I led by example, side-by-side with Bill Solomon, Joe Alcantar and other Dallas Together Forum corporations. PNI Industries annually hosted the Pettis Norman Celebrity Golf Classic that benefited El Centro Community College in Dallas. We worked very closely with the Dallas

Citizens Council, the Greater Dallas Chamber of Commerce, the Dallas Black Chamber of Commerce, and Paul Quinn College, to name a few.

In 1993 the Minority Business Development Council recognized PNI as a TXU Gold Star Supplier. As always, our focus mixed philanthropy with business while supporting the Covenant and hiring an ethnically diverse staff.

In short, we understood the need for the Dallas community at large to stand and deliver on the promise of equal opportunity and then personally step up to volunteer outside of the corporate realm. PNI Industries continued to encourage and promote corporate responsibility and efforts to help "the least of these" while ensuring economic parity to every citizen in the City of Dallas.

It turned out that not just Dallas was impacted. We got calls from Austin, San Antonio, and other cities outside Texas, and most notably, a call from overseas.

Charter

After three years, I stepped aside to allow others to lead the Dallas Together Forum (DTF). That term limit of service was incorporated into our charter, making room for a new slate of co-chairs and continued momentum. What we eventually discovered was that many Fortune 500 companies went through their own cycles of leadership. As CEOs stepped down and new CEOs came on board, their focus was on corporate stability (and, at times, restructuring). This didn't always translate to DTF membership as a priority.

The initiative eventually lost steam after three-quarters of a billion dollars had flowed from Dallas companies in the form of contracts or business to minority and women-owned firms. I do believe DTF served its purpose during that era. The concept of minority hiring was sustainable and is evident in the city today. There is always room for improvement, but Dallas is more diverse, more colorblind, and has a healthier business climate because of the fine efforts of Bill, Joe, and the members of the Dallas Together Forum.

I thank them all from the bottom of my heart, for they changed not just the business structure of the city, but in many ways, the social structure. Our corporate culture became more minority-focused, sounder, and more robust because so many great leaders in Dallas cared. It turned out that people in other countries cared as well, evidenced by an overseas phone call described below.

Japan

What I appreciated most about the Dallas Together Forum was its usefulness and applicability in other cities, states, and even nations. A case in point — as DTF was making inroads, I received a conference call from Japan in the mid-'90s. A group was interested in our equality initiatives for women.

My understanding was that the nation of Japan was a rather homogenous population, differentiated mainly by gender. What did we have in common? Patriarchal dominance and the unfair treatment of women left much to be desired in both countries. A women's rights movement had been percolating for some time in Japan, culminating in their Equal

Employment Opportunity Law in 1986. This first-ever gender equality law was credited to the Women's Bureau of the Ministry of Labor.

I was informed that more progress had been made. In 1994, the Cabinet of Japan added a headquarters for the Promotion of Gender Equality, leading to the concept of "Womenomics." This was the first I had ever heard of that term, but I knew it had to do with women and the economy. Obviously, Japan was serious about women's civil rights but faced centuries of stubborn tradition and entrenched cultural norms.

I empathized and understood very well what it meant to take on the established ways of doing things and seek reform. Despite our distant locales, the people I conversed with were obviously unified with the Dallas Together Forum's quest for gender rights. It was an amazing dialogue.

I shared background information that led to the formation of the Dallas Together Forum, including issues facing minorities and women in the Dallas business sector and the solutions we enacted through corporate involvement. I was asked for details about our Covenant and how best to implement a Japanese version of the Dallas Together Forum. It impressed me that across the vast North Pacific Ocean and despite a bit of language barrier, we had a productive and fascinating phone conversation.

It was thrilling to be able to help, and I realized at that moment how powerful and far-reaching our efforts in Dallas had become. Although I never received a follow-up phone call, my impression was that some version of the Dallas Together Forum Covenant would be drafted and deployed in Japan. I hope very much that our initiatives in Dallas made a difference for women in that country.

Chapter Seventeen: Other Voices of Dallas Together Forum

Equality and economics go hand in hand.
~ Pettis Norman

I treasure my long-term relationships with some very special business leaders involved with the Dallas Together Forum. While writing this book, I touched base with some key participants and realized how much they had to say, even today, about minority inclusion and equality. It really merits an entire chapter — how fascinating to look into the hearts and character of these influential men and women who operated out of a sense of fairness and equality.

Front row: Joe Alcantar, Pettis Norman, William Solomon. Back row: Jim Washington, Ron Haddock, Robert Huesh, Erle Nye, Tom Lazo. Photo credit: *Minority Business News DFW*

While we are all different, these fine business leaders realized the dynamic, collective impact on economics and community. I am honored to share their insights and reflections.

Bob Crandall

Robert "Bob" Crandall, former President and Chairman of American Airlines, is a prime example of a person who gives back. I'll never forget that he donated $1 million to help save Paul Quinn College. We can also thank him for many corporate innovations, including the concept of frequent flyer miles. Not surprisingly, a "Bring Back Bob" movement has been afoot, harkening back to the days "when customers, employees, and shareholders ALL benefited."

Many may not know that Bob is a voice in the cause of social justice as well. In June 2019, he spoke at a global forum for Operation Hope. His speech titled "Why Inequality Matters and What to Do About It" included a profound statement: "Unequal societies have higher crime rates, particularly in low-income areas. Unequal societies have higher levels of obesity, mental illness, homicides, teenage births, incarceration, drug use, and child abuse. Inequality diminishes social cohesion, which was very high in the U.S. in the '40s and '50s and is very low today."

The work of the Dallas Together Forum in the '90s addressed inequality — discrimination and wage inequality — through measurable means. Bob's participation in the Dallas Together Forum was crucial. It was great working with him in yesteryear and even better touching base with him to prepare this section of the book. What a wonderful person with a heart of gold who is so powerful and respected throughout our nation. I'm proud to call him my friend.

Contributed by Bob Crandall

The Dallas Together Forum was unusual in the context of that day and time. Pettis turned the notion of minority inclusion into a "topic" we could all rally around. It was a very appropriate movement, and I was glad to have an opportunity to provide support.

I think the Dallas Together Forum had a long-term favorable impact on minority-owned businesses and on the economic momentum that has carried Dallas forward in the years since.

Robert Decherd

No one in Dallas is more plugged into the media than Robert Decherd — former Chairman of the Board, President, and Chief Executive Officer of A. H. Belo Corporation of Dallas, the parent company of the *Dallas Morning News*, among other publications.

He began his career as a writer for the *Harvard Crimson*, became a servant leader on many boards, and steered his enterprises through industry challenges and amazing innovations. His newspaper evolved with the city, a bird's eye view of all things Dallas. I enjoy reading the *Dallas Morning News* and searching its time capsule archives, which are so vital to the City of Dallas.

Robert is a good friend and has supported many of the causes that I held close throughout the years. Above all, he truly has his fingers on the pulse of the people — the movers and shakers, the underdogs and "least of these" — and recognized the importance of change. It was incumbent on us all to improve race relations and offer minorities a fair shake. Robert helped make that happen with the Dallas Together Forum and through other organizations.

It was so good to work with him, elbow to elbow, as we pushed for a more fair, in-depth, and panoramic measure of progress in the business community. I reached out to him regarding his recollection of the Dallas Together Forum and what it meant to the city. He has incredible memories of those long-ago years.

Contributed by Robert Decherd

The Dallas Together Forum may seem Dallas-centric, but it was responsive to a situation being experienced in cities all over the country at that time. Dallas' issues were not isolated. We committed to addressing the participation of minorities and women comprehensively and effectively in all aspects of business, weighted in private-public access to capital.

We wanted to ensure that everyone had the same opportunities in business and career advancement. It took work and dedication, but I believe we made huge inroads. What we did truly mattered for many minority- and women-owned businesses.

Pettis is one of the true citizens of Dallas who cares, a former sportsman who devoted half his time to civic matters and never sought notoriety after his football career. He was always a person who exhibited calmness and had an innate insightfulness in his approach to very complex problems — calm and reasonable. He could lead men and women because he was just extraordinarily respected. Everyone was in the same place in their regard for Pettis.

I remember when he approached me about the Dallas Together Forum. 'We need to do this,' he said, just dogged about the need and obligation to make it work. I agreed. It is hard to say no to Pettis, and the city is a better place because of it.

Joyce Foreman

Joyce is a good, longtime friend. Her insights as an African American businesswoman and CEO of Foreman Office Products Inc. were valuable to the Dallas Together Forum.

Joyce has been a community leader for as long as I can remember and was recently recognized and honored in 2017 as a Master Trustee by Leadership TASB, the nationally recognized leadership training program sponsored by the Texas Association of School Boards. She was elected to the Dallas ISD Board of Trustees, representing District 6 in June 2014, and began serving on the Dallas ISD Bond Advisory Committee in 2002.

Like me, she is passionate about a fair business culture and preparing our students to be the best and brightest in our city. Her involvement in the Dallas Together Forum back in the '90s helped pave a path of inclusion and economic hope for all.

She weighs in below regarding the work it took to impact corporate Dallas.

Contributed by Joyce Foreman

I have had the privilege of meeting and working with many individuals in Dallas in my lifetime, but none like Pettis Norman. He showed great intensity in making Dallas a better place by improving the inequities of racial injustice, education reform, and minority business development. These were very controversial issues in Dallas but never swayed Pettis Norman from getting involved and making a positive difference.

Being a former Dallas Cowboy player was not his ticket to the community. Pettis gained a deep understanding of the problems and then implemented his ideas through a collective lens that benefitted the entire community. With that in mind, I remember his work on the Dallas Together Forum around 1992 when Dallas was struggling with racial problems. Pettis, along with Bill Solomon and Joe Alcantar, led a racially diverse group to grapple with the racial divide in the city.

There were some very tense and painful meetings to address the concerns of all, but Pettis kept a steady hand on the situation and worked for positive outcomes. Because of the Dallas Together Forum, corporations better understood what was needed to move forward.

Ron Haddock

My great friend Ron Haddock, former President and CEO of FINA, was instrumental in the success of PNI Industries. He mentored me and my companies through several expansions, and I can't thank him enough for his selfless leadership.

Ron reminds me of a quote by Thomas John Watson Sr. – "To be successful, you have to have your heart in your business and your business in your heart." He was absolutely determined that FINA participate fully in the development of minority businesses and was a trailblazer in this concept before it was a common practice.

Ron's social conscience is reflected in all he does for the community, including his work on behalf of the American Heart Association. I considered him a role model inside and outside the corporate world, for he supported many causes. Even today, decades after our business collaborations, we still enjoy spending time together.

Karen Jones Griggsby, FINA's program manager for the Minority Women Business Enterprise Program, also took time to share her insights, incredibly reflective of the "boots on the ground" work she did for the Dallas Together Forum.

Both Ron and Karen weigh in below.

Contributed by Ron Haddock

FINA never subsidized other businesses but rather gave equal access and opportunities to large and small enterprises alike and minority and women-owned businesses. As a global firm, our corporate culture emphasized inclusion early on, and we were serious about it. When opportunities emerged to mentor smaller businesses, we did so, and Pettis' was one of the most dominant participants.

Our corporate efforts segued with the goals of the Dallas Together Forum, and I personally participated in this worthy initiative. Pettis, Bill Solomon, and Joe Alcantar were the first co-chairs, and we maintained this same Black, Hispanic, and White leadership ratio once their terms expired.

Jim Washington of the Dallas Weekly, Tom Lazo of Lazo Technologies, and I comprised the next set of co-chairs and endeavored to carry on the good work of the Dallas Together Forum. I feel FINA made a difference, and the Dallas Together Forum made a difference, and collectively Dallas is a better city because of it.

Contributed by Karen Jones Griggsby

I felt both honored and challenged to work for Ron Haddock. He had such a belief in fairness and equality; I saw his character and what he envisioned for FINA. 'Because you are our program manager,' he said, 'you will be the secretary of the Dallas Together Forum.' My role was to meet with the other co-chairs and talk about the agenda before meetings, take minutes, and eventually coordinate plans with every major player at the table.

As the Minority Women Business Enterprise Program Manager, I enjoyed an outstanding relationship with different organizations. The social aspect was notable; FINA would sponsor a table at fundraisers, sometimes located at a sports venue, and Magic Johnson and Pettis Norman would attend. Lamar Hunt, George Will, and other notable opinion leaders attended as well. It was remarkable!

Ross Perot's company, EDS, was very involved with the Dallas Together Forum. Ross was such a wonderful and unpretentious man. At times I'd see him at one of his favorite restaurants, a salad place off I-35, and he'd come to the table and say hello. He was such a gentleman.

Major General Hugh Robinson, formerly head of Southland Corporation's Cityplace project, thought the world of Pettis. The major was one of the few Blacks on the Dallas Citizens Council — noteworthy in that day and age. May General Robinson rest in peace. I believe Pettis could have served in any government position had he wanted to but he chose to lead outside of public office.

Also noteworthy were the major corporations that supported our initiatives of minority- and women-owned business inclusion. Frito-Lay, JC Penney, Southwestern Bell, Minyard Food Stores — eventually, all the large companies participated. Ron went after businesses that weren't yet on board and continued to build important alliances. Other corporations across Texas reached out to learn more about what we were doing to improve representation and opportunities — the Dallas Together Forum was a very well-respected organization. It made me feel good to be a part of it.

Ashok "A. K." Mago

I cannot say enough good things about my friend Ashok Mago, Chairman & CEO of Mago and Associates, a Dallas-based business and investment consulting company. I appreciate his perspective on our work in the Dallas Together Forum; his insights on behalf of minority-owned businesses were unique to Dallas and benefited all minorities.

A.K. helped ensure that the focus wasn't exclusively on African American, Hispanic, and female inclusion, but also the inclusion of Indian Americans and Asian Americans. This resulted in a much-needed perspective from all ethnicities in the business sector.

I will never forget the wedding celebration he hosted at a restaurant for Ivette and me — a fun gathering of friends and associates, many who supported the Dallas Together Forum. Throughout the years, we've watched Dallas grow, learn, adjust and become a better version of itself.

I am proud to call this amazing businessman a friend and fellow servant leader.

Contributed by A.K. Mago

Pettis tells me his most prized award was the 'Humanitarian of the Year' from the Lions Sight and Tissue organization, calling it a huge honor. The organization helps people who have issues with their eyesight, primarily an alliance extension with a concern for the prevention of blindness. I was president of the organization and considered our city leaders' civic and business contributions and their devotion to our society in the metropolitan Dallas area. Pettis contributed so much to the people of Dallas and their families. He was a successful, caring business person and earned the award through his tireless volunteer efforts.

Bill Solomon, Joe Alcantar, and Pettis were the initial co-chairs of the Dallas Together Forum. Joe and I were in the same Leadership Dallas class. Later, I served as a co-chair to get more minority businesses involved and encourage larger businesses to sign contracts with them, keeping in mind the importance of diversity in business. African Americans, Anglos, Hispanics, Indians, Asians, and women — these business leaders focused on opportunity and also gained attention from media corporations regarding inclusiveness. Pettis played an important role in that.

We found that the business community wanted to address minority issues, and the CEOs of major corporations came to the table to help, thanks in large part to Pettis and the efforts of all in the Dallas Together Forum.

Liz Minyard

My admiration for Liz Minyard dates back to the mid-1970s when we first became friends. She served as the former Co-Chairman and Co-Chief Executive Officer of Minyard Food Stores and held the titles jointly with her sister Gretchen Minyard Williams.

Liz exemplified the power of an entrepreneurial spirit as a woman overseeing what became approximately $900 million in annual sales. Her business acumen and energy level surpassed the gender barriers that many women encountered in those days. Even with a vast enterprise to oversee, she found time to give back to the community as a philanthropist and volunteer.

Liz is someone to emulate, a true role model for other women who dream of success in a world still dominated by males. Her participation in the Dallas Together Forum was beyond helpful — it ignited change in the 1990s. We drew on her expertise in strategy, investment, finance, and public affairs.

Below she shares insights I will always cherish.

Contributed by Liz Minyard

Pettis worked on several City of Dallas committees, which gave him a foundation for the Dallas Together Forum. He was always respected in the community, and this was vital. To change things, we have to respect the change leader. His wife Ivette and daughters worked with him in his family business. A lot of people assumed that being an athlete had advantages, but it takes more than a name to be successful. You have to demonstrate ability and desire. You have to go above and beyond, and Pettis did.

Pettis' first wife died when we were envisioning the Dallas Together Forum and he married Ivette a few years later. To see such a variety of business associates of all ethnicities at his wedding was wonderful. Their presence was a gesture that reflected what we were trying to accomplish — doing business together, socializing together, and developing a trust factor regardless of race or gender. It was really special.

More communities would be better off if they could change perspectives and value one another, especially those from different cultures and countries. Doing so helps solve equality and pay problems and enhances respect for women who work really hard to contribute to the economy.

The Dallas Together Forum brought real improvements to the city. Becoming more inclusive nearly 30 years ago meant something. The initiative ended when people felt it had run its course — some moved, some retired. In hindsight, we might have taken some time off and regrouped, perhaps not meeting as often — maybe twice a year — to continue the focus. The whole purpose was to impact younger generations and continue to influence our communities about how we treat each other and respect each other. It's frustrating to see the same issues cast by different characters today. How often do we have to keep solving this problem and re-teaching people?

We still have a ways to go. Pettis has worked very hard in his life to help us get there. He should be proud that he persevered and didn't give up, even in the most challenging decades. Everyone says the same thing — they are proud of Pettis and proud of the purpose and strides made through the Dallas Together Forum.

Erle Nye

Erle, former President and CEO of TXU Electric, was more than an associate; he became a dear friend over the course of many years. His service to Dallas in general and through the Dallas Together Forum specifically did a lot of good for the minority business community. There are a lot of great stories about Erle, but the one below is my favorite.

At dinner one night, the former Mayor of Atlanta said, "I know something about you."

Erle said, "I hope it's not bad."

The mayor said, "No, your company in Texas bought more services from minorities than the entire State of Texas."

The Mayor of Atlanta was correct, and what a tribute to Erle. TXU became well-known as a company that cared. Under his leadership, TXU became a leading industry example that proved minority- and women-owned businesses could deliver if simply given the opportunity. I am proud to call him my dear friend; he is an incredible, selfless leader.

I'm reminded of a Thomas Carlyle quote that fits Erle well —"Everywhere in life, the true question is not what we gain, but what we do."

Contributed by Earl Nye

Pettis and I met in passing in the 80s during our civic work around the city. I got to know him well when he founded PNI Industries. I hired his company to haul fuel for TXU, and Pettis received a TXU Gold Supplier Award for PNI Industries for great service.

Our company was aggressive in our approach to this award, which suppliers coveted. People went to great lengths to win the gold star, and Pettis' nomination was based on pricing, the bidding process, and his ability to deliver right to the site, which was a breakthrough. He also came up with some good ideas and thus earned the award.

Pettis never used our friendship to influence business but worked through the process to earn contracts based on hard work and great service. The award meant something to him. It's amazing what motivates suppliers. Yes, they are trying to make a living, but recognition is just as important.

We'd invite suppliers and key players to an evening ceremony at Symphony Hall or some other venue and host a reception with food and drinks, and then announce the honors. I still see former gold star suppliers who remember receiving the award 20 years later; it was that important and motivational.

I joined Pettis in the Dallas Together Forum and later became a co-chair after Bill Solomon's term expired. I believe Pettis' best claim to fame was creating a program that included minority and women-owned businesses in mainstream Dallas. We focused on large corporations that were in a position to help small businesses. TXU was interested in creating a new culture in approaching procurement. Price was still a significant factor, but we sought ways to make minority businesses more competitive.

When small suppliers had a hard time getting the bonding and insurance needed to compete, we helped them when possible. These small businesses were not in a position to bid on larger projects, and we endeavored to solve this by breaking jobs down into parts so small businesses could compete. If smaller producers and minority transporters could deliver ten or fifteen% of the requirements, they could bid.

Pettis and I worked on this concept together, generating millions in procurements for diverse smaller companies. I believe this had to do with Pettis' extraordinary politeness. He always kept his composure and carried himself so well, a big fellow who could have been loud and direct, but to the contrary, was soft spoken, kind, and thoughtful. He was the voice of reason, a modest person and a gentleman first, last, and always.

We'd go into these tense meetings, and the big companies would resist, thinking the Dallas Together Forum was a giveaway program. 'No, this is valuable,' Pettis explained. When Pettis spoke, people listened. I remember that he'd hold up his hands as he talked, and we'd see his bent fingers, old football injuries. He held his water until the right time to express his thoughts. He was diplomatic and made a point, and had a lot of perspective. In this remarkable way, he persuaded people to come around and join in the Dallas Together Forum mission.

Pettis' service to the community and humankind was very notable and admirable. I appreciate his charm and great sense of humor. If he's your friend, he's your real friend.

Pete Schenkel

Pete Schenkel, former President and Principal owner of Schepps Dairy, has one of the shrewdest political minds in Dallas, and I'm not the only one to say so. What I found most remarkable about him was that early on, he broke bread with White and Black business leaders without exclusion. This made him one of the few true bridge builders in the Black and White power structure going back decades.

As a major employer in a minority neighborhood in southeast Dallas, Pete encouraged the strengths and abilities of all regardless of race. He never compromised the trust placed in him and was always sensitive to the needs of the disenfranchised. I admired that he took a chance on people, giving them opportunities to excel.

I always thought of Pete as a "big picture" type of leader. Pete was a board member of the Citizens Council, the North Texas Commission, the State Fair of Texas, and past chairman of the DFW Airport Board and the Methodist Health Care Foundation. But most of all, he remains one of my good friends, and we still enjoy meeting up for lunch.

Contributed by Pete Schenkel

I first met Pettis when he was drafted by the Dallas Cowboys and arrived here from Charlotte. Back then, he was a good listener regarding the politics and the happenings in Dallas, staying more or less on the sidelines. That's when I met him on the sidelines. His ears perked up, and he decided this was the type of city he wanted to be connected with.

After a year or two, early on, he started to get involved in the community and then left to be a San Diego Charger. Fortunately for the citizens of Dallas, he came back and made a home here, raised his family, bought some Burger King franchises, and was very successful. One thing I admired is that he managed his money well. He got involved politically and had a keen interest in education and the Dallas Independent School District. Then he became quite an entrepreneur in the fuel distribution and transport business. I believe I was one of his first PNI customers. I picked up the phone, he came over, and I told him I wanted to buy fuel from him, assuming it was the right fuel and right price. Yes, I wanted to do business with Pettis Norman.

There is no telling how many successful minorities in this town owe Pettis a thank you. He opened doors for many of them through the Dallas Together Forum. Sometimes people need a break to grow their businesses, and minority business owners are no exception. We'd see people like Pettis and Richard Knight and others who made the city a better place and encouraged others to do the same.

When I was chairman of the DFW Airport, we led a charge for minority participation. At the time, there were few, if any, minority-owned concession stands, and now it's 40%. All of that comes from meeting people like Pettis Norman. He is such an ambassador in the arena of inclusion and states that people of color have the same needs and abilities as White people.

Pettis always provided a helping hand regardless of skin color. He wanted to help people prosper in the business front and the education system. He wanted Dallas to be the best in the country, especially while he was raising his family.

We went out to lunch at Luby's recently with our mutual friend Tom Dunning. Pettis couldn't eat his food because so many people came to our table. "Remember me, Pettis? I'm so-and-so," they'd say. Pettis got up from his chair and treated them like they were the most important person in the room. It made them feel special, and that stuck out in my mind.

When his first wife passed away, I'll never forget sitting in church and watching a figure come down the aisle singing 'Amazing Grace.' I knew I had seen that face — it was Jesse Jackson. He gave the eulogy. Later on, Pettis married Ivette, and I attended their wedding at Paul Quinn College. There was Jesse again, officiating the wedding.

I'll always remember and appreciate Pettis for standing up for the right things in political circles. I know it was hard for him sometimes, but he acted for the right reasons.

Pettis opened doors in the community, and more so for the African American community that had encountered closed doors for a long time. Now those doors have swung wide open. Young African American and Hispanic kids today are doing well financially because of Pettis Norman. I really believe that. He has a quiet professional manner, and I've never heard him brag. He is never one to pat himself on the back, so I'll do it for him.

James "Jim" Washington

Jim Washington is an iconic media and public relations leader with deep insights into the track records of elected officials, community activities, minority businesses, chambers of commerce, and the CEO culture. I have a lot of respect for him as one of the Legends of the National Association of Black Journalists and the publisher of *Dallas Weekly*, a trusted voice in the African American community. Not many Black publishers existed at the time — how gratifying that this successful news source was available week after week without fail.

Today he lives in Atlanta, Georgia and it's wonderful to reconnect and pick up where we left off. His legacy is still felt in Dallas — Jim's son now owns and operates the *Dallas Weekly* print and digital enterprises.

After the co-chair terms of Bill Solomon, Joe Alcantar, and myself expired, Jim stepped in with Ron Haddock and Tom Lazo to fill the positions. It was a huge undertaking, and below, Jim shares his retrospective view.

Contributed by Jim Washington

The Dallas Together Forum began with a small group of CEOs, Anglo, African American, and

Asian, who got together to discuss race relations. I was fairly new to the city at the time and give a lot of credit to Bill Solomon for introducing me to key people. This gave me access to the inner workings of Dallas, and I became aware of the concern shared by many CEOs about racial disparity in the city.

There was no agenda for a while; we spent time bonding and learning to trust one another. We explored how to get to know each other, including dinners at each other's homes and engaging at a level where race was not an obstacle. I credit everyone because no one held back. We were able to speak our minds frankly, knowing how critical every perspective was. Eventually, we all became friends, led by Pettis, who was a co-chairman for three years.

We met for two years privately, and at first, no one in the city knew what we were doing. We didn't want to politicize it. Then the Rodney King tragedy occurred. When I look back from a historical perspective, this debacle became a catalyst in Los Angeles and erupted throughout the nation. Many in Dallas, as I recall, felt something should be done before the Los Angeles scenario happened in Dallas.

We decided that as CEOs, we could blow up barriers in hiring practices, and that's when we decided to go public. As a public presence, we officially changed the name of our initiative to the Dallas Together Forum and needed officers, bylaws, goals, and objectives. We honed in on the focus and purpose of our organization, which was to empower business opportunities for minorities and women.

So that people wouldn't think we were a subversive group (oddly enough), we first approached public entities — the airport, city government, and other groups — always cognizant of purchasing, hiring, and contracting more minorities and women. Early in the game, we were successful and decided to approach corporations as well, CEOs visiting other CEOs.

The goal was for corporations to track spending and put a benchmark out there to be measured as time went by. We tilted the city in a lot of ways, but not without challenges. I became very close with Robert Decherd, and we noted that mid-level White executives might look at these initiatives as threatening their livelihood. It wasn't just waving a magic wand and changing institutional behavior and mindsets. Convincing corporate Dallas that this was the right thing to do — and a beneficial thing to do for all — took a lot of effort.

Erle Nye had an interesting perspective and said, 'I can't take any pleasure that your end of the boat has a hole in it because we're all in the boat together.'

We set the example in our own companies. If any of us had a terrible track record, we addressed it honestly and tapped each other for help. By the time I stepped in as co-chair, we had become a more formal organization and a model for other cities to do likewise.

After six years, we assessed where we were and the progress that had been made. Most companies in Dallas had fair employment and contracting practices in place. Every chamber of commerce and the Citizens Council had now adopted diversity in spending and hiring. We had moved the needle and didn't want to be in a position of duplicating someone else's mission. We took a vote and decided to *sunset ourselves, knowing we had made a difference.*

I will say this about Pettis — he is a rare human being. He walks with the proverbial "every man" with confidence and comfort. From community and civic icon to corporate leader, he is one man who is respected by all, even when his courage demands he stand alone. I am grateful and appreciative that he has stood with me and I with him on many a battlefield. Even when I may have doubted victory, his presence on my side let me know there was no question we would ultimately win out. I call him friend.

Chapter Eighteen: One Door Closes and Another Opens

True love is not something that comes every day. Follow your heart; it knows the right answer.
~ Pettis Norman

I made the decision to sell the restaurants, apartments, and real estate holdings in 1986 to focus on humanitarian endeavors. At the same time, I began to envision something commercially larger and more far-reaching. In 1990, I founded PNI Industries as a sole proprietorship, while Margaret continued pouring her heart into our hair care company, Liquid Love.

During this transition, my soul shook when I lost Margaret unexpectedly in 1991 due to heart failure. There were no warning signs; she was here one day and went to heaven the following day. I sought answers, but the mystery was never solved; my world was upended. I share more about my loss in the "Legacy" chapter.

As humans, our hearts are resilient, and life is expected to go on. I stopped and pondered for a while to reflect on our beautiful union and thought about how difficult it would be going forward without my lifelong partner by my side. While this unbearable loss stopped me for a good while, PNI, my newly-founded business, helped create a diversion from the pain by keeping my mind focused on the future. I began working on behalf of presidential hopeful Bill Clinton as his campaign surrogate for Dallas in 1992. Later, President Clinton invited me to the National Prayer Breakfast, which meant another meaningful trip to Washington D.C. It felt like a blessing of sorts as if God had His steady hand on my new startup and me after losing Margaret.

That same year in 1992, I was awarded the "Doers, Dreamers and Unsung Heroes" Award from The Real Estate Council of Dallas, which I thought was a nice commendation based on the businesses I had built and planned to build going forward.

Also in 1992, the sky opened and an angel dropped in my path. Her name was Ivette Hightower, and while I was not looking for love, she appeared in the right place at the right time. Ivette was the Director of Sales & Marketing for US Airways (later American Airlines) and felt it would be a great opportunity for the company to sponsor a Paul Quinn College fundraiser at the Meyerson Symphony Center. Her responsibility was to get exposure for her employer, but she believed this was also a wonderful way to support a Historically Black College and attend an enjoyable event. US Airways raffled two airline tickets as part of the sponsorship.

It was a high-profile gala with more than 500 people, entertainment from Hollywood, and many friends. I was reluctant to attend the gala that October, but a close friend, Comer Cottrell Jr., called and said, "You have to come to this fundraiser. It will be good for you to get out of the house." Comer donated the land for Paul Quinn College. What a blessing! God rest his soul.

It was raffle time, and Ivette announced the lucky winner and awarded two round-trip tickets anywhere in the USA. She stirred the names for the raffle, pulled out a slip of paper, and announced, "The winner is ... Peeetis Norman," unsure how to pronounce my name. She was new to Dallas and did not know me. During the drawing, I was conversing with people at my table when suddenly, a thunderous noise erupted. Everyone stood up, looked at me, and began clapping. "YOU WON! YOU WON!" In disbelief, I walked up to claim my prize.

"Thank you very much," I said, locking eyes with Ivette as she extended the two vouchers. "Congratulations! When you get ready to travel, let me know, and I will arrange your travel plans," she answered.

Later that evening, after attending the VIP Reception, Ivette and I happened to arrive at the valet desk at the same time, part of God's plan when I think back on it. I thanked her again for the tickets, and she reaffirmed her willingness to make arrangements when I was ready to travel. That was it — no more conversation between us until six months later when I called Ivette's office and said, "I need a ticket to Charlotte."

She arranged for the ticket to be picked up at the airport and said, "Have a nice trip." That was it.

Three months later, Margaret's uncle died, and I called to claim my second ticket. I had to leave almost immediately for Charlotte, so Ivette was kind enough to make last-minute arrangements at the gate to ease the stress on this unexpected trip. She had everything set up upon my arrival at the airport.

"Just pick it up at the gate," she said.

"How nice of you," I replied.

On the way home from Charlotte, I reflected on how kind Ivette had been to me without any expressed interest or overtures. There was a meekness to her that I liked, something special that I wanted to know more about. After I returned from the funeral, I called Ivette.

"Would you like to go to dinner?" I asked.

"Sure," she responded.

We bonded that evening over our tragic mutual losses. Ivette lost her mother Cora suddenly in April 1991, two months before Margaret passed suddenly in the same year. We were both hurting, and neither of us knew it. Our pain was raw, and we helped each other, talked about our significant losses and the reason why it took so long for us both to be ready for our first date. From that day forward, we talked every day, two or three times a day. I noticed an uptick in my mood and spirit; this felt good.

Her passion is travel and history; mine handicapping and the lineage of thoroughbred horses. We merged our passions and began a beautiful journey of travel and horse racing. They say opposites attract, but I disagree. I believe there must be common interests in a relationship, and we had them. Ivette and I shared the same values and cared about the same causes. She had a selfless spirit about her and cared deeply about people — always has.

We joined Concord Missionary Baptist Church, where the late Dr. E. K. Bailey was pastor. We both had a strong faith and placed God as the head of our lives. We began attending many events together — I loved the way she interacted with people so graciously. I introduced her to my family in Charlotte and Lincolnton, and they embraced our relationship. They grew to love Ivette as a person, as did my daughters, and welcomed her into our family.

I recall starting the 1994 New Year by escorting Ivette to an Anti-Defamation League Dinner honoring EDS president and CEO Les Alberthal Jr. Ivette was with me when I received the "Minority Supplier of the Year" Award from the Dallas/Fort Worth Minority Business Development Council. She was with me when I received the "Distinguished Service Award" and "Doctor of Humane Letters" from Paul Quinn College. She was always my biggest cheerleader and always so proud of my accomplishments. I frequently traveled with her on business to different parts of the country, and we became inseparable over time.

Long story short, we fell in love, and I secretly began designing an engagement ring. I presented it to Ivette on her birthday, February 11, 1994.

"Will you marry me?"

"YES, YES, YES!" she exclaimed as we embraced and prayed for God's blessings in this new exciting journey of love and marriage. The next day we set our wedding date for May 13, 1995. We knew our union was not just about us, but the importance of Ivette becoming a surrogate mother, grandmother and embracing important customs and traditions in each other's families. Ivette met my daughters early on and was at the hospital for the birth of our grandson Alex, who became our ring bearer in our wedding.

She never liked the word "stepmother," so my daughters and grandson endearingly called her "Mima." She couldn't replace their mother, but she could put them first, and that's what she has done.

The Nuptials

I'd like to share some observations about our wedding by those who know us well and how this demure and quiet woman completely transformed my life.

Dr. Lee Monroe, the president of Paul Quinn College who so graciously prepared the campus chapel, says:

> *I'm fond of Ivette and Pettis and was aware that Ivette loved the chapel at Paul Quinn College. Pettis was such a generous contributor and fundraiser, and it was only fitting and proper that we would move up putting the chapel in proper condition to host the wedding for this wonderful couple. We worked diligently to refurbish and beautify the venue and make Ivette's dream come true.*
>
> *Ivette was such a lovely bride and brought a certain calmness to Pettis. This is true today, as well. She has a steady, understated energy that is pleasant and accommodating. I noticed her personality was (and is) an excellent complement to Pettis' personality. Out of all the potential partners in the world, Pettis was drawn to her for these qualities. He made an excellent choice, for Ivette has been steadfast*

in supporting his business and servant leadership efforts. He has been able to achieve a lifetime of goals with her in his corner.

Although Ivette has a quiet presence, her reach extends quite far. She is able to arrange surprise events for Pettis by coordinating with guests from all over the country and even internationally. The last time I saw her at Pettis' 80th birthday, I noticed that it took a tremendous effort to make the celebration so meaningful and noteworthy, truly a labor of love.

Yes, Ivette is quite a lady, very gracious and committed to Pettis' wellbeing. It's hard to believe their wedding at the Paul Quinn chapel happened more than a quarter-century ago, and I'm so pleased they are enjoying a long, happy, and successful union.

My lifelong friend Butch Walker also has fond memories leading up to our wedding. I would say that Butch is an "expert witness," knowing me so well and wanting the very best for me in the "spouse department."

I fell in love with Ivette the very first time I saw her. I thought Pettis was one of the luckiest guys to walk the earth to find this lovely woman. He brought her to Homecoming at JCSU, and she struck me as elegant, intelligent, and so very, very nice.

You have to remember that Pettis was single at the time. I'm sure many women would have loved to be in Ivette's shoes. But Ivette was "the one" — that special person Pettis chose to be his wife. And I certainly approved of the match.

Ivette was a stunning bride, just beautiful. Ray Charles and Stevie Wonder could see that! Pettis and I have been friends since 1958 as a freshman at JCSU and we graduated together. So it was nice that my wife and Ivette hit it off. I will say they are two of the classiest ladies you could ever hope to meet outside of my mother. Come to think of it, perhaps I am the luckiest person in the world, with Pettis a close second.

It's been one heck of a trip, being lifelong friends with Pettis. I'm so glad we have maintained our friendship as husbands to two wonderful partners. It feels like Ivette has been there for the whole journey, a part of the trip from the very beginning, although she married Pettis in 1995. I was a groomsman and so happy to see him exchange vows with someone so very, very likable. It was like he got the brass ring on the merry-go-round, especially at that point in his life and career.

Believe me, Pettis is blessed. And there isn't anything I wouldn't do for him and Ivette.

Another eyewitness to our beautiful union was Justine Norman, a close relative. The fact that Justine and other family members embraced my wife-to-be meant a lot to me.

My father and I traveled from Georgia to Texas to celebrate the beautiful nuptials of Pettis and Ivette. They were truly a match made in heaven. Ivette, dressed so beautifully, appeared to have stepped out of a fairytale as she marched down the long aisle, love gleaming from her eyes, anxious to meet her husband at the altar.

Ivette is such a special person, modest and quiet with a sweet spirit. I've never heard her say a cross word. She's a peacemaker, a giver, and thinks of others first — the epitome of a truly loving partner. Throughout their relationship. I witnessed selfless love and a caring heart in action. She engaged in every aspect of Pettis' life, always providing gentle support, kindness, and understanding. Obviously, they were best friends when they exchanged vows, and their bond has been blessed beyond measure due to Ivette's commitment, sweet attitude, and graciousness. I have always been impressed with their deep and relentless love, and I am certain Pettis thanks God every day for sending him this gift, his angel.

The Norman wedding was royal from beginning to end. The host hotel and reception venue, the elegant Adolphus Hotel, was a retreat in the heart of downtown Dallas known for its modern conveniences and big Texas hospitality. Lodging there was a wonderful way to connect with family, meet new friends, and gush over the excitement. The party started the moment we arrived, and I immediately became keenly aware that the Dallas Cowboys ruled the land. People at the hotel were asking, 'Who's getting married?' and the response was 'A Dallas Cowboy!'

Their choice of Paul Quinn College, an HBCU, as the venue to exchange their vows and start their new life together made my heart smile. It was a decision that I loved! Officiated by an iconic pastor Dr. E.K. Bailey and civil rights leader Reverend Jesse Jackson, the ceremony had tangible energy felt by all in the chapel. The mutual admiration and respect I witnessed that day has grown over the years.

Pettis and Ivette inspired so much love and happiness on their wedding day, just as they do now. When it comes to true love, it's rare, unique, and beautiful, and it's wonderful that they found it.

Wow, I must say Ivette was breathtakingly stunning. The wedding was almost as beautiful as she was and quite a large gathering. Who better to describe it than Ivette? Below she reflects on that special day and our honeymoon.

Reflections From the Bride

> "This kind of certainty comes but just once in a lifetime"
> ~ Robert Kincaid

I absolutely loved our wedding venue, the unused chapel at Paul Quinn College (formerly Bishop College). I remember touring several possible locations, but when we entered the chapel escorted by President Dr. Lee Monroe, something just "spoke" to me. The long aisle, the altar, the pews — everything was grounded in history. Both Pettis and I knew this was a special place to exchange vows.

I woke the morning of May 13, 1995 to a beautiful sunny day, feeling rested and peaceful. I felt the presence of our Lord and Savior and knew that our marriage was a gift, an amazing blessing from God. I sat with my cup of coffee and reflected on our special courtship, and recalled our first date.

Family portrait. Photo credit: Reggie's Exclusive Photography

With my beautiful bride. Photo credit: Reggie's Exclusive Photography

THE PETTIS NORMAN STORY

I wasn't looking for love; I had a successful, professional career, was very happy, and had no plans for marriage. Our first date was so special. Pettis knocked on my door and greeted me with a dozen red roses and a bottle of Cabernet Sauvignon. I remember thinking to myself, Chivalrous men are a dying breed, but Pettis' presence at my door proved otherwise. The chivalry did not stop there; it continued throughout the evening and ended with a soft hand touch as we said good night. As I looked into his eyes that evening, I thought how special it was to date a man who still values the tradition of courting and appears to be a respectable human being; and yes, handsome too.

My mother Cora would have loved him, and I wish she could have met Pettis. I reflected on the very close bond I had with my mother and the important lessons she taught and lived by. She was a selfless wise spirit who demonstrated the importance of giving, sharing and kindness. She grew up with modest means but had an enormous amount of spiritual wealth. She was a happy soul and no matter where I lived, we talked every single day – she was my best friend.

The years flew by, and our love grew stronger. I noticed Pettis had a way of engaging and befriending people he didn't know. This captured my heart and mind early on — he's never met a stranger. Football fans adored him, naming him 'Man of the Year,' his teammates both in college and the NFL praised him, and the community leaned on him for his wisdom. I kept asking myself, Is he real? Does this kind, gentle man have any flaws?

As we counted down the days to our wedding, he never changed. Pettis never portrayed himself to be anyone other than himself. The wedding was sacred and beautiful. I was happy to have our daughters and grandson be a part of our special day. It was important to me because I was not just marrying Pettis; I had the awesome task of becoming a loving surrogate mother and grandmother. So, this day had an even deeper meaning. We understood our sacred marriage covenant included our children.

I found the most beautiful dress in Dallas and a one-of-a-kind tiara that complimented the dress perfectly during a shopping spree in New York with my sister Janet. She was so excited for me, and I was blessed to have her shuttle me around to find the perfect headpiece.

I arrived at the hotel and was greeted by my daughters, sisters, and bridesmaids, who showered me with hugs and kisses. My oldest daughter Shawn pulled me aside and said, 'Mima, I have someone to do your makeup; I want you to be beautiful today.' That was a small detail I hadn't thought about, but my thoughtful daughter had my back. Shortly thereafter, we were en route to the church. My youngest sister Xiomara could not be there, but I felt her loving spirit.

My father, Harry Hightower, a proud Naval Officer, was waiting to walk me down the aisle. He whispered, 'Walk slow; I want to show you off.' That brought a huge smile to my face. He loved Pettis and was eager for us to marry. We had 13 bridesmaids and groomsmen in our bridal party, all of them beloved family and long-time very dear friends.

As always, the adorable children stole the show. The flower girls were my niece Olivia Davis and Margaret Ivey. They were charming in their beautiful dresses and shiny shoes. Charles Davis and

Alex Norman, my cute-as-a-button nephew and grandson, were the ring bearers. Alex, who was 1 ½ years old at the time, boldly walked down the aisle until he realized no one was with him. When he saw all the eyes fixated on him, he turned and ran back. He eventually made it to the altar with the encouragement of Pettis and family friends. It was a precious moment and brought a smile to everyone.

Helping my bride into our 1933 Buick Model 57 Sedan. Photo credit: Reggie's Exclusive Photography

After the wedding Pettis drove his 1933 Buick Model 57 Sedan, a prized possession for many years. With Pettis behind the wheel looking happy and handsome in his tuxedo, it served well as the lead vehicle in the procession from the church to the hotel reception. Our first dance, 'At Last' by Etta James, says it all. We both found love and were on a new journey embraced by our favorite biblical verse, 1 Corinthians 13:4-8. Interestingly, one of our most prized wedding gifts was from my sister Yolanda, who gave us a beautiful ceramic book sculpture engraved with this Bible verse. It is prominently displayed in our room and is a constant reminder of our love.

The day after our wedding, we took off on a ten-day dream honeymoon. First, we took a flight to Greece where we visited the historic Parthenon and enjoyed Greek culture. Then a flight to Israel where we walked in the footsteps of our Lord and Savior, visited Tel Aviv, the Sea of Galilee/Mount of Beatitudes, Jerusalem, Bethlehem, and the Dead Sea. On our final flight to Egypt, we toured the

Pyramids of Giza on camelback, saw the mysterious Sphinx, bonded with the Egyptians, and visited several underground, multi-roomed burial tombs of the Pharaohs. What an exciting trip, one that will always remain entrenched in our hearts.

Today, we are connected in so many ways and are now approaching our 27th wedding anniversary as I write this; we have been in a loving relationship for almost 30 years. I married an amazing man who taught me so much about love, selflessness, and forgiveness. He made me a better person, and I am so happy he is mine, and is it any wonder?

Pettis frequently whispers to me, 'The best is yet to come.' How exciting! His love is worth a thousand skies!

Paul Quinn College

I'd like to share a bit more about Paul Quinn College, which holds such a special place in my heart. As mentioned previously, Ivette and I met due to a Paul Quinn College fundraiser and exchanged vows at the chapel on campus.

None of this would have happened if Paul Quinn College had not relocated from Waco to Dallas in 1990 onto the vacated campus of the defunct Bishop College. The relocation was beset with many issues, including both financial and crumbling facilities. Since I was involved throughout the community, a corporate associate asked me to get involved with Paul Quinn. I joined the board of trustees and partnered with Joe Zimmer, a Texas Instrument executive and chair of the board's executive committee.

Joe and I were tasked with recruiting a leader for Paul Quinn's major fundraising campaign. We recruited my good friend Robert Decherd, the Chairman of the Board and CEO of the A.H. Belo Corporation. Robert, Joe, and I, along with the new president, Dr. Lee Monroe, began the drive. We called on more than 100 corporations and individuals, raising more than $30 million. No one said no. The funds were used wisely; the campus was purchased and refurbished, an endowment was established, and, most importantly, the enrollment grew to about 900 students from throughout the country and several foreign countries.

Another event added to the excitement of this time period. In 1996, Paul Quinn College and the United Negro College Fund sponsored the first Presidential Awards Gala. Notably, I received a Doctor of Humane Letters, conferred as an honorary degree from Paul Quinn College on May 2, 1998, to recognize my humanitarian and philanthropic work. I received the diploma at the college's graduation ceremony wearing a cap and gown with my wife Ivette, daughters Shandra and Sedonna, and grandson Alex in attendance.

This experience was very humbling and inspired me to consider ways to give back to the community under the PNI Industries umbrella.

Paul Quinn College

Dallas, Texas

On the recommendation of the Faculty and by virtue of the authority vested in them the Trustees of the College have conferred on

Pettis B. Norman

the degree of

Doctor of Humane Letters

together with all the rights, privileges and honors appertaining thereto. In recognition of the satisfactory completion of the course prescribed by the Faculty of the College.

In testimony whereof, the undersigned have subscribed their names and affixed the seal of the College at Dallas, Texas, May 2, 1998.

John R. Bryant — Chairperson of the Board of Trustees

Lee E. Monroe — President of the College

[Secretary of the Board of Trustees]

Charles A. Humphrey — Vice-President of Academic Affairs

Chapter Nineteen: PNI Industries — We Go the Distance for You

Company branding must be more than a slogan; it should be a way of life.
~ Pettis Norman

I diversified PNI in 1994 by adding several companies, classified as "Certified Minority Business Enterprise (MBE)" and "Historically Underutilized Business (HUB)." Eventually, more than 50% of our managers were female in what can only be described as traditionally male-dominated industries.

By hiring PNI, customers reduced their costs and risks and experienced improved efficiencies. It helped to build brand loyalty, and our customers trusted PNI – this loyalty meant the world to us. Under the PNI umbrella, five companies were formed during an exciting and adrenaline-filled decade.

(1) PNI Distribution
(2) PNI Energy
(3) PNI Transportation
(4) PNI Best Value
(5) PNI Fleet Services

PNI Distribution

I'm asked quite often, "How did you get into the wholesale fuel business?" First, I credit my good friend Ron Haddock, former President & CEO of FINA, Inc., for my entry into the industry. I met him when he staked out the issue of race relations in his role as Division Vice Chairman of Community Development for the Greater Dallas Chamber. His selfless mentorship, generous guidance, and partnership with PNI Distribution inspired me to expand my operations. Ron Haddock and FINA were trendsetters back in the '90s and set a powerful example of mentorship with minority-owned companies.

Ron trail blazed these efforts by initiating and formalizing FINA's minority mentorship program. Before this was a large focus within major corporations, he took the lead and mentored several companies throughout the Dallas-Fort Worth area. He felt it was important to diversify beyond an all-White and all-male system of business leadership and believed this change would be good in corporate cultures across our city and the nation. He was right. I credit Ron with taking a leadership role with race relations in our city, and I am grateful to have crossed paths with this visionary man, who remains a good friend today.

Pettis Norman in his office after launching PNI Industries. Photo Credit: Gittings Photography

As our partnership with FINA expanded, PNI's role in this successful mentorship program was highlighted in President Bill Clinton and Vice-President Al Gore's BusinessLINC (Learning, Information, Networking and Collaboration) initiative that encouraged corporate mentorship opportunities across the United States. The Small Business Administration and the Department of Defense Office of Small and Disadvantaged Business Utilization organized BusinessLINC meetings around the nation. Many thanks to the office of Mayor Ron Kirk for organizing the Dallas BusinessLINC Regional Meeting; his effort helped highlight this important initiative for businesses in our area.

BusinessLINC took us to the next level. What a blessing that FINA and the city and national government targeted economically distressed urban and rural areas to build business-to-business relationships and enhance the competitive strengths of small businesses.

PNI Distribution qualified as a Small Business Partner Firm because we were successful with the necessary "stages": (1) the concept stage, (2) the early growth stage, (3) expansion, and (4) stabilization and maturity, the stage at which we were fine-tuning operation and production and looking for additional opportunities.

It was gratifying that the success of PNI Distribution and FINA's partnership was included in a report to Vice President Al Gore dated January 1, 1998:

BusinessLINC
Learning, Information, Networking, and Collaboration:
Business-to-Business Relationships that Increase
the Economic Competitiveness of Firms

A Report to Vice President Al Gore
Presented at the Second White House Business and Entrepreneurial Roundtable

New Opportunity, a Stronger Economy
By Clifton G. Kellogg
January 1, 1998
Department of the Treasury

Pettis Norman founded PNI Distributors in Dallas as a wholesale fuel supplier almost ten years ago. Today, PNI revenues are $16 million with over 75 employees. PNI's relation with FINA, Inc., a $4 billion petroleum company, demonstrates how firms of different sizes in the same industry can benefit from sharing business expertise.

Ron Haddock, President and CEO of FINA, Inc., says, "The relationship is based on a strong mentor commitment: through our relationship, FINA assisted and guided PNI almost as though it was a division of the FINA company."

FINA management asked PNI to develop 3- and 5-year business plans and expected a level of financial accountability. Haddock had to be convinced that mentoring a firm is ultimately in Fina's shareholders' interest for two reasons: first, because the relationship draws on company resources, and second, because the shareholders' interest is also critical to long-term, broad-base employee commitment to the relationship. "Without our employees seeing the logic of this relationship, says Haddock, "their commitment would decline over time."

The PNI relationship meets this standard, both through increased product sales and by helping FINA earn the respect of all members of the community. FINA assisted PNI in accessing new markets and diversifying into the retail convenience market business. PNI supplies FINA fuel to retail outlets and, with the support of FINA bought 25 retail outlets (some of which had been owned by FINA). FINA offered PNI assistance with marketing, preparing financing requests, administrative support, technology, and business strategy guidance.

After an extensive evaluation and assessment of PNI's capabilities and limitations, FINA and PNI signed an agreement focusing on three areas to help PNI double its revenues: increasing the number of PNI-owned gasoline stores; linking PNI with new customers in the fuel hauling business; and suggesting how PNI could diversify into other business areas.

With my dear friend, Ron Haddock. Photo courtesy of PNI Industries

Diversifying into other ventures is precisely what we did. Our partnerships included key refineries such as Koch, Fina, Motiva, Citgo, La Gloria, Delek Refining, Ltd., Valero, Chevron, Shell, and Exxon. We became a large-scale wholesale fuel distributor by modernizing our operations with leading-edge dispatch and IT systems and flourished because we hired experienced industry professionals who understood the market and our competition. These were not salespeople, but managers trained to provide exceptional service and build brand loyalty.

Our products included liquified natural gas (LNG), compressed natural gas (CNG), diesel, and regular, mid-grade and premium gas. We expanded our customer base to include major entities and corporations such as DART, DFW Airport, refineries, and convenience stores. It was a matter of mastering the industry from the bottom up — and quickly — for government regulations and customer expectations were vast.

To handle this aggressive expansion, I needed high-level experienced management. I also knew the best way to retain long-term employees was to offer an attractive benefits package that would rival any Fortune 500 company. Allow me to commend a few of our key executives — Mel Ottinger and Karl Simmons, Directors of Transportation; General Manager John Foster; CPA Amenta Rasa; and Dispatch Managers Russell Thrasher, Pat Wade, and David Neveling. My nephew George Bolton was also indispensable in running the businesses early in PNI's operation. Their expertise was invaluable to our operation, and I leaned on them in several ways to keep our operation successful. Our staff was paid at the higher end of the pay curve for this industry and received a generous benefits package.

When it came to random audits by the IRS, I was always confident we would pass. "If everyone operated their business like this, we wouldn't have jobs," one agent told me. I trusted Amenta Rasa with maintaining excellent accounting records, and I trusted her as a person. She continues to handle my remaining corporate and personal business, and I consider her to be a very close friend today.

During this time, I served as the chairman of the Greater Dallas Chamber of Commerce Minority Business Development Committee, which interacted with several minority chambers, including the Black Chamber, the Hispanic Chamber, and the Native American Chamber. This extremely important collaboration created greater opportunities to address minority concerns and helped raise their visibility.

PNI Distribution would become an important platform upon which other PNI business ventures were launched. In 1995 and 1997, we were awarded the "Minority Supplier of the Year" Frito-Lay Certificate of Appreciation, which was extremely gratifying. We had two evergreen philosophies: *"Do unto others as you would have them do unto you"* and *"My word is always my bond."*

PNI Energy

Likewise, an opportunity arose to develop, supply, and manage battery programs, both automotive and commercial. PNI Energy launched a partnership with Frito-Lay in Plano, Texas, to provide wholesale automotive battery distribution. I decided the most cost-effective way to run this operation was through a partnership with Exide Batteries, rather than to bring the operation in-house.

Frito Lay signs a contract with PNI Fleet Services to provide Exide batteries to 16,000 route trucks and over-the-road tractors in the United States and Canada. Back row: Bob Gonzales, Group Mgr. Minority Business Development, Ted Phillips, Fleep Operations Mgr., Larry Caldwell, National Fleet Senior Group Mgr., Dennis Selle, Fleet Operations Mgr. Front row: Paul Zmigrosky, Vice President Purchasing North America, Pettis Norman, President & CEO, PNI Fleet Services. Photo credit: *Minority Business News DFW*

This entity, under PNI Industries, was a big success, and this strategic decision secured our bottom line. It allowed us to expand rapidly without compromising service to Frito-Lay. PNI Energy eventually served a fleet of 16,000 route trucks and over-the-road tractors across the USA and in Canada.

The economy of South Dallas was depressed, and few minority-owned businesses were open in the area. Unemployment was the result, and I wanted this enterprise, and all PNI enterprises, to be a center of opportunity in our community. I later added several dozen employees to my staff of 60 to expand our corporate office.

We took PNI's Energy program with Frito-Lay one step further and piloted a one-of-a-kind program in California, Florida, and New England. This was an intensive "trial run," in which we tracked each battery's location, documented if it worked or was returned due to failure, or if there was theft or possible abuse. We used a closed-loop system to handle all billing and provided consolidated reports for each fleet location and data on each truck battery.

Bob Gonzales, Group Manager of Minority-Women Business Development for Frito-Lay, said, "PNI provides us with a 'one-stop shop' for batteries. They take care of everything." Paul Zmigrosky, Vice President of Purchasing for Frito-Lay North America, said, "The service level and attention to detail are important. Price is important too, but not as important as getting the right battery for end-use applications. PNI delivered a quick turnaround on battery orders."

With that high bar to maintain, we added forklift, stationary, UPS, specialty, industrial, telecommunications, and Gel Cell products and services to our portfolio. We also offered PNI private-label batteries.

I was focused on both the economy and the ecology of the world and therefore searched for opportunities to convert waste into reusable materials. The batteries themselves were environmentally friendly, and we expanded our agreement with Exide to send used batteries to a licensed smelter for recycling. In short, we were one of a handful of energy distributors in the country offering this unique program and level of accountability. Therefore, people who protested the loudest about the environment usually came on board and were our biggest supporters.

The bottom line was ensuring we stood behind our service, our people, our customers, and our communities throughout the United States and Canada. This was the right way to do business and a hallmark of our reputation.

PNI Transportation

PNI Transportation was founded in 1994 after a request from several of our large PNI Distribution customers who needed transportation of fuel to their various centers. Never afraid of a challenge, I researched the requirements for tanker transportation of petroleum products, located a company that I trusted for equipment, and initially leased/purchased five trucks and tankers. We had experienced management already in place, Mel Ottinger, who ran the inside operation, and Russell Thrasher, who understood the tanker business and became a driver dispatcher. I wish I had ten more drivers like Russell; he was incredibly loyal and became part of my inner family circle until he went to heaven. God rest his soul; we miss him.

This new PNI entity offered wholesale fuel and transportation services for large and small businesses, truck stops, major oil companies, municipalities, school districts, corporations, transit authorities, DFW airport, and the Murphy USA gas stations located in front of Walmart stores.

This business expanded rapidly by word of mouth. Several acquisitions included other key customers such as Shell Oil Products, Atmos Energy, Motiva CM&D, Schepps Dairy, Texas Instruments, Delek Refining, Ltd., TU Mining, American Airlines, TXU, Frito-Lay, Foremost Dairy, and Dallas Area Rapid Transit (DART).

Speaking of DART, we hauled fuel (specifically a special blend of diesel) to DART facilities in Dallas. I recall their buses were the first to use this type of diesel (mixed with bio and called biodiesel). The process was straightforward. Typically, my drivers removed a hose from the truck, hooked it up to the trailer valve, and connected it to a tank on the ground. DART, according to industry regulations, had a vapor recovery system in operation. When the caps were taken off the tanks, the fumes could not vent into the air. I was pleased to receive the following quote from one of DART's top executives:

> *Summer 1998, a fleet of 488, new, state-of-the-art buses were delivered to DART. PNI's job was to transport fuel for the more than 80 million passenger trips per year on the DART network. This period was critical because of air quality standards and to ensure our vehicles met the needs of our community. PNI maintained our schedule and delivered on-time in the quantities needed. PNI was a proven, dependable, good contractor.*
>
> ~ Victor H Burke, Executive Vice President /GM Retired

Our 24-hour-a-day operation grew to over 40 trucks and tankers, and more than 50 drivers took shifts to deliver fuel around the clock. PNI Transportation was branded with the words: "From sunrise to sunrise, we go the distance for you." It was a sincere company-wide call to action to provide our customers on-demand, timely service for any petroleum products they needed throughout Texas and neighboring states.

Our refineries were located in South Lake, Fort Worth, Dallas, Tyler, and Houston. Orders arrived continuously in the Dallas office electronically in our fast-paced operation. Three dispatchers coordinated deliveries and relayed information to our drivers with state-of-the-art equipment installed in our trucks to communicate deliveries.

I was pleased to receive the following testimony from Shell Oil:

> *PNI has been a contract carrier in the Dallas-Fort Worth metropolis since the beginning of 2003. In this period, their performance has been exceptional. They have been responsive to our service demands and have performed all operations in a quality manner. They have helped us achieve better than 'world class' results in the areas of customer service stock outage, redirected deliveries and customer satisfaction. We will continue to look for opportunities to expand our business relationship with this high-performance company."*
>
> ~ George D. Maar, Delivery Manager at Shell Oil Products

Taking advantage of various cutting-edge technologies was a company-wide endeavor. We installed "People Net" fleet management software in our trucks, giving us end-to-end vehicle tracking. We captured information on travel logging, navigation, routing, fleet performance monitoring, and safety compliance. Additionally, our inside operation was equipped with TMW software to monitor repairs and maintenance. This software maximized asset utilization to reduce empty miles and lowered operating ratios to maintain productivity.

Finally, safety was always paramount in my business. We kept a tight grip on our fleet by implementing the Smith Systems Accident Avoidance Program, GPS monitoring, spot training of our drivers, and an aggressive drug-testing program. As a result, we ran a safe operation with very few accidents.

Our fleet of late-model, well-maintained freightliner tractors and 4-C \ 5-C trailers were branded as well. They were painted silver with blue and white stripes in a nod to the Dallas Cowboys. Our large PNI logo, a star, appeared in the middle of the tanker, again painted in Dallas Cowboy colors. These were good-looking machines, and we received a lot of positive comments on the aesthetics. We also employed drivers in Denver, who transported bulk petroleum products in parts of Colorado. This meant the Mile-High State got a dose of Dallas Cowboys spirit from the Lone Star State!

PNI truck tanker. Photo credit: PNI Industries

Our branding wasn't always well received when football rivalry came into play. One of my top drivers drove through Louisiana to deliver motor oil and never understood why people gave him dirty looks. Then it occurred to him that some New Orleans Saints fans became riled up when they saw our Cowboy-themed trucks in their "territory." The folks in Louisiana love their Saints.

Several of my very best drivers were ticketed for speeding, and a few were taunted by Saints fans in pickup trucks. My top driver, Roland Brown, told me, "I got a ticket down there for *not* speeding." I called the judge and told him, "I was not speeding," and he said, "I believe you, son, and the best thing you can do is pay. We just want your business." The next week, another driver experienced the same thing but decided to fight his ticket in court and was basically given an identical speech.

I don't really blame the passionate Louisianans for their reactions. After all, who knows what would have happened if New Orleans Saints-themed big rigs rolled through Dallas! In the scheme of things, I believe our Cowboys branding helped inspire pride in our company — pride from our employees and pride from the community.

We kept up with the latest in IT requirements, which was very important, especially as we integrated as many PNI company systems as possible. Driver Safety Compliance was vital because our company was governed by the Department of Transportation. Past references, drug testing, previous driving history, motor vehicle reports, maintaining current commercial driver's licenses, accidents, performance — all had to be documented. Of course, we also maintained and closely monitored records relating to loans, payments, fixed assets, various reports to the government, fuel tax rates — the whole nine yards, with state-of-the-art software. This technology and hands-on approach to management kept our company safe and profitable.

Pettis talks with Mel Ottinger, Director of Transportation in front of branded PNI trucks.
Photo credit: PNI Industries

I am truly proud of the PNI family and feel blessed to have had a loyal group of employees who captured the vision and helped our company grow.

The Personal Touch

I should mention that PNI Transportation was very much a family affair. My wife Ivette, two daughters Sedonna and Shandra, and my nephew George worked in the businesses. Early on, Margaret also worked at PNI and took on various roles while pouring her heart into running Liquid Love, a company I talk about in the "Legacy" chapter. Even Alex, my much-adored grandson, spent time after school serving as our paper shredder. We all had a hand in raising him; he was a joy to have around.

Shandra proved to be extremely valuable and productive in our accounting department while pursuing her Bachelor of Arts degree from SMU. Ivette and I were proud parents when she graduated and left PNI to apply her skills in corporate communications with the Greater Dallas Chamber of Commerce. Today she works with the Texas Real Estate Commission and was recently promoted to Member Benefits Manager. Shandra has always been very talented with a brilliant mind, and I am proud of her accomplishments.

Sedonna was excellent in customer service and remained employed with PNI until she obtained her real estate license. She branched out into residential and corporate real estate in Dallas and became very successful in her own right. Sedonna took off to California and anchored down in Los Angeles to continue developing her real estate business. I was not happy when she left the nest, but this move allowed her to expand her business and be close to the entertainment industry, a key part of her business development. She is like a magnet; people are drawn to her personality, intelligence, and expertise in real estate.

My oldest daughter, Shawn, did not work at PNI but ventured into the music entertainment business in New York, where she managed and worked with high-profile clients. I could never live in New York, but she thrived in business and fell in love with the bright lights in a city that never sleeps. Her work with notable clients was impressive, and I enjoyed meeting and getting to know many of these entertainment icons. Tragically, we lost her in 2014, and I also share more about this significant loss in the "Legacy" section. She's an angel in heaven now and I carry her beautiful spirit with me daily.

George Bolton, my nephew, has been a special part of my life for quite some time. Back in the mid-'70s, I encouraged George to relocate from Charlotte to join me in business. He always had a brilliant mind, an excellent work ethic, and brought new innovative ideas to my business operation. Bottom line, I felt he could make a valuable contribution and take my businesses to the next level. He first began working for me when I built The Golden Helmet apartments as our Operations Manager, where we housed several teammates and maintained 100% occupancy.

George transitioned with me to my new Burger King franchise operation and became a valuable member of the management team, responsible for managing operations, staff, and promotions. He then joined Margaret and me when we launched Liquid Love from the heart of our kitchen and was steadfast with growing and expanding our line of hair care products throughout the Metroplex.

After launching PNI Distribution in 1990, George became one of my key executives and educators for automotive batteries, fuel, and oil. As a result of his passionate commitment and visionary leadership, we built successful companies and sustained long-term success year after year. Here is how George Bolton describes our relationship and friendship over the years:

> *My uncle Pettis was a role model for me. I loved hanging around him while we were growing up. We were close in age, and yet he was so inspiring to me. I watched him closely as I tried to pattern my life after my uncle. He taught me to never give up, never quit. He helped me believe that I was capable of doing anything and that I should never, ever say 'no' to any challenge. I appreciate his loving guidance, and my mother, his sister Ida Helen, loved him dearly.*

While they say never work with your spouse, Ivette and I were partners in business for 20 years; she was my anchor. Ivette preferred to remain behind the scenes and took on a very critical role in our companies. She helped us stay on top of the complexities of meeting state, federal, and safety requirements, as well as corporate professional standards, accepted business practices, and internal standards for all of our companies. She was always a multi-tasker and had an integral part in building our exceptional team at PNI. At 3:00 p.m., she was off to her second job, supporting our family, especially our grandson Alex who had basketball, soccer, and football practice. Her home-cooked meals were a great way to finish the day, and dinnertime was always enjoyable, especially when our grandson was visiting.

Finally, to my genius grandson Alex. I have never seen a child do homework while watching TV, listening to music, talking on the phone, and making the honor roll every year while in school. Also, he excelled in sports at a very young age and became the team captain, role model, and leader on the football team at Bishop Dunne High School — I am proud of him!

He was selected as one of 100 high school student-athletes across our nation to play on the "Under Armour, All-American" game in Orlando, Florida; what an accomplishment. I was pleased when almost every Division One university began pursuing him in high school for their football programs; he worked very hard to get this well-deserved recognition. But he was laser-focused on only one offer, The University of Texas at Austin. He got a full-ride scholarship, played football, and most importantly, graduated with honors. I am so proud of Alex and always tease him that he is a "chip off the old block."

PNI Best Value

The fourth company, PNI Best Value, was a logical offshoot of the other PNI enterprises and our mentoring partnership with FINA. I was already sourcing and transporting fuel for gas pumps at convenience stores and decided to buy and operate FINA branded convenience stores. Ron Haddock, CEO of FINA, and I worked closely together to identify the best convenience store locations for our operation. He cradled this new venture from start to finish until we consummated the deal. This was another example of Ron's selfless commitment as a mentor to PNI.

After our due diligence and closing, Ivette and I took off to South Africa for ten days.

Nelson Mandela was in office, and we toured Cape Town, Johannesburg, Soweto, and Sun City. This trip is and forever will be the favorite of our international travels. It was refreshing to see that apartheid was now illegal. This country no longer permitted five million Whites to control over 30 million Blacks. South Africa had the right leader in place, though it was just the beginning of a long and treacherous journey. Ivette and I had a joyous and yet emotional trip.

Upon my return, my convenience store locations escalated to a dozen Best Value stores staffed with polite, well-trained employees. This was probably my most challenging business because it was a decentralized operation based on market trends and the important needs of the community.

With the help of our General Manager John Foster, I implemented the successful Burger King training model and approach to customer service. While we had some success in changing the culture and attitudes of inherited staff through retraining, we still needed significant changes to build a cohesive team of employees to run this operation. It took patience and time for us to get our arms around this new venture.

We named our convenience store chain "Star City." I recently came across an old rendering for one of those Star City stores and its FINA gas pumps. It reminded me of Coach Landry and my football buddies because there, front and center, was our own star logo, another nod to the Dallas Cowboys — gray, blue, and white. It was displayed on the outer architecture of the convenience store. Clean, aesthetically pleasing, and functional — when we said, "Best Value," we meant it and demonstrated it in these stores.

As time passed, PNI Best Value became my most difficult division to operate. We experienced uncharacteristic turnover, theft, inventory challenges, revenue management, and a robbery that took the life of a beloved employee. After several years of managing this operation, I felt it was in the interest of our overall operation to sell these stores and redirect my energy and effort to fleet services, transportation, and distribution. Failure was never an option, and I knew it was time to sell my convenience stores and focus on my profitable divisions.

PNI Fleet Services

In 1992, we were honored to receive the Minority Business of the Year for Outstanding Performance Award from Southwestern Bell, a company we successfully served through our PNI Transportation business.

A few years later, I got a call one day from the corporate office of Southwestern Bell. "Pettis, I need you to fly to El Paso. I have a proposal for Fleet Service that I would like you to handle." I had never been in the repair business, although we certainly serviced our own PNI vehicles. To my delight, based on our success with fuel sales and transportation as a top service provider, we were awarded a new contract with Southwestern Bell (which later became AT&T) to provide fleet repair service.

"We go the distance for you" became the motto at PNI Fleet Services, just as it was with PNI Transportation. Our services included full-service vehicle repairs and maintenance; generator service and repairs; hydraulic repairs; auxiliary trailer repair; utility truck bodies, doors, ladder racks, modifications; and emergency road service.

I launched this venture with the existing employees onsite and hired Alex Parga, who became an instrumental part of the success of this operation. He was knowledgeable and proficient, exactly what I needed to run an operation from a distance. I provided education on who we were at PNI and stressed the importance of understanding the difference between the old and new practices. The employees knew their jobs but needed to understand the cultural differences between Southwestern Bell's former contractor and PNI.

Since my reputation demanded that we have a record of excellent service and repair, we hired skilled ASE certified master technicians and experienced pickup and delivery drivers, thus equipping us with a great team who could diagnose with accuracy, provide safe pickup and delivery of vehicles, and ensure satisfactory service with a quick turnaround.

As always, I believed that employee retention resulted in superior customer care. We employed women, which was novel in the industry. We implemented a state-of-the-art software program that tracked performance reviews, technician productivity, inventory, workplace regulations, on-time performance, and invoice accuracy.

PNI Industries Fleet Repair Shop in San Antonio, Texas

Our technicians were required to have excellent interpersonal skills, an accident-free and clean work area, follow OSHA safety guidelines and workplace regulations, and participate in unannounced drug testing. Ivette was instrumental in implementing and managing these important programs and made sure we consistently met all regulations. I'm proud to say we met and exceeded OSHA safety audits, Environmental Protection Agency compliance, and AT&T's environmental, health and safety policies during every evaluation period.

Within one year of operation in El Paso, AT&T granted us an opportunity to expand to San Antonio and Austin. Of course, we accepted this new opportunity, and PNI Fleet Services became a "one-stop-shop" for AT&T in Texas. In addition, we were recognized as being one of AT&T's top-performing Fleet Maintenance operations in the country.

My success with this operation could not have been accomplished without two outstanding Fleet Service Managers. First, Alex Parga ran an excellent operation in El Paso and became our Fleet Service Trainer, IT Manager, and interoffice Fleet Service liaison. Alex was not only an excellent manager but a great family man too. We have stayed in touch with Alex and his family and are blessed to call them friends. I appreciate his kind quote below:

Pettis was my boss for over ten years. He was more than just a boss; he was family. I always say that if I could work for him again, I would do it in a heartbeat. I really miss his daily business phone calls. He is a real class act.

Randy Bivens, Manager in San Antonio, recently shared some kind words on his employment with PNI Fleet Service:

> *Working for PNI Fleet Services has been the best career opportunity that anyone could ever imagine. The management and decision-making skills that I learned from Pettis prepared me for a successful future in fleet management. Pettis Norman was the best boss, teacher, and friend anyone could ever expect to have. Thank you for still being my mentor and friend.*

I truly appreciate these kind words from Alex and Randy. It's not every day that you find employees with this level of devotion, hard work, and tenacity to do whatever it takes to get the job done. It was a pleasure to have these exceptional managers on the team.

We were now running four companies under the PNI Industries umbrella and doing it quite well. I learned that it takes a variety of people who perform a multitude of important tasks, cohesively and consistently, to make a company run efficiently — a tremendous challenge as I reflect, but we were successful.

As our expansion snowballed, I reminded myself of important life lessons such as honor, trust, commitment, and performance that I learned from four important people — my mother, my father, my college coach Eddie McGirt, and my professional football coach Tom Landry, who I believe was the greatest coach in NFL history.

Chapter Twenty: Revelations of a Serious Man

When you hear laughter, move toward it. It is an essential ingredient for living healthy and building successful relationships.
~ Pettis Norman

Readers Digest is onto something when they state: "Laughter is the best medicine." I remember that special feeling as a child, instinctively knowing how to have fun and giggling over random, silly things. Perhaps you remember this too, back when you were a younger version of yourself and blessed with buckets of energy. But joy, wonder, unbridled laughter, and hijinks are not exclusive to childhood. Grownups should have fun too.

Sure, it's easy to get bogged down with some of life's problems and become too serious, too intense, and too "one-dimensional." We are multi-dimensional people with a full spectrum of emotional needs, one being a need for laughter and joy. All work and no play should never be a motto, for the reality is, we all need to play. It's like food for our souls, and science backs me up on this — numerous studies prove the many benefits of playtime in adulthood.

This gives us permission to sing our favorite "oldies but goodies," goof off, joke around, prank each other, play games and tickle the funny bone. The results are increased creativity, productivity, a sense of well-being, and a closer bond with the people we enjoy and love the most.

For those who are busy planning weekly calendars, please schedule time for play. Yes, we all need to strategize with staff, review reports, improve the bottom line, and figure out how to make more money... but scheduling time for fun makes these tasks more bearable. Put fun in your schedule; if you don't schedule it, it's less likely to happen.

Those who know me well can attest to this lighthearted (and often scheduled) part of my life, a side of me known by a handful of best friends and beloved family members. I want to share a few favorite escapades, most planned but some a complete surprise that brought respite from my busy schedule — a glimpse of personal and corporate moments in no particular order that will forever bring a smile to my face.

Guess the Celebrity

As a way of showing appreciation to PNI employees, I hosted an annual summer picnic at Sandy Lake Park in Carrollton, Texas, beginning in 2003. We offered a full buffet of food, refreshments, carnival rides, and games, with the backdrop of a beautiful lake.

Giving back to our employees was an essential part of my value system. The gifts ranged from turkey giveaways at Thanksgiving, cash bonuses at Christmas, and birthday cakes. We also made it a point to get personally involved in the lives of our employees and their families. Our planned annual picnic was an extension of the office but in a very fun way. I got to know husbands, wives, and children — an important part of bonding with employees.

We also handed out awards to our employees for outstanding service to the company, notably "Employee of the Year" and "Driver of the Year." The grand prize was a coveted "President's Circle" Award for the top performer in the company. The President's Award came with a significant bonus and the recipient's name prominently displayed on a beautiful large plaque in our office reception area along with previous awardees. Our President's Award reminded all employees to strive for excellence in their positions.

After the presentation of the awards, we asked our employees to join in the fun and display their talent for 1st, 2nd, and 3rd place monetary prizes. This set the stage for the main attraction, a "Hollywood celebrity" who provided entertainment and was kept secret until the performance began. Then drum roll… and the party grew loud with chatter and buzzed with anticipation when a stretch limousine pulled up to the stage. Who could it be? The energy from the crowd began to grow as the megastar sat in the limo, teasing the anxious crowd. Who could it be?

Finally, six PNI "security guards" and six PNI "FBI agents" surrounded the limo in preparation for the show. Screams of excitement could be heard miles away. Who could it be? The medical staff was on hand for adoring fans who fainted, and security was prepared to tackle rowdy groupies.

Who could it be? Why, of course, me, ready to rock the house, costume and all.

Only at PNI could you see…Elvis "Pettisley" Presley; MC "Cool P" Hammer; Michael "Hee Hee, I'm Really Bad" Jackson; the artist known as Prince "Prince of Whales" from Purple Rain and finally, Tino "Gonna try to take you higher" Turner.

Preparation for these performances was very serious and required months of watching videos, studying moves, tons of aspirin, and the occasional spa day to relieve the stress. Once I perfected the choreography, with Ivette's help, it was showtime!

The hard work paid off every time. Word circulated throughout the park, and the venue was packed to capacity. This really boosted my ego, and I felt talent of this caliber could not be contained. The demand was so high, we decided to take the show on the road to family reunions. For a minute, I contemplated a career change.

Yes, I gave my best renditions as a celebrity impersonator to much applause and even more laughter. My favorite was Michael Jackson. I had all the accessories — the sequined socks and glove, vest, hat, high-water pants, and yes, the wig to look the part. The fun thing about being "Michael" was learning the moonwalk. I mastered the fine art of sliding and gliding backward while appearing to move forward, at least in my opinion. My family and employees suggest otherwise.

As for Tino Turner, well, Ivette made me vow never to impersonate "the queen of rock" ever again. She refused to go dress shopping with me, and perhaps that's why I had a wardrobe malfunction. Yes, *that* type of wardrobe malfunction, where the inserts that filled out the chest kept slipping down and plopping on the floor. My barber for 60 years, Lee Williams (a.k.a. Lee

Photo Credit: Bobby's T-Shirts

Cool "P" Hammer

Photo Credit: Bobby's T-Shirts

Prince of Whales

"Let's Go Crazy"

Photo Credit: Bobby's T-Shirts

the Barber), served as Chief of Security and was in charge of picking up those inserts. I kept adjusting, and they kept slipping. I guess my dance moves to "Rolling on the River" were just too much. The process became a dance in itself — drop, pickup and tuck; again drop, pickup, and tuck. The waves of laughter were loud, but the show went on. I'm sure I looked far from feminine despite performing in high heels: shiny gold sandals two sizes too small and a beautiful red thigh-high dress topped off with red fishnet stockings.

How sad I was when Ivette gave my red dress and sandals away, commenting, "Tino will never take you higher again." Some of those old photos are hilarious. The memories are priceless; it was great while it lasted. But I'm not finished. Maybe one day I'll make it to "America's Got Talent."

By the way, I still trust "Lee the Barber" with my hair. I first met him at one of the largest barbershops in Oak Cliff. He is a legendary professional, styling many of my teammates, including Rayfield Wright, Jethro Pugh, Bob Hayes, Reggie Rucker, Don Perkins, Mel Renfro, and other NFL and NBA players. Lee isn't just a great barber, but a great man. We've maintained a very good friendship, him with the scissors and me in the chair. He weighs in on those early days:

> *I met Pettis Norman in 1964 and have been his barber ever since. He came through the door and began talking — a great guy who enjoys doing the right thing for all people. He was a great football player and now works on behalf of the community. As a Christian, he believes in the greatest biblical saying, 'Do unto others as you would have them unto you.' I have never seen him waiver over the years.*

Beverly Hillbillies

Back in the '50s, I enjoyed *I Love Lucy* and Lucille Ball's zany adventures with her husband Ricky, and their neighbors Ethel and Fred. The show was the pinnacle of popularity at that time. In 1962 I bonded with another family in the oil business — the Clampetts from *The Beverly Hillbillies*. For those who are not familiar with this famous bunch, they were a poor backwoods family from the Ozark region who struck oil, became millionaires, and moved to Beverly Hills. During the show's heyday, *The Beverly Hillbillies* ranked among the top 20 most-watched programs for many, many seasons, and at one point, ranked twice as the number one series on television.

My love and affection for the Clampetts began during the height of running several businesses, taking a leadership role in our community, and continuing to help "the least of these." As a respite from a busy day, I'd race home for my daily bowl of soup and peanut butter crackers and turn on the television at noon to watch my favorite show. Then I'd take a power nap. Nothing could interfere with this routine — it was scheduled — but if I missed the noon show, it returned at 1:00 p.m. So, I had a backup plan.

You may ask why I was attracted to this famous family. The answer is simple. They made me laugh. This show took me away from the hustle and bustle of everyday life. I escaped my own world and joined Jed, Elly May, Jethro and Granny for 30 minutes, enjoying their unpretentious reactions to the Beverly Hills lifestyle. Their shenanigans were boisterous and funny.

My favorite character was Jed, the fearless head of the family. In my head, I can still replay his catchphrase, "*Welllll*, doggies!" Hilarious! If you are not aware, he made the decision to move to Beverly Hills after discovering a huge oil pool in his backyard swamp. Since his money was just as good as anyone else's, the Clampetts rags-to-riches journey took them into awkward social situations. They were untouchable due to their vast fortune and could be as "hillbilly" as they wanted, including raising chickens and a menagerie of livestock on their finely manicured estate.

I vividly recall the year my family planned a "Beverly Hillbillies" birthday for me with all the characters and trappings of a 30-minute showing. First, my family presented me with an 8-track series of the show with more than 20 episodes to delight me during my lunch hour, and more importantly, when I traveled. What a fantastic gift! After the singing and birthday cake, my daughter Shandra asked me to have a seat in the den for part two of our celebration.

After waiting for what seemed like an eternity, *The Beverly Hillbillies* theme song began playing, and out came the Normans dressed as their favorite Hillbillies characters. I could not believe what I was seeing. My daughter Sedonna was "Granny," and she looked the part. Ivette dressed as "Elly May," pigtails and all. Alex was Jethro in high water pants while Shandra directed the show. If I had to give an Academy Award for best performance, Sedonna nailed it all the way down to hair, dress, and talk; she was Granny's double.

Yes, I still search for the series today, but it's hard to find. I suppose the 8-track tapes that I converted to DVDs will have to suffice. Here's a shout-out to the actors in *The Beverly Hillbillies* — Buddy Ebsen, Donna Douglas, Max Baer Jr., and Irene Ryan for lightening my load during stressful times.

Outspoken Characters

"This is the big one! You hear that, Elizabeth? I'm coming to join ya, honey!" This exclamation by TV character Fred G. Sanford brings a smile to my face every time I hear it. Fred was a cantankerous and crotchety junk dealer whose television series debuted in 1972. The character, played by Redd Foxx, actor/comedian with one of the quickest minds on the planet, was a sensation. He was the first African American to headline in Las Vegas and appealed to Blacks and Whites. Everyone loved Redd not because of his ethnicity but because he was funny. Humor is a wonderful bridge.

Demond Wilson, the perfect foil for Fred, played his long-suffering TV son Lamont. The pair had me in stitches; the intergenerational exchanges and arguments reflected the dynamics in many families, I'm sure.

I think my admiration for *Sanford and Son* centered on the sitcom's grown-up jokes and somewhat risqué humor, which took audiences right to the brink without crossing the line. Sanford & Son was NBC's answer to CBS's *All in the Family*, which had begun airing the year prior. Fred Sanford and Archie Bunker lobbed culturally insensitive comedy bombs into living rooms across the nation in the 1970's. I admit nearly cringing at some of the more outrageous and brazen dialogue but laughing nonetheless — and that was the point. Fred Sanford said what the rest of us couldn't or wouldn't, at least not in polite company.

In 1975, George, Louise, Lionel, and Florence amused America in *The Jeffersons,* another successful Black sitcom that appealed to all audiences. I just laughed and laughed at Sherman Hemsley's portrayal of George, the impatient and short-tempered businessman who had "moved on to the Eastside." Isabel Sanford played his level-headed wife Louise, and Marla Gibbs was the irritable and sassy maid Florence. As a bit of trivia, Ivette and I were thrilled to meet and spend an evening with Marla Gibbs at a charity event. She was very kind and gracious, nothing like her TV character.

This was at a time when we could still laugh at ourselves and others goodheartedly, all the while aware of issues with race relations and the social chaos of the 1970s. At that time, we didn't have the overbearing political correctness and the over-the-top censorship of today. Perhaps back then, we were secure enough to chuckle at it all, embracing the fact it was depicted on television. It became conversation starters at water coolers and lunchrooms. I believe this type of experimental television tested the audiences' reactions and willingness — or not — to accept the outspokenness of the characters.

The Madwoman

As a child, I learned a lot about the cemetery up the road from my parents' house. It served as a burial site for a few people in Lincolnton. I remember spending time admiring headstones, reading epitaphs, looking at wreaths, and wondering about the lives of the men, women, and children entombed there. At that age, it was both a scary and sacred place, about half a football field away from our home.

I suppose I come by my sense of humor from a childhood that included plenty of good old-fashioned pranks. Many were directed at me, for I was the youngest and most gullible, and my reactions got a lot of laughs. Not even my mother spared me from these jokes; in fact, she was sometimes the instigator!

Yes, my mother once concocted a trick that had me running for my life. I don't think I've ever sped away as fast as I did the day a terrifying visitor appeared out of thin air. This prank took some planning and coordination between my mastermind mother and my sister Sarah who had the starring role. I replay it in my mind, on the one hand admiring their choreography and on the other hand remembering the fear associated with the prank.

Here's the backdrop. There was always talk around town that a mad woman named Laura being on the loose. I remember my parents and other relatives talking about Laura, and we were always on the lookout for a lady who fit the description. You see, in the country, untruthful gossip would sometimes spread, and it would become a topic of conversation among family and friends.

My mother usually asked my older siblings to get the mail, but one cloudy day she made me feel like a "big boy" by asking me to run to the mailbox. This presented the perfect opportunity to scare me out of my wits.

Mami sent me out with a warning: "Get the mail, but be careful."

"I'm always careful," I assured her.

"Because a madwoman was spotted close to the cemetery."

"A madwoman?" I repeated. "A crazy woman?"

"Yes, so be careful around the graveyard and keep a watchful eye out for her."

I was a little uneasy but wanted to be brave for Mami and took off on my errand about a block down the road past the cemetery. My head was on a swivel, and I kept glancing at Mami for assurance as she remained in full sight. I arrived at the mailbox feeling confident and safe, grabbed the contents, and turned to walk briskly back home.

At this point, I had no fear; Mami and my sister Gladys were still in sight on the porch as I passed by the cemetery. Then I thought I heard an eerie moaning sound. Unsure of what it was, I froze and searched the landscape but saw nothing. As I gathered my composure, the sound occurred again, much louder and very close – *hmmmm*. I gulped, searched my surroundings, and spotted a figure wrapped in a full-length fur coat stumbling and wailing. I think my heart stopped, but my body went full throttle. In my head, I kept saying, *it's her, it's her, the madwoman!* But unbeknownst to me, it was my sister Sarah dressed in disguise.

Mami saw how afraid I was and began waving her hands. My sister Gladys did the same in an attempt to calm my fears. Instead, I took their waving to mean "Run baby, run!" I took off with an adrenaline rush. My sister Sarah got scared when she saw Mami frantically waving and thought she was telling her to get out of the graveyard and run for her life too! To a little kid, this was a scene right out of a horror film! I'm told it looked like my feet were running in the air as I raced back to my mother with the "mad woman" not too far behind!

Mami realized the joke went bad when her two children raced down the road, fearing for their lives. Worse, I thought the madwoman might be after my Mami too. All sorts of terrible scenarios raced through my mind as I leaped onto our porch, panting. "Mami, Mami, the mad woman's coming." I pointed and yelled at the top of my lungs, "There she is!"

"No, no, stop running! It's a joke, baby. It's really Sarah!" Of course, my mind was still spinning, and I couldn't process what Mami or Gladys was saying. I wanted to keep running!

I was shaking when "the mad woman" reached the porch. After I got a close-up look, I realized my sister Sarah was in disguise, and I wasn't sure whether to run down the steps and confront her or drop to the ground in relief. After the shock wore off, we all began laughing hysterically, especially Sarah, who got spooked by the spoof.

The "Mad Woman" story still gets lots of chuckles from my family and is often retold at reunions. Oh, I laugh now, but back then, I think I nearly hyperventilated!

Seinfeld

Seinfeld has ranked among the best television shows of all time, and I wouldn't be surprised if my personal fandom increased the Nielsen ratings. I taped every show I could find, and nothing else could be added to our DVR at home because it was filled with the antics of Jerry, Kramer, George, and Elaine. This was my show to watch in the evenings, a point of contention in our home.

With the hilarious Jerry Seinfeld

I recall heading to my recliner one evening after dinner to pick a Seinfeld recording. To my shock, they were all gone. I took my family, mainly Ivette, through Judge Norman's family court to determine why and how these recordings were missing. In hindsight, this investigation could have been its own Seinfeld episode.

I had multiple hearings during my "mediation" process to unlock the mystery of who and why anyone would erase my Seinfeld recordings. I included our cable company during the "discovery" process; they came out to investigate but did not find any plausible answers.

Unfortunately, I could not convict anyone, although I tried really hard to convict Ivette since our children did not live with us. Ivette requested a "motion to dismiss." I never did get a "verdict," and I never found the DVR recordings. My suspicions linger today; I still might "appeal" this travesty.

I don't care how many times I have replayed these sitcoms; each viewing is like the first. I had an amazing opportunity to meet Jerry Seinfeld in Las Vegas, and it was special. After all my years of watching Seinfeld, I never thought that I would finally shake hands with the man who entertained my family and me for so many years. It was a great meeting; he was very kind and cordial. Seinfeld continues to be taped on my DVR, and Ivette will confirm that I continue to be very protective of these recordings.

Creepy Crawlers

I'm not thrilled with this recollection, although it makes people laugh. "Bullet" Bob Hayes, my college buddy and fellow Dallas Cowboy, knew I had an irrational fear of crickets, grasshoppers, and creepy crawlers in general. At our first training camp, he began slipping them down the back of my jersey and watched as I jumped around. He thought it was very funny, but the nicest thing I can say is that these practical jokes and new friendships with teammates helped my homesickness. It did nothing, however, to alleviate my phobia.

I think I have good reason to be squeamish, for I am allergic to bees, wasps, and hornets. Therefore, I probably transferred my fear of stinging bugs to all bugs. Since we live close to a wooded area, we keep the exterminator busy at my house; but I still can't fully escape Mother Nature. It reminds me of a safari adventure that nearly had me jumping out of my skin. For those who have never been, I hope to describe it well enough so that you can live vicariously through our escapade.

It just so happened that Ivette and I decided to go on a safari and checked out several options. We chose Kruger National Park, a fenced camp located in northeastern South Africa, one of Africa's largest game reserves. Its high density of wild animals includes the Big 5: lions, leopards, rhinos, elephants, and buffalos, and we saw them all. Hundreds of other mammals make their homes there, as do diverse bird species such as vultures, eagles, and storks, and we saw them too. What a picturesque landscape — the rugged mountains, bush plains, and tropical forests were breathtaking.

Our camp was enclosed by an electric fence designed to keep dangerous animals out, but other camps were wide open. I'm sure the openness adds an adrenaline rush for people who like to live on the edge and want to see animals up close and personal... but I am not a fan of tempting fate. We had plenty of adrenaline surges just spotting hyenas that lurked outside the fence and lions peering from the bush, targeting their next prey.

Even within the relative safety of the fence, my senses were on high alert during this exotic vacation. We learned that African animals have a sense of smell hundreds — if not thousands — of times more sensitive than humans, so our heads remained in swivel mode during this three-day excursion. I've never used my peripheral vision quite as intensely.

We arrived at our casita in the bush, our home for three nights. It was a circular structure with modern conveniences and two twin beds —nothing fancy, just the basics. The first evening, the local tribesmen escorted us to our tour vehicle, equipped with a bank of three rows of seats rising behind the driver. Everybody got a great view forward and to the side, plus one hell of a bumpy ride. Someone shouted "leopard," and we all searched with a light in every direction to get a glimpse of this elusive animal, only to witness its tail disappear into the dark.

Next, a pride of lions rested across a pond about 20 yards from our vehicle. They were fully aware of our presence and, in my opinion, too close for comfort. A lion's roar causes a primal gut reaction. A *Smithsonian* article describes it as a sound up to "114 decibels, about 25 times louder than a gas-powered lawnmower." We heard that rumbling out in the night, perhaps a territorial call that went down into the earth and straight up our spines!

"Well, you've tackled lions before — Detroit Lions — ha, ha!" Ivette whispered nervously.

Now, I take my role as protector in chief of my family very seriously, but fending off wild beasts seemed a bit of a stretch. Apparently, my expression didn't instill confidence because Ivette said a quick prayer. Thankfully, God was listening, and the big cats ignored us. The infamous hyenas, however, did not. They kept following the vehicle and pretended to be friendly, but we knew they were awaiting an opportunity to snatch someone's hand.

After two hours, it was time to return to our casita. We were on guard until safely inside, then peered out of our window into the wilderness. An abundance of shiny eyes flashed in the darkness, on the hunt for their next meal. Then Ivette and I laughed; it was really like a reverse zoo, with uncaged and free-roaming wild animals examining us while we were trapped in a truck.

Exhausted, we settled in for the evening, still filled with a sense of uneasiness. For good measure, we moved the twin beds together. Just as we were about to drift off, we heard a loud "plop" on the bedspread. Ivette grabbed for my hand, and with a white-knuckled grip, whispered, "What's that?"

After waiting a split second, we both leaped out of bed. Ivette darted for the door while I fumbled for the lights. And what did we behold? An intruder decided to join us… the largest praying mantis imaginable, maybe five inches long. My aversion to bugs had me hopping around as I always did, especially when confronted with one the size of my hand. It didn't help that I knew a thing or two about the appetite of this species — a large praying mantis in Africa could feed on insects, mice, small turtles, and even snakes — and I didn't want it mistaking us for dinner!

After saying a quick prayer myself, I grabbed my gear and went about saving my shrieking bride from the unwelcome invader. Out of the casita it went, and I slammed the door behind it. Of course, we inspected every nook and cranny of our casita for additional trespassing crawlers. I had a case of the heebie-jeebies for the remainder of our safari. We enjoyed the next two days of giraffe and rhinoceros sightings, and on our last day, saw a small herd of elephants. A mother elephant briefly charged us because we got too close. Her ears spread out to the side, an intimidation tactic to make her seem larger than life. She simply wanted to chase us away from her calf and was quite successful — we high-tailed it out of there!

We left the camp and proceeded to our next stop, Johannesburg, and then on to Sun City. On the way, we drove through a troop of baboons, the meanest and sneakiest variety who love to swarm cars and steal food. We soon learned that if you stopped to stare at them, they rushed your vehicle, climbed all over, attacked suitcases on the luggage rack, and would attempt to get in through the windows. Thankfully, we had already closed our windows to keep the bugs out.

As we sat frozen in the car, I closely watched their behavior, intellect, and judgment. This invasion had approximately ten baboons, one, in particular, leading the pack. You could spot the so-called leader, the one that was loud, aggressive, and territorial with others in the group.

This encounter recalled an article in the *Dallas Morning News* dating back to 2004, titled "Baboons give peace a chance." It summarized a study led by Dr. Robert Sapolsky, a neuroscientist at Stanford University who documented the movement of baboons in Kenya, where the culture within a certain group went from aggressive to peaceful after the dominant male died. Dr. Sapolsky's research contradicts the old adage that violence and aggression in humans and primates are inevitable. He went on to state that if peaceful leadership is in place, along with the right social environment, the old stricter hierarchy eventually softens, and peaceful interactions prevail.

How amazing that the common thread seemed to be: if you are treated kindly, you will treat others kindly, too. Sound familiar? Luke 6:31? I think there's a lesson here for humans as well. Think about it!

Finally, Sun City was quite a fantasy land, their version of Las Vegas — a manmade beach in the desert, a reenactment of an erupting volcano, casinos, and performances from Hollywood. It was a nice refreshing change from the room we shared with the praying mantis.

On a serious note, we visited other parts of South Africa as well. It was an emotional experience to reflect on Nelson Mandela's impact on the country. At the time of our visit, President Mandela had been in office for three years and survived a total of 27 years in prison. We made it a point to explore his footsteps, including Robben Island, where he was incarcerated, where he built his law practice, and where many tragic and triumphant events played out during the revolution. What an amazing life President Mandela had; it's an inspiration to us all.

Modeling Stint

Here's an anecdote you might find interesting. It has to do with the world of advertising and one of the nation's favorite soft drinks. Imagine my surprise when a team from Dr Pepper

DISPLAYS

Negro Display Plaque

Item Number L-391

Development of the Negro Display Plaque is the result of a specific need for promotional materials directed to that segment of the population where, virtually, the full sales potential still exists. Conventional point-of-sale may be highly effective in areas outside of negro populated centers, but that same point-of-sale may, totally, lose its effectiveness when not directed, specifically, at the negro consumer.

The precedent for ethnic point-of-sale has already been set by many of the major manufacturers. The contribution-to-expanded-sales factors of ethnic materials is firmly established. Break old buying patterns and establish new purchases with this semi-permanent and prestige point-of-sale display. The plaques are in full color, and are of durable, wonderflex embossed material.

This point-of-sale piece will assist in the development of Dr Pepper in an area of marketing where only ethnic materials will effectively perform.

Item Number L-391
Packed in Units of 25
Shipping Weight: 17 lbs.
Dimensions: 15" x 22"
Unit Price: $58.58

Section 9
Page 7
November 1968

Image courtesy of the Dr Pepper Museum

arrived at training practice one day and recruited me for an advertising campaign. Notice there is no period after Dr — the new spelling became part of their redesigned logo sometime in the 1950s. I know this because Dr Pepper hired me as their first-ever African American professional football "model" in the 1960s.

At this point, I had posed for plenty of publicity photos but had never been hired as a model. To me, modeling meant gracefully walking a catwalk in some newfangled outfit, and that would have been quite a sight. But in reality, all I had to do was take direction and strike a pose. I was happy to do so because the photoshoot paid the equivalent of what I made in three Dallas Cowboy games! This was quite a windfall financially and turned out to be great fun.

Honestly, I had forgotten most of the details of this event; it wasn't until I began researching information for my autobiography that I reached out to the Dr Pepper Museum for context. The museum staff was extremely helpful and searched their archives. What they found filled in the missing pieces.

The photoshoot was sports-related (Don Meredith of the Cowboys and golf legend Lee Trevino were recruited separately). The ad I appeared in was meant to appeal to African American consumers — a "Negro display plaque," as they referred to it back in the day, intended to increase sales within a minority population that had not yet been tapped for its full consumer potential. It was a nationally targeted ad.

These particular ads were referred to as "foil pieces," made of durable wonder flex embossed material. Collectors of advertising memorabilia might recognize that description. Apparently, my featured ad was packed in units of 25 and sold for $58.58 per unit. Even more interesting, the Dr Pepper Museum also found an article written in the January/February 1969 issue of the *Clock Dial*, an internal publication by Dr Pepper corporate for salespeople and the Dr Pepper bottlers franchise system. It featured my wife Margaret and me. I am overjoyed to have this memento and the accompanying *Clock Dial* article, reprinted with permission:

> *Dallas Cowboy tight end Pettis Norman will be greeting Dr Pepper shoppers from a newly distend point-of-sale piece which is now going into stores.*
>
> *The bright piece features the nimble-fingered Norman clutching a Dr Pepper and a girl model pouring one.*
>
> *'Our bottlers are impressed with the sign,' said Cuyler Caldwell, point-of-sale advertising manager, 'and initial orders have been excellent.'*
>
> *'It's a great merchandiser from several points,' said Caldwell, 'not the least of which is that it's very subtle. We're not hitting people over the head with the fact that it's Norman in the photo. We think the customers will know who he is.'*
>
> *The success Dr Pepper is having in identifying with sports figures is tremendous. First Don Meredith, the Cowboys quarterback, gave our football premium promotion impetus. And then Lee Trevino, the*

U.S. Open winner, is doing a great job promoting Dr Pepper.'

'Norman is an outstanding athlete who has compiled an impressive record with the Cowboys, and we are delighted to have him with us,' said the p-o-s manager.'

Image courtesy of the Dr Pepper Museum

Well, the ad was highly successful from a corporate viewpoint, but few recognized me as "nimble-fingered Norman." No national newspapers came rushing in to interview me, although my role in the campaign helped Dr Pepper stay on par with Coca-Cola. Honestly, I wasn't interested in acclaim. I just endeavored to "look pretty," flash my pearly whites, collect a check, and take Margaret shopping. I smiled all the way to the bank but became inordinately fond of Dr Pepper. I later served plenty of the beverage in my Burger King restaurants.

No one seems to remember the name of my co-model; I hope to locate her and revisit that moment in time. The City of Dallas has close ties to Dr Pepper, and the Dr Pepper Museum in Waco is a fascinating place. If you have a chance to check it out, do so! I highly recommend it. It's another locale for a book signing, and I anticipate visiting there often.

Chapter Twenty-One: Horse Whisperer

The heart of a boy and the heart of a horse collided, and my life changed forever for the better.
~ Pettis Norman

I'll begin this chapter with a humorous story that took place during my first training camp with the Dallas Cowboys. I was seated in the first row of the plane and wore a yellow plaid sports jacket. It must have had a vivid hue because Gil Brandt teased, "Hey, we're not going to the Kentucky Derby!"

Honestly, I was worried about not having a sports coat at all. I couldn't afford to buy one and had borrowed money from my brother in the hopes of finding something suitable on sale. I really liked the yellow jacket and thought it was a good-looking purchase, but it drew attention for all the wrong reasons. I can laugh now, but not then. Gil's quip now seems almost like a foretelling, for indeed, I became a big fan of the Kentucky Derby and horse racing in general.

Ross Perot and Miss Bee

This brings me to another anecdote from the early 1960s. I was playing for the Cowboys and held down an off-season side job at Sears & Roebuck in downtown Dallas. I was a salesman in the sporting goods department, and in walked a young man by the name of Ross Perot. I believe this was just after he founded Electronic Data Systems, known as EDS.

We had a nice conversation in the camping section, and I told him about my childhood horse, Annie. He smiled and told me that he, too, had a childhood horse. I vaguely recalled that his horse's name started with the letter "B" but vividly recalled that she was Ross's paper route partner. It was obvious he loved that horse just as much as I loved Annie.

From there, I ended up selling Ross a high-end camping tent. This memory has stayed with me all these years and still makes me smile. He told me, "I never intended to buy a tent, but I was so impressed with you as a salesperson, I bought it."

So, this very nice fellow who didn't need or want a tent graciously helped me out with a sale. I thought about our long-ago conversation as I was writing this book, just as Ross passed away in July of 2019. With a bit of research, I learned his horse was named Miss Bee and found a reference to this conversation in the February 28, 2010, edition of the *Fort Worth Star-Telegram*.

I reached out to the Perot family with my recollection. I wanted to commemorate the mutual love of horses shared by Ross and me, as well as commemorate his kind purchase of a camping tent, but only with their blessings. Ross Perot Jr. phoned back and said they'd be honored, which just reconfirms to me how special this iconic Dallas family is.

Ross was a brilliant businessman, philanthropist, and presidential hopeful; God bless him. He left such a meaningful legacy to his family, the tech industry, his beloved City of Dallas, and our nation. He, too, was a trailblazer when it came to diversity and minority inclusion, and I'll never forget Ross' company Electronic Data System (EDS) and his loyal support of the Dallas Together Forum.

Prissee's Honor

I credit my childhood love for Annie for sparking a lifelong passion for equestrian sports. It led me to breed racehorses, and by 1986 I had interests in six thoroughbreds. I'll take this opportunity to mention them briefly.

First, I owned Prissee's Honor, foaled February 22, 1990, a beautiful Texas-bred roan filly. She was my favorite and would always perk up when I arrived at the stable and dance around to welcome my visit. Shortly after Ivette and I met, I took her to meet Prissee's Honor, and they fell in love with one another and had a playful relationship.

What a personality! Prissee's Honor began her career as a two-year-old in 1992 at Trinity Meadows racetrack, one of the first tracks opened in Texas after legalized pari-mutuel betting was approved. That maiden special race was five furlongs on the dirt track, and she was disqualified from 6th to 9th place, quite common for two-year-olds just starting out.

She ran four times in the maiden special weight category, meaning races for the top quality maiden horses that are generally expected to win quickly, move up in class, and are not for sale. Then she was dropped to a maiden claiming race for horses that have never won a race and are for sale for a pre-determined price. Prissee's Honor came in third, building her confidence, after which she was brought back up in class to a maiden special race. She won on October 30, 1992, at odds of 4/1 with trainer Robert Anderson and jockey Terry Stanton.

Prissee's Honor had 38 starts resulting in three wins, four seconds, and four thirds. I went to the Winners Circle three times. Horse racing is fun, but owning a horse and going into the winner's circle is the ultimate racing experience.

I'll also mention my other horses. I had a 50% interest in Alleged Wager, a gorgeous dark bay colt foaled in 2000. I had 25% interest in Tomorrow's Vision, a dark bay filly foaled in 2000 that matched Alleged Wager in looks. Both horses were from Champion Racing Stable in Weatherford, Texas.

I bought a 25% interest in Sister Char, a bay filly foaled in 2001. I had an interest in Hondo County, a chestnut gelding foaled in 2001, who enjoyed a successful career. Finally, I bought an interest in Simply Sider as well, a beautiful dark bay filly foaled in 2002. I think she, above all the others, was the best horse as far as wins, but I admit I loved them all regardless.

These horses raced mostly in Louisiana and California and taught me so much about diversity, love, and morality. Federico Tesio, the famed Italian thoroughbred breeder, once stated: "A horse gallops with his lungs, perseveres with his heart, and wins with his character." I could not say it better myself.

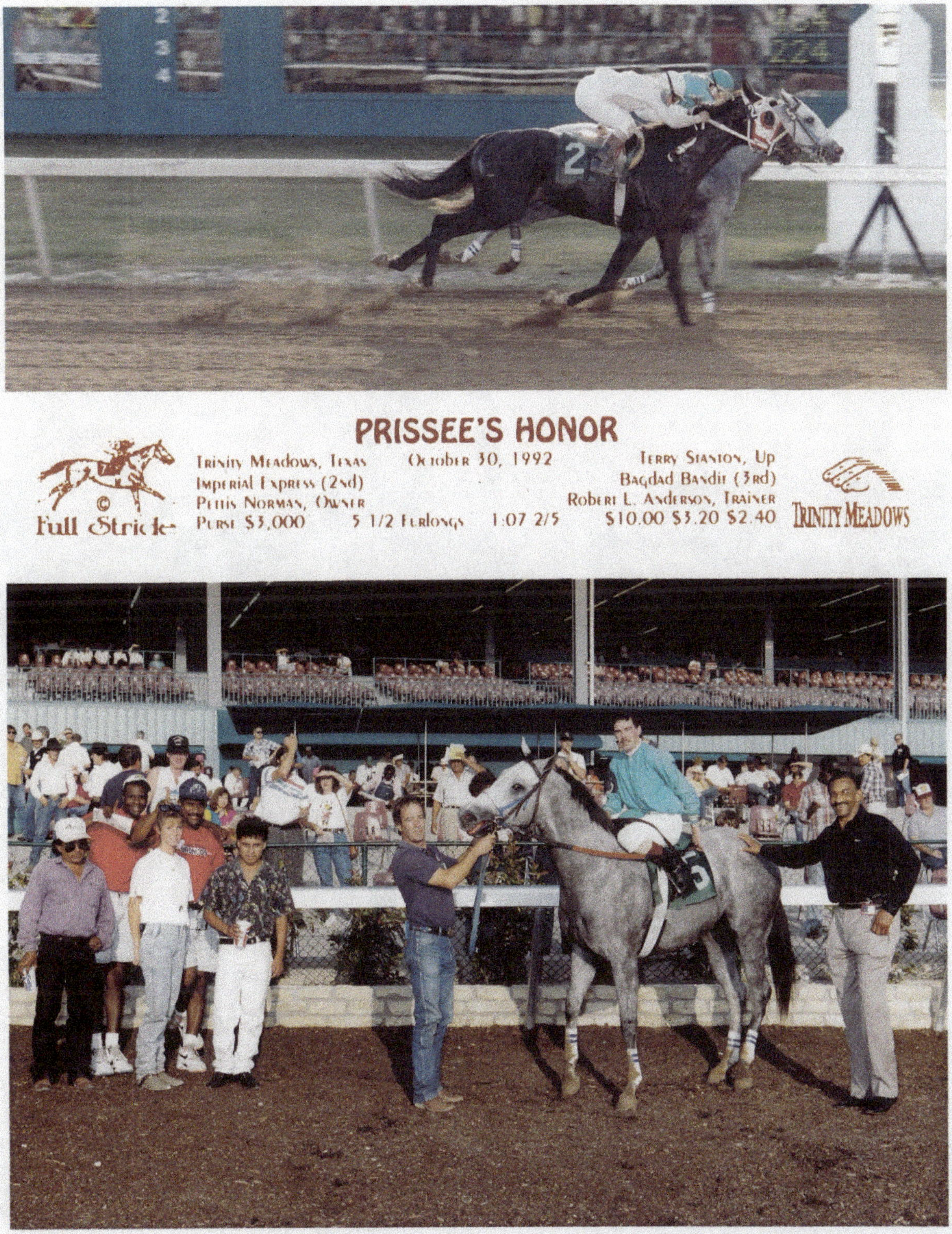

PRISSEE'S HONOR

Trinity Meadows, Texas   October 30, 1992   Terry Stanton, Up
Imperial Express (2nd)   Bagdad Bandit (3rd)
Pettis Norman, Owner   Robert L. Anderson, Trainer
Purse $3,000   5 1/2 Furlongs   1:07 2/5 $10.00 $3.20 $2.40

Headline Photo

In 1992, the *Dallas Morning News* ran an important story. The headline was, "Rather than run for office, Pettis Norman hopes to implement change with an initiative he created — the Dallas Together Forum." While the Dallas Together Forum meant so much to me, a photo taken by *Dallas Morning News* photographer David Woo captured the lion's share of attention. There I was on a full-page spread with a close-up of two beloved thoroughbreds. One nuzzled me behind the neck while the other nuzzled my chest. The smile on my face said it all.

My two beloved horses. Photo credit: David Woo/*Dallas Morning News*

In the aftermath of the Rodney King beating and the riots in Los Angeles, not to mention the smoldering racial undertone that threatened to engulf Dallas, this image revealed pure joy rather than worry. My thoroughbreds were a respite. They were beautiful. I invested whatever little spare time I had with them. I traveled as frequently as possible to Louisiana Downs (now known as Harrah's Louisiana Downs Casino & Racing) to watch the races and took Ivette along on our second date. She was a good sport and eventually embraced a future filled with family, horses, business, politics, activism… and squirrels.

Yes, Ivette is impressed with my ability to train the squirrels around our yard. One, in particular, my favorite, had a hole in her ear, and we knew her by that marking. We named her

"Ebony." I'd coax her down the tree, always with a treat, while the others watched. She began appearing when I called, and the rest followed their fearless leader, except on the day I changed my cologne. Ebony tilted her head suspiciously as if I was a perfect stranger, and it took a while before she trusted that it was me and not an imposter. Ivette commented that it was the new cologne that confused the squirrel, and she was right!

Surprises

My favorite tracks are Saratoga Springs in New York and Santa Anita Park in Arcadia, CA. Back in the '80s, I frequently raced my horses at Louisiana Downs and Santa Anita, where a few of them did quite well. Ivette knew early on that handicapping and racing were two of my passions in life, so she got busy trying to understand this new sport that she had never been exposed to in the past. She learned quickly and became a good handicapper. We traveled to several tracks throughout the United States; it was a wonderful getaway from our busy schedules and quickly became our favorite pastime as newlyweds.

Ivette took it a step further; she always believed marriage should be fun and full of surprises, and I certainly needed an occasional respite from work. She'd secretly book hotels and airline tickets to various tracks, namely, The Travers in Saratoga Springs, Louisiana Derby, Florida Derby, and Santa Anita Breeders Cup. She planned some of these surprises with the help of our youngest daughter Shandra and grandson Alex.

"Pack your bags," she'd announce.

"Why?" I questioned.

"Just pack your bags," Ivette would insist, and we'd show up at the airport. She'd tell the skycaps and security not to give me a clue (airport protocols were not as strict at that time), and then we'd arrive at the gate. Then, and only then, did I know our destination.

"You're kidding!" I'd exclaim. After all the initial resistance, I took charge and led her full steam ahead down the jet way and onto the plane. Those surprises were so special, but the "big" one is still the one I reflect on today. Somehow, Ivette coordinated a trip to the Kentucky Derby with the help of the chairman of Lone Star Park in Grand Prairie, who then called the chairman of Churchill Downs and got us seats on the finish line. Wow!! We could literally touch the horses walking by on the track — a real treat.

I looked at Ivette and said, "How did you do this?" She just smiled and gave me a kiss.

I still shake my head at the energy and effort Ivette has put into our marriage, creating these lasting memories. It's funny — she can no longer surprise me with these getaways because I now know the Derby schedule.

With Ivette at the Kentucky Derby

A Dear Derby Duo

We met Mark and Carolyn Isabelle on one particular trip — we sat beside them on Derby Day because they had extra seats in their box. What a beautiful time we had with this couple; it began a wonderful 20-year friendship. Amazingly, we've met them at the Kentucky Derby at least 15 times and many other racetracks such as the Florida Derby, Travers in New York, Keeneland in Lexington, and finally Belmont Park to witness a failed Triple Crown attempt by a horse called Smarty Jones.

We are blessed to have such good friends. In fact, Mark is an excellent thoroughbred historian and helped research Prissee's Honor for me. He is a professional when it comes to handicapping, and I am fortunate to have his insight.

Ivette recently spoke with Carolyn to reminisce over the adventures we've shared, and it turns out that Carolyn was willing to share a reflection in this book. Her words mean so much to Ivette and me. We value her recollections of our long-term friendship.

Contributed by Carolyn Isabelle

We've known Ivette and Pettis for over 20 years and met in an unusual way. Mark and I had been going to the Kentucky Derby for a few years and had nice box seats. It just so happened that Ivette decided to surprise Pettis with a trip to the Derby that year and ended up in our box. They sat right next to us, and we introduced ourselves and were able to spend two days with the fabulous Normans.

My husband is a huge Dallas Cowboys fan and couldn't help but notice Pettis' Super Bowl ring. This initiated a conversation about football and business ownership. Ivette and I hit it off because she had lived in the Miami area and worked for an airline. I'm from South Florida and worked for a hotel chain — we were both in marketing and sales. Ivette said, 'I probably put people in your hotels!' She was so incredibly friendly, kind, and funny. We had such a great time with these strangers who became close friends and have been there for us in difficult times and great happy times. Pettis and Ivette love to help people and are generous with their time. We have trust and faith in each other.

Art and Science

After spending so much time in various arenas as a player, I discovered that horse racing is a great sport to enjoy as a spectator. Horse racing appeals to all the senses — the sight of horses running full out with jockeys on their backs, the roar of the crowds, the rush of adrenaline, and even the smell of the horses if you are fortunate enough to sit close to the action.

For those of you who are not familiar with racing, allow me to share what makes thoroughbreds tick as well as the elements of wagering. I won't go into all the nuances of wagering — suffice it to say that straight wagers entail win, place, and show across the board, or win/place, place/show. Exotic wagers entail betting on multiple horses in a single bet, such as exactas, quinellas, trifectas, and superfectas. We also key horses to minimize our wager while increasing our payout *if* we pick our horses correctly.

But the method to it all lies in the art of handicapping (intelligently picking the horses to bet on) — something I absorbed over time and after much effort and patience. Everyone seems to have an opinion on handicapping, and it really is a learn-as-you-go experience.

First, I became familiar with the four race classes: maiden races, claiming races, allowance races, and stakes races. I poured over race day programs — the stats of each horse, how they performed on the surface type (dirt and grass or all-weather artificial tracks), the jockey's performance, and more. All of it matters to the horse, and that is the bottom line. Handicappers have to know the horse and its ability to perform optimally under any circumstance. Attending to those details increases the odds of victory.

But handicappers also watch for telltale signs, such as the horse's body language and behavior in the paddock and post-parade, nervous sweat, and even their reaction to the weather. Handicapping can become an addictive hobby, that's for sure, but I enjoyed it greatly to participate from the sidelines and wield a bit of control over the odds.

Saratoga Springs

Ivette and I won $50,000 — the biggest payout in the history of the Saratoga Race Course back in 2010. Ivette picked the horses, and I placed the bet — what an amazing sight it was to see three long shots cross the finish line with the favorites in last place. Ivette's emotions were uncontrollable; I think the entire racetrack knew we won. I'll never forget the race.

I am so fond of this venue and Saratoga Springs as a city. This picturesque area is known for its breathtaking views of the Adirondack Mountains and beautiful lakes around town. I am blessed to have a niece and nephew-in-law who live in the area, Joyce and Benji James, and we have many fond memories of breaking bread together and celebrating family and horses.

As part of my surprise 80th birthday celebration, Joyce planned a special gift. She approached Saratoga Springs Mayor Meg Kelly to request a proclamation on my behalf. Joyce and Benji then hopped on a flight to Dallas to attend my surprise party and hand-delivered the document in person. I was so touched when they read the proclamation out loud.

What an honor and pleasant surprise to hear from Mayor Kelly and ring in my 80th year, especially since it commemorated the horse racing excursions that I enjoyed so much in Saratoga Springs. Joyce, my niece, also sent me a sweet note.

> *The only highly successful person I could relate to while growing up was my Uncle Pettis. He was the youngest of ten children and the only one to go to college and be invited as a free agent by the famous Dallas Cowboys to play professional football! Not only was he our family's role model, he was also a real-life HERO to our friends, teachers, and the entire community.*
>
> *Pettis' life story is inspiring and worthy of chronicling. It will prove to be a highly profitable study for this generation. I am extremely excited to know that so many others will have the opportunity to see the world through his lens and be encouraged by the genius of his life-long success!*

I truly appreciate these kind words from Joyce. I am so proud of her accomplishments as an investment analyst with Merrill Lynch and owner of multiple McDonald's franchise restaurants with her husband, Benji. It is Joyce who sets a beautiful example of success in our family.

A Decade Comes to a Close

My trips to the racetrack were wonderful diversions, but my various PNI companies and volunteer work were never far from my mind. I admit wanting to "race" back home to attend to business at the end of each surprise trip — sometimes to other surprises in the form of impressive awards.

I was honored by the John Ben Sheppard Public Leadership Forum in 1997, received the Minority Business Enterprise of the Year Award from the Minority Business Development Council and the Outstanding Citizen of the Year Award from Theta Alpha Chapter of Omega Psi Phi Fraternity.

That year I was also inducted into the Central Intercollegiate Athletic Association (CIAA) Hall of Fame. I hosted El Centro's Third Annual Pettis Norman/Cowboy Alumni Scholarship Golf Tournament as well.

There's more, and I'm so grateful! I received a certificate for being the longest continuous major S.M.E. contributor to Circle 10 Boy Scouts of America in 1998. I was also honored with the Liberty Bell Award from the Dallas Bar Association and the Humanitarian of the Year Award from the Lions Club International District 2-XI. I was so proud of the kids and adults who were involved in these worthy organizations. It kept me feeling "young" as I participated and supported them in their ventures.

How special that the decade concluded with a Certificate of Appreciation from the State of Texas and Senator Royce West of District 23 for the Dr. Emmett J. Conrad Leadership Program — an initiative supported wholeheartedly by PNI Distribution. This recognition took me back to the days when Dr. Conrad had partnered with me as we built the Golden Helmet apartments. He was a remarkable man; the apartments could never have gotten off the ground without him.

Chapter Twenty-Two: Turn of the Century

We should always look back at what was done and undone and left to do, and then tackle that too.
~ Pettis Norman

The '90s had certainly been a busy roller-coaster decade, and I wondered what the future would bring, never imagining the gigantic loss of the greatest football coach in the NFL. Yes, tragedy struck like a bolt of lightning once again in the new century; losing Tom Landry felt a lot like losing my father and mother.

How can I begin to articulate what it felt like to receive the news that Tom Landry passed away from leukemia on February 12, 2000? What a terrible shock it was — we had hoped and prayed that he would beat his diagnosis.

As far as I was concerned, this coach, mentor, and friend was 75 years young and indomitable. It did not seem that death could claim someone who was larger than life, a stoic figure in a fedora, tie, and sports jacket who had served in the Army Air Forces in World War II. Not even 30 combat missions in Europe could stop him, not even a crash landing in France with him as co-pilot. Yet cancer took his life.

I'm sure the nation pictured him standing on the sidelines with folded arms, looking stern and unemotional. What the fans may not have known was that he was a man of faith. Under that tough exterior was a follower of Christ who served as a goodwill ambassador for the Fellowship of Christian Athletes. I was so saddened when he was abruptly severed from the Cowboys after 29 incredible years at the helm.

His funeral and burial were private, with about 400 of us in attendance. I'll never forget Roger Staubach's eulogy or that Tom's son, Tom Landry Jr., placed his fedora inside the casket before it was closed. The 21-gun salute and a flyover by F-16s and World War II-era military planes reminded us all of his service to the nation. Tom had joined his daughter Lisa Landry Childress in heaven, who died after a four-year battle with liver cancer. I would later remember Tom's grieving over Lisa's passing when my own child, Shawn, was also taken from me too soon.

Tom had two memorial services; I attended both. The one held at the downtown symphony center was an emotional experience. I saw his classic portrait on stage next to one of his iconic fedoras and an open Bible, and that's how I'll always remember him — a good man who cared for his players and prayed with those of us who needed it.

This brings to mind a special quote from Coach that has remained embedded in my mind: "When you want to win a game, you have to teach. When you lose a game, you have to learn."

I have carried this quote in my heart and mind since I left football and applied it to every aspect of the game of life and business. God bless him for the man he was and the imprint he left on my life and the lives of those who loved him.

By the way, not everyone knows that Tom Landry died a Giant's fan, no surprise due to his sudden termination from the Cowboys. His team of choice in no way affected how the City of Dallas and Cowboys fans felt about him. The section of I-30 between Dallas and Fort Worth, formerly the Dallas-Fort Worth Turnpike, was renamed the Tom Landry Freeway in his honor. Dallas drivers can catch glimpses of his fedoras on this stretch of interstate, which always tugs at my heart. From June 15, 2010 through February 6, 2011, I-30 was temporarily designated as the "Tom Landry Super Bowl Highway" to commemorate Super Bowl XLV, played at Cowboys Stadium. Coach Landry will always be well loved.

Texas Black Sports Hall of Fame

Now I was in my '60s, the age when most people start pondering retirement, but this was the last thing on my mind. I was about to become busier than ever! By then, I had served on hundreds of boards and committees, but the decade ahead would be marked with some of the most heartwarming recognition I would ever receive.

In 2001, I was inducted into the Texas Black Sports Hall of Fame at the La Meridian Hotel. Houston Oiler Earl Campbell was among the 17 athletes who were honored. Earlier that day, we were on hand for the Family Day Sports Clinic held at the African American Museum in Dallas.

Dr. Harry Robinson, visionary President and CEO of the African American Museum, established the Texas Black Sports Hall of Fame in 1996 to herald the contributions of African American Texans in the world of sports. Under his leadership, a new facility was built in 1984 in Fair Park and has evolved into a nationally recognized destination for people all over the world.

The city of Dallas is proud to have Dr. Robinson as one of our own. He has served as President of the Association of African American Museums and the African American Library Association. In 2003 President George W. Bush appointed him to the National Museum Services Board, and on May 26, 2005, he was re-appointed to The National Museum & Library Services Board of the Institute of Museum and Library Services (IMLS). Well done, my good and faithful servant. Dr. Robinson's kind words about me:

> *Pettis Norman is the epitome of athlete, scholar and gentleman. He is an example of what can come out of an HBCU. We point to him as a role model, especially for our younger athletes. His activities off the field have been exemplary. His character and integrity are unquestionable. He is compassionate, yet firm. Pettis and Ivette have been staunch supporters of the African American Museum. Pettis honored the Museum by permitting it to induct him into The Texas Black Sports Hall of Fame. His legacy as a servant leader will inspire us for years to come.*

It was gratifying to be recognized for my corporate efforts in addition to my sports career.

The DFW Minority Business Council named PNI Industries Regional Supplier/Distributor Firm of the Year. In 2003, I received the Tom Unis Award for Valuing Diversity from the Greater Dallas Community Relations Commission, the Outstanding Service Award from Southwestern Bell Telephone Company, and the Sam Lacy Pioneer Award from the National Association of Black Journalism. In 2006 I received the Medal of Recognition Award from the Dorie Miller Post 1406 DFW.

It was such a good feeling to have been a part of these great organizations, and as my parents had always encouraged, "Make life count for others."

The Kindness of Jerry Jones

Tom Landry wasn't the only football legend we lost early in the new century. I was worried about Bob Hayes' health and contacted Jerry Jones with the idea that Bob should be included in the Ring of Honor for the year 2001. For years, Bob lived right up the street from me and we hung out as neighbors. Many years later, he came to visit and it was obvious that his health challenges had taken a toll.

For this reason, time was of the essence. I was gratified that Jerry ushered Bob into the Ring of Honor in 2001; I know he carried that great achievement in his heart, and it meant a lot to him. I remember his quote: "I'm thrilled, I'm grateful, I'm blessed. I played for the world's greatest professional sports team in history. Once a Dallas Cowboy, always a Dallas Cowboy." He died in Jacksonville, Florida, the place of his birth, in 2002.

The next time I had contact with Jerry, it was he who graciously reached out to me. After Bob lost his battle, Jerry called and said, "Gather a group of teammates, and I'll fly them to the funeral." What a great, kind gesture! Sure enough, several of us boarded the plane and recalled the exploits of our departed 1964 Summer Olympian, who competed in Tokyo, tying the world record for the 100-meter sprint. Mind you; he did so in borrowed shoes! Yes, Bob had inadvertently misplaced one of his spikes, but this didn't stop him from setting another world record in the 4×100-meter relay, earning him another gold medal.

We also recalled his feats with the Cowboys. The year I left for San Diego, the Cowboys won their first-ever Super Bowl in 1972. This made Bob an icon — the only athlete to win an Olympic gold medal and a Super Bowl ring. In 2009 he was posthumously inducted into the Pro Football Hall of Fame. It was long overdue and well deserved. I am so proud of my friend and teammate and for the kindness of Jerry Jones.

Contributed by Jerry Jones

Bob's induction into the Ring of Honor was very important to me. It was also important to many of our former players, like Pettis, who played with Bob and understood not only his impact on the Dallas Cowboys organization — but also on the evolution of professional football.

Bob's speed and natural athletic gifts changed the way the game was played in the 1960s and early '70s. The predominant pass coverage that defenses played in the earlier days of pro football was man-to-man, which was usually effective in a game that was mostly built around a strong running game on the offensive side of the ball.

Jerry Jones and Bob Hayes. Photo credit: Dallas Cowboys

When Bob Hayes came into the NFL, with his Olympic gold medals and the title of "The World's Fastest Human" under his belt, he was an electrifying presence on NFL playing fields. His blazing speed put him in a position to break past individual coverage and be a dangerous deep threat who could score from any position on the field.

And the fact that Don Meredith had the ability to throw the ball all over the field — and especially the deep ball — created great excitement for Cowboys fans and great concern for defensive backs all across the league.

Bob's presence with the Cowboys was very unique because of his great fame as an Olympian. He was able to excel in two sports at the highest levels, and he was one of the first truly colorful and explosive players in Cowboys history.

As an Olympic champion and a Super Bowl winner, I felt that he was more than worthy of selection into both the Ring of Honor and the Pro Football Hall of Fame, and I was proud to be a part of both of those recognitions for Bob. He was an iconic figure in two sports. He was a man with great pride and someone who had a wonderful heart.

We inducted Bob into the Ring of Honor in September of 2001, in our first game after the 9/11 tragedy. It was a very emotional day for our fans at Texas Stadium, and having Bob Hayes be honored—as an American sports legend—made the day all the more special and rewarding.

Unfortunately, he had passed away before being inducted into the Pro Football Hall of Fame. His funeral was inspirational and highlighted by a wonderful turnout of friends and former Dallas Cowboys players.

Heartwarming Occasions

I was featured in the *Fortune 500 Magazine* for the Outstanding Service Award from Shell Oil in 2007 and received the Altruistic Award from the Dallas/Fort Worth Hall of Legends, quite an honor. Then an event tugged at my heart in 2010, a momentous occasion.

The decade began with the loss of Tom Landry and ended with a celebration of his life ten years later at the Hall of State at Fair Park. An important exhibition — "Remembering Tom Landry: The Personal Collection" — was displayed by his wife, Alicia. Ivette and I attended the sneak peek with Eddie LeBaron, Don Meredith, Roger Staubach, Craig Morton, Danny White, and their families.

It felt good to see my old friends and honor my beloved coach. He was such an important person in my life, and I still mourn the loss. At 15 years my senior, he was almost old enough to be a father figure, and definitely the right age to be a mentor.

I called him coach but also called him friend. I have always been fond of his wife Alicia, their two daughters, and his son Tom Jr., who continues to be very supportive of me on special occasions. He is a great friend, and I cherish his quote: "Like my mom, I admire Pettis very much, and he's one of my all-time favorite Cowboys, too! I can't say enough about Pettis —

he's a great person."

Another momentous event had to do with Johnson C. Smith University's highest honor, the Arch of Triumph. This award was so meaningful and took me back to my launching pad, JCSU, where my close friend and Cowboy teammate Calvin Hill introduced me that evening and provided some history on my life's journey.

Equally, it was truly heartwarming to have Nate Edwards in attendance, the man and my angel, who introduced me to Coach McGirt. As I shared in an earlier chapter, this led to the JCSU scholarship that set my life in motion. Sitting with him was Ivette, my siblings, and many of my classmates to celebrate this tremendous honor.

What a wonderful feeling it was to sit among my co-honorees John Crosland, Jr., Wintley Phipps, and Smithite Bertha M. Roddey at the Charlotte Convention Center. Other attendees included former Mayor Harvey Gantt, Representative Mel Watt, Urban League President Patrick Graham, and numerous elected officials and city leaders. Interestingly, Dr. Condoleezza Rice from the Bush Administration was the keynote commencement speaker for JCSU's graduation ceremony the same year.

Arch of Triumph with Calvin Hill and JCSU President Ronald Carter. Photo credit: JCSU

This tribute took place on April 17, 2010, during the 143rd-anniversary Founder's Day Celebration. The Executive Board of the National Alumni Association of the university thanked all supporters at the convention center for our participation and contributions toward the university's goals. Dr. Bertha M. Roddey of the Theodore and Bertha M. Roddey Foundation, noted educator, community leader, and co-founder of Harvey B. Gantt Center for African-American Arts & Culture, was the co-honoree.

I felt extremely blessed that my alma mater was so well represented and can't begin to tell you how many letters and congratulations I received after being given this honor. This was very special to me because I will always believe my attendance at Johnson C. Smith University was due to miraculous and Divine intervention.

I've said it before, and I'll say it again — it really was the start of life as I know it today.

Bishop Dunne Catholic School

On April 29, 2015, John Wooten of the Cleveland Browns and I stepped up as co-chairs for Bishop Dunne Catholic School's "Evening with Legends Dinner" featuring NFL legends Roger Staubach, Bob Lilly, Drew Pearson, and Joe Greene. The theme was Reminisce to Raise Funds for Oak Cliff's Bishop Dunne at AT&T Cowboy's Stadium.

It was meaningful to co-host this event because of the positive impact this private school had on my grandson Alex and daughters Shandra and Sedonna, who were graduates of this school. Bishop Dunne had a great curriculum and equipped my children with an excellent education, especially Alex, who graduated not only with outstanding grades, but with an impressive offer to attend UT Austin on a football scholarship.

Many thanks to Bishop Dunne's head football Coach Michael Johnson and assistant Coach Walton for their mentorship of Alex while he was in school, and even today. Their love and devotion to my grandson have been a blessing to him and our family. It was a great evening, and raised scholarship money for deserving students who endeavored to receive a quality college preparatory education.

On another note, I felt completely humbled when I received the Commission of Civil Rights Award from Alpha Rho Chapter of the National Sorority of Phi Delta Kappa, Inc., and the Distinguished Service Community Award on behalf of the Association of Black Students at Southern Methodist University. I was inducted into the Hall of Fame at Johnson C. Smith University and received the Charlotte Business League Award.

Two Golden Footballs for West Charlotte

In 2016, I credited the NFL and my high school for bringing a special light to my life. As part of the nationwide Super Bowl 50 celebration, the NFL began a new program for high schools. I thought it was a fantastic initiative and liked the NFL's program slogan: "We're all just a kid from somewhere, and that's hitting home for some Super Bowl champions."

With my beloved grandson, Alex

The Super Bowl High School Honor Roll program acknowledges schools that have directly influenced Super Bowl history by graduating a player or head coach that later appeared on an active Super Bowl roster. Golden Wilson footballs were awarded to each high school for every individual Super Bowl player or head coach. West Charlotte High School received two golden footballs — one for me and another for Mo Collins, who played for the Oakland Raiders. A special assembly was held in the high school auditorium to commemorate the occasion.

The entire school was invited to the NFL Super Bowl Honor Roll ceremony; what an amazing program for an alumnus who had graduated more than 59 years prior. The West Charlotte high school band, which has a lot of history and tradition, played. Cheerleaders performed, and the football team was there along with the student body.

It was a grand affair, a tremendous honor, and I treasure it to this day. I must say the sportsmanship, values, and accountability I learned at West Charlotte High laid the foundation for my life. I was honored to receive the Wilson Golden Football Award from the NFL.

Stephanie Wilkerson, Assistant Athletic Director at West Charlotte High at that time, said:

> *Pettis' accomplishments in the sports world and business world speaks to the kids at West Charlotte. The fact that he walked the same halls that they do now, played on the same fields, came from the same community, and did great things with his life, greatly impacts our students, faculty, and staff. He's very inspirational.*

I sincerely appreciate Stephanie's kind words, and especially her impressive coordination of this important event.

I prepared my acceptance speech but became ill the night before and was not feeling well enough to travel to Charlotte from Dallas. I asked my niece, Melissa Hasty Taylor, to speak on my behalf. She has always been there for me, and that night was no different. Here are the key points I asked Melissa to deliver to my alma mater:

> *Character is the foundation for any and all that you will do successfully in life. Character is who and what you are at the very core. It reflects the principles you hold dearest and highest — and it is the line you draw, over which you will not cross.*

Melissa closed her speech with a quote from an unknown author: "People with good intent make promises; people with good character, keep them."

After the speech, the principal made a special announcement on behalf of the NFL Foundation, which donated one million dollars for the Super Bowl Honor Roll campaign. West Charlotte High could now apply for a grant of up to $5,000 to support their football program and character education curriculum.

More than two thousand high schools and about three thousand players and coaches were recognized in 2016, and this tradition continues annually. It felt good to bring this opportunity to my high school alma mater, where my football days began.

The Super Bowl 50 Pettis Norman Golden Football. Photo credit: Lawrence Jenkins Pictures

Fellow recipient Mo Collins was a lineman on the Oakland Raiders' 2002 Super Bowl team and played for the Raiders from 1998–2003. He later coached the West Charlotte Lions football team. Tragically, Mo passed away in October 2014, at the young age of 38. His contributions to football and the school were also honored during the ceremony.

This was a very appropriate and meaningful wrap-up of my football career at West Charlotte High, but more wrap-ups were on the horizon.

Mecklenburg Sports Wall of Fame

John Love, a long-term friend of our family, nominated me for the Charlotte Mecklenburg Sports Wall of Fame, and I was chosen as one of the honorees in 2017. This just pleased me on so many levels, taking me back to my roots and those formative years.

The award recognizes outstanding Mecklenburg County athletes, coaches, and teams who contributed significantly to the development of athletes, contributed to the excellence of sports programs in the area, and brought national or international recognition to Mecklenburg

County.

I could not attend the ceremony held on May 18, 2017, because it was on the same day as my grandson's commencement ceremony at UT Austin. Ivette and I were such proud grandparents and would not miss Alex walking across the stage to receive his hard-earned bachelor's degree. I am sure he heard the family whooping and hollering from the audience as he walked across the stage; we were all so happy with this milestone in his life.

Once again, I asked my faithful niece, Melissa Hasty Taylor, to step in on my behalf to accept the award and share a few words during the ceremony. I asked her to speak of my humble beginnings in Lincolnton, Georgia, and the Bible verse Luke 6:31. She also shared how I tried my best to "make life count" for others by giving back to my community and selflessly supporting passionate causes throughout my life. I felt blessed, knowing my effort to make a difference in this world was being recognized in such an honorable way.

Melissa did an outstanding job. Below is a portion of her thoughtful words titled "A few attributes about my Uncle Pettis as I see them…"

- Strong personality – "Pettis' capacity to motivate, inspire and call others to action is rooted in his strong personality. His strong character helped him fight for social justice issues, regardless of how controversial they were."
- Compassionate – "Pettis has always felt that we have an obligation to fight for the world as it should be."
- Self-confident – "One of the many lessons that Pettis learned while growing up was to always stay true to yourself and never let what someone else says distract you from your goals."
- Perseverance and persistence – "Many of Pettis' accomplishments require a significant amount of time and hard work. He was keenly aware that the only time 'success' appears before 'work,' is in the dictionary."
- Inspirational – "Pettis' life story has been inspirational to thousands of people, some he will never know. He has shown that the power of the individual is paramount, and why you shouldn't underestimate your ability to inspire real change in your community."
- Honesty – "Success doesn't count unless you earn it fair and square as far as Pettis is concerned. As a great leader, he has always believed in being honest about his strengths, weaknesses, and expectations."

Melissa's kind, thoughtful words touched my heart. I thank her from the bottom of my heart for making me feel that I made a difference in her life too.

After Alex's graduation, Ivette decided the Mecklenburg Wall of Fame Award was such an important recognition that it deserved a reenactment. On May 26, 2017, with the help of James Alsop, Park and Recreation Manager at the Wall of Fame, Ivette invited more than 40 family, friends, business associates, including West Charlotte's Athletic Director and JCSU Director of Alumni Affairs, to another ceremony that included special presentations and a luncheon.

Me, with my sister Gladys in the background at the Mecklenburg Hall of Fame Ceremony.
Photo credit: *Charlotte Post*

Wanda Foy-Burroughs of JCSU, the Athletic Director from West Charlotte, and close friend Butch Walker were on the program. During the Revolution Park Sports Academy ceremony, the speakers talked about my contributions and gave me some mementos for their gratitude. I was so appreciative that these important people in my life came to celebrate this very special recognition, especially since many missed the formal presentation the week before.

Finally came the most riveting part of the ceremony — the unveiling of my plaque on the Wall of Fame. It meant so much to see my name among so many distinguished leaders, and it meant even more to have my close friends, family, and JCSU associates present. After the program, I was all smiles as I viewed the plaque on the Wall of Fame and believe a "YouTube" video exists of my acceptance speech even today.

Ivette never misses an opportunity to celebrate me and my achievements. Her loving energy brings me so much joy, and she noted that this was yet another important milestone in my life that deserved recognition. I was starting to see a pattern. Perhaps I should bask in these accomplishments and take time to smell the roses.

Chapter Twenty-Three: It's Who You Know

God bless the voices in the media who keep us informed and connected.
~ Pettis Norman

On June 3, 2007, Nelson Mandela shared a message with the 14th congress of the World Editors Forum in Cape Town, South Africa. He said, "Newspapers allow us to hold a mirror up to ourselves, and we must be brave enough to look squarely at the reflections."

Looking back at the media coverage I've encountered in sports, corporate endeavors, and civic duties, I feel these words are spot on regarding newspapers and the broader world of radio, television, and online platforms. Much of it hinges on the opinions of news reporters and broadcasters and how they perceive "people in the news."

Fortunately, I have the honor of knowing some notable media voices and developed friendships with many of them. Early on, I watched and learned a bit of the trade from these personalities I so admired. Honestly, it wasn't what I knew but *who* I knew that helped me find my voice behind a microphone. This positioned me to step into broadcasting and television — not on a large scale, but in interesting ways that allowed me to stretch as a communicator.

The Quality Touch Show

My earliest appearances were on the Quality Touch Show, WFAA-TV, ABC Channel 8 at the Communications Center of ABC, a broadcast service of the *Dallas Morning News*. I joined my good friends Don Meredith, Don Perkins, Mel Renfro, Dave Manders, and Jim Boeke for some fun and informative banter that the audience seemed to enjoy. I certainly had fun — these nostalgic off-field antics hold a cherished place in my memories, especially since some of my old teammates are no longer with us.

On this same station, award-winning Sports Director Wes Wise (future Mayor of Dallas) featured human interest stories on important sports developments — part of the sports beat in 1960's Dallas. Some might remember the *Sump'n Else* live teen dance television show on WFAA-TV as well. WFAA Studios is a legendary part of Dallas-Fort Worth broadcasting history and added technological advances to local news. As you'll see, it laid the foundation of many famous sportscasters today.

The World Football League

After I retired from the NFL in 1973, I became a sports agent and ventured into restaurant franchises. I assumed football would become a thing of the past, but I was wrong. The World Football League (WFL) approached me in 1975 and offered me a position at the WRET station as a television announcer for the Charlotte Stars/Hornets, one of many teams in the WFL.

I'm fairly certain my stint as a former NFL player and sports agent influenced the offer, and I was interested. It would allow me to maintain a relationship with football and remain involved with a sport I loved, although from the opposite end of the camera. Plus, I was accustomed to juggling multiple jobs and traveling, so this new gig was intriguing.

At this time, I appeared in television commercials as a spokesperson for my Burger King restaurants, so I was prepared, at least somewhat, to work behind a microphone — thanks to the examples of announcers like Bill Mercer, Verne Lundquist, Brad Sham, Dale Hansen, and Jack Buck. I had followed their careers and enjoyed their on-air personas. Their approach to broadcasting was something to emulate. In fact, I developed friendships with these larger-than-life announcers, who kindly weigh in further in this chapter.

The Charlotte Stars were originally called the New York Stars, but financial problems caused them to leave New York and settle in Charlotte. The Stars were renamed the Hornets and were a great success at the box office as the first professional team in Charlotte.

The WFL was founded in 1973 by attorney and businessman Gary Davidson of the American Basketball Association and World Hockey Association and held its first season in 1974. That first year was known as a WFL rollout effort beset with some chaos and a lot of debt. The "WFL II" emerged the next year, savvier and seemingly able to pay bills on time, another reason I agreed to become an announcer.

The WFL signed numerous NFL stars, including a few of my former teammates. Calvin Hill signed with Hawaii, and after an injury, was replaced by Duane Thomas, who had played with me — both a Dallas Cowboy and a San Diego Charger. Craig Morton played with Houston.

The Super Bowl champion Dolphins saw their backfield duo of Larry Csonka and Jim Kiick, the celebrated "Butch" and "Sundance," join wide receiver Paul Warfield in signing with the WFL. Raiders quarterbacks Ken Stabler and Daryle Lamonica also signed with the new league.

Other "WFL jumpers" who had been active on NFL rosters included Dallas Cowboys Mike Montgomery, Jethro Pugh, and Rayfield Wright for WFL Birmingham, and D.D. Lewis for WFL Memphis. San Diego Chargers included Virgil Carter for WFL Chicago; Ron East and Greg Wojcik for WFL Hawaiians; Danny White for WFL Memphis; and Ron Holiday for WFL Philadelphia. I have to hand it to these players — they were willing to sign with a new and experimental league, one that initially showed some promise. I recall talk of expanding WFL teams into Tokyo, Europe, Mexico City, and more.

The WFL only lasted the 1974 and 1975 seasons, but that was long enough to change the course of NFL history. The loss of Csonka, Kiick, and Warfield denied the two-time Super Bowl champion Dolphins key offensive weapons and opened the door for the Steelers and Raiders to dominate the NFL in the mid-1970s. During its brief existence, the WFL played one World Bowl (1974) and added some innovative rules to the game of professional football, some used by the NFL today. For instance, the WFL moved the goalposts to the back of the end zone and started the season in July (the NFL followed suit), and played a Thursday night game, now known as "Thursday Night Football" by the NFL.

Unfortunately, the Hornets were less of a success on the field, losing their final four games in 1974. The team struggled on the field and financially in 1975, drawing some 10,000 fans to home games, less than half the capacity in American Legion Memorial Stadium, and going 6-5 before the WFL folded.

The telecast was fascinating while it lasted — the WFL was known for its brightly-colored team uniforms, so vivid on the screen. I remember the station's "chroma-keyed" promotional spots, and the director asked us to wear clothing with tan hues. When we traveled to games, we could wear blue blazers.

The WFL often broadcasted on WRET TV 36 (Charlotte, NC), WGHP TV 8 (High Point, NC), and WCTG TV 17 (Atlanta, GA). The renowned John Sterling was the play-by-play announcer, and I was the color commentator. In context, play-by-play announcers are the primary speakers due to their ability to articulate events in a fast-moving game. Color commentators have experience and insight and are often asked questions by play-by-play announcers. That was my working relationship with John — he talked and bounced questions off of me, and I weighed in.

We had been gearing up for a game scheduled for October 23, 1975. The WBT-AM 1110 radio announcers Harold Johnson (play-by-play) and Matt Snorton (color) were scheduled to air. The *Charlotte Observer* and the *Charlotte News* were on assignment for the start of a Charlotte Hornets four-game home stand under head coach Bob Gibson. The game was to be played at the American Legion Memorial Stadium in Charlotte against the Hawaiians and head coach Mike Giddings.

Suddenly, on October 22, 1975, we learned the league had been canceled one day before the big game. The WFL abruptly disbanded 12 games into the season while shouldering unsustainable debt. Still, the news was stunning. Unfortunately, fans showed up with tickets and were turned away. I felt especially bad for the incredible players who had pinned their hopes and dreams on the World Football League. I knew many of them personally and shared their devastation.

Some made their way back into the NFL, others retired, and some, like me, made hay in corporate America. I believe I was left with a few unpaid WFL travel expenses. Yet, in the scheme of things, I was simply thankful I had been blessed with this opportunity and had the Burger King restaurants to operate.

For those who remember the WFL, check out the nostalgic videos and interesting posts on the World Football League's Facebook page. It's a recommended walk down memory lane and helps keep the history of the WFL intact.

I thought it would be interesting to catch up with my media friends who happen to share a few common denominators — their career longevity and that unforgettable, still fascinating Ice Bowl game. The players themselves have shared reflections in this book, but the press box announcers have their own "take" on the action. What a treat to get their bird's eye views.

JAMES THRASH
President
General Manager

July 29, 1975

Mr. Pettis Norman
777 South R.L. Thornton Freeway
Dallas, Texas 75203

Dear Pettis,

Enclosed are your tickets and the check for the Memphis game on August 9. As soon as the team decides what their hotel will be, I'll let you know.

Pettis, we were very happy with the telecast from San Antonio. You guys took a losing second half and did an outstanding job of keeping the Hornet spirits at home as up as possible.

Let me clear up a misunderstanding we had on clothing (which is our fault). Because we were going to chroma-key the promotional spots at the station, our director asked us to use solid tans. However, that doesn't mean we have to at the games. We can wear any color. So - if you want to wear a blue blazer, or another jacket, please do so. For the next two summer games, Memphis on 8/9 and Jacksonville on 8/30, we can stay with the leisure suits. Please wear your jacket whenever you are on camera. Then, beginning September 21, in Birmingham we will require coats and ties when you are on camera for the rest of the season.

Good luck in Memphis, and I look forward to seeing you in Jacksonville.

Sincerely,

Jim

JT:dm
Enclosures

Brad Sham

The year 2018 was a landmark year for announcer Brad Sham, his 40th anniversary with the Dallas Cowboys organization. Remarkably, he's held the distinction of being the "voice of the Dallas Cowboys" longer than any other broadcaster with the team. He joined the Cowboys in 1976 as a color analyst and worked with Verne Lundquist, who did play-by-play.

To be honest, I can't imagine anyone replacing Brad. Our community has grown to trust his broadcasting, and his voice will always be synonymous with the Cowboys. We may not see each other often, but our bond from those long-ago days is still very special.

Although I had left the NFL prior to Brad's Cowboys broadcasting career, I became a fan of his weekly columns for dallascowboys.com, as well as his work for Westwood One, the NFL on Fox, TNT Sunday Night Football, and the NFL on CBS, and the Texas Rangers.

He's such an important fixture in the Dallas Cowboys franchise, but what impresses me most about Brad is his thoughtfulness and mindfulness regarding the social problems we face today. I was thrilled to catch up with him and absorb some of his thoughts, which I feel are timely for this moment in history. He speaks about some of the most weighty issues that plague our nation today, namely racism, and I agree with him wholeheartedly.

Contributed by Brad Sham

My greater memories of Pettis are of his work as a civic leader. I remember being aware of his presence as a community leader as I started my career as a reporter. I came to town in 1970, just a cub reporter, and then left to work for a different station. I came back to Dallas in 1976 to work with Verne as 'second banana,' and by then, Pettis had retired.

I realized that Pettis is a person who did the right things for the right reasons and maximized his reputation to cause change for the greater good. He made a tremendous difference as a football player but an even greater difference as a citizen. He's an inspirational leader and really understands what the '60s and '70s meant for minorities, more so than most folks. He led by example and still does and has such high character. It's as if he realized early on that his life was meant to be bigger than football.

I was in the National Guard, like Pettis. He served almost a decade before I did, and his reason for enlisting was pure — he wanted to serve his country. I, on the other hand, enlisted because I was worried about the draft. A lot of people my age had terrible lottery numbers and would have been sent to Vietnam. So, we both served, but Pettis did so with no other motivation than to support the nation.

As I write this in 2020, there were a lot of unknowns, like the pandemic and our social consciousness that seems to be expanding at rates that could not have been previously predicted. I know Pettis has always been concerned with social causes, and it brings to mind the kneeling issue we see in sports today. We have no way of knowing what the end result will be, but it has caused a lot of discussion and soul-searching. I'll expand on this topic because it has gained momentum and can no longer be ignored. It also ties into what Pettis has worked toward his entire life — racial harmony, equality, and mutual respect.

It's an individual thing. I think each of us can only speak for ourselves when it comes to the kneeling dilemma. When the first players began to kneel three to four years ago, I was a little uncomfortable. Still, I understood the motivation, although it was controversial that athletes used the most visible pulpit in the land to call attention to racism. They were publicly cursed in a manner that was completely unnecessary and exacerbated the problem.

It brings to mind my training for infantry combat. Never, not once when I put on my uniform, did it occur to me that I was training to protect only people who thought like I did. I have a very deeply held belief that we are born into a nation of dissenters. That's who we are at our core. It never occurred to me that there was only one way to respect the flag and that only one group was right.

I'm Jewish and don't understand how people of my faith, people who have relatives who were persecuted, cannot feel empathy for those who are moved to kneel. Any oppressed group should be able to identify. Living as a Black person carries with it certain peril that those of us who aren't Black can't fully understand. But we should at least sympathize.

Kneeling was never about the flag to begin with, but a lot of people don't want to see that. They are bull-headed or blind not to understand that this social action, kneeling, is not about the flag. It's about justice. In my opinion, it didn't just happen overnight. George Floyd was the last straw.

'Find a different way to protest,' some say. My response is, 'What else will get that level of attention?' All men are created equal, but Black people haven't been afforded that equality for 400 years. So, if I was a coach, I'd be tempted to kneel with the players. It's time for fundamental change. If an athlete kneels while the National Anthem plays, and raises a fist to drive the point home, then I'm right there with them.

Who we are, what we believe, and how we process life matters very much. I'm indebted to people like Pettis, who blazed a trail and emboldened us to speak out.

Bob Johnson of the *Charlotte Post*

When it comes to journalists who know me best, Bob Johnson is at the top of the list. We go back to our junior high school days and I value him as a newspaper publisher. He shares memories below that transport me to my earliest interest in sports as well as my transition from Georgia to North Carolina. It's nice to have a friend who has preserved these shared experiences.

Contributed by Bob Johnson

The Charlotte Post was first started in the AME Zion church in 1878 and moved to the secular community in 1906. My father bought the paper in 1974 after working for the Charlotte News. He especially enjoyed covering sports. The Charlotte News wrote a lot about Pettis, especially about his high school and collegiate football performances. The Charlotte Post has covered Pettis even after he retired from the NFL.

I will say that my father, a real newspaperman, left his footprint in our community. Before he passed in 1986, he taught my younger brother, Gerald, and me all about hard work, honesty, and manners. Growing up, we feared him — not in a negative sense, but in the sense of respect and reverence. He didn't believe that parents should be friends with their children. Parents should be parents. I took this philosophy with me into the classroom as a 6th-grade teacher. My role was not to be the students' friend. My job was to impart knowledge, and my classes were well-behaved throughout the decades. I thank my father for that.

My father also taught my brother and me about the newspaper business. I worked full-time as an educator, and Gerald worked as a banker when we inherited the newspaper. We ran the paper while still working full time in our respective careers and thus wore many hats. I wrote a weekly column about community events called 'What's Happening' and also focused on circulation. Gerald handled the business end. When we retired from academia and finance (me in 1994), we exclusively devoted ourselves to the newspaper. Gerald is the publisher and CEO. I'm the publisher and general manager.

It's been amazing to see the Charlotte Post *grow and adapt to the changing times, yet some things are eternal. Our devotion to the community is the same. Our focus on African American accomplishments and challenges are the same. But, we've kept up with a modern world both in print and digital coverage — News, Sports, Life, A&E, Health, Business, and our work with the Pulitzer Center. It would have made my father proud to see the progress.*

I'm very flattered that Pettis has included me in the media chapter of his book, for he's an icon in Charlotte, and I've known him since junior high. He moved from Georgia when he was ten after his father's death and met Margaret, his future wife, in junior high. They were quite the couple — 7th-grade sweethearts.

Because Pettis loves Mecklenburg County, he told me he wanted to honor the City of Charlotte, the Charlotte Post, *and his long acquaintance with me in his autobiography, which is gracious of him.*

We have a strong connection. I played sandlot football and wanted to try out for the team as a high school sophomore. The coach asked, 'Johnson, why are you here?' After all, I was short, and the prospective players were much bigger. The coach slapped a clipboard in my chest and said, 'You're the statistician.' Well, being the statistician all the way through college meant I covered Pettis' games at West Charlotte High School and Johnson C. Smith University, our alma mater. I don't think anyone knew Pettis better as a sports hero. He was big, could catch passes, played both sides of the ball, and had talent.

We didn't necessarily run in the same circles because Pettis didn't belong to any particular clique. He focused like a laser on grades, sports, a few clubs (like the photography club), his multiple after-school jobs, and Margaret, of course.

Yes, Pettis was the cool one, but not many people know that he also took care of his mother, who was ill. He was a very good son and way too busy to socialize much. Yet, he was never standoffish. Pettis was always friendly but disciplined. Stoic. That's why he's been able to accomplish so much as an athlete, entrepreneur, and servant leader. It's remarkable what he's done with his life.

He's the same guy today as he was in our childhood, and I am blessed, like many others, to know him.

Jack Buck

Here's a bit of humor, thanks to the late Hall of Fame sportscaster Jack Buck, father of current sportscaster Joe Buck. Jack became CBS' regional voice for Cowboys broadcasts in 1966-67 after Frank Glieber left Dallas to become the voice of the Browns.

I spoke with Jack on a number of occasions when I played in the '60s. As many football fans know, Jack often switched up my name. "Norman Pettis," he would say, sometimes correcting it to "Pettis Norman" and sometimes not. I took it in stride and thought it was amusing, for he certainly wasn't the only person to confuse my first and last names.

Sportscaster Verne Lundquist was working for the ABC affiliate in Dallas at the time and recalled that Jack cringed every time Meredith threw a pass to me. Jack knew he was going to mistakenly refer to me as "Norman Pettis" — you'll see Verne and others weigh in below on this topic. Suffice it to say; the bloopers got plenty of media coverage. When the Cowboys played, people couldn't wait to see if Jack would get my name wrong. It wouldn't have surprised me if a few friendly wagers were made. KRLD got calls from angry fans who deliberately mangled the sportscaster's name as "Buck Jack."

Many still ask me about that period in football history and continue to be curious if Jack's slips of the tongue were playful or purposeful. I assure them these were just inadvertent gaffes, captured in NFL lore and all in good fun. Honestly, it brought additional attention to both Jack and me, and neither of us minded it. Jack later told me in jest, "You're the guy who made my career."

We all miss Jack. He passed away in 2002, a national loss to the sports community. Not long ago, I read an old article in the *Fort Worth Star-Telegram* written by Ray Buck (I'm not sure if he's related to Jack) about those long-ago days. It was gratifying to see a quote from Jack: "Norman Pettis … Pettis Norman. He's good. Both of 'em." Jack was fond of sharing that one, and I am fond of sharing memories of him.

Bill Mercer

What can we learn from a radio personality born in 1926 and is as active and intellectual today as he was more than half a century ago? Plenty, as it turns out. Bill provides a "different take" on glory days — a fascinating peek behind the broadcasting scene.

He was one of the first media icons who took an interest in my career and has remained a friend over the decades. At the time of this writing, he's 94 years old and an encyclopedia of sports knowledge.

Bill has maintained dear friendships with many players, me included, and I'll brag on him a bit. He is so very accomplished, having served in the Navy and earning a master's degree from North Texas State University. He has broadcasted NTSU/UNT sports, created and managed the university's radio station (KNTU), and taught the art of sports broadcasting to more than 700 students from 1966-2006. Bill trained many of the best sports announcers in Texas, affectionately known as the Mercer Mafia. This included Craig Way (University of Texas), Mark Followill (Dallas Mavericks), Dave Barnett (Texas Rangers, ESPN, UNT), Ted Emrich (ESPN), Lisa Burkhardt Worley (KENS San Antonio), George Dunham, and Craig Miller (the Ticket), just to name a few.

What a legend, a rare breed. Among his numerous awards and honors are the Texas Pro Baseball Hall of Fame, North Texas Athletic Hall of Fame, Texas Radio Hall of Fame, Oklahoma Broadcasting Hall of Fame, Dallas Press Club "Living Legend of North Texas Journalism," UNT's Apogee Stadium Bill Mercer Press Club, and the UTD-Dallas Athletic Hall of Honor. Bill is also the oldest, living past president of Dallas-Ft. Worth SAG-AFTRA having served during the 1960s. He was inducted into the Texas Sports Hall of Fame in 2020.

What an honor that he weighs in below about the glory days of the Cowboys.

Contributed by Bill Mercer

I began broadcasting in 1949 in Muskogee, Oklahoma, my hometown, and had the opportunity to broadcast all the sports — football, basketball, boxing, professional wrestling, and my favorite, professional baseball. KRLD TV needed an announcer for live professional wrestling, and I auditioned. They hired me, and that's how I came to Dallas.

As I was announcing football in North Texas, I decided to get my master's degree so I could teach and work in radio at the same time. The Cowboys called in 1965 and asked me to do color commentary with Jay Randolph, who left in 1966. I took over his spot and started broadcasting.

That's when I got to know Pettis and thought he was the finest young man I had ever met in my life. I told Pettis he was a good leader, an important trait in football. He is such an intelligent person with a great personality, congenial and one of the good guys. He succeeded as a football player, but more importantly has always been dedicated and hardworking. He was interested in everything and held down a lot of off-season jobs, and this helped prepare him for a successful post-NFL career.

In 1967, my color announcer was Blackie Sherrod, a famous columnist with the Dallas Morning News. *Blackie was a different kind of color commentator, intelligent and occasionally witty. We covered the Ice Bowl game, which was such a crazy thing. It was 35 below zero when I woke that morning, and by game time had warmed up to 20 below. I can hardly describe the suffering in the press box, which wasn't heated. The windows iced over and we couldn't open them — they were frozen shut. We used a couple cans of de-icer so we could see what was going on.*

What a great game. The fans might not think so due to the loss, but the Cowboys played their hearts out. Little things caused the defeat, interesting mistakes caused by the weather. It's one of the most talked about football games of all time, and considered the third best of all time.

Verne Lundquist was hired at WFAA Channel 8 sports and worked with me as a color commentator with the Cowboys. Verne hadn't done play by play, and after I resigned I talked to Tex Shramm, who gave Verne a shot as a play-by-play announcer. Verne and I covered the Cowboys at the Super Bowl in 1972. He became one of the best national sports broadcasters.

In one way or another, Verne Lundquist and Brad Shams' careers intersected with mine. Dale Hansen, on the other hand, turned into a really good commentator on current events. A small group of us are still around to reflect on those early games of the 1960s and 1970s, and I'm glad we are all sharing memories in Pettis' book.

If you ask what the differences are from then and now, I'd say the size of the football players. Back then, players were more of an average size — still big, but not huge like today's players. I enjoyed watching plays in those days, faking in the back field, handing off. It was really the best of times in the NFL. I was impressed with the quality of the individuals like Pettis and the fact they were on the forefront of tackling issues like discrimination.

I know Pettis was very fond of Tom, and vice versa. Underneath the tough exterior was a good heart and a sense of humor. I think those of us who are still around agree that the early days of the Dallas Cowboys were like no other era. I had an incredible level of respect for Tom Landry as a coach and a person.

Verne Lundquist

I have many great things to say about Verne Lundquist, a sportscaster extraordinaire known as "The Golden Throat." He began his broadcasting career with WFAA in Dallas and joined the Cowboys Radio Network in 1967, the year of the Ice Bowl. I have immense respect for his decades in the field and his eye-witness accounts of incredible moments in sports history.

One of the things I love about Verne is his humbleness — the telecast was never about him. His voice captures listeners, no matter the sport he broadcasts, and my recent favorite has been the Masters. I'll never forget our annual reunions; my bond with Verne and others in the industry is so very special.

Verne was inducted into the Sun Bowl Hall of Fame in 2005 and the National Sportscasters and Sportswriters Association Hall of Fame in 2007. In 2020, I was proud to learn about his Lifetime Achievement Award from the Texas Golf Hall of Fame. Amazingly, he has been a part of 35 Masters and 27 PGA Championship telecasts — what versatility. He is a very busy man, and I appreciate the insights he shares below.

Contributed by Verne Lundquist

Pettis and I go back a long way. I first heard about him when he joined the Cowboys in 1962. Five years later, I came on board as a broadcaster with the Cowboys Radio Network and met him in person. Pettis was a gregarious and humble man and still is. We knew a lot of the same people and have been friends ever since.

The wonderful thing is that we were all around the same age. I was 27 in 1967, and the players and I grew up together. When I think of friendships back then, I think of Pettis, Calvin Hill, Mel Renfro, Walt Garrison, Lee Roy Jordan, and Jethro Pugh. Fortunately, most of us are still walking upright, and our health is good. For about ten years, we had 'get-togethers' once a season. These friendships were forged because the team was special, and we had so much in common — youth and a passion for the sport — and it created a lot of memories.

For anyone who played in the Ice Bowl game like Pettis did or covered the game as I did, it was a once-in-a-lifetime experience. I covered the pregame and post-game shows, half-time, and the post-game locker room show. I flew up Thursday with the team and officials and stayed at the Northland Hotel in Green Bay, press headquarters. We planned a press conference with coaches Lombardi and Landry. It was a small-scale event — nothing like the big, splashy interviews we have today.

Vince Lombardi agreed to speak with the Dallas media, and Tom Landry agreed to speak with the Green Bay media. The public relations team arranged for me to do a televised one-on-one interview with Vince Lombardi after the writers got through with him. Lombardi agreed. When the meetings in the press box were over, the cameraman was already set up and waiting.

Lombardi was seated in front of the cameras, and just as I was about to sit down and join him, I was told, 'I'm sorry, he's not going to do it.'

'But I brought a photographer to do this interview,' I said, flabbergasted.

Lombardi got up and walked out.

'You promised me. Give me five minutes,' I pleaded.

Lombardi came back in. 'Just so you know,' he said, 'I don't do television without a coat and tie.'

'Coach, if it will make you feel any better at all, I'll take off my sports coat and tie,' I offered.

'No, let's just get it done,' he said and spoke about the $80,000 heating system under the field, the first of its kind that would, under no circumstances, ever freeze.

Coach Lombardi was wrong — Lambeau Field did freeze. The interview aired Saturday night, and we woke Sunday morning to temperatures at 13 degrees below zero. They chartered three buses to get us to the game. The third bus was filled with media and front office staff. We drove through the snow and arrived at Lambeau Field around 10 a.m.

The sun was out, but the weather remained breathtakingly cold. None of us had looked at the forecast and had no idea that everything had iced over. The late Frank Luksa, a writer for the Dallas Times Herald, *carried his old-fashioned typewriter in a briefcase. All he had on was a tan jacket. He took one step off the bus and skidded pell-mell into a ditch but managed to save his typewriter. When we pulled him out of the ditch, he was frozen and full of snow.*

Dallas Times Herald columnist Blackie Sherrod also wrote stories, and Bill Mercer covered the play by play. I knew all the guys who wandered into the CBS booth during the first half. They cracked the window to get some ambient noise from the crowd. I was standing behind Frank Gifford and saw him put a cup of coffee down on the window ledge. When he reached over and brought it to his lips, he kept turning the cup over because it was frozen solid.

I remember the locker room show interview with Don Meredith. He didn't have permanent frostbite, as far as I know, although he was suffering. There have been other games almost as cold, but the significance of the Ice Bowl game and the wind chill factor made history. The wind blew throughout the whole game.

For Cowboy fans, it was the saddest trip home. The New Year's Eve party at Tex Schramm's house was almost morose. The front office was there, but no players. Midnight came and went, and no one noticed.

The Cowboys made amends a couple of years later. We lost Super Bowl V in Miami at the Orange Bowl and won Super Bowl VI the year after Pettis was traded to the San Diego Chargers.

There was such an aura around the Dallas Cowboys. I still remember that during the Super Bowl VI game, owner Clint Murchison forgot to line up a band for the post-game party they were going to hold, win or lose. We were at the Galt Ocean Mile Hotel in Fort Lauderdale (long gone). On the Wednesday of that week, Clint looked up and said, 'We don't have a band lined up.'

Someone said, 'Let me make a phone call to a guy named Willie Nelson,' and he did. 'Can you get down here and play post-game party?'

Willie said, 'I'll be glad to do it, but I need 15 tickets.'

After some discussion, Clint said, 'You tell Willie he'll have his 15 tickets,' and so Willie showed up with Waylon Jennings and Jerry Jeff Walker in '71 before they hit the big time.

Even though it took a while to win, all the Cowboys' successes helped ease the stigma of the Kennedy assassination. They played such a positive role in getting Dallas over the hump — Landry and Meredith and Pettis.

In those days, unlike today at CBS or Fox, they assigned announcers to games. Frank Glieber, the NFL on CBS broadcaster, was a Cowboy announcer and worked for Eddie LeBaron, former quarterback and executive vice president of the Atlanta Falcons. Frank took a job in Cleveland and considered it a promotion. He brought in an announcer from St. Louis named Jack Buck, one of the all-around announcers in the business.

For one or two years, Jack Buck covered the Cowboys. Pettis was a starting tight end, and for some reason, Jack could not pronounce his name correctly. Pettis Norman became Norman Pettis. 'It's a block by Norman Pettis, a catch by Norman Pettis,' he'd say, and then correct himself. It became such a running joke that Pettis became as well known for the mispronunciation of his name as his athletic skills.

Pettis is absolutely one of the nicest, kindest human beings I've ever been around. I've never seen him be disrespectful, whether it be to a fan or a writer. He just has a sense of dignity about himself and the way he carries himself. I'm proud to call him my friend.

Dale Hansen

WFAA, ABC's Dallas affiliate, employs a unique talent I've grown to admire through the decades — Dale Hansen.

He's made a career out of sports media and was the weeknight sports anchor on the 10 p.m. newscast. Dale and I have known each other since he moved to Texas in 1980. Throughout his long career, he's championed many causes and has been an outspoken critic on many social justice issues.

Dale's reporting on the SMU football scandal in the 1980s prompted an NCAA investigation that ultimately led to the cancellation of the Mustangs' 1987 season. He has delivered commentaries condemning homophobia in the NFL and supported the NFL's "Take A Knee Protests" against police brutality. Like Coach Tom Landry, Dale is a big fan of anyone who doesn't follow the easiest path.

Dale gave me a moving tribute when he said, "While Pettis' time as a Cowboy player has faded from the memory of most, what he has meant to the city of Dallas should be remembered forever."

I thank Dale for those kind words and have a few of my own. I was proud when Dale received a Lifetime Achievement Award from RTDNF – The Radio Television Digital News Foundation, created to set standards in the journalism field and protect the US Constitution's First Amendment. He joins an elite group of distinguished journalists and First Amendment leaders who are carefully chosen each year for this award. What an honor and so well deserved!

Finally, I can't thank Dale enough for his friendship, and his selfless support of me on special occasions. He retired in September 2021 and is the quintessential sports and entertainment anchor of my time. We are blessed to have this shining star in our community.

He sheds light on some of the most important trending topics below.

Contributed by Dale Hansen

While I was a high school kid in Iowa, Pettis was playing for the Cowboys. I was a fan and watched him on TV.

My real opinion of Pettis developed in later years when I moved to Dallas and witnessed him as a great activist for civil rights and equality. The City of Dallas has a great deal of respect for someone who could have taken an easier path because of his celebrity but used his platform to make a better community.

It wasn't easy being a Black football player in the '60s — same for the '70s and '80s. Pettis faced roadblocks others never had to hurdle. The NFL saw improvements, and in the middle of that was Pettis. He spoke out to end segregation and showed courage as he dealt with the blowback. He focused on solving the issues.

Dallas earned its reputation — it had a huge problem with race relations. Pettis played a big part in getting government and business opportunities to expand for minorities.

This was crucial because people were leaving Dallas, not wanting to live in such a racist, fractured city. Every place in America has its problems, but I've lived in Dallas for 40 years because Pettis made it a better city.

We still don't have a perfect union. I was doing a podcast a couple of days ago and spoke of the single most frustrating thing about being my age — 72. No, not the backaches, but coming out of high school in the '60s and believing my generation would change the world. We were going to fix discrimination — I played a role, I tried. I wrote letters, marched, and wore armbands.

Dr. Martin Luther King Jr. marched for years but got real attention when Bull Connor set those German shepherds and fire hoses on peaceful protestors, men and women; CBS captured it. When Americans saw the images on their televisions, the whole thought process changed. Thank heavens we had that footage.

I come from the old-school era of responsible journalism. Back in the day, everything was filtered through the networks with layers of vetting and double-checking. Now a guy sits in his basement, bangs out conspiracy theories, and it goes viral without any fact-checking at all.

That's the conundrum with social media. On the surface, it may seem that social media is out of control and full of misinformation. Yet, if George Floyd's murder had not spread across Facebook and Twitter, we wouldn't have seen the nation rise up.

I watched the service for John Lewis, a civil rights icon. A racist element still exists 40 years after civil rights should have been a fixture in society.

Every time someone tells me that old racist attitudes are dying out, I can watch TV and see people marching with Nazi flags.

So, here's where we are in 2021. We still have work to do, and Pettis has never wavered in his efforts to bring equality to our nation, even today.

Monday Night Football

"Dandy" Don Meredith, Frank Gifford, and Howard Cosell — what a trio! From 1971 to 1973, this magical mix of personalities became a primetime phenomenon. Football fans loved them. Many NFL players did too, me included, and I was glad to see them reunite in the late '70s.

I had a special friendship with Don as both a teammate and ABC sports announcer. He signed with the Cowboys in 1960, two years before I joined the team. We played together until he retired in 1969, and by then, I had become very fond of Michael, his son. I liked that Michael explored the chemistry between Howard Cosell, Frank Gifford, and Don Meredith as broadcasters. I've mentioned Michael Meredith in this book more than once, and further below, you'll read some of the film projects he produced in honor of his father.

It was an adjustment for me personally when Don left the Cowboys, and I followed his post-NFL career with great interest. He became a color analyst in 1970 — lightning struck the following year when he joined Frank Gifford and Howard Cosell on Monday Night Football telecasts. I was so proud of him. It was an absolute delight to watch the nation relate to his folksy, funny, "every man" personality, which earned him movie and television roles.

He received the coveted Pete Rozelle Radio-Television Award by the Pro Football Hall of Fame in 2007. When we lost him in 2010, I believe the world dimmed a bit. While we have "turned out the lights" for Dandy Don, I won't forget the memories. Don was a special human being and a great friend.

Frank Gifford was another great NFL player and sports commentator. In fact, he recommended Don Meredith for the Monday Night Football position. Fortunately for me, I knew Frank before he became a play-by-play announcer. I vividly recall playing against him in 1963 (the New York Giants beat the Dallas Cowboys 34-27) and again in 1964 (the Cowboys beat the Giants 31-21). He impressed me as a player and later as a color commentator who covered my plays.

Frank spent his entire football career with the Giants and began his broadcasting career in 1965. He was the color announcer during two iconic Dallas Cowboys vs. Green Bay Packers championship games, the first in 1966 with Jack Buck and Ray Scott as play-by-play announcers and Pat Summerall as the sideline reporter. They covered us a second time in 1967, although Tom Brookshier stepped in on the sidelines.

Not everyone may know that Frank shared a birthday with his wonderful wife, Kathie Lee. Like Don, he acted in several television shows and earned the Pete Rozelle Radio-Television Award. We lost him in 2015, and I'll always remember him as a giant both on the field and in the booth.

Of course, Howard Cosell was another famous component in the Monday Night Football triad — a lawyer, sports journalist, and a larger-than-life personality. Interestingly, he rose to prominence in the early 1960s covering boxer Muhammad Ali and represented Willie Mays on some legal matters. He was already a household name before joining Don and Frank, and everyone recognized his unforgettable staccato voice.

Howard was the intellectual of the bunch. I remember he was never afraid to touch on controversial issues, and everyone accepted the fact that he built a reputation around his catchphrase, "I'm just telling it like it is." I believe this is why so many were attracted to the show.

Just one meet-and-greet with him was enough to leave a permanent impression. Fans either loved him or not. I happened to admire him and wish I knew him as well as I knew Don and Frank. It was natural for me to stay in touch with fellow football players, and Howard ran in a different circle. But he did leave me with one strong memory — he, too, recalled Jack Buck's struggle to get my name right, and never once did Howard mispronounce it.

I appreciate Don, Frank, and Howard, especially because their Monday Night Football antics happened to coincide with my years as a San Diego Charger. These three legendary characters impacted the national sports psyche and made an impression on me.

Bob Costas and Revisiting Kennedy

In 2013, I appeared with Roger Staubach, Bob Lilly, Lee Roy Jordan, Gil Brandt, Pittsburgh Steelers chairman Dan Rooney, presidential historian Michael Beschloss and others on the Bob Costas Tonight Special, *No Day For Games: The Cowboys and JFK*. The NBC Sports Network's show was based on the 50th Anniversary of JFK's assassination, as experienced through the lens of football players who were personally impacted by the horrible event.

"For a league that has no presence in Los Angeles, the Dallas Cowboys are as close to Hollywood as it gets," Costas said in the opening of the show. "But half a century ago for the Cowboys of 1963, it was fear — not football — that was on their minds."

Living through the assassination in real-time was one thing, but reflecting upon it a half-century later was another. While it was good to connect with old buddies, it was painful to recall those somber moments, taking us back to our reactions as players... the booing, the shock, and the wariness of being targeted ourselves, just two days after JFK's death.

Television viewers saw present-day interviews, archival footage, and NBC News coverage from November 1963. "As symbols of the city where the President was murdered," Bob continued, "the Cowboys soon found some of the nation's anger directed towards them."

When asked how I felt during this terrible time, I answered, "I felt totally lethargic on how I would approach this game." Indeed, the team had to function in a fog of grief and disbelief, appearing on the television screens of citizens who were also reeling.

But things did turn around. "When Dallas started winning," I noted, "that was a transitional thing for this whole city. And it began to wipe away a lot of the negative things that people felt about Dallas."

Bob Costas agreed. I remember him stating, "After bearing a measure of the nation's anger for a crime that took place in their city, the Dallas Cowboys had become a phenomenon: America's Team."

And that is how I will remember the Cowboys — as America's Team.

Back in Film

In 2017, Michael Meredith, Don's son and an independent film director, screenwriter, and producer, created a documentary based on his father and the Dallas Cowboys in the '60s. Most of it was filmed at the Cotton Bowl at Fair Park.

I was invited to be in the film playing myself and was in good company. Michael also interviewed Bart Starr, Walt Garrison, Ralph Neely, Mel Renfro, Rayfield Wright, Roger Staubach, Gil Brandt, Don's widow Cheryl King, Lee Roy Jordan, Donny Anderson, Jerry Cramer, Bill Mercer, and peripherally, Willie Nelson on his bus, among other amazing people.

I liked the documentary's premise, titled *First Cowboys*, told through the eyes of original Cowboys who made "America's Team" great during those early days in the boomtown of Dallas.

Earlier that year, Michael invited me to be featured in The Ice Bowl, again playing myself. This was filmed for *The Timeline* TV series documentary and explored the most memorable cold-weather playoff game in sports history. The film was balanced with insights into the ordeal that both teams experienced.

Again, a wrap-up that added two additional film credits on my IMDb page. I admit not even being aware that I had an IMDb page until I began to write this book, but it shows all my appearances in televised games. After 12 years in front of a camera, there is a robust list.

Michael has become a great friend, and I've enjoyed working with him immensely. He shared some very generous comments about me:

As far back as I can remember, my dad spoke fondly of his 'Buddy ol' pal, Pettis.' Later in life, when I became friends with Pettis myself, I understood why. He has that rare combination of grace, courage, and fierce determination. I feel very lucky to know him and to have worked with Pettis on several of my film projects.

Michael Granberry

I am impressed with the work of Michael Granberry of the *Dallas Morning News*. His continuing coverage of the "Old School" Dallas Cowboys, particularly the documentaries by Michael Meredith, keep the legacy alive. Michael's remembrances are a treat, and it's nice to hear them through the lens of an experienced multi-talented writer.

Pettis' involvement with the Dallas Cowboys goes back to the era of Clint Murchison, Jr., who founded the team. Murchison's son, Burk, and I recently completed a biography of his dad — it is also a history of the Cowboys —in which Pettis is quite favorably mentioned. Pettis was a force for good in helping the Cowboys become a racially integrated team. I applaud Pettis for his efforts on behalf of civil rights on and off the field.

In 1959, when I was a second grader, I saw my first football game in the Cotton Bowl — Don Meredith, the quarterback of Southern Methodist University, played against Navy. I was smitten with football after that. I also vividly remember when President Kennedy was assassinated in 1963. It shook us all when Dallas was called the "city of hate." What healed Dallas, in my opinion, was the Cowboys — Pettis, his teammates, and the good will the team generated. It made all the difference, and I became an even more passionate fan.

My main memory of Pettis was in the first NFL title game played after the AFL–NFL merger. It took place in the Cotton Bowl on January 1, 1967, during the Cowboys' seventh season. They faced the Green Bay Packers, an agonizing game. During a key moment, Don Meredith threw to Pettis, a terrible throw, and Pettis literally had to go all the way to the ground to catch it. Dallas lost 27 to 34.

Like Meredith, I attended SMU. I studied journalism and interned for the Washington Post *between my junior and senior years in 1973, when Watergate was erupting. Bob Woodward and Carl Bernstein were covering the story. Of course, Don Meredith was a sportscaster by then, and Pettis was finishing up his NFL career in San Diego. I went on to become a sports editor for the* Anchorage Times, *covering the Iditarod, among other events. I was a Sunday magazine feature writer at the* Dallas Morning News *from 1976 to 1978 and then worked for the* Los Angeles Times *for 19 years, the first three as a sportswriter.*

I really wanted to go back to Texas at some point and was fortunate to return to the Dallas Morning News *in 1997. I have been with* The News *the last 24 years, focusing on the arts, lifestyles, and entertainment. There's a lot going on, and like Pettis, I'm working on a book during the pandemic. I'm so very honored to be featured in his autobiography and have always looked up to him as a player, business leader, and now an author.*

Scott Murray

For three decades, Scott Murray was the Sports Director/Anchor on the local NBC Nightly News in Dallas/Fort Worth and Washington, DC. He was named Sportscaster of the Year 17 times by various news organizations and a Living Legend of Journalism by the Press Club of Dallas. He's also a recipient of the Silver Circle Lifetime Achievement Award from the National Academy of Television Arts and Sciences.

Scott has covered it all during his impressive career, from U.S. Presidents to U.S. Opens, the World Series to the World Cup, to 35 Super Bowls and the Olympics.

I should also mention that Scott is a multiple Emmy Award winner. One special Emmy was based on a 70th Anniversary D-Day project filmed in Normandy, France, that absolutely touched the hearts of many. Well done!

I admire Scott for his professional accomplishments, and on a personal note, for his selfless spirit. He is a humanitarian and volunteers his time to many sports organizations, charitable and civic causes. I have been the recipient of his selfless acts of kindness, and I can't tell you how much it meant to me. Below he shares insights on these important projects and more.

Contributed by Scott Murray

I've bumped into Pettis for years, usually at a gala or fundraiser for a worthy cause. He's always kind, courteous, respectful — and elegant too. He has such presence! As a kid, I certainly knew who he was, the great tight end who played with other iconic players in the '60s. After all these years, I still call Roger Staubach, Mel Renfro, Bob Lilly, and Rayfield Wright all great friends as well. They don't make 'em like that anymore. Pettis' era was a golden era, the very beginning of what was to come.

Aside from making a name for himself as a former NFL player, Pettis is even more noteworthy as a civic leader in Dallas. He's passionate about people, no matter their walk in life, and is particularly interested in the welfare of his fellow veterans. The Armed Services is another thing that connects us.

I remain very involved with countless military endeavors. When my son graduated from college 15 years ago, he and I started a television production company. I retired from nightly television news and went straight to Murray Media and worked on videos and A/V presentations and projects. We made little profit at first, but the work was certainly rewarding. From Veterans Day parades to Military Balls, it has been a true honor to serve as master of ceremonies for decades. In addition, I also remain on the boards of countless military organizations and veteran endeavors. It is, indeed, a great privilege to support our heroes in uniform, both past and present, and the commitment they've all made so we might enjoy the freedoms we do every single day. So, thanks to Pettis and all the men and women who so bravely served, putting their lives on the line to keep us all out of harm's way.

When my son and business partner, Doug, and I were asked to cover the 70th Anniversary of the invasion on D-Day, we traveled to Normandy, France, with two dozen WWII veterans. I can hardly express how special it was to tour by bus from Belgium to Luxembourg to Germany and back to Omaha Beach for two weeks with these heroic veterans of the Greatest Generation. It was the ultimate "bucket list" trip. When we returned, the documentary we created, produced and hosted, aired locally on NBC, and allowed both of us to receive an Emmy for our efforts. Two years later, we were asked to travel to Pearl Harbor on the 75th Anniversary of the attack on Dec. 7, 1941, and produce another documentary. That was part of our Emmy award-winning weekly television program, Conversations with Scott Murray.

I've also immensely enjoyed serving as host of two weekly radio programs for years, The Scott Murray Show and Leading the Way Today, where we have spoken to CEO's of prominent Fortune 500 companies, addressing strategy, culture, diversity and leadership within their organizations. I'm presently co-host and co-founder of a show entitled Leadership America, where we "Create Champions of Change through a Culture of Civility."

Pettis has been all too kind in congratulating me on what I do and the honors I've received, saying it was the equivalent of winning a Super Bowl. Not sure about that, yet coming from him, that's quite a comparison and certainly something I will forever cherish. But, in the grander scope of things, his career in the NFL, and maybe even more importantly, his tireless servant leadership in the community, is tough to top.

I relate to Pettis because he's one of the hardest working people around, not for fame and glory, but because he cares about being a difference-maker. He exemplifies the words I share with my listeners as I close out my radio show each and every week: "Live your life as a Go-Getter… Share your life as a Go-Giver!

Brady Tinker

Brady Tinker is a renowned broadcaster and an amazing storyteller. This special gift sets him apart — he doesn't just "report" on a topic but takes his audience on a deep dive into the "story behind the story."

Brady recently invited me to interview on his podcast, *A Cowboy Life,* and took me back to those long-ago days, growing up as a sharecropper's son and soaking up the values my parents taught me. Gil Brandt chimed in with a recollection of the signing bonus he offered me when I became a Dallas Cowboy. What fun, and what a great presentation. Brady really knocked it out of the ballpark.

Brady is a busy guy — President of Brady Tinker Sports, Tinker Productions, and ScrewTop Media. Back in 1996, he helped create the first fantasy sports national TV show as well. As a TV Host at KTXD TV Dallas/Fort Worth, he grew the NFL player's fantasy football show and the MLB fantasy baseball, aired on the Primetime sports networks.

Below he shares his interesting background and talks about our interview. I'm so glad we connected — he's a genuine talent.

Contributed by Brady Tinker

I invited Pettis to A Cowboy's Life podcast because I knew he had a fantastic story to tell. He lived an amazing life and is the kindest and most intelligent person you'd ever want to meet. He reminded me of Marques Haynes, a pro basketball player, and Harlem Globetrotter. I was around Marques for a year or so, and the era he grew up in was filled with adversity. He was 13 years older than Pettis and overcame many challenges and became such a remarkable person.

Like Marques, Pettis strikes me very much the same way — a phenomenal work ethic, smarts, and concern for the community. As anyone will tell you, it's a great honor to get to know Pettis. He left me with a feeling that we are friends, and I think everyone feels that way.

I had always wanted to be a broadcaster, a play-by-play man, and moved to Dallas with my wife in my late twenties. I ran into Norm Hitzges at a Mavericks game, a Radio Hall of Famer. We hear him today on SportsRadio 1310 The Ticket. When I shared my broadcasting goals, he said, "Don't do it!" But when he realized I was doing it anyway, he opened some doors for me. I was hired at KLIF talk radio but in sales. My role was to introduce prime sports TV to advertisers on two shows. In the meantime, I watched the announcers and learned to read the teleprompter, etc. A year later, I sold nearly a million dollars in advertising.

My bosses were reticent to give me a chance on the air, but luckily for me, they did. Fox SW Regional took over the show, and I stayed on, an amazing stroke of luck. Now I've built several companies and noticed how big podcasting had become over the last few years. It's a lot of fun and has connected me with fascinating people like Pettis.

I enjoyed having Pettis and Gil Brandt together on my show, a real honor. Gil has recruited many of the people I've interviewed, and I was present at his Hall of Fame Ceremony.

Pettis paid me a real compliment by referring to me as a storyteller. That, indeed, is what I do, inspired by people like Ira Glass of This American Life. We need more uplifting stories in the world — not the mass-produced headline stories, but stories from the heart.

That's what Pettis gave my audience — a heartfelt story that inspires others to do their best, persevere, and leave the world a better place. He has lived an amazing life and still has more to do. What an example for us all.

Retirement is great — time for Ivette and me to smell the roses. Photo credit: Sonia Trevino

Chapter Twenty-Four: Retirement

For me, retirement was just an opportunity to do more, undistracted by a paycheck.
~ Pettis Norman

I remember looking at Ivette and saying the words: "It's official!" We sold our last business and honestly didn't know what to do with ourselves, at least initially. I think we were both a bit stunned, for work had defined us for as long as we could remember. A tangle of emotions hit me when I finally embraced the infamous "R" word I had avoided for so long — retirement.

Yes, I am still working, but without a paycheck, as I continue to pursue humanitarian causes. I can't help myself — when duty calls, I answer. But I did learn to transition into a more relaxed way of living. I must admit, I'm enjoying my newfound freedom.

I found there is plenty to occupy my time and discovered amazing things that can be accomplished in my golden years. First, I am spending quality time with Ivette and our family as never before, without the stress of business deadlines. Holidays with our daughters, grandson and great grandchildren are fun and our times together are priceless.

For nearly 30 years, Ivette has worked, played and prayed by my side. But for the first time we both experienced what it is like to smell the roses and be completely "off the clock." Maya Angelou once said: "I've learned that making a 'living' is not the same thing as 'making a life.'" This is so true, and for the remainder of my life I plan to continue to make life count for Ivette, my family and others.

Another perk of retirement is enjoying my vast extended family. Today, Ivette and I feel like free birds and can take off with absolute freedom to visit loved ones far away. It's indescribable, this upside to retirement, and being able to spend more time with the people we cherish. Their genuine love and presence in our lives is the one thing that makes me wonder why I didn't retire sooner.

The Milestone Surprise Birthday and More

I was treated to quite a "ringing in" of 2019, grateful that I am in good health and have lived such a long, eventful life. My daughters planted the seed and they worked with Ivette to put together an unbelievable surprise party for my 80th year on earth. The backdrop, on the 48th floor of the Tower Club, was beautiful and overlooked downtown Dallas.

It was elegantly decorated thanks to the contributions of my thoughtful niece Teresa Hasty Ray, affectionately called "Ree," who was present from Charlotte, North Carolina. She and my other niece Melissa are precious gifts to their mother, my sister Sarah, who went to heaven in November 2020. Also present was my beautiful sister Gladys and four of her children

(Lynda, Judy, Joyce & Natalie) and spouses, who flew in to celebrate my special birthday. Gladys, now 92, whom I adoringly call "Gippy," is my only remaining sibling and someone who has always been an inspiration to me.

My lovely sister, Gladys

As the evening began, there was live entertainment along with a photographer and videographer to capture these special moments. My daughter Shandra planned an amazing array of scrumptious appetizers and a lovely dinner buffet for those who came hungry. My other daughter Sedonna, created the most stunning birthday cake I have ever seen. I did not want to cut the cake; it was so beautiful.

Our two masters of ceremony for the event were my close friends Shirley Ison-Newsome and Reverend Zan Holmes. Ivette tells me the dates and venue changed several times, and my buddies rolled with the changes by clearing their calendars to be there for me. The famous Socrates once said, "Be slow to fall into friendship; but when thou art in, continue firm and constant." I am so grateful for Zan and Shirley's friendship and their selfless contributions to my life and this very special evening.

Shirley Ison-Newsome and Zan Holmes. Photo credit: Jesse Nogales Photography

While initially planned as a birthday party, the event evolved into a special program in which my family and friends recognized my contributions personally and professionally. This was totally unexpected; I was not prepared to receive all the accolades shared that evening. I was truly overwhelmed with emotion.

Amazingly, more than 25 people flew in from Wilmington, Charlotte, Houston, Louisiana, and New York. In all, a total of 125 attendees came to share their love.

Of all the gatherings I have attended, this was something special! Family, civic leaders, JCSU alums, football greats, and Hall of Famers attended, including Mel Renfro, Rayfield Wright, Tom Landry, Jr., Mean Joe Green, John Wooten, Joe Washington, and Jim Ray Smith.

There were so many close friends that I have known for decades in attendance. While there are too many to name, I was grateful for their attendance.

Gil Brandt, who was inducted into the Football Hall of Fame in 2019, tweeted:

> *Pettis Norman's 80th birthday bash is underway at the Tower Club in Dallas. So proud of him, all of his business accomplishments post-football. And he was so influential in creating social change with the Cowboys during the Civil Rights era. Wish more people knew his incredible life story.*

I enjoyed this happy soiree very much and was thrilled that my family took the time to fly to Dallas and celebrate my birthday. My nieces Melissa Hasty Taylor, Lynda Gresham-Moore, and Veverly Joyce James shared beautiful reflections that moved me deeply.

80th birthday festivities. Photo credit: Jesse Nogales Photography

Congresswoman Eddie Bernice Johnson so beautifully captured my life story in the 2010 Congressional Record, featured in the foreword of this book and a second Congressional record for the birthday milestone. My emotions were raw when I was awarded Civic Resolutions for Outstanding Service to the Dallas Community from Senator Royce West, Mayor Pro Tem Casey Thomas, Representative Yvonne Davis, Commissioner John Wiley Price, DISD Representative Joyce Foreman, Mayor Meg Kelly of Saratoga Springs and from JCSU, Christy Bryant, Wanda Foy-Burroughs and Jeanette Praylor. Mayor Mike Rawlings was also present and took time from his busy schedule to send me a kind note.

I received "Letters of Recognition" for outstanding contributions in Dallas from Pete

Schenkel and Erle Nye — another special honor. There were also plenty of kind words from my longtime friends Bill Solomon, Ron Haddock, Vernell Sturns, Dr. Lee Monroe, Butch Walker, and the late Nate Allen.

The only extraordinary people missing that evening were my children, who were involved in a major car accident while driving to Dallas from Austin, Texas, to surprise me. We found out about the accident three hours before the party and contemplated canceling the event to be with our daughters.

Sedonna, sitting in the front passenger seat, had serious injuries and was rushed to the hospital with several bone fractures. Shandra, sitting in the back seat, re-injured her knee.

Ivette and I were so alarmed by this accident; our hearts nearly stopped as we frantically contacted Sedonna to check on her condition. She calmed our nerves and assured us that while she was in pain, her condition was not life threatening. She insisted that we go forward with the party. After hearing her voice and speaking with Shandra about her condition, we were relieved and felt much better about proceeding with the party. It was a blessing that our great-grandson and a family friend in the car were not seriously injured.

Sedonna emailed a statement that was shared with our guests and me that evening by her long-time friend, Carol Jones. Here are her words, so special, so loving…

> *Daddy, we wanted to let you know how profoundly blessed we are that God blessed us with you as our father and grandfather. There comes a time in most children's lives when it all begins to make sense. The guidance, advice and lessons. To know that family and friends have traveled from far away to honor you is no surprise to us. You have given tirelessly and endlessly to our family and our community. It is only fitting that we pause and take this night to celebrate you.*
>
> *We know that Mom and Shawn are there in spirit, and so are we. You are truly the epitome of grace. When we show our friends photos of you, no one believes that you are turning 80 years young! You've somehow found a magical fountain of youth and have mastered aging in reverse. If we had to guess your secret, I'm sure it would be a combination of your life's recipe given to us for a well-lived life. Do unto others, work hard, speak words of kindness, listen more than you talk, and forgive others. When life knocks you down, get back up and above all else, always give thanks.*
>
> *So, although we would never have missed this night for anything, we will always be with you. We love you, and most of all, we thank you for living a life that has been of service and passion. We would like to thank Ivette, Aunt Sarah, and Gladys, our cousins, friends and everyone who made time to share in this beautiful night.*
>
> *Love,*
>
> *Sedonna, Shan, Alex, and the great-grandkids*

These beautiful words touched the hearts of everyone at the party and made me feel blessed. Still, my heart was heavy that evening as Ivette and I tried to put on our happy faces but continued to worry about the well-being of our children. It was difficult. I am happy to report that Sedonna and Shandra recovered from this accident and are doing well today.

Then, it was party time, and the dancing began. I must say it had been a while since I shook-a-leg but was told that I still had it going on. We didn't get to bed on that special night until 4 a.m.! Ivette kept the celebration going with a catered brunch the following day for all of our out-of-town guests and close friends. What an amazing two-day celebration! Everyone should have a party like this on their 80th birthday and I thank my daughters and Ivette for making it special.

To put a period at the end of this fun-filled and exciting weekend, Ivette framed the awards and letters that I received, and they are now prominently displayed on an entire wall in my office, along with my other corporate and civic accomplishments. In addition, she put together the most beautiful photo album to reminisce upon this very special evening.

Spare Time for Trivia

Now with more leisure time on my hands, I could explore the historical roots of my favorite pastime — football. The early evolution of football helmets caught my eye, thanks largely to a gift from my good friend Calvin Hill. He sent me a replica of a vintage leather helmet used by football players in the '20s and '30s. While he and I were fortunate to play during the era of modern-day helmets offering more protection, those who played the game back in yesteryear had quite a different experience!

Of course, I had to try on this vintage helmet and it roused my curiosity. So I searched the internet, very much an amateur sleuth, to learn more. This particular replica was made for the Disney movie, *Angels in the End Zone* starring Christopher Lloyd.

Due to its popularity, some people wear them to games and tailgate parties, or display them in collections. These replicas are also presented as awards, commemorative gifts, or used in fundraisers. In case you are interested in a vintage-looking helmet, contact Marv Lubinsky with Past Time Sports (pasttimesports.biz) which sells these replicas.

I found two people credited with the development of original leather football helmets worn in actual games and there are possibly others. Apparently, in 1893, an injured player, Joseph Reeves, had a protective leather harness created (with the help of a blacksmith) so that he could play in an Army-Navy football game. In 1896, George Barclay invented what would eventually become "executioner-style" helmets composed of brown or black natural leather. These were threatening-looking helmets that give the appearance of a hooded executioner. My research indicates that versions of this helmet were worn on college campuses, including the University of Michigan and elsewhere.

Another interesting fact is that nearly all of the games in this era were played in unadorned helmets —school colors and mascots were rarely used. As rivalries grew, colleges and high schools began to paint the leather. This helped the receiver spot the quarterback at long distances.

In the vintage helmet given to me by Calvin Hill. Helmet credit: Past Time Sports (pasttimesports.biz)

Photo credit: Chris Hornung/AntiqueFootball.com

For professional sports, molded nose-protector head harnesses were introduced in 1921 by P. Goldsmith & Sons and marketed as "a good helmet for linesmen." It was the first American football helmet with integral face protection, a molded leather mask. The first-generation styles were simply attached to a standard Western-style head harness. In the mid-1920s, the design included fiber reinforcement in the crown, and most major sporting goods manufacturers offered this second-generation helmet.

Though unpopular among players, the nose-protector head harness allowed injured players to avoid rubber nose masks. Can you imagine the discomfort, not to mention the limited vision? But linesmen chose face protection over field visibility.

I recently posted on my personal and official Facebook pages about the "executioner helmet," which generated great interest. If you are as fascinated as I am about this subject, you may recognize some early great pro players and teams who wore these leather helmets — Red Grange, Jim Thorpe, the early Packers team, the early Bears team, the early Giants team, and more. Then in the late 1940s, plastic replaced the leather, and logos were displayed on the helmets. It seems some leather helmets survived through World War II and into the 1950s and then faded into history, a very rare find today.

If you would like to own one of these vintage helmets, contact Chris Hornung at AntiqueFootball.com and check out his amazing array of helmets. He shared "executioner helmets" similar to the one above sell between $7,500 and $12,500 depending on condition. But you better move quickly; only 30 to 40 originals have survived since the 1920s.

Family Reunions

They say families who play together stay together; that's the Normans. Our family reunions, called Glaze, Murray, Norman, have taken place for over 50 years and are rooted in African American customs.

The tradition of our reunions goes back to Africa and the love of family. Although Africa is a vast and diverse continent, one similarity at the center of African tradition is the family, which is also the religious, economic, and political unit encompassing a wide circle of extended family members.

During slavery, women often took care of children that were not their own, and many slaves protected each other despite tribal or language differences. When slavery ended, women and men went about trying to put the family back together.

Our ancestors survived the worst of circumstances. They survived because they helped each other, took care of each other, and extended themselves to blood relatives and others. This is still our tradition today. Our family reunion cements these ties because it provides a sense of unity.

For most of our family members, it's the most anticipated time of the year, and they arrive from all over the country. Each summer, they pile into cars, jump on trains or hop on airplanes, and travel hundreds (or thousands) of miles to attend our family reunion.

Our three-day event is a fun-filled program with a variety of activities. Friday night is generally our informal cookout, catching up with all that has occurred over the past year.

Saturday is filled with a variety of field trips and bonding activities during the day and a banquet in the evening. We have a lovely dinner during our banquet, reintroduce ourselves, present our family lineage, and finally play and dance at the end of our program. On Sunday, the final day, we unite for breakfast and worship services; departures are planned shortly thereafter.

The Glaze, Murray, Norman family reunion provides a sense of belonging to a group of people who love and care unconditionally. It is central to strengthening the ties of our families because it brings everyone together — young and old. Stories are shared about times past, including reflections on those who paved the way for us and have gone on to glory.

This celebration is held in a different state each year — North Carolina, Georgia, Illinois, and New York, have all served as reunion locations. Our focus is "reconnecting," "reviving the legacy," and "finding the rest of who we are." Most importantly, it's our road map from the past and our guide to the future.

I thank my nieces, Melissa Hasty Taylor and Lynda Gresham-Moore, two of our reunion organizers who are passionate about researching, collecting, and maintaining historical data on our family and very supportive in contributing information about the Glaze, Murray, Norman reunions.

A Political Spectator

Three occasions cause me to hang my "do not disturb" sign: televised horse racing, football games, and presidential debates. I might view text messages in case of a family emergency, but otherwise am in the cave with the remote in hand. During televised horse racing especially, I can predict "win," "place," and "show" horses without placing a wager. As I've shared previously, it's my passion, and I remain in my cave for as long as the program is running.

The current political climate has me counting just how many presidents served during my lifetime — 14, and several for multiple terms dating back to Franklin Roosevelt. It does cause a bit of "time travel" to the days when I was heavily involved in supporting presidential candidates. But today, I am merely a spectator on the national scene. Perhaps I can describe it best by comparing it to my retirement from the NFL. I still love football, but from the comfort of my couch, and likewise with national politics.

However, local politics is something altogether different. I still attend galas and fundraisers in Dallas, one recently for my favorite Congresswoman Eddie Bernice Johnson, and still financially support the campaigns of leaders who care for "the least of these." We should all be involved locally, and monetary donations are not the only way to do so. Many can't afford a contribution, but they can support candidates through social media, yard signs, rallies, and telling others why they favor one candidate's platform over another. Sometimes word of mouth is the most convincing way to sway people who are straddling the fence.

Most of all, especially at this age, I cherish the right to vote — something others around the globe may not be able to do. I continue to pay close attention to the choices I can make as a citizen. All our votes are valuable; I hope everyone exercises this important privilege. We cannot complain about the outcome of elections while ignoring the ballot booth — remember, every vote counts.

Soul Work

Perhaps retirement is the very best time to focus on the "here and now" as well as the "hereafter." I must give God credit, once again. I've done a lot of reflection about Him as the head of my life and how I've passed this culture of Christian beliefs to my offspring. The Lord has led me to be a better man, spouse, father, grandfather, and great-grandfather — I'm not sure what life would have been like for all of us without Him, and I'm thankful I never had to walk alone without the guidance of my Divine Savior.

My goal has always been to protect and provide for my loved ones, and my prayer throughout all these years has been to be a blessing to others. And then along comes a book project that acts as a mirror. I was suddenly wondering if I had honored my roots, lived up to the sacrifices of my parents, and practiced my faith as fervently as they would have expected. Was I the best father I could be? Was I the best husband? Friend? Mentor? Boss? Servant leader? Did I give of myself appropriately, fairly, wisely? Had I hurt anyone, failed anyone, or let an opportunity to help someone slip by? I continue to raise the answers privately and meticulously to these questions.

That is what you can expect when you write an autobiography. It was easy to say that I had no regrets, but delving into the decades caused me to ponder the past and question the quest. It became a great soul-searching task and sparked a deep desire to mend whatever was broken. I call it "soul work," for it's more than frolicking through memories; it's fretting about what more could have been done. Honestly, it was quite an eye-opener for me.

It had me reflect, once again, on one of my favorite Frank Sinatra songs, "The Impossible Dream," and I wondered, *Did I run where the brave dare not go? Did I right the unrightable wrong? Did I try to be far better than I am? Was I willing to give when there's no more to give?*

Ivette tells me that I have been true to my quest and not to worry. She feels this book is a raw and honest account that captures the essence of "effort." I liked the ring of that, for effort does matter. I did put in the effort, lots of effort, and must trust the good that came out of it.

Forming a family and passing on traditions has been a blessing. So have civil rights breakthroughs, a functional school system, and most importantly, a city that operates more fairly in the workplace and government. Yes, effort matters, and I hope it inspires others to do the same selfless volunteering in their communities.

Of course, Ivette's biased. I often tell her I could not have done it without her. And I am so thankful we both were raised in families of strong believers and hard workers, and we know that God has full reign in everything we have done and continue to do. As my partner in life, I dedicated this book to her for many reasons. I am deeply grateful for her continuous encouragement, guidance and devotion to this ten-year project. Without her support and self-sacrificing spirit, this book would likely never have come to fruition.

True love. Photo credit: Lawrence Jenkins Pictures

I feel that my love for Ivette could encompass an entire manuscript by itself. I love her more today than when she first caught my eye nearly 30 years ago. I cannot imagine life without her. We have forged an amazing relationship beyond all expectations — we truly are soulmates. She has been a wonderful partner to me through the highs and lows, the triumphs and defeats, and the most challenging and blessed moments in our lives. We have suffered devastating losses and healed together from them. We have challenged and inspired each other during our journey together, and we have reached a place in our marriage where the landscape is beautiful. Our love is worth a thousand skies and the best is yet to come.

I also thank God for my greatest gifts — my daughters, grandson, and great-grandchildren, whom I love dearly. On Father's Day, I shared an important inspirational message with them and hope they'll never forget the words:

*I want you to believe deep in your heart that you are capable of achieving
anything you put your mind to;
that you will
NEVER LOSE —
you either win or learn.
Just go forth and aim for the skies.
I can't promise to be here for the rest of your life,
but I can promise to LOVE YOU, for the rest of mine.
~ Author Unknown*

Sedonna, Shandra and Alex

To my children I say... think of life as a book. You have laid the foundation, but the book is yet to be complete. Some chapters are very exciting vignettes, others are intended to share wisdom, some are sad, and others will share your personal growth and success.

As you walk through these important chapters in your life, remember the life lessons that I taught you…Do unto others, a good reputation is more valuable than money, integrity is paramount, every action has a consequence, forgive, no easy path to financial independence, and ethical work leads to success in business and in your personal lives. There are many more lessons that I hope you remember. It's great that your book is still being written – so turn the page and make me a proud dad and grandfather.

Sedonna, you are my inspiration having transcended many obstacles with such grace. Your intuition and intelligence shine as your guiding lights. Shandra, you are resilient and have wisdom far beyond your years. You are anchored in thought and laser focused on your goals. Alex, you have a heart of gold, a magnetic personality and a remarkable intellect. Never forget, it's not where you start, it's the finish that matters.

Finally, I hope that I've taught you about unconditional love — my selfless love that surpasses all behavior and is in no way reliant upon any form of reciprocation. While I have held your hand for a short while, I will carry you in my heart forever. Never forget, that you are a child of God and must make life count for others.

Photo credit: Jesse Nogales Photography

This may be one of the shortest chapters in the book, as my "retirement" is still relatively new, and I have more living to do in the years ahead. I leave you with a quote from John Newberry, who divided people into three groups: "those who make things happen, those who watch things happened and those who wonder what happened." Which group will you belong to when you are called to serve? So onward and upward!

Finally, a cherished look at my ancestral beginnings in the last chapter below, as well as reflections on the dear ones who are no longer with me.

Chapter Twenty-Five: Legacy

Our ancestors began the journey; our descendants will carry it forward.
~ Pettis Norman

In the spirit of gratitude, a theme throughout this book, I dedicate this final chapter to beloved family members who are gone but never forgotten. I pay tribute to them beginning with my late wife, Margaret, and first born, Sharneen, and ending with my siblings.

Tribute to Margaret

We were married for 29 years. What a lovely person she was; life was great. By the grace of God, we created a beautiful family, had a wonderful life together, and were blessed in so many ways. She was a great mother and "second mom" to many of our daughters' friends and those who came to our home. She was a Christian woman, beautiful both inside and out, who sang in the choir at Golden Gate Baptist Church, our home church.

On June 12, 1991, we were sitting at home, a normal evening. I was watching television in the den when Margaret expressed concern about a tingling sensation in her left arm. We walked down to our neighbor's home, who happened to be a trusted doctor. After checking her vital signs, he could not diagnose any serious condition.

We returned home, and Margaret appeared to feel better. She returned to our bedroom with our youngest daughter Shandra by her side. Shandra was home from the University of Texas and was with Margaret in her closet when I heard, "Dad, Mom fainted! Come quickly, she's in the closet."

I flew back to our bedroom where I found Margaret on the floor without a pulse. I tried feverishly to administer CPR until the ambulance arrived to take her to Charlton Methodist Hospital. My other two daughters, Shawn and Sedonna, arrived swiftly.

Margaret never had any serious health challenges in the past, and I certainly had no reason to believe this incident would take her life. After waiting hours in the hospital, the doctor emerged to share words that I will never forget:

"Mr. Norman, we tried persistently for one hour to bring her back. I am so sorry for your loss. Her heart just stopped working."

The rest is too painful to explain.

We were comforted by the words spoken by Reverend C.B.T. Smith and Jesse Jackson as they eulogized Margaret. Other kindnesses meant a lot, as well. Commissioner John Wiley Price opened his home to my relatives who had flown in for the service and, as always, was there for me. Many friends checked on the girls and me throughout the following weeks. We appreciated that they brought food and words of encouragement. I remember thanking God for blessing me with a beautiful marriage, sustaining me as a widower, and anchoring my daughters through the storm.

Margaret and I were also partners in business, and the following recollections are a tribute to the company she inspired — Liquid Love.

It just so happened that in 1982, Margaret was very particular about having healthy hair. She was given a sample from her beauty shop and fell in love with the product. It made her hair so soft and healthy, and she encouraged me to try the formula. I did, and loved it! I visited the shop the following day to speak with Charles Smoots, a.k.a. "Sir Charles," the owner of the formula.

"I want to buy the formula. How much would you like for it?" I asked. We agreed on a price, consummated the deal, and laid out a vision on how to handle this new venture. We launched Liquid Love from the heart of our kitchen. Beginning with one product, a moisturizing activator serum. We bottled, labeled, and boxed the products with all of our love.

The popularity of our initial products came out of the heyday of the curl activator and Jheri curl craze, but overall, our hallmark was revitalizing and maintaining the integrity and texture of our customers' hair. People fell in love with the green apple fragrance and the signature purple, pink, and white motif on product bottles. Best of all, our customers were "falling in love" with their hair.

With Margaret's lovely touch and me running Burger King and later PNI Industries, our little side business grew into something quite amazing. It was gratifying to see the demand for our products continue, thanks in large part to word of mouth and glowing reviews. Our products were made from the highest quality cosmetic grade ingredients, paraben, phosphate, and sulfate-free, beautifully packaged, and became the "talk of the town."

We moved the operation to a manufacturing facility in Fort Worth, where we could offer complete turn-key service and the ability to expand rapidly in the market. Eventually, we sold our products to beauty supply distributors who shipped products all over the country from Washington state to Washington D.C. and many states in between. We kept expanding into retail stores and grocery stores, and also developed a website. We sold our products online, supported by YouTube videos and bloggers who featured Liquid Love products with a passion.

As I reflect on the good times, the kitchen became the place where Margaret shared her love with family, friends, and acquaintances, whether making a new batch of Liquid Love, pouring her energy and effort into a scrumptious meal, or just playing and laughing about life and family.

Today as I look back on our beautiful marriage, I am so grateful for her love. God rest her soul; her contributions to my life are immeasurable.

Margaret

Tribute to Sharneen

I had a very close relationship with Sharneen — known as Shawn — as my oldest child. Our Liquid Love enterprise is part of her legacy as well. I asked her to move from New York back to Dallas to take the helm of Liquid Love in 2010. She had a brilliant mind and the social media skills needed to expand through online sales. She implemented a number of changes that included rebranding, repackaging, new promotions, and fresh marketing materials that placed a bright spotlight on Liquid Love and took us to the next level in this industry. All of her hard work and energy paid off, but we tragically lost her in December 2014.

Grief is a painful journey, a solitary one for me. I know this from the loss of Margaret and many of my beloved siblings. I am reminded of a Bible verse, Psalm 127:3 — "Children are a gift from the Lord; they are a reward from Him."

God's reward was taken away from me the day I lost my daughter to a senseless murder at the hands of the man she was dating on December 1, 2014. Another unspeakable tragedy in my family. He shot her and later committed suicide. I kept trying to understand, but I could not.

I did not know the man she was dating other than two brief visits during their short-term relationship. Why would he take my daughter's life? She was private, and like most women in an abusive relationship, was not ready to talk. Could I have protected her? I relied on my faith to help me through this storm.

Verses such as Proverbs 3:5-6 anchored me. God tells us to take whatever trust we have and put it in Him. He tells us to lean NOT on our own understanding, especially in grief.

Shawn had a brilliant mind, was successful in business, and had the spirit of an angel. She called me "Papi," and I miss her dearly. She was also very close with her sisters, Sedonna and Shandra. They talked daily no matter how far apart they lived. Shawn loved her nephew Alex and always gave him life guidance and loads of love. They continue to struggle with the loss of their big sister and aunt but have found their own personal ways to heal from this tragedy. She referred to Ivette as "bonus mom," and Ivette loved Shawn dearly. They had a special bond, and Ivette misses her beautiful spirit.

Her favorite mantra was: "Surround yourself with people who are outrageously optimistic, fly with others who are truly, madly, and deeply in love with life, move in the company of kindred spirits who build you up and give you wings to fly."

My heart still yearns for her, but I stopped asking "why" and began celebrating the beautiful relationship we had for 50 years. After she went to heaven, I found a letter during my research for this book; I will always treasure it:

Dad, I know that sometimes you might have thought I'd never grow up. Then, as I grew older, it may have seemed like I didn't need you as much as I used to. Well, I may not run to you with every little thing anymore, but with things that really count. I can always come to you, and I know you'll be there for me. You see, no matter what else may change, I'll always need you, and I'll always love you.

~ Shawn

My oldest daughter, Sharneen (a.k.a. Shawn). Photo credit: Steve Foxall

Africa to America

Without the sacrifices of my ancestors, I would have no legacy at all. I believe this is also an appropriate chapter to discuss my ancestors, an accumulation of strong men and women who braved obstacles I can only imagine. I've mentioned some of my relatives previously in the book, but this section digs deeper.

My ancestral story begins in the mid-eighteenth century on the continent of Africa. Imagine Africans, my ancestors, being hunted, handcuffed, shackled around their necks and feet, stripped of their clothing, chained together, and forced onto ships in preparation for the notorious "Middle Passage" across the Atlantic.

They were labeled "chattel" — an article of property that could be bought, sold, loaned, used as collateral, willed to another, punished, or even murdered at an owner's whim. African slaves were brought to America against their will and were kept here against their will. They were not recognized as "persons" in the eyes of the law and had no legal rights upon their entry into the new American Colony.

I raise this not to bring up the ugly truth about our history, but to challenge my brothers and sisters today about a reckoning that must take place to address 250 years of enslavement and 100 years of legal separation based on the color of one's skin. Several proposals from leaders across our nation have raised questions on how to address our past sins. Do we begin with a formal national apology? Should we focus on reparations? How do we right the historical wrong? I am still pondering the best approach — this section was written as the nation grappled with George Floyd's death — but an apology should be the beginning, something vital to rededicating our American values.

As history and records reflect, it appears my lineage was grounded in courage, strength, wisdom, and faith, beginning with my great-grandfather Isaac Norman, a warrior as far back as can be recollected. I would like to think that some of Isaac's genes were passed on to me to carry on the fight for unity, peace, racial equality, and justice for all people during my lifetime.

As background, Isaac Norman was born into slavery in the State of Virginia in 1846. As a lone wanderer at an early age, relying on his strength and his faith, Isaac Norman left Virginia. He migrated to Lincoln County, Georgia, my hometown, where he rapidly established himself as an upright and respectable man. On July 25, 1867, he was issued voter registration card #122 by the registrar of the 29th registration district of the State of Georgia, making him one of only a few Black men allowed to vote during that time; whereas most others were not awarded that right until the Voting Rights Act of 1965.

Further records, produced by the Georgia Production of Agriculture, show that by 1880 Isaac Norman owned 75 acres of land, which at that time was worth $400. It was extremely rare for a Black man to own land during this period in America, let alone in rural Georgia.

Isaac soon met and married his beloved Winnie. Little is known of Winnie prior to her marriage to Isaac, but together they produced and raised six children: Aaron, William-Otis, Lucinda, Simon, Ella, and my grandfather Jesse.

The exact time of Isaac's death is not certain. However, the 13th census of the United States

(1910) indicates that Winnie was then a widow and head of her household. It also indicates that Winnie was an educated woman who was able to read and do arithmetic.

Only God knew how the life of a certain slave woman by the name of Hannah Glaze would eventually intertwine with the lives of Isaac and Winnie Norman. According to the Last Will and Testimony of a slave owner by the name of Suzanna Glaze, Hannah was awarded to Suzanna's daughter Elizabeth upon her marriage to John Knox. In March of 1868, Hannah Glaze bore a daughter fathered by a White man, John Murray. She named her daughter Helen. Being bi-racial, Helen was usually referred to as a Mulatto by census reports.

The relationship between Helen's mother, Hannah Glaze, and her White father, John Murray, appeared to be a cordial one, as he continued to take care of Hannah and their daughter Helen. Helen grew into a beautiful woman and soon caught the eye of Jesse, the son of Isaac and Winnie Norman. As time went on, Jesse Norman and Helen Glaze fell in love and united in Holy Matrimony on December 28, 1886. Their union grew in love and in family, and together they produced eight children: Pearl, Lois, Rosella, Gertrude, Francis, Isaac, Clifford, and my father Fessor.

Jesse cared for his family as a sharecropper, while Helen was a homemaker who cared for their home and reared their children. They spent the next 39 years of marriage nurturing their children, grandchildren, and great-grandchildren. Jesse and Helen became lovingly known as Pa Jesse and Ma Helen. Helen also maintained a close relationship with her fully White half-brother, William Murray.

On May 7, 1925, Pa Jesse became ill with liver disease and remained under a doctor's care. On Friday, May 10, 1925, at 11 in the morning, a heart attack claimed his life. He was 58 years old. Both Helen Glaze Norman and William J. Murray signed his death certificate.

After the loss of her beloved Jesse, Ma Helen continued to thrive for many years. She was a farm laborer for a short while, then a full-time homemaker who spent most of her time with a large and loving family of children, grandchildren, and great-grandchildren. She also spent much time at her family church, Tabernacle Baptist Church, which the Norman family was instrumental in founding in 1886. To date, Tabernacle is still the Norman family church. Many of my ancestors are buried on the church grounds, including my parents, Fessor and Elease "Eloise" Norman. Many Normans still fill the pews and serve in many offices and capacities. Ma Helen also served in this great church until 1952, when she quietly passed away.

Leaving a rich heritage and an amazing legacy for their children and their children's children and beyond, Isaac and Winnie Norman, and Jesse and Helen Norman, laid a foundation of faith, values, and principles, filled with courage, strength, and wisdom.

The current most senior Norman generation (the fourth generation) continues to build on that rich foundation. Our family name is respected far and wide as an example of amazing strength. We continue to demonstrate the content of our character as we walk in faith and in love.

And now, I'll introduce you to my siblings, all born from the strong genes of our ancestral heroes.

My Siblings

I have warm memories of our close-knit sharecropping family and have collected remembrances of my nine siblings — seven sisters and two brothers. I remember growing up as the baby and youngest brother to Ruby, Winnie Pearl, Eva, Ida, Fessor Lee, Elizabeth, Gladys, Tony, and Sarah, and I feel compelled to document their lives and my memories of each. It turns out that I had an additional sister as well — Dora Norman.

Only one of my sisters, Gladys, is still here on earth and enjoying life with me. While our two departed brothers and six departed sisters dance with the angels, Gladys and I are holding each other closer now and we frequently reminisce about our family members. Known as "Gip," Gladys was born May 4, 1929 and is 92, healthy and blessed. She married Roy Gresham. She and my sister Elizabeth married two brothers, Floyd and Roy Gresham. Gladys has nine children: Johnnie, Lynda, Dempsey, Judith, Veverly Joyce, Michael, Roderick, Janice and Natalie. After the death of her husband, she left Lincoln County and moved to Charlotte to raise her children.

Gladys began her career as a domestic worker and retired as a manager for IBM Corporation more than 30 years ago. Like our siblings, she is quite witty and still very active, and loves to dress stylishly, travel, and sing in her church choir and the Citywide Hymn Choir. She is a member of "The Friendly 13," a group of 13 female senior citizens who meet monthly, take trips to dinner theaters, the mountains, and the beach, and contribute to organizations like the Salvation Army. They have a big soiree at Christmastime. Gladys is the epitome of "90 as the new 70."

My departed siblings have earned their wings, and I can imagine them reveling in their great heavenly reward. Below, I share small vignettes of what my siblings mean to our family and me. I don't want them to ever be forgotten.

Ruby

My firstborn sibling, Ruby, arrived on December 22, 1916, and married John Fred Carr. She had one child, Phyllis Diane. Ruby retired as a domestic caretaker after working for the same family for more than 30 years. She loved flower gardening and baking — I'll never forget the chocolate and coconut cakes she gifted us at Christmas. She gave each family household half of a chocolate cake and half of a coconut cake, wrapped in gift paper. We all really looked forward to this treat every year. Ruby was feisty, comical, and did not bite her tongue. As the oldest sister, she was definitely "the boss" and kept the family connected. I remember she called all of us almost every single day, and never failed to send her siblings birthday and holiday cards. She died on January 5, 2013, at 96 years of age.

Winnie Pearl

Winnie Pearl was my quiet and soft-spoken second oldest sister, born April 28, 1918. She married Sylvester Norman, and his last name and her maiden name were the same. Interesting result — she became Winnie Pearl Norman Norman! They had six children: Charles (Buddy),

Melvin, Shirley, Marvin (Ray), Wallace, and Ben Jasper. Winnie was a career homemaker and lifelong active member of the family church, New Tabernacle Baptist Church. She died on May 10, 2009, at 91years of age.

Ida Helen

Known as "Sister," Ida Helen was born on January 21, 1921 and married George Bolton. They had three children, George, Emylean, and Randy. She was a schoolteacher in the Lincoln County, Georgia school system from 1943 to 1948. After relocating to Charlotte, North Carolina, she worked as a social worker for Mecklenburg County for more than 29 years and retired in 1984. Ida was an avid volunteer and loved helping others. She was very active in her Garden City Neighborhood Association and loved to entertain. On any given Sunday, family and friends gathered at her home after church for food and fellowship. Her home was the "gathering place." She died on July 4, 2010, at the age of 89.

Eva

Known as "Baby," Eva was born April 18, 1923, and married Wade Bolton (she and my sister Ida married two brothers, Wade and George Bolton). Eva had six boys and one girl: Thomas (Sonny), Luevornia, Willie McArthur, Robert, Paul, Larie, and Fessor Leon. She was a homemaker, an exquisite quilt maker, and very active in the Norman family church, New Tabernacle Baptist, where she served on the Mother Board, the Usher Board, and the choir. She was a member of the Eastern Star Lodge #597 and a member of the Lincoln County NAACP #5213. She died on June 1, 2010, at the age of 87.

Fessor Lee

Known as "Bish," Fessor was born August 9, 1925, and married Azzie Lee Garnett. He had eight children: Douglas, Lonnie, Taffy, Eugene, Chauncey, Kenneth, Antonio, and Antron. Fessor was self-employed and owned Norman Woodworks. He was an accomplished and highly sought-after master carpenter; a craft passed down through generations from my father Fessor. He was soft-spoken, very generous, and loved to dress up and go dancing. He served in the United States Armed Forces in WWII and has a section in this book devoted to his service. Fessor died of pancreatic cancer on April 11, 2012, at the age of 86.

Elizabeth

Born July 12, 1927, Elizabeth married Floyd Gresham. They had two children, Rudy Dean and Pearlean. She later married Clarence Partlow. Elizabeth worked as a domestic in the Lincoln County community, had an unmatched sense of humor, and always kept us laughing. The children in our family were amazed at how she tended to the henhouse and quickly dispatched chickens for dinner. She was an excellent cook and a warm, compassionate spirit who died on March 2, 1992, of a massive stroke at the age of 65.

Tony Edwin

Tony was born March 25, 1932, and died on July 1, 2011, at the age of 79. He married Annie Pearl Garnett and had two children, Sherrow and Rowena. He retired after many years as a school system custodian and owned his own pallet business, Norman's Pallets. He was a natural comedian, a compassionate man, and member of the Masons Lodge #7 (PHA). No matter where you were, somebody knew him. He was known for visiting the sick and shut-in at home, nursing homes, and hospitals. This was his way of giving back to the community. He and Gladys loved to hit the road and travel together, visiting family and friends near and far.

Sarah Frances

My youngest sister, Sarah Frances, arrived May 27, 1934, and passed away on November 14, 2020, at the age of 87. She married Wallace Hazel Hasty in 1952 and shortly after had two children, Melissa and Teresa Marcel. Sarah retired as an OB/GYN nurse after 35 years of service and was also an entrepreneur, owning a wedding/catering business. She loved spending time with family and always went out of her way to assist family members when needed. Sarah had an impeccable fashion style and was definitely "The Fashion Diva." She never stepped out anywhere without everything in place. She also loved home decorating, and traveling with her husband, Dwight Lacy Jones. One of her favorite events was attending the Kentucky Derby with me, her "little/big" brother, and my wife Ivette … hats and all! Sarah was always my "baby sister," even though she was five years older than me.

Dora Norman

It turns out that I had a surprise sister, Dora Norman. She was born when my father was 22, before he met my mother. Dora was raised in Pisgah Forest, North Carolina, and attended family reunions, but I only knew her as a "cousin." My older siblings knew she was our sister but never mentioned it to me until the writing of this book. I suppose this is because I was much younger than my siblings, and as the baby of the family, wasn't included in conversations.

I'm so happy to know I had a "bonus" sister, although Dora passed away in 1983. She left a legacy of children: Susie Mae who became a principal; Ollie; Rosella (named after one of Dora's aunts); Jeanette; Grant Jr.; Walter Lee; and Emma, a stepdaughter she raised.

The Game of Life

And now it is time to part. I hope very much that something within these pages inspired you. I'm passing the ball to all the readers who have finished the book and wish you the best as you reach for your goals. I'll leave you with this message — something I stumbled across and refer to frequently — as you play the game of life:

Rules of the Game

I'm giving you the ball, son,
and naming you the quarterback for your team in the game of life.
I am your coach. So, I'll give it to you straight.
There is only one schedule to play. It lasts all your life. But consists of only one game.
It is long with no time out and no substitution. You play the whole game — all your life.
You'll have a great backfield. You are calling the signals,
but the other three fellows in the backfield with you have great reputations.
They are named Faith, Hope and Charity.
You'll work behind a truly powerful line. End to end, it consists of honesty,
loyalty, devotion to duty, self-respect, sturdy cleanliness, good behavior and courage.
The goal posts are the gates of heaven.
God is the referee and sole official. He makes all the rules.
And there is also an important ground rule.
It is 'As ye would that men should do to you, do ye also to them likewise.'
Here is the ball. It is your immortal soul! Hold onto it.
Now, son, get in there and let's see what you can do with it.
Think of these words now in relation to your task.
The need, time, opportunity, your youth coordinates as your coach.
You are the quarterback for your team in your community.
You are young — God will hold you responsible.

~ Author Unknown

ACKNOWLEDGMENTS

★ ★ ★ ★ ★

The outpouring of love and collaboration that has been shared throughout this project humbles me.

I could not have captured all the historical details in this autobiography without the help of my immediate and close-knit extended family. Their collective memories merged with my own to weave a beautiful, colorful tapestry. A very special thanks to my only living sibling Gladys Gresham, and Sarah Jones who contributed to this book before her passing. Nieces Teresa Hasty and V. Joyce James, family historians Lynda Gresham-Moore and Melissa Hasty Taylor, and nephews George Bolton, Robert Bolton, William Kenneth Norman, and Kent Norman, and first cousins Bertha Hill, Jesse Norman and his daughter Justine Norman. These beloved relatives honor our family legacy with their recollections.

Many thanks to writer, managing editor, and collaborator Melanie Saxton. She oversaw this project and shaped the many overlapping moments in this story arc into a wonderful "look back" at my childhood, scholastic endeavors, family life, business enterprises, and humanitarian causes. She also assisted with social media, book signings, and my website content. We are so thankful we found her website, www.melaniesaxtonmedia.com, and that she was available to work on the project.

Thanks to Ed Gruver, (egruver60@msn.com) collaborative writer, author, sportswriter, and subject-matter expert on football, for his contributions in several exciting gridiron chapters covering my college and NFL career. He brought those glory days to life.

I would also like to express my sincere gratitude to Dr. Helen Benjamin for embracing this project during a busy time and being a guiding light with developmental editing and professional proofreading of the book.

I give enormous thanks to Mark Wittow, Attorney and Partner at K&L Gates (mark.wittow@klgates.com) who has been so valuable to this project. I appreciate his subject matter expertise, guidance, selfless spirit and assistance in getting this book to the finish line.

I give mammoth thanks to Holly Chervnsik with SuburbanBuzz.com who created my website, brand designs and social media platforms for this book. Her creativity is unmatched, and I am grateful for her one-stop operation that provided formatting, editing and preparation of this book for publication.

Finally, I want to thank the Dallas Cowboys, San Diego Chargers, colleagues, friends, media, organizations, libraries, museums and the National Archives and Records Administration, who have touched my life in so many ways and contributed to this autobiography. While it is my desire to list everyone, it's quite a list, and just know that I carry you in my grateful heart and my spirit.

www.ingramcontent.com/pod-product-compliance
Lightning Source LLC
Chambersburg PA
CBHW080632170426
43209CB00008B/1553